PAPERS

OF THE

LIVERPOOL LATIN SEMINAR

1976

*Classical Latin Poetry/Medieval
Latin Poetry/Greek Poetry*

ARCA

Classical and Medieval Texts Papers and Monographs 2

THE LIVERPOOL LATIN SEMINAR
IS GRATEFUL TO THE FACULTY OF
ARTS OF THE UNIVERSITY OF
LIVERPOOL FOR A CONTRIBUTION
TOWARDS THE COST OF PRODUCING
THIS VOLUME.

PAPERS

OF THE

LIVERPOOL LATIN SEMINAR

1976

*Classical Latin Poetry/Medieval
Latin Poetry/Greek Poetry*

Edited by

FRANCIS CAIRNS

X

FRANCIS CAIRNS

© 1977 Francis Cairns

Published by Francis Cairns, School of Classics,
Abercromby Square, University of Liverpool, P.O. Box 147,
Liverpool L69 3BX.   All rights reserved.

ISBN   0 905205   00   6

Printed in Great Britain in the Administrative Department of
The University of Liverpool.

CONTENTS

I CLASSICAL LATIN POETRY

Christopher Tuplin: *Cantores Euphorionis* 1
I.M. LeM. Du Quesnay: Vergil's Fourth *Eclogue* 25
E.L. Harrison: Structure and Meaning in Vergil's *Aeneid* 101
Alex Hardie: Horace *Odes* 1,37 and Pindar *Dithyramb* 2 113
C.W. Macleod: Propertius 4,1 141
Summary:
R. Seager: Horace and the Parthians 155

II MEDIEVAL LATIN POETRY

P.G. Walsh: *Pastor* and Pastoral in Medieval Latin Poetry 157
S.F. Ryle: The Sequence: Reflections on Literature and Liturgy 171
Mark Davie: Dante's Latin *Eclogues* 183
Summaries:
A.B.E. Hood: The Cambridge Songs 199
Michelle Levy: The Poetic *Persona* in Twelfth
Century Latin Lyric 201
R.B. Kevin Maguire: The Revision of the
Breviary Hymnal under Urban VIII 203

III GREEK POETRY

J.G. Howie: Sappho *Fr.* 16(LP): Self-Consolation and Encomium 207
Gregory J. Giesekam: The Portrayal of Minos in Bacchylides 17 237
Giuseppe Giangrande: Three Alexandrian Epigrams:
APl. 167; Callimachus *Epigram* 5(Pf.): *AP* 12.91 253
Giuseppe Giangrande: Aspects of Apollonius Rhodius' Language 271
Francis Cairns: The Distaff of Theugenis— Theocritus *Idyll* 28 293

Papers of the Liverpool Latin Seminar 1976 collects most of the papers given at the meetings of the Liverpool Latin Seminar in the academic year 1975-76 either in revised, and sometimes expanded, form or in summary form, together with supplementary papers contributed by members of the Seminar at the invitation of the editor.

The conventions of reference, etc., found in the volume are editorial impositions. Contributors quoting from foreign scholarly works have been asked to do so in translation. The amount and distribution of Greek has been controlled editorially, primarily for economic reasons. The principle has been that Greek has been quoted only where it is necessary as the subject of linguistic comment. Otherwise transliterations and translations have been used.

Some Latin and Greek quotations have been accompanied by translations. The guiding principle here has been the extent to which it was felt that a paper might be useful to those not engaged primarily in the study of Latin or Greek.

The publication of this volume was made possible in two ways: first, through the generosity of the Faculty of Arts of the University of Liverpool, which made available a subvention for this purpose; and second, through the valuable cooperation of the Administrative Department of the University of Liverpool where the printing was done. Special thanks are due to Mr. Walter Hare and Mr. John Owen for administrative assistance; and to Miss Val Taylor for her patient and resourceful oversight of the composing.

Francis Cairns   Liverpool, August 1976

CANTORES EUPHORIONIS

by

CHRISTOPHER TUPLIN

(University of Liverpool)

For many years now the idea of the so-called "neoteric" movement in pre-Augustan Latin poetry has exercised a baleful fascination over students of Latin literature.[1] The stimulus for such an idea lies in three Ciceronian comments about contemporary poets in a letter to Atticus, the *Orator* and the third book of the *Tusculan Disputations*, which refer respectively to *neoteroi, poetae novi* and *cantores Euphorionis*. In this paper I wish to make a new suggestion about the identity of the last of these groups. It should be made clear, however, that it is not my purpose to make any specific assertions about the relationship in fact, or in Cicero's mind, between the three groups. That should be regarded as a separate problem whose solution might be assisted by, but cannot consist in, the identification of any one group.

In *Ad Atticum* 7,2,1 (November 25(?) 50 BC) Cicero writes: *Brundisium venimus VII Kal.Dec. usi tua felicitate navigandi: ita belle nobis "Flavit ab Epiro lenissimus Onchesmites". Hunc σπονδειάζοντα si cui voles τῶν νεωτέρων pro tuo vendito.* In *Orator* 161, after commenting that it used to be thought quite elegant (*politius*) to drop the final 's' of '-us' terminations, whereas it now seems to be *subrusticum*, he adds: *ita non erat ea offensio in versibus quam nunc fugiunt poetae novi*. Finally in *Tusculans* 3,45 where he has been quoting Ennius in support of his philosophical argument, Cicero suddenly interjects the comment: *O poetam egregium! quamquam ab his cantoribus Euphorionis contemnitur.* The temptation to combine these three references, especially the first two, where *neoteroi* appears to be simply a Greek translation of *poetae novi* suitable to a private letter, has not always been resisted. Crowther (*loc. cit.* n.1 above) has reminded us that it should be. He concentrated on the difference between the characteristics attributed to the various groups; but two other differences which draw attention to and distinguish the third group deserve stress as well.

(i) *Hi cantores Euphorionis* is a rather specific phrase of denotation. *Poetae novi* and *neoteroi* have also tended to take on an air of exactitude thanks to the use in modern scholarship of terminology like "New Poets" or "Neoterics"; but this exactitude is not there in Cicero's words. *Poetae novi* on the face of it means simply modern or recent poets, as it does in an entirely different literary world in Seneca *Apocolocyntosis*

1

12, 29; and even with allowances for overtones in the word *novus* (Lewis and Short *s.v.* B), the poets in question are not fixed by Cicero any more accurately than as people whose poetic art is not that of the second century BC. The apparent tautology of *nunc* and *novi* hardly implies special overtones in *novi* amounting to the creation of a technical term. The situation is similar with *neoteroi*. It is worth bearing in mind the evidence of the Homeric scholia for the use of the term *neoteroi* in literary historical criticism, particularly of post-Homeric poets and their characteristically 'uncanonic' forms of stories and language.[2] The usage is confirmed for the first century BC by the fragmentary commentary in *P.Oxy.* 1086 on *Iliad* 2,783, and it is worth noting that Pindar can be one of the "moderns" at this date. Later grammarians, both Greek (e.g. Hephaestion) and Latin (e.g. Gellius, Pompeius, Servius) use the term *neotericus* as a title for all non-classical or "non-canonic" authors, or in connection with items which even in an authoritative poet like Vergil seemed to lapse from the proper standards of Latinity. Notice that in all these cases, as with *Ad Atticum* 7,2,1 and *Orator* 161, usage, not aesthetic quality, is the centre of interest.[3] Much earlier, Aristotle distinguished the *neoi* among writers of tragedy (*Poetics* 1450a25,b7), and one might compare the distinction of 'old' and 'new' comedy. In fact the differentiation of new and old is a theme recurring throughout ancient literary criticism from the *Frogs* onwards and at times acquiring an illegitimate status as a yard-stick which provoked disquiet in some quarters (e.g.Cicero *Brutus* 39; Horace *Epistles* 2,1,34; Tacitus *Dialogus* 15f).[4] Moreover two facts about *Ad Atticum* 7,2 should be noticed. (a) Cicero's last letter to Atticus (7,1; 16 October) had been unusually full of references to Homer and old Latin poetry, 2,4 (*bis*); 9(*bis*), elicited by the difficult political situation facing him (cf.7,3,5; 7,6,2). (b) Atticus was, as ever, in a discriminating mood, as is shown by his comments about Cicero's use of *in Piraeea* (6,9,1), to which Cicero replied in 7,3,10 with quotations from Caecilius and Terence. It is tempting to imagine that somewhere in the letters to which Cicero is replying in 7,2(cf.3) was a sardonic comment from Atticus about his friend's predilection for the old poets, and that this accounts for the reference to *neoteroi*. In any event, if *neoteroi* in Cicero has anything of the character of a technical term it is one of literary-historical scholarship, perhaps introduced parodically, and nothing specifically to do with Roman poetry. It appears possible consequently that Cicero had some more precise object of reference in mind in the *Tusculan* passage than in the other passages.

(ii) In *Orator* 161 Cicero does not display any very strong or clear

2

feeling about the *poetae novi*. The comment *quodsi indocta consuetudo tam est artifex suavitatis quid ab ipsa tandem arte et doctrina postulari possumus*? relates to the general argument about *natura* and *analogia* and no judgement is being passed on the poets.[5] The passage in *Ad Atticum* has more colour. Cicero is not so much showing off his skill in writing a *spondeiazon* (*pace* Crowther) as apparently teasing Atticus for having more sympathy for the *neoteroi* than he himself does. For that view of the matter, rather than the supposition of a shared joke at the expense of a common enemy, support may be found both in *pro tuo vendito* and, more distantly but more interestingly, in the figure of Q.Caecilius Epirota, a freedman of Atticus and the man entrusted with the responsible task of teaching his daughter. He was later noted as an enthusiast for up-to-date poetry and a pioneer in its use in teaching, presumably in place of the old classics (Suetonius *De Grammaticis* 16). That perhaps gives us a measure of Atticus' literary tendencies, and we may suppose that the real focus of the remark in Cicero's letter is Atticus and not the *neoteroi*, about whom Cicero is asserting no particular attitude. The situation is very different with the *Tusculans* passage: (a) the word *cantor* has a pejorative tone in Plautus (*Pseudolus* 366) and Cicero (*De Oratore* 1,236). It is also used of the unpalatable Hermogenes and Tigellius in Horace (*Satires* 1,3,129; 1,2,3) and a similar overtone attaches to *cantare* in *Satires* 1,10,18f. This will be the effect that Cicero is seeking in *Tusculans* 3,45.[6] (b) Cicero's opinion of Euphorion was not high (*nimis etiam obscurus, De Divinatione* 2,133), so that reference to a taste for his poetry is hardly intended as a compliment. Moreover the disreputable character attributed to Euphorion in some of the *testimonia* (e.g. Plutarch *Moralia* 472D; Athenaeus *Deipnosophistai* 436E; 477E; Suda *s.v.*), which at the least may reflect impressions gained from the reading of his poetry – impressions that we can still understand from the fragments of that poetry – make him a particularly colourful counterweight to Ennius. The group in question may well have had other characteristics than a love for Euphorion; Cicero's selection of that single characteristic may smack of exaggeration and animus. (c) There is bitterness in the attribution to the *cantores* of contempt for Ennius rather than merely disapproval. Again there is an air of exaggeration.

Tone is not always an easy thing to judge, but it does seem as if Cicero is taking up a strongly defined position about these people in a way that is not true of the *poetae novi* or the *neoteroi;* and this special engagement of prejudice once again raises the possibility of a more specific target and one more readily identifiable, at least in the context of

Tusculans 3,45, by the contemporary reader. In short, the notion of attempting to identify the *cantores* seems *a priori* more reasonable than that of identifying the "new poets".

Some have regarded the comment, taken in isolation, as nothing more than a purely literary judgement on Ennius and his adversaries, comparing *praeclarum carmen! est enim et rebus et verbis et modis lugubre* just below (46), apparently equally purely literary. Thus J.F. D'Alton quoted *Tusculans* 3,45 as a rare case of a purely aesthetic criticism in Ciceronian literary appreciation.[7] Yet there is surely more to it than that, and the key lies in the context. In the latter case (46) the degree of excellence in the evocation of misery is directly relevant to the philosophical argument insofar as the proper reaction to extremities of distress is what is in question and Ennius is being quoted for an example of such distress; this is made immediately clear by what follows: *eripiamus hanc aegritudinem.*

The philosophic relevance of *O poetam egregium . . .* is no less clear. Immediately after that sentence Cicero justifies his judgement with the remark *sentit omnia repentina et necopinata esse graviora.* This is a comment related to a particular aspect of the general topic under discussion in the third book of the *Tusculans*, the alleviation of distress. The relevant train of thought goes back as far as section 28, where it is said that the Cyrenaics consider that not all evil causes distress, but only *insperatum et necopinatum malum.* Cicero agrees that unexpected evil is considerably worse. He mentions some lines illustrating this truth from Ennius' *Telamon*, quotes Euripides *Fr.* 964 (Nauck[2]) for a statement of the belief that it is important to ponder on possible future ills to fortify oneself and adds the well-known story of Anaxagoras' reaction to his son's death: *sciebam me genuisse mortalem.* The argument continues with a development of the Euripidean principle; and the policy of seeking total comprehension of *humanae res* with a view to finding nothing unexpected is called *praestans et divina sapientia.* Further illustration comes from Terence (*Phormio* 2,1,11) and fables about the imperturbable Socrates. In section 32 we discover the point of this lengthy insistence. Epicurean theory denies the principle of pondering future ills, and indeed makes *avocatio a cogitanda molestia* one of the two cardinal sources of the alleviation of distress. It is attack on this, and more particularly on *revocatio ad contemplandas voluptates* that is the concern of the argument that follows. This moves back and forth between the nature of Epicurean *voluptas* and the sufferings of tragic heroes; and it constitutes the context of section 45.

4

Insisting that Epicureanism advises attention not to virtues (36f.) but to physical pleasures (37f.) Cicero pours scorn on the notion that someone suffering the ills to which tragic heroes are liable can be rescued by application of the Epicurean way of life. The example of Thyestes, Aeetes and Telamon are mentioned, the last-named with further quotation from Ennius' tragedy. There follows renewed treatment of the topic of what type of pleasure is contemplated, and reference is made to Epicurus' *Peri Telous* to show that physical pleasure is the aim. Is this the way to relieve Telamon? If you find someone broken by grief, do you give him an *acipenser* rather than a *Socraticus libellus*, urge him to listen to water-organs rather than Plato, or give him flowers to look at or sniff – not to mention the other forms of pleasure: is Thyestes to be given a goblet of *mulsum* or Andromache put into a soft bed and treated to harp music, incense and sweetmeats to afford relief from their griefs so finely expressed in the verses of Ennius? It is precisely here that we come upon the comment about the *cantores Euphorionis*; and it can now be seen how closely it fits into the context of an extended and polemically brilliant, not to say captious, attack on the hedonistic aspects of Epicureanism. The idea that the remark is only an aside will hardly commend itself in view of the fact that this whole attack highlights the Epicurean inability to cope with certain types of passion and suffering, namely those represented so excellently in the stories of tragic heroes and heroines found in the great works of literature. That is, the poetic aspect is a very intimate part of the skein of the argument, not just an illustrative adjunct; and one could justifiably suppose that Cicero all along has in mind the point that Epicurean moral principles would necessarily have an undesirable literary counterpart, if only because the presentation of the people in distress, an activity evidently regarded by Cicero as of literary and moral worth, would be a breach of the principle of avoiding thought about *molestiae*. This encourages one to think that, though the clear contrast of poetic character between Ennius and Euphorion makes for a certain suitability in mentioning the latter poet and his supporters, that is not the whole of the matter, and that Cicero's anger at the *cantores* is not based purely on aesthetic grounds but has philosophic overtones.

There is another consideration that perhaps has some bearing on Cicero's outburst, but equally does not provide the whole explanation. This is that the particular Ennian passage to which Cicero appends his comment seems to have been a special favourite of his. It is quoted in his works even more often than the famous opening of the *Medea*, which is the only part of Ennius' tragic output to receive more quotations by all ancient authors than Andromache's speech has by Cicero alone. Moreover, it had special associations for him, to judge from *Pro Sestio* 110ff. (esp.

5

121f.). Here he recounts the reactions of a theatre crowd to the news that he had been voted an honorific decree (116). The passage starting *O pater . . .* (which appears in *Tusculans* 3,45) is said to have been taken as a reference to the *pater patriae* (i.e. Cicero), and Aesopus drew tears from all with his declamation of the lines down to *haec omnia vidi inflammari*, which seemed to reflect the contemporary political situation. But all this at best serves to explain why it is quotation of this particular passage to which Cicero adds his comment in *Tusculans* 3,45. It does not explain *cantores Euphorionis*.

It seems to me that the general context as outlined above makes it very tempting to suppose that the *cantores* are not entirely innocent of the views of Epicurus, in addition to any views they may have about Euphorion and Ennius, especially since the latter provides not only examples of grief beyond cure by physical pleasure but also a text for the non-Epicurean view that grief is to be anticipated (28). That is, it would be suitable if the adversaries were in some sense Epicurean poets, especially if their Epicureanism were reflected in their literary theory and poetic practice. Moreover, viewing the matter without prejudice, in the phrase *his cantoribus Euphorionis* there is no reason why the word *his* should be taken, or taken solely, in the sense of "present to the mind because contemporary" (whence translations like "modern imitators", J.E. King, Loeb Classical Library) rather than "present to the mind because relevant to the argument". So Cicero may even actually be saying that there is a connection between the *cantores* and his philosophical adversaries. In any event, the general argument from the context remains. "Epicurean poets" seems at first to evoke thoughts of Lucretius, but clearly he is not in question, being no *cantor Euphorionis* nor for that matter a *contemptor Ennii*. There is, however, another tempting possibility.

Recollection of the date of the *Tusculan Disputations* will help to direct attention the right way. Exact determination of the date of composition is not really possible or necessary for the present purposes, but it can safely be put in the second half of 45BC.[8] The point is that the work is part of the philosophical flowering late in Cicero's life and that the literary world in which he is writing, and to which he might refer, is not that of the "Catullan Revolution" but rather of the civil war. A feature of that world was the Epicurean circle at the Bay of Naples, centred on the figures of Siro and Philodemus[9] and including people of poetic importance and interest. Vergil's association with Siro is well known both from references in the *Catalepton* (5,9; 8,1) and information in grammarians and commentators,[10] while a text from the Herculaneum library of works

6

of Philodemus himself appears to refer to Vergil, Varius, Horace or Plotius.[11] The friendship of Vergil, Varius, Horace and Plotius is of course known from other sources as well, including Horace *Satires* 1,5,40f., where one can detect the Epicurean ideal of friendship, and Probus 43 (Diehl): *vixit pluribus annis liberali in otio secutus Epicuri sectam insigni concordia et familiaritate usus Quintili, Tuccae et Vari.* Philodemus himself is noted, among other things, as a writer of epigrams of a slight and frequently erotic nature and as a literary critic. More will be said of his latter role below. My suggestion is that it is in this area that we ought to look for the *cantores Euphorionis.* We need at least experience no doubt that Euphorion was known to them. The quantity of fragments preserved suggests his importance in Hellenistic literature; his appearance as an example of obscurity as easily recognisable as that of Heraclitus in a work of Cicero (*De Divinatione* 2,113) affords strikingly relevant confirmation; and Philodemus' quotation of the *Mopsopia* in his *Peri Eusebeias* (T. Gomperz *Herculaneische Studien* II Leipzig (1886) p.16 on the subject of the three births of Dionysus clinches it.

The idea of course needs immediate qualification and restriction. Any confident naming of individual Roman poets as *cantores* would carry dangers. Just to take the names already mentioned, in the cases of Vergil and Horace the period is at the very beginning of their poetic careers; so it may be difficult to judge the suitability of their being dubbed *cantores Euphorionis* on the basis of their later works. Horace is in any case a frankly uncertain member of the set (cf.n.8). In the other cases we are dealing with figures who are obscure at any date though one might, for example, observe that the view that Varius' *De Morte* was "un synthèse d'Ennius et de Lucrèce"[12] is not particularly well-founded. Moreover, the Roman poet most readily associated with Euphorion is at first sight nothing to do with the Neapolitan circle. That poet is of course Cornelius Gallus. The exact nature of his debt to Euphorion does not need detailed discussion here; and some might think that it is not susceptible of it anywhere. That it existed may be accepted (cf. Vergil *Eclogue* 10,50f.), even if the commentators sometimes described it in unhelpful terms (*translatus* etc.). Parthenius' *Erōtika Pathēmata* compiled for Gallus included stories from Euphorion (nos. 12, 26 and 27) and Parthenius' own poetry struck the Emperor Tiberius at least as of a type with that of Rhianos and Euphorion (Suetonius *Tiberius* 70), so that Gallus was hardly remote from Euphorionic influence. The way that Propertius 2,34b,91f. which is likely to reflect Gallan material, matches Euphorion *Fr.* 43 (Powell) is also rather striking. Moreover, there is no cause to doubt that Gallus was already poetically active in the mid-forties.[13] Hence he could be relevant to *Tusculans* 3,45 and has sometimes been mentioned in this context: "what better candidate for membership (sc. of the *cantores Euphorionis*) than Gallus, the imitator of Euphorion?"[14]

But Gallus is not normally thought of as an Epicurean. It is true that Cytheris came in reality from an Epicurean household, that of P. Volumnius Eutrapelus,[15] but that is hardly a weighty consideration. More important is that Gallus was notoriously the friend of Vergil, who does have a place among the Neapolitan Epicureans. It is not possible to say anything about Gallus' serious philosophical inclinations, but for the present purposes it would be sufficiently interesting if some connection with the Campanian group, through Vergil, could be supposed. One might tentatively mention a few apparent facts: (i) Vergil was taught Greek by Parthenius (Macrobius *Saturnalia* 5,17,18); (ii) this could have been at Naples (e.g. Boucher *op.cit.* p.76); (iii) Parthenius was a friend and mentor of Gallus (cf. the *Erotika Pathemata*); (iv) Gallus is asserted to have been Vergil's *condiscipulus* (Probus *Proemium ad Bucolica*); (v) since he was by origin a Transalpine Gaul[16] he is more likely to have studied with Vergil not at the primary level in Cisalpina, but later in life and at Naples, the part of Vergil's education in which the sources show most interest. It is not beyond the bounds of possibility that Gallus at some time had to do with Vergil's Epicurean friends as well as with Parthenius; and in general one should recall that the Bay of Naples was not exactly an out-of-the-way place at this time. Rather, it was a fashionable area to which a man like Gallus would surely have been drawn.

However, what there is to be said about Gallus is presented most tentatively and the overall argument does not stand or fall by it. The tendency to associate Gallus particularly with Euphorion is perhaps the accident of the thinness of surviving information;[17] and in any case Cicero, in mentioning Euphorion, may have had in mind not so much that the people he referred to were active proselytisers for Euphorion and nobody else, as that Euphorion conveniently represented a certain trend in Hellenistic poetry in which they showed an unhealthy interest, to the detriment of more proper, and Roman, poets. Certainly it is not easy to discern Euphorion in Vergil. Servius draws attention in the *Aeneid* commentary to passages of Euphorion at which he thought Vergil hinted or where he saw him adopting a different version.[18] Presumably Vergil know Euphorion's treatment of the Trojan War, a prominent piece to judge from the quantity of fragments and, it might be added, one particularly to the point for Cicero in *Tusculans* 3,45 who is quoting Ennius' *Andromache*. But when he acquired this knowledge cannot be

8

said. Again, passages of the *Eclogues* sometimes produced to demonstrate recollection of Euphorion are not very cogent.[19] All the same, "to be a *cantor* (leaving aside the derogatory overtone) is only to be an adherent . . . and Vergil could have been that, especially given his tribute to Gallus" (Bramble *op.cit.* (n.4) p.182 n.1).

Equally difficult would be the discovery of Euphorion in Horace; but more relevant, perhaps, the fact that at least later he was open to the view that exaggerated respect for Ennius and other second century poets was undesirable (*Epistles* 2,1,50f.) and could criticise Ennian dramatic works — which are, as it happens, what are particularly in question in Cicero — with some sharpness (*Ars Poetica* 258ff.: *hic . . ./ . . .et Enni/ in scaenam missos cum magno pondere versus/aut operae celeris nimium curaque carentis/aut ignoratae premit artis crimine turpi.*) Quinn has remarked "it would not greatly surprise us if Cicero had said of Horace (supposing that he had lived long enough to be familiar with his poetry) what he here says of the *cantores Euphorionis*".[20] That seems fair comment and is worthy of note even if Horace was not one of the Neapolitan group of 45BC but was only befriended by them at a later date. The epic grandeur of the *Aeneid* makes it seem less natural to think of Vergil as hostile to, or at least discriminating about, Ennius. But it would not necessarily be incorrect to do so. With all due circumspection one might bear in mind one ancient reader's reaction to the *Aeneid: Vergilius quoque noster non ex alia causa duros quosdam versus et enormes et aliquid supra mensuram trahentes interposuit quam ut Ennianus populus agnosceret in novo carmine aliquid antiquitatis* (Seneca *ap.* Gellius *Noctes Atticae* 12,2,10); the manner of expression is almost satiric, but the implication is that Vergil was not by nature given to the Ennian manner. In any event, the immense fastidiousness and subtlety characteristic of both Horace and Vergil in all their different poetic incarnations might belong to minds that, especially in youth could even have been scornful of the old master; and for Horace at least we have the slight confirmation of the passages already mentioned. Moreover, to a post-Callimachean generation, the Ennian national epic had all the wrong associations and characteristics.

Be that as it may, the argument must not be made to turn too much on over-precise speculation about the state of mind of the young Vergil or Horace but rather, more simply, on the identification of a group involved in both Epicureanism and the contemporary poetic and literary world. The proposition that *cantores Euphorionis* is a pejorative reference to the Neapolitan circle of Siro and Philodemus must next be tested in the light

9

of such evidence as there is, both direct and surmised, about Cicero's attitude to this circle. For most of the individuals in question there is none; and of some we know very little in any connection. These include Siro himself, despite the passages noted below. It is only for Philodemus that there is anything extensive; and this amounts mainly to consideration of his literary-critical writings and of Cicero's likely reactions to them, to which I will turn shortly. As for Gallus, if he is at all relevant, we have a letter from Asinius Pollio to Cicero, written in 43 BC (*Ad Familiares* 10,32), in which Pollio advises Cicero to consult Gallus to obtain a copy of a *praetexta* (§ 5). In addition it is sometimes thought that *Ad Familiares* 10,31,6 (March 43 BC) refers to Gallus and shows Cicero in close contact with him. But this evidence is not particularly illuminating, especially as it comes from one and a half years or so later than the *Tusculans*.

It is more interesting to notice that the year of the *Tusculans* sees a sudden spate of references to Siro and Philodemus in Ciceronian writings.

(i) *De Finibus* 2,119, written in 45 BC, though set some five years earlier, shows us Torquatus saying that he can refer to other more learned men on the topic under discussion. These prove to be Siro and Philodemus, who are then described by Cicero as *familiares nostros . . .cum optimos viros tum homines doctissimos*. No-one will be naive enough to suppose that this tribute precludes a covert attack in the different, and emotive, context of a separate philosophical work. In view of the Cumaean setting of the dialogue, the reference to the two Epicureans has special point if Cicero has in mind specifically their Neapolitan circle. One may legitimately wonder whether Torquatus had spent some time in their company and reflect also that all sorts of people may have passed in and out of the circle at different times and with different degrees of serious interest in Epicurean philosophy – a point which is relevant to what was said about Gallus above.

(ii) The reference in *De Finibus* 1,65 to Epicureans living in a small house *quod fit etiam nunc ab Epicureis* might be not, or not only, a reference to the contemporary Epicureans of Athens, with whom Cicero had come into contact on his way to Cilicia (*Ad Familiares* 13, 12f.) but to Siro and his associates. Compare Vergil *Catalepton* 8,1 (*villula quae Sironis eras et pauper agelle*) and Philodemus' invitation to Piso to come to his "simple hut" for dinner (*AP* 11,44). Certainly *etiam nunc* shows that something specific is in mind and not just an undifferentiatedly "Epicurean" habit going back to Epicurus himself. But despite the other reference to Siro in *De Finibus*, secure identification of this allusion is perhaps impossible.

(iii)   In *Academica Priora* 2,106 we find a good-humouredly critical reference. Cicero is considering the question of the comprehensibility of false concepts and remarks that on the hypothesis that false concepts are not comprehensible and that therefore they cannot be remembered, the dogmas of Epicureanism must be true, since Siro can remember them. This is the *reductio ad absurdum* offered to the other side in the argument. What is interesting is the way that Siro comes to mind as the "typical" Epicurean. The *Academica* was written in 45 BC prior to the *De Finibus*, though reworking of parts of it is contemporary with work on the latter.[21]

(iv)   *Ad Familiares* 6,11,2 again has *noster amicus Siro*. Here Cicero wants Trebianus to praise him in Siro's presence, *quae enim facimus ea prudentissimo cuique maxime probata esse volumus*. One feels that the relations of Cicero and Siro are not in fact all that close. When he says *noster amicus* he means his and Trebianus', and no doubt Trebianus was very much closer to Siro since it appears that he had been devoting himself to philosophical studies in a period of political and material deprivation (cf. *Ad Atticum* 6,10b,4; *Ad Familiares* 6,10f.).[22] Since by the time of *Ad Familiares* 6,11 Cicero had secured Trebianus' reinstatement and therefore his departure from the Neapolitan "school", Siro may not have been very predisposed to listen to Cicero's praises.

(v)   Siro may also appear in a letter of 46 BC (*Ad Familiares* 9,26) as a philosopher to whom Paetus had made a flippant remark about dinner being the main object of his inquiries. This depends on the correction of *Dioni* to *Sironi*, the main arguments for which are the unidentifiability of Dion and the fact that Paetus was an Epicurean in the Naples area (cf.*Ad Familiares* 9,23). The tone of the reference to Siro, if it is he, is a little difficult to estimate. He is called *ille baro*, a word used of Epicureans also in *Ad Atticum* 5,11,6, and *De Finibus* 2,76, in the latter case with strong irony. Even granted that two of the contexts in which it is applied to Epicureans are playful and that in the Atticus letter Cicero is teasing the Epicurean Atticus, the word, whose primary sense seems to be the sort of man who has rather more brawn than brain,[23] hardly evinces much kindness, and Cicero elsewhere shows himself fond of sneering at Epicurus' supposed stupidity or ignorance (*In Pisonem* 69; *Academica* 2,97; *De Natura Deorum* 1,85; *De Divinatione* 2,103; *Tusculans* 3,50).

It is clear, therefore, that in 45 BC Cicero is conscious of Epicureanism being represented by Siro and his friends: such figures as Amafinius (*Tusculans* 4,5-7), if indeed he is contemporary,[24] Catius (*Ad Familiares* 15,19,2) or Rabirius (*Academica* 1,5) do not compare.

Consequently we can see (quite apart from the indication of the reference to Zeno, Philodemus' teacher,[25] in 3,38 that recent authorities are being used) that when writing of Epicurean views in *Tusculans* 3, Cicero would be very likely to have Siro in mind; and this consideration seems to strengthen the view that a connection should be seen between the *cantores* and the circle of Siro and Philodemus. That is, having Siro and Philodemus in mind for philosophic reasons, he can hardly have failed to have in mind the circle's literary aspirations and activities, especially when he was using so much literary exemplification for the philosophic argument. That being so, when he suddenly drops a reference to some sort of group of poetically interested people, it would be odd if the Siro/Philodemus circle were not the object.

On Cicero's attitude to Philodemus the most famous evidence is undoubtedly *In Pisonem* 68-72, but this is ten years earlier in date and in any case rather ambivalent. In view of the nature of Roman invective it is dangerous to use the contents of such a work as evidence of Cicero's views on a peripheral figure like Philodemus. It is indeed not uncommonly said, and perhaps in the context of an invective thought, to be of particular significance, that Cicero shows a marked tendency to conciliate Philodemus, despite the attack on Piso. Thus Nisbet (*op.cit.* n.9) speaks of "restrained criticism" of Philodemus and says that "the pomposity of 71-2 should not be taken too seriously". But if by the latter remark he means that the charges are not true, and that Cicero did not think them true, while this might well be the case. it is not the same as saying that in writing 71f. Cicero did not intend to be taken as making an attack. The truth is, rather, that the treatment of Philodemus is a carefully designed part of the overall assault on Piso. Cicero is painting a picture of the barbarous Piso led astray by the well-meaning but innocent Greek philosopher who is so naive that he writes poems revealing Piso's iniquities. Notice, for example, the humane Philodemus who did not, as might have been expected, spurn the friendship of the distasteful Piso *iam tum hac dis invisa fronte*, or the gentle Philodemus unable and unwilling to stand up to the misconceptions of his grand friend (*imperator populi Romani*, 70). The good qualities attributed to Philodemus appear solely to allow the creation of contrasts unfavourable to Piso. One cannot conclude from them Cicero's real thoughts, but more telling perhaps are *philosophus tantus* (69, sarcastic?) and *graeculus, adsentator, poeta advena* (70). In 68, *cui generi* allows Cicero to avoid implying too much approval of Philodemus in particular. The failure to name Philodemus may not be due to a desire to protect his reputation so much as to the feeling that he is individually insignificant; after all, *Pro Sestio* 24 is not very commendatory either. In short, not much reliance can be placed on the *In Pisonem*, but insofar as anything emerges from it, it is not respect for Philodemus

Before going on to Cicero's likely attitude to Philodemus' literary theories, there are a number of other pieces of real or supposed evidence to be noticed. (i) In *Ad Atticum* 12,6,2 (June 45 BC) Tenney Frank (AJP 41(1920)p.282) proposed to introduce the name of Philodemus in place of a word meaning "loving knowledge" (*phileidemon*), but the latter is more suitable and better defended by the manuscript tradition. In the same article he also, probably rightly, rejected attempts to amend †*arasira*† in *Ad Quintum Fratrem* 2,8,3 into *a Gadara Syra* or *a barone Syro* (i.e. Philodemus). We must make do with secure references. (ii) The idea has sometimes been canvassed that Philodemus dedicated one of his works to Cicero.[26] The evidence consists of a passage of *P.Herc.* 986, *Fr.19* which refers to "the man sent to the Cilicians by Rome" (the textual supplements are fairly certain). Despite F. Sbordone's new and improved text (*Atti del I Congresso Internazionale dei Studi Ciceroniani* Rome (1961) pp.190f.) this is no less uncertain now than when Nisbet so described it (*op.cit.* p.186). But if a reference to Cicero is involved, the idea of a dedication appears very dubious; indeed it is not at all obvious that the reference is a friendly one. The incidents which Philodemus would have in mind are those of *Ad Atticum* 5,10 and one could detect a certain ironic contrast between Philodemus' words and Cicero's professions of honesty in that letter. However, the interpretation is probably best left open. (iii) Finally there is the question of Cicero's use of Philodemus' philosophical writings as a source for his own works. The case for this centres on the comparison of the *De Natura Deorum* and Philodemus' *Peri Eusebeias*, and is not all that strong. The claim that the layout of the two books shows similarity (advanced by J.B. Mayor[27]) is over-stated. The first 64 pages of Gomperz's text correspond to two sections of *De Natura Deorum* (1, 2-3) which follow the doxographical section that is supposed to correspond to the second par of Philodemus' work (pp.65-89G) and are so highly compressed that it is not very meaningful to claim them as a summary of pp.1-61G. The argument that section three of Philodemus (pp.93-151G) proceeds "not unlike *De Natura Deorum* 1,44f." (Mayor *op.cit.* p.xlix) is satisfactorily answered by Mayor's own qualifications (*ibid.*) so that the case such as it is comes down to the doxography, and there are weaknesses here as well. (a) From the list of philosophers in Philodemus Cicero omits both Heraclitus and Prodicus. The claim that this is because their views were like those of the Stoics and Persaeus

13

respectively[28] is specious but not quite satisfactory, despite the fact that the relevant similarities are pointed out by Philodemus. Even if Cicero had decided to copy out Philodemus on the Stoics and Persaeus and omit the separate sections on Heraclitus and Prodicus, there was no reason to remove also the passing references to those two philosophers in the sections on their later counterparts, which were after all the justification for making any omissions at all. It is easier to believe that the source, whatever it was, did not have any mention at all of Heraclitus and Prodicus. (b) The fact that both Cicero and Philodemus put the Xenophontic Socrates straight after the Platonic one and before Antisthenes is not all that significant. It would be quite natural to put the Xenophontic and Platonic Socrates together and ahead of Antisthenes, merely a Socratic figure, not the master himself. There is no need to hypothesise copying by Cicero. (c) Cicero appends comments and criticisms to each name in the list, whereas Philodemus on the whole reserves them for the end, and then produces different ones from Cicero: there is, for example, hardly any agreement on Parmenides. The theory of a common doxographical source, and a fairly old one since the review stops at Diogenes (died *ca.* 150 BC), seems the most persuasive solution.[29] This conclusion does not involve the belief that Cicero was unfamiliar with Philodemus' philosophical works, only that he did not respect the *Peri Eusebeias* sufficiently to use it as a source, which is a different matter and not a very surprising one.[30]

Still less probable would be the view that Cicero was unfamiliar with Philodemus' writings on literary topics, especially as he had long known of him as *litteris, quod fere ceteros Epicureos negligere dicunt, perpolitus* (*In Pisonem* 70). These were matters in which Cicero had been professionally interested for much longer, and also ones on which Philodemus could be claimed to be very different from his fellow Epicureans and therefore particularly worth reading. That is, even from the anti-Epicurean point of view of someone like Cicero, a perusal of Philodemus on literature could add something to one's knowledge in a way that might not be so true of his work in other fields of a more traditional Epicurean sort. It is therefore legitimate to reflect on Cicero's likely attitude to Philodeman literary theory, and such reflection will serve to strengthen the plausibility of the proposition that the damning comment in *Tusculans* 3,45 is directed at Philodemus and his associates.[31]

Since the days of Plato and Isocrates there had been a good deal of argument about the relative importance of rhetoric and philosophy in education.[32] The familiarity of the topic does not, however, diminish the importance of realising how far Philodemus was a protagonist of philosophy, particularly in ways that amount to a rejection of Cicero's ideals in *De Oratore* and elsewhere. Philodemus did not write with Roman rhetoricians in mind, but from the point of view of Cicero's reaction to him that matters less than the fact that the Greek rhetorical theory which he attacks was very congenial to Cicero. That this should be so is scarcely surprising in view of the hostility of the traditional Epicurean to rhetoric (cf. e.g. Cicero *De Oratore* 3,63f.; *Academica Posteriora* 5). There is in this sense a very fundamental Epicurean colouring to the whole rhetorical corpus which, combined with the exceedingly polemical style of discourse, would rapidly alienate someone in Cicero's position. In addition, Philodemus has a characteristically Epicurean distaste for the political life as such (cf. 1,234; 237; 238; 2, 139-67). That helps to get the whole discussion off on the wrong footing from a Ciceronian point of view.

Philodemus draws a distinction of type, and a corresponding qualitative distinction, within the realm of *rhetorikē*. On the one hand there is practical rhetoric of a judicial or deliberative type, the reserve of people he calls the *empraktoi*, who include Demosthenes, Lycurgus, Themistocles, Pericles and Callistratus (2,97,10f.: 233,11f.). This type of enterprise cannot be thought of as an art (2,97 (*Fr*.8), 1f., cf.2,68(=101) where the reference to Critolaus suggests a context similar to that of 2,97) and is little regarded by Philodemus so far as one can tell. The situation is otherwise with the other type of rhetoric, *sophistikē*, the epideictic side of the coin (1,48,26f.; 1,122,30f.; 2,135,28f.), sharply contrasted with the realm of the *empraktoi* (1,122,25f; 2,97,11; 256,7f.) and represented above all by Isocrates (2,97.10f.; 233,11f.). Here we are dealing with something of comparable theoretical status with *poetikē* (1,123,36f.) and possessing the character of a *technē*. The second book of Philodemus' *Rhetorica* was largely devoted to assertion of this last fact, in part against other Epicureans who maintained that there was no trace of the view in Epicurus' writings (1,78,2 – 89,10; 120,10,22f.; *supplementum* 25,15; 28,14f.; 54,11f.).

Nonetheless *sophistikē* has its shortcomings when viewed in terms of claims made for its educational value; and this reflects particularly on Isocrates who notoriously had a theory of education through rhetorical training which he even tended to call *philosophia* (e.g. *Antidosis* 50). At the beginning of book 4 Philodemus referred slightingly to the tendency of some rhetors to arrogate to themselves an ill-defined sort of *philosophia* (1,148,13-16), and the Isocratean method came under this criticism (1,147 col.2). The significant thing about this in the present context is that Cicero was a follower of the Isocratean point of view. *De Oratore* was announced as being Isocratean as well as Aristotelian (*Ad Familiares* 1,9); praise is frequently bestowed on Isocrates and his pupils in this and other works (e.g. *De Oratore* 2,94; 3,10; 57; 141; *Tusculans* 1,7; *Brutus* 32; *Orator* 42); and in general there is no doubt about the affiliations of the ideals of rhetorical education that Cicero expresses.[33] Philodemus takes a directly opposite position at most points. For example, Cicero's praise of the Isocratean pupils, which redounds to the credit of the educational system, is to be contrasted with Philodemus' criticism (2,250,23f.): they have neither political skill nor the ability to perform in court or assembly without making the audience die laughing. The Isocratean method was of course supposed to fit one for practical affairs. Despite occasional criticisms of court rhetoric (e.g. *Antidosis* 47), a passage like *Antidosis* 260-2 which insists that the Isocrateans are concerned with *politikoi logoi* and, as contrasted with scientists or students of eristics, of much more use in public and private matters (cf *Antidosis* 99;285) is not unique; and both Isocrates and Cicero make bold statements of the thesis that there is an ideal union of politician and rhetor (*Antidosis* 230-6;306-9; Cicero *De Oratore* 3,57-60;137f.). The *doctrina bene dicendi* and *doctrina recte faciendi* are not separate (*De Oratore* 3,57).

The last part of Philodemus' *Hypomnematikon*, by contrast, considered the question of whether a rhetor is a good politician *qua* rhetor, and decided that he is not. Cities are kept safe not by rhetors acting as politicians but by good men (2,271,8f.). The *sophistikos* does not strike a discordant note in panegyrics and prose-writings, but in the law courts and assemblies nobody takes any notice of him (2,135,27f.). "It is not in the nature of sophistic rhetoric to have political employment (or to be an exercise for *politikoi* (?)), not even in addition to other employment. Political power is not a product of the rhetorical schools, nor are *politikoi andres* of the sort able to make rhetorical displays in practical discussions and to come forward in assemblies and other meetings of the people. It is not the case that rhetoric as such is naturally connected with *politikē* in any way, or that the rhetor is a politician and a demagogue; we refuse to concede to those who claim that in some cases such a connection has occurred. We say that not only is the rhetor not straightforwardly a politician, but that he is not one at all ... " (2,240,15 – text and interpretation are not at all points certain). It is admittedly only in political matters that rhetoric can have any chance of getting things done (1,10,19-11,25); but there is no commitment to the view that rhetorical training will ensure that result, let alone that what is done will be rightly done. That would depend on political skill and morality.

Isocrates claimed that his teaching made men better (*Antidosis* 278, cf. Grube *op.cit.* p.39) and that he was better at this than others who professed the same aim because he preached a generally recognised sort of virtue (*Antidosis* 84).[34] This claim was recognised as characteristic of Isocrates by Dionysius (*De Isocrate* 1) and incorporated by Cicero (e.g. *De Oratore* 2,96; *Brutus* 93). Philodemus' attitude to such professions is not one of conviction (1,223,22f.) and he disapproves of sophistic praise of Busiris or Polyphemus and preference for Clytaemnestra over Penelope, or Paris over Hector, (1,216,19f.). Such things encourage wickedness.

More extreme passages of attack are found at 1,213,221 and 2,269,272; and it seems that the third book of the *Rhetorica* took the topic of the rhetor as politician at length: "In that book it will be shown why political power is no more the product of the sophistic schools than it is of the grammarians or philosophers, and that possession of it is often the cause of significant harm and not of good fortune in the real struggles of life" (1,135,4). "We do not assert that rhetoric is in itself a bad teacher, though it gives weapons to evil men, only that it does not carry implications about the proper use of power and the attainment of what we recognise as good and just" (2,142,4f.).[35] *Sophistikē* will not conduce to the happy life (1,250,29f.), unlike philosophy (1,270,32f.). Nor, as we see from 1,223,11f. and 2,231,8f., is it educationally valuable in the sense that it leads the student to gain all sorts of knowledge to form the material of his sophistic performances, an (Isocratean) idea often found in Cicero (e.g. *De Oratore* 1,17; 20; 59; 72; 213; 2,5; 68; 3,59; 72; 76; 141; *Orator* 14-16; 113-121). In the longer perspective, the notion of speech and persuasion as great forces in the advancement of civilization (cf. Isocrates *Nicocles* 5; *Antidosis* 253; Cicero *De Oratore* 1,32f.; *De Inventione* 1,2f.) is countered by the praise of philosophy as the improving force in human society (2,133; *Fr.*4).The conflict is very sharp, and there is no softening it by, for example, detecting in Cicero a Philodeman distinction of sophistic rhetoric and the *genus iudiciale/deliberativum* (A. Rostagni *Scritti Minori* Turin (1955) pp. 372f.). It is the value judgement that matters (cf. Grube *op.cit.* p.199 n.2).

Another potential source of conflict would be the matter of rhetorical styles. In *Orator* Cicero propounds the view that perfection in rhetoric lies largely in command of the different styles and the ability to use them at the appropriate moments. Compare the whole of 69f., including the extensive survey of the three styles (75-99), and the authoritative conclusions stated at 100f. and 123 (*haec enim sapientia maxime adhibenda eloquenti est, ut sit temporum personarumque moderator . . .is erit ergo eloquens qui ad id quodcumque decebit poterit*

17

accomodare orationem). The Philodeman position appears quite contrary to this. There is one style which is the "naturally fine *logos*" (1,151,7f.) and which is generally applicable. The rhetors are at fault in not allowing only one style (1,152,10-20). Philodemus moreover has a strong feeling against elaboration of style, just as against complication in the numeration of styles, so that his one style will be the plain one (cf. Grube *op.cit.* p. 204). The reference to different types of style in the context of ornamentation (1,165,2f.) is not very clear and cannot overturn the impression gained from the other passages. The same applies in the context of poetry (to which Cicero also applies his concept of the appropriate style, *Orator* 74), as we see from *Poetics* 5,31f.: it is simply mad to speak of matching style and matter, and the supposed achievement of such matching cannot be the criterion of a good poet. Philodemus can take a very cavalier attitude to style when it suits him – we will see more of this in a moment – and this could hardly appeal to Cicero, always the supremely conscious stylist. For Cicero the wielding of different styles in a rhetorical context is the way to persuasion. For Philodemus those who teach style do not teach persuasion (cf. Grube *op.cit.* p.201). The divergence is total.

Philodemus' views on rhetoric cannot therefore but have seemed antipathetic to Cicero. The same would go for his ideas on poetry. I select three areas for comment.

(i)   Cicero had a great interest in tragedy, not least from the point of view of its value in moral terms. That is a fundamentally Aristotelian view of the matter: one can view the Aristotelian *Poetics* as a sort of sustained polemic against the Platonic devaluation of literary art. So it is not unlikely that Cicero would have found fault with Philodemus' assault, in the fourth book of the *Poetics,* on Aristotle's poetical theory (cf. F. Sbordone *Richerche sui papiri ercolanei* I Naples (1969) pp.289f.). The attitude to tragedy that emerges there, including the distinct preference for epic poetry, is of course of particular relevance to *Tusculans* 3,45.

(ii)   Philodemus laid great stress on the content of poetry as against its form and sound, criteria that had received, he thought, too much recognition from certain critics. The followers of Crates, for example, held that apart from sound everything that people praise in poetry is common to all, be it good or bad; and though Crates allowed that, despite the fact that the "natural differences" of poems are judged by hearing, poems are accounted good or bad not if they please the ear but if they satisfy the apparently wider theoretical principles of art,[36] Philodemus will have none of it, regarding the position as inconsistent.[37] He himself, of course,

18

attacked judgement by ear as opposed to reason.[38] Similar disapproval goes to Aristomenides,[39] while Heracleodorus, who considered that *synthesis* (*compositio*) was of supreme importance,[40] that thought in itself, whether or not artistically expressed, has no aesthetic effect[41] and that it can even be obscurely expressed without harm resulting,[42] is also berated.[43] Quality can of course depend on *synthesis* if thought and diction happen to be the same.[44] and, in general, importance can attach to aspects other than content, when purely borrowed material is in question.[45] But by and large it is content that remains central. Characteristically, for Philodemus, unlike other critics, *metathesis* affects thought and meaning,[46] while his comments on *poēma, poēsis* and *poētēs* are susceptible of interpretation as part of the desire to keep content to the fore.[47] To some extent this stress on content is corrective rather than definitive, and Philodemus' more positive point of view does involve an indissoluble relation between the various constituents of a poem which others tended, at least for pedagogic purposes, to separate.[48] How far he took this is a matter of dispute;[49] but in any event the favour for *dianoia* is indubitable, as is the exasperation with over-subtle stylistic analysis (e.g. *Poetics* 5,3-5). Cicero was a man with high regard for the formal aspect of poetic creation (D'Alton *op.cit.* pp.141f.) and above all a consciousness of style, of the sheer manner of expressing ideas. For him poetry is characterised in terms of rhythms, *verba, ornandi genera* in which the poet was the greater or lesser relation of the orator (*De Oratore* 1,70ff). This manner of speaking is outlawed by Philodeman theory, while Cicero's fundamental interests and the objects of his basic sensibilities are set at a low level of importance. This could scarcely have led him to favour Philodemus.

(iii) Antiquity as a whole is full of the idea that poetry has a certain utility and a consequent moral duty, and this idea was certainly shared by Cicero. It is evident in his well known stand on the lyric poets whom he had never read (cf. Seneca *Epistulae* 49,5) or in the curious notion that the sheer quality of poetry could make it "dangerous" (cf. *Tusculans* 1,106; 2,49). Torquatus is approved in *De Finibus* 1,72 because he only peruses poets who teach useful things and not those who provide childish amusements. Other relevant comments are found at *Ad Quintum Fratrem* 2,15,2; *De Oratore* 2,239; 242; *Orator* 88; and the treatment of Archias is telling (*Pro Archia* 12f.). Above all, Cicero's own widespread use of poetic texts in philosophical works demonstrates his position on the matter. Philodemus took a different view; the *dianoia* for which he is so passionate an advocate is not considered to be useful or morally

19

improving, or at least not necessarily so. He is most critical of other theorists' failure to be specific about the nature of the utility they supposed to be the purpose, in part anyway, of the good poet (*Poetics* 5, *Fr.*2,23f.; col. 1, 1f.; 15f.; 13,13-22; 29 *passim*) and the whole theme is frequently touched on in the fifth book of the *Poetics*. Two succinct statements must suffice: "For a poem does not by its nature produce any *opheilēma* either by its language or its thought" (5,22,30f.); "Even if a poem does have a useful effect, it is not *qua* poem that it does so" (5,29,17-9). The only striking passage that seems at first to attempt to introduce a moral tone into poetic criticism is *P. Herc.* 1074 col.105 (=VH[2]IV,201).[50] This refers to the attraction for the Greeks of Archilochus, Hipponax, Simonides and certain dubious parts of Homer and Euripides (material related to *ponēra prosōpa*), and might be thought to be attacking such preoccupations. However, although the fragment breaks off at the crucial point, it looks as though the context was the familiar one of the importance of content and that the point was going to be that the question of whether a man is a good poet has nothing to do with whether he is a good man. A similar view appears in the rhetorical writings, 2,226,12f. (wickedness does not stand in the way of technical excellence), and is of course connected with what is said above about the non-educative value of study of *sophistikē*. So the general impression of Philodeman artistic amorality, which applied in other fields as well,[51] is maintained; and we can only suppose that Cicero would have greatly disapproved.

I would conclude this sketch of Cicero's reaction to Philodemus the *litterateur* by reiterating two points mentioned above in connection with rhetoric. (i) Epicureans were traditionally hostile to literary arts (cf. e.g. *Tusculans* 1,6; 2,7; *De Finibus* 1,14; *Ad Familiares* 15,16; *In Pisonem* 70; and other passages cited in Pease's commentary on *De Natura Deorum* 1,72). While this would tend to increase interest in literary theory from the pen of an Epicurean, it would also make Cicero come to the reading of that theory with a mind not entirely open. (ii) The manner of Philodemus, quite apart from being stylistically far from attractive, and therefore confirming the bias just mentioned, is viciously polemical (cf. Grube *op.cit.* p.204; Sudhaus *op.cit.* I, p.xxiii). It would inevitably produce in those who disagreed with it not just disinterest but distaste and antipathy.

The presumptive case for Ciceronian hostility to Philodemus thus seems strong, and to it may be added Philodemus' own poetry, about which little need be said, as the point is very obvious. Playful, erotic epigram is not a genre calculated to appeal to Cicero very much, at least in his philosophically self-righteous moods. That I devote little space to this should not be taken as implying that it is of minor importance. On the contrary, Philodemus' authorship of such things would show as clearly as did his literary theory that poetically his heart was in the wrong place, and might assist in eliciting the tag *cantores Euphorionis*. For the lack of moral seriousness about human suffering that characterises much of Hellenistic epigram could also seem discernible in the distasteful complexities of Euphorion. Still, since the specific naming of Euphorion might have a correspondingly specific explanation that we cannot now discover, Gallus being an admittedly tenuous link, this may only be an ancillary consideration.

It is time for a summary of the argument. (i) The comment about the *cantores Euphorionis* is distinguished by precision and animus that call for explanation. (ii) The context, an impassioned attack on Epicurean hedonism, provides part of that explanation and suggests Epicurean overtones to the *cantores*. (iii) We know of a pair of eminent Greek Epicureans, one of them a poet and literary man, who were often in Cicero's mind at this time, and in whose company Roman poets were to be found. (iv) There is every reason to suppose that Cicero will have had a low opinion of this group, especially in literary connections. It is worth noting that at this date there will hardly yet have been any saving grace in political considerations (cf. A. Momigliano *JRS* 31(1941) pp. 151-5). The attacks on Antony from Varius — *Fr.* 12 (Morel), and from Philodemus — *On the Gods* 1,25,23-7 (Diehl), *On Death* 34,15-35 (Kuiper) are yet to come, and *On the good King in Homer*, often thought to be a covert political tract, may have been fourteen years old (O. Murray *JRS* 55 (1965) pp.161-182), if it too was not still unwritten. While the "republican" disposition that produced these works may already have been discernible, and may even account for the apparent friendliness in some of Cicero's references, it will count for little in a literary and philosophical context.

The state of the evidence about the poetical world of the forties BC precludes certainty in this and other hypotheses. At the same time the importance of that period as a link between republic and principate in literary as in political matters imposes upon the literary historian a duty and privilege of speculation. It is only to be hoped that this privilege has not here been abused. [52]

NOTES

1. Some bibliographical reference in N.B. Crowther CQ n.s.20 (1970) pp.322-8.

2. Cf. Sch. Hom. *Il.* 1, 59; 103; 108; 516 etc; T.P. Wiseman *Cinna the Poet* Leicester (1974) p. 51; L. Alfonsi *Mnemosyne* ser. 4, 2 (1949) p. 217.

3. See for details A. Cameron *Poetae Novelli* (forthcoming). The whole of this paper is important on the essential vagueness of titles like "new poets". I am very grateful to Professor Cameron for the opportunity of using it ahead of publication.

4. J C Bramble *Persius and the Programmatic Satire* Cambridge (1974) pp. 181f.

5. The analogy argument and "newness" come together again in Gellius *Noct.Att.* 11, 1, 5; 16, 7, 13; 17, 2, 15. This may be a significant coincidence.

6. H. Bardon *La Littérature latine inconnue* I Paris (1952) pp. 359f.

7. *Roman Literary Criticism: a Study in Tendencies* London (1931) p. 149.

8. T.W. Dougan *Tusculan Disputations* Cambridge (1905), introduction. Alterations in the datings of some Atticus letters by Shackleton Baily do not greatly affect the issue.

9. Cf. R.P. Westendorp Boerma *Catalepton* I Assen (1949) pp. 99f; R.G.M. Nisbet *In Pisonem* Oxford (1961) pp. 183-188; R. Philippson *BPh.W*29 (1910) pp. 740f.

10. Eg. Servius *ad Ecl.* 6, 13; *ad Aen.* 6, 264; Schol. Veron. *ad Ecl.* 6, 10; Donatus *Vita* 79 (Diehl); Phocas *Vita* 87 (Br.), cf. N. de Witt *CPh.* 17 (1922) pp. 104-110. The date of summer 45 for Vergil's presence in Naples is of course at best a *terminus ante quem.*

11. Cf. A. Koerte *Rh.M* n.f.45 (1890) pp. 172f. On the Plotius/Horace controversy, E. Bickel *Symb. Osl.* 28 (1950) p. 22; M. Gigante *Cronache ercolanesi* 3 (1973) pp. 86f

12. H. Bardon *La Littérature latine inconnue* II Paris (1956) pp. 29f.

13. J-P. Boucher *Caius Cornelius Gallus* Paris (1966) pp. 103f.

14. Bramble *op.cit.* p. 181, cf. Boucher *op.cit.* p. 77 n.30.

15. A. Momigliano *JRS* 31 (1941) p.152.

16. R. Syme *CQ* 32 (1938) pp. 39f., more convincing than Boucher's advocacy of Voghera.

17 Cinna at least should not be forgotten. Cf. Wiseman *op.cit.* (n.2) pp.47f.

18. *Frr.* 55, 62; 69; 70; 71 (Powell).

19. 7, 25/*AP* 6, 279 (contrast Gow-Page *ad loc.*); 9, 13/*Fr.* 48 (Powell); 10, 66/*Fr.* 58 (Powell); 8, 21/*PSI* 1390 C 29.

20. *The Catullan Revolution* Cambridge (1959) p.20.

21. *Ad Att.* 13, 12; 13, 16, 1; 13, 19, 4f.; Dougan *op.cit.* p.xv.

22. A. Rostagni *Riv. Fil.* 61 (1933) pp. 449f.

23. Petron. *Sat.* 53, 11; 63, 7.

24. Controversial: cf. D. van Berchem *MH* 3 (1946) pp. 26f.; H.M. Howe *AJP* 72 (1951) pp. 57f.; P. Boyance *Lucrèce et l'épicurisme* Paris (1963) pp. 8f.; M. Gigante *Ricerche Filodemee* Naples (1969) ch.1.

25. Philodemus *On Methods of Inference* p. 66 (de Lacy); *Peri Eusebeias* p. 118G; *Against the (Sophists)* 11, 6 (Sbordone).

26. H. Diels *Abh. Preuss. Akad.* (Phil.-Hist.-Klasse) 1915, no 7, p. 99.

27. *De Natura Deorum* I Cambridge (1880) pp. xlvif.

28. H. Diels *Doxographi Graeci* Berlin (1879) p.125.

29. See also M. van Brawaene *Cicero De Natura Deorum Livre I* Bruxelles (1970) pp.18f.

30. That Cicero had not read Latin Epicureans (*Tusc.* 2,7) has no bearing.

31. Reference to Philodemus' rhetorical works are to volume, page and line of the edition of S. Sudhaus, 2 vols, and supplement, Leipzig 1892/1896 and 1895. The fifth book of the *Poetics* is quoted from Jensen's edition, Berlin 1923. Other papyri are quoted from the second collection of *Volumina Herculanensia* (VH^2) and in the case of pap. 1676 also from Heidmann's edition reprinted in *Cronache ercolanesi* 1 (1971). All use of papyrological evidence is subject to the dangers consequent on supplementation, and much of the work of Sudhaus and Jensen is rather bold in this respect. But the argument of this paper does not, I think, turn unduly on hazardous supplements.

32. Cf. H. von Arnim *Dio von Prusa* Berlin (1898) pp. 4-114.

33. G.M.A. Grube *The Greek and Roman Critics* London (1965) ch. 11; H.M. Hubbell *The Influence of Isocrates on Cicero* New Haven (1913) ch. 2.

34. Cf. *Antidosis* 180f.; 255; 271; 277; 262; *Sophist.* 2-8; *Panath.* 26-30; *De Oratore* 2, 96; *Brutus* 93.

35. Cf. further Grube *op.cit.* p.200; Sudhaus *op.cit.* I pp. xli-xliv.

36. *P. Herc.* 228 = VH^2 VIII 165; *Poetics* 5, col. 25.

37. *P. Herc.* 994 coll. 21-5 = VH^2 VI 170-4 = *RAAN* 30 (1955) pp. 29-33.

38. *Poetics* 5,20f.; 23, 30-5; 24f.

39. *Ib.* 21; VH^2 IV 113.

40. *P. Herc.* 1676, 6, 4-7 = VH^2 XI 159 = p. 101 Heidmann(=H).

41. *P. Herc.* 1081 *Fr.* 23 = VH^2 VII 100.

42. *P. Herc.* 1676 *Fr.* 3 = VH^2 XI 148 = p. 94H.

43. *Ib. Fr.* 11/col. 1 = VH^2 *ib.* 153 = p. 97H.

44. *Ib.* coll. 6-7 = VH^2 XI 159-160 = pp. 101/2H.

45. *Ib.* col. 1 = VH^2 XI 154 = 97-8H; *P. Herc.* 1081 col. 9 + *P. Herc.* 1074 col. 14 (cf. F. Sbordone *RAAN* 31 (1956) pp. 170f.).

46. *P. Herc.* 1676 col. 8 = VH^2 XI 163 = p. 103H; cf N. Greenberg *TAPA* 89 (1958) pp. 262f.

47. N. Greenberg *HSCP* 65 (1961) p.281.

48. Often in *Poetics* 5(coll. 5, 9, 10-13, 26); cf. *P. Herc.* 994 col. 34 = VH^2 VI 183 = *RAAN* 30 (1955) p. 42; Grube *op.cit.* p. 196.

49. Cf. N. Greenberg *HSCP loc.cit.* p. 283.

50. F. Sbordone *RAAN* 32 (1957) p. 176; V. de Falco *Aegyptus* 3 (1922) p. 290.

51. L.P. Wilkinson *CQ* 32 (1938) pp. 174ff.

52. Thanks for various assistance is due to Alan Cameron, John Bramble, Donald Russell and David Sedley, and special thanks for encouragement at the beginning and end of the project to Margaret Hubbard and Francis Cairns.

VERGIL'S FOURTH *ECLOGUE*[1]

by

IAN M. LE M. DU QUESNAY
(University of Birmingham)

Eclogue 4 is a complex and difficult poem. This paper offers a new interpretation that attempts to account for all the various elements in the poem. Inevitably, in view of the vast secondary literature,[2] it is necessary to state again some well-known explanations of some details in order to achieve any degree of completeness or comprehensibility. On the other hand a special effort has been made to avoid preconceptions and to question prejudices that inevitably gather round such a well-known poem.

The problems presented by *Eclogue* 4 fall into two different, though not quite distinct, categories. First there are those that are accidental, the result of the intervening gap of two thousand years. These are here discussed as historical problems (§§1–5): the character and biography of the addressee, the exact date of the poem, the nature and significance of the occasion it celebrates, the identity of the child and the meaning of the change of *saecula* as it was seen in the first century. A contemporary reader would have knowledge of all this, but we have to extract it from meagre evidence. Yet this historical context provides the undertones and overtones, general associations and specific point for words and phrases that seem neutral when it is not considered.

The main part of the paper is that which examines the other set of difficulties (§§6–8). These are posed by Vergil to be solved by his sophisticated reader and involve imitation of and allusion to specific poems and manipulation of the commonplaces of ancient literature. The solving of these problems is part of the enjoyment of the poem. In order to further understanding of the relationship of *Eclogue* 4 to its models, Theocritus *Idyll* 17 and Catullus 64, Vergil's techniques of imitation and allusion have been studied in combination with his handling of the generic material suggested to him on the one hand by Theocritus *Idyll* 17 *qua* basilikon and on the other by Catullus 64 *qua* epithalamium. This can be done only after *Eclogue* 4 has been properly assigned to its genre and analysed in the light of the conventions of that genre. The poem is then considered in relationship to the *Sibylline Oracles* (§ 9) and the study is completed by a brief analysis of the most striking stylistic features of the poem (§ 10).

1. C. Asinius Pollio

Since the importance of Pollio to Vergil as the poet of the *Eclogues* and his role in *Eclogue* 4 are too often minimised, it is worth stating briefly what we know of him and how it illuminates the poem. Born in 76 BC,[3] Pollio was about five years older than Vergil, and ten years younger than Catullus, in whose social circle he moved as a young man.[4] When he visited Greece at the age of nineteen (56 BC)[5] Helvius Cinna wrote for him a propemptikon, one of the most famous poems of the day.[6] A poet himself, he composed *nova carmina* and tragedies in imitation of Sophocles.[7] In 43 BC he referred to C. Cornelius Gallus, the *cantor Euphorionis*, as his *familiaris*; and he apparently secured for this protégé a training with the leading consular, orator and *novus homo* of the day, M. Tullius Cicero.[8] About the same time or a little later he suggested to Vergil that he should write the *Eclogues* and become the Roman Theocritus[9] and Vergil expressed his gratitude for Pollio's support in *Eclogue* 3, one of his earliest poems (42 BC).[10] It is interesting that the three poets who have links with Pollio at this stage are also the three known to have been associated with Parthenius: Cinna, Gallus and Vergil.[11]

After his triumph Pollio built, with the booty from his campaigns, a monument to the now dead republic, the *Atrium Libertatis*, Rome's first public library.[12] He resumed his interest in letters, originated the practice of recitation, supported various writers and wrote his *Historiae*. He early achieved a considerable reputation as a critic.[13]

Pollio was also a highly successful soldier-politician. He began in 54 BC by attempting to prosecute the tribune C. Cato, who was defended by Scaurus and Calvus and acquitted through Pompey's influence.[14] Perhaps as a result of this case he incurred the enmity of some unknown powerful persons and threw in his lot with Julius Caesar, whom he served loyally and well until his death in 44 BC. He had a deep personal affection for Caesar but still professed his love for the old order, the Republic.[15] This is unlikely to have been hypocrisy: he was ambitious to succeed within the system and would not want the system changed and his achievement of prestigious office devalued. After his praetorship (45 BC?) he commanded Hispania Ulterior, probably as proconsul. There he waged war against Sextus Pompeius;[16] and he was in Spain when Caesar was assassinated. He remained neutral until it became clear that the Republican party was in fact the Pompeian party resurrected.[17] Octavian was at that moment flirting with these enemies of Caesar; and Pollio declared for M. Antonius, at the time Caesar's obvious successor and known to Pollio, presumably, from earlier days. Antonius commanded his loyalties until his withdrawal from politics in 39 BC.[18]

At the formation of the triumvirate in November 43 BC[19] it was agreed that Pollio should be one of the consuls for 40 BC at the age of thirty-five.[20] This was to be his reward for taking command of the key province, Gallia Cisalpina, in the previous year (41 BC). Gallia Cisalpina was one of Antonius' provinces according to the division of 43 BC. But when Octavian returned to settle the veterans after Philippi, he claimed that it was to be made part of Italy.[21] There is no suggestion that Pollio submitted to Octavian's claims, but when Agrippa routed Pollio's forces while they were attempting to relieve L. Antonius besieged at Perusia, Octavian took over the province.[22] It is often stated that Pollio was in charge of settling veterans in Cisalpina; but there is no evidence to support this idea[23] or its concomitant — that Vergil came to know Pollio through the confiscation of his father's[24] Mantuan estates. Vergil knew Pollio in 42 BC;[25] and there is no evidence either to support the common belief that Pollio was in charge of Cisalpina in that year.[26]

During the whole of this period there is no doubt about the political allegiance of Pollio. He had declared for Antonius in 43 BC; he was Antonius' nominee for the consulship in 40 BC; he was Antonius' legate in Cisalpina in 41 BC. In 41 BC he had warded off Octavian's attempts to annex Antonius' province, and he had been drawn into the Perusine War on the side of the Triumvir's brother, L. Antonius *cos.* 41 BC. Macrobius preserves a bitter epigram written against Octavian.[27] When Pollio was forced to withdraw to Venetia,[28] it was clear that he had been robbed of his consulship by Octavian and his generals. Through the next six months of 40 BC Pollio was busy preparing for the return of Antonius and for the new war against Octavian. When he reappeared for the negotiations at Brundisium, he acted for Antonius, as did Maecenas for Octavian.[29] Even when Pollio left active politics (39 BC) he never ceased to assert his independence of Octavian.[30]

It is not too difficult to suggest connections between these facts and *Eclogue* 4, although inevitably some of the suggestions will be more tentative than others. It is clear that, when the man who was his friend and, in some sense at least, his patron reached the summit of his brilliant, if unorthodox, career and held the consulate seven years early, Vergil must have felt a certain obligation to honour him. The obligation brought a challenge. For not only was Pollio himself a practising poet and an austere critic but a standard had inevitably been set by Cinna's famous propemptikon, a poem evoked by a far less momentous occasion. No wonder then that Vergil resolved to sing *paulo maiora*, to make his *silvae consule dignae* (*Eclogue* 4,1; 3). But it was Pollio who had urged him to become *Theocritus Romanus*: this was no moment to forsake his model. So the poem opens with an invocation of the *Sicelidae Musae*. Vergil acknowledges that Theocritus is not universally popular (*non omnis arbusta iuvant*, *Eclogue* 4,2); but Pollio was not one of the undiscerning masses. When Vergil turned to Theocritus for a model for a poem to be written in honour of a Roman consul, *Idylls* 16 and 17, both written for βασιλεῖς, would easily have suggested themselves; and it was *Idyll* 17 that he chose as a model. This is in itself to be seen as a compliment to Pollio, an acknowledgement of indebtedness both for p tronage and for literary inspiration.

Catullus 64 is the poem's chief Latin model, as has long been recognised. Pollio cannot have been displeased at this allusion to the *magnum opus* of a now famous poet whom he had known as a youth. There may be more to the choice of Catullus as a model than is now apparent: in another poem dedicated to Pollio (*Eclogue* 8) Vergil Romanised *Idyll* 2, a poem which the Elder Pliny seems to imply had previously been 'translated' into Latin by Catullus.[31]

Two further possibilities are worth mentioning although the evidence is suggestive rather than conclusive. Vergil may be glancing sideways at a poem of the other protégé of Pollio, C. Cornelius Gallus; and he may also be alluding to a lost description of the Golden Age in Pollio's own poetry. That Vergil is alluding to Gallus[32] seems to be suggested by a number of similarities between *Eclogue* 4 and the poetry of Propertius and Tibullus. At *Eclogue* 4, 53f. Vergil expresses a wish that he may live to sing the deeds of the *puer*. This same topos is used by Propertius in 2,10,19f. with reference to Augustus; and this same poem of Propertius ends (2,10,25f.) with a well known echo of Vergil's account of the *Dichterweihe* of Gallus in *Eclogue* 6,64ff.[33] Moreover, Vergil goes on to claim that in singing of the deeds of the *puer* he will surpass Orpheus and Linus; and Propertius in 2,13 (a companion piece to 2,10) couples a reference to Orpheus with the claim that his poetry for Cynthia will make him *Inachio notior arte Lino* (2,13,8).

A common debt to Gallus might also explain the similarities that exist between our poem and Tibullus 1,7. Both poems are of almost identical length (63 lines, 64 lines); both have a similar structure, an outer frame and an inner panel; in both poems the poet honours his patron (Pollio, Messalla) for his achievement (the consulship, the triumph); in both the occasion itself is confined to the frame while the centre panel celebrates one who brings about the joys of a rustic paradise (the *puer* in the future; Osiris in the past); both clearly echo the refrain of Catullus' Song of the Fates (64,321f.; 327, cf. *Eclogue* 4,46f.; Tibullus 1,7,1f.). But the similarities here may be due to direct influence or similarity of occasion and genre.

The hypothesis that Vergil is alluding to a lost work of Asinius Pollio is based on the evidence of the *Eclogues* alone.[34] *Eclogues* 3, 4 and 8 are all addressed to Pollio; and all of them contain Golden Age descriptions based on the idea of a reversal of nature. In *Eclogue* 3, in connection with the direct address to Pollio, Vergil expresses the wish (89): *mella fluant illi, ferat et rubus asper amomum.* This finds a parallel in *Eclogue* 4,29f.: *incultisque rubens pendebit sentibus uva/et durae quercus sudabunt roscida mella;* and in *Eclogue* 4,25: *Assyrium vulgo nascetur amomum.* In *Eclogue* 8 the lovesick shepherd says (52ff.): *nunc et ovis ultro fugiat lupus, aurea durae/mala ferant quercus, narcisso floreat alnus,/pinguia corticibus sudent electra myricae.* Apart from the echoes of *Eclogue* 4,29f. there are also parallels in *nec magnos metuent armenta leones* (4,22) and in *humilesque myricae* (4,2). It is, moreover, these similarities of detail and conception that differentiate these passages from the descriptions of the *locus amoenus* elsewhere in the *Eclogues*. The obvious explanation is that Vergil is here alluding to some work of Pollio himself as a compliment to the addressee.

To sum up: Vergil has taken as his models in *Eclogue* 4 Theocritus *Idyll* 17 and Catullus 64; and both these poets have a special relevance to Pollio. In addition there is some slight reason for supposing that Vergil may also be glancing sideways at a poem by Gallus written for this or an analogous occasion, and that he might also be colouring his poem with phrases and ideas from Pollio's own poetry. It is clear that Vergil has carefully written his poem to reflect and to compliment the literary tastes of his addressee.

Pollio in *Eclogue* 4 is not just a patron of letters. He is addressed as consul and we must therefore expect the attitudes and actions of Pollio as soldier, statesman and politician to be equally relevant. One point must be stated bluntly at the outset. We should not expect a poem written in honour of Pollio to reflect glory on Pollio's political enemy Octavian any more than we would expect a poem written in honour of Maecenas to reflect glory on Antonius. We know nothing of Vergil's political leanings at this period beyond what is revealed in the *Eclogues*. It is not however the political allegiances of an unknown Alexandrian poet that are relevant but those of the dedicatee, a leading politician and soldier, whose political attachments would be known to any reader of the poem.

2. Date

Pollio is addressed in this poem as consul (3,11). This suggests three possible dates for the composition of the poem:

(1) Late 43 BC. It was at the formation of the Triumvirate that Pollio learned that he was to be consul in 40 BC. But there are serious objections to accepting this early date. It would mean that *Eclogue* 4 was one of the very earliest of the *Eclogues*. We would have to accept that Vergil could speak with confidence and hope of the coming of a new age immediately before the triumvirs launched their campaign against the assassins of Caesar, that is, before a war of unknown duration and outcome in which many of Vergil's Epicurean friends chose to fight against the triumvirs.[35] It would also imply that Pollio would not have found it tactless to have his consulship immortalised as the gift from a selection board of three and not as a recognition of worth by the *SPQR*.

(2) Late 41 BC. This date has been widely canvassed[36] and rests on lines 11f.:

> teque adeo decus hoc aevi, te consule, inibit,
> Pollio, et incipient magni procedere menses.

It has been suggested on the basis of these lines that not only the new age but also Pollio's consulship lie in the future. This is a patently false deduction, since there is no reason why someone who has just taken up an office should not be told that something will happen while he holds it. There are additional severe objections to dating the poem to late 41 BC. It became increasingly clear from the summer of 41 BC on that the civil war was worsening; and in these circumstances it must have appeared ever more unlikely that Antonius' legate,[37] Pollio, would be able to take up his consulship on January 1st 40 BC. Indeed in the first weeks of that year Pollio was engaged in open hostilities with Octavian and his generals and he was soon driven from Italy altogether. It is certain that he could not in fact have taken up his office until after the treaty of Brundisium.[38] Not all the details are clear, but it seems inconceivable that in the circumstances prevailing from summer 41 BC to summer 40 BC Vergil could have written with confidence of a new age of peace that was to dawn in the consulship of his patron.[39]

(3) September 40 BC. Pollio did not enter Rome to take up his consulship until after the treaty of Brundisium, that is probably early in September.[40] He left for Macedonia before the end of the year, probably in late November.[41] This was the moment when the threat of civil war in Italy was averted, contrary to all the expectations of the previous months, and the moment which exactly suits the mood of our poem.[42] At last the new age, bringing peace not destruction, which had been promised intermittently by the propaganda of the moneyers, could actually begin.[43] This date and this date alone suits our poem.[44]

3.   Identity of the *Puer* and Historical Setting

This question is one that has taxed scholars since the first century BC,[45] but it is a question that must be faced, not avoided. The first decision to be made is whether the birth of the child is thought of as having already taken place or as being imminent or as an event lying in the more distant future.

There is no doubt that the new age has not yet begun. This is made clear by lines 11f. (*inibit; incipient*) and line 52 (*venturo saeclo*). Nor is there any doubt that the beginning of the new age is linked with the birth of the child: *nascenti puero quo ferrea* (sc. *gens*) *primum desinet* (8f.). Therefore the birth of the child must lie in the future.

If the event were imminent we would expect the poet to show more concern for the mother and for the safe delivery of the child than he does. But the only indication that the birth might be imminent is the past tense in line 61: *matri longa decem tulerunt fastidia menses.*[46] This past tense and the unusual scansion of *tulerunt* as an anapaest have caused problems since Roman times. The manuscripts offer, in addition, the readings *tulerint* and *tulerant;* and Servius in his note on the line records the suggestions of others that *abstulerint* should be the reading.[47] The manuscripts of Servius offer the variations *adtulerunt, attulerint, abstulerunt.* In spite of this confusion in the tradition there is no need to doubt the authenticity of *tulerunt.* The last four lines of the poem consist of two balanced couplets, each introduced by *incipe, parve puer.* The first couplet concerns the mother, the second the father.[48] This kind of balance is characteristic of Theocritean poetry and, as we shall see, of this poem.[49] The past tense *tulerunt* must therefore balance *dignata est* in line 63. The parallelism also makes it clear that *tulerunt* is not a true perfect indicating that the dramatic temporal setting is at the end of the period of pregnancy, just before birth. It must rather express a general truth, which

31

is given as the reason for the impe ative *incipe* in the preceding line, in just the same way as *dignata est* is given as the reason for the second *incipe* in the final line.[50] These lines may therefore be translated: 'Come, little fellow, acknowledge mother with a smile; ten months bring (a) mother endless discomfort. Come, little fellow: those who do not smile at father, neither a god thinks him worthy of his table, nor a goddess of her bed.' Such playful sententiousness is typical of nursery talk.[51] Line 61 cannot, then, be taken to indicate that the birth of the child is an immediate prospect, much less that it has actually happened.

There can be no objection to these lines being addressed to an unborn child, since there is a parallel in Statius *Silvae* 1,2,269ff.: *tuque ipse parenti/parce, puer, ne mollem uterum, ne stantia laedas/pectora.* These lines come at the end of an epithalamium and the same topos occurs in a slightly different form in Catullus 61,209ff. at the end of another epithalamium: *Torquatus volo parvulus/matris e gremio suae/porrigens teneras manus/semihiante labello.* These parallels provide an important clue that the occasion of Vergil's address to the child was a wedding. This was the only occasion on which it was appropriate to talk of an unborn child, at least of a real child that had not yet been born.[52]

It may seem strange that Vergil should prophesy about an unborn child, for to make such a prophecy was clearly a hazardous undertaking. Awareness of the danger of being proved wrong was doubtless a factor in making Vergil cautious about identifying the child explicitly. Indeed such vagueness is characteristic of any prophet who wishes to safeguard his future reputation. Nonetheless Romans clearly did not shrink from making such prophecies and predictions in their poetry. So, for example, Tibullus prophesies a triumph for Messallinus (2,5,113ff.) which he did not win until after the poet's death; Martial predicts a *puer* for Domitian (6,3) which was never born.[53] It is especially worth noting that such prophecies were so commonplace that the rhetoricians prescribed them for writers of epithalamia.[54]

The next question to be raised is whether the child is a real child or not.[55] No attempt to explain the child as an abstract, a symbol or as identical with the age itself will be convincing, since the child, though indissolubly associated with the new age, is distinct from it. Lucina will attend his birth (10); he has a father (17) and a mother (60); the earth will bear him gifts (19ff.); he will be educated in the Roman manner (26); he will perform *facta* (54). On the other hand it was argued above that the child has not been born. It is therefore envisaged as a real but unborn child, full of potential, the sum of all human possibilities as they were conceived by the ancients, unlimited by such accidents as being born deformed, dead or a girl. Vergil does not tell us directly who the child is to be, or who the parents are. Nor are we told explicitly when the child will be born, only that it will be conceived during the consulship of Pollio.[56] Because of this specific indication of time and the association of the child with a real man and a real event – Pollio's consulship – it is inevitable that the reader should wish to identify the child; and it is a historical fact that attempts to do so have been made since the first century BC as the following passage shows:

> quidam Saloninum Pollionis filium accipiunt, alii Asinium Gallum, fratrem Salonini, qui prius natus est Pollione consule designato. Asconius Pedianus a Gallo audisse se refert, hanc eclogam in honorem eius factam.

Servius Auctus *ad Eclogue* 4,11[57]

But there are two serious objections to the child being a son of Pollio. First, Pollio is nowhere said to be the father, either implicitly or explicitly, nor is the mother said to be Pollio's wife. Secondly, the line *pacatumque reget patriis virtutibus orbem* cannot refer to a consul or to the son of a consul.[58] Moreover none of the observable characteristics of the child (see below) fit with anything known about Pollio. It has already been shown that a date in 41 BC is impossible; and this excludes Asinius Gallus who must have been born in that year if not earlier.[59] Asinius Saloninus was not Pollio's son but his grandson, the son of Asinius Gallus. Saloninus was mistakenly thought to be a son of Pollio because of the association of his name with Pollio's capture of Salona in Dalmatia.[60]

It is widely believed that the *puer* is the expected son of Octavian and Scribonia.[61] This belief is founded essentially on the undoubted admiration for Octavian that Vergil expresses in the *Georgics* and the *Aeneid.*[62] However, to proceed backwards through the poet's works is clearly an unsound procedure. Octavian and Scribonia were indeed married in 40 BC. But this was in the spring when Pollio was still being kept out of his consulship and Italy, and was preparing for Antonius' return and civil war. Moreover the marriage of Octavian and Scribonia was intended to cement a bond between Octavian and Sex. Pompeius, Pollio's two known enemies.[63] Some very explicit indication that Vergil's *puer* was to be the son of Octavian and Scribonia would be needed to surmount this objection. This is not provided by the mention of Apollo (11) and the

33

indications that the child is descended from Jupiter (49) and a second Hercules (see below) which are, at the very most, ambiguous. Nor is it easy to understand why, if the child was to be Octavian's, this should have been forgotten so soon.

There is in short only one child that fits the circumstances, the date and the indications given in the poem. This is the expected child of M. Antonius and Octavia.[64] Their wedding is intimately connected with Pollio and his consulship. He, as one of the negotiators at Brundisium,[65] was at least partly responsible for making the match. He was the friend and loyal supporter of the husband.[66] The marriage was the outward, symbolic act that guaranteed *concordia* between Octavian and Antonius, and *pax* for the people of Italy.[67] Pollio's consulship marked the return of constitutional government and normality.[68] Octavia was to marry less than ten months after the death of her previous husband and permission had to be gained from the senate.[69] Who would have been better placed to obtain this permission than the new consul? Every Roman wedding had its *auspex*; again who would have been a better *auspex* than Pollio, friend of the groom, matchmaker and consul? Unhappily these last two suggestions must remain pure guesses. But it is clear that Pollio must have been a guest of honour at the wedding and that the celebrations in honour of the bridal pair and the celebrations in honour of the new consul must have been indissolubly associated in people's minds.[70]

There is moreover no moment more suitable for this poem during these years. From mid 41-40 BC Italy experienced the most extensive, the most bitter and the most bloody fighting since Sulla's wars nearly half a century earlier.[71] It was clearly more traumatic than Pharsalus or even Philippi. The ferocity of the war was heightened by a combination of two factors. Some fought to protect their land and their livelihood, others for the rewards of long and particularly difficult terms of service in the army. Many however saw the war as a last chance to recover the old form of government, a battle for *libertas* against the new tyrants. The grim tale of civil war with the execution and betrayal of the proscribed, split families, shortage of food and frequent riots is detailed in Appian and Dio.[72] The sack of Perusia brought a brief respite and rumours that three hundred senators and knights had been sacrificed *divo Iulio* on the Ides of March.[73] Through spring and summer the confiscations and their associated horrors continued, while Pollio and other Antonian generals prepared for Antonius' return and everyone waited for the inescapable renewal of war. Antonius and his forces landed and the inevitable happened. They began to make a series of quick punitive raids into southern Italy. Then the soldiers refused to fight and the leaders were forced to negotiate. As a result the provinces were redivided, plans were formulated for the conquest of Parthia and other future arrangements, and the *concordia* was sealed by the marriage of Antonius and Octavia. The threat of a final and wholly destructive civil war had been averted.

Normal life seemed to have been restored. The consuls entered office at last.[74] The wedding was celebrated in Rome. Octavian and Antonius were each voted an *ovatio*, not for any victory but *quod pacem fecit*.[75] Games and celebrations must have been almost continuous through Pollio's months of office. The new *concordia* was widely advertised on coins and with inscribed statues.[76] Everyone was pleased since *concordia* between the triumvirs meant *pax* for all.[77] The empire would soon be restored when the invincible[78] Antonius defeated the Parthians and revenged the defeat of Crassus, as Caesar had intended to do four years earlier. Then a new age could begin.[79] No one at this moment could have failed to think of Antonius and Octavia as the parents of Vergil's *puer*. If they did, their suspicions would be confirmed by the text.

Apollo (10) should not at this date lead inevitably to thoughts of Octavian,[80] since the radiate crown of Apollo appeared on the coins of Antonius, not Octavian, after Philippi.[81] But it is not certain that Apollo's appearance here has any political significance at all. He could be an indication of the new age, as Servius thought.[82] At any rate, joined with Lucina, he might reflect the symbolism of the change of *saecula*.[83] Given the association with a wedding, it is worth noting that Apollo's presence is normal in epithalamia,[84] as are prayers to the *genethlioi* (Lucina).[85] Alternatively, given the relationship of *Eclogue* 4 to Catullus 64 the presence of Apollo and his sister may be intended to underscore the differences between the poems, since the gathering of the gods for the wedding of Peleus and Thetis is marked by their absence.[86] There is of course no reason why several of these factors should not be operative.

Magnus Achilles (36) is sometimes seen as a reference to Antonius, and the new Trojan war (36) as a reference to the new war against Parthia.[87] This draws some slight support from two facts: that the Trojan war was commonly considered the first of the wars between Europe and Asia,[88] while this new Trojan war will presumably be the last; and it was a commonplace to compare the bridegroom with Achilles.[89] However there is no evidence that the Parthian campaign was presented elsewhere as a new Trojan war or that Antonius ever attempted to associate himself with

Achilles. There is no historical reference in Tiphys or Argo (34); and there is probably none here. Moreover to see the new Trojan War as the war against Parthia involves crediting Vergil with a most unlikely forecast for these events. He would be implying that the Parthian wars would not begin for fifteen years or would still be in progress fifteen years later. The only solution to this problem would be to assume that the *puer* shared with other gods and heroes a preternaturally rapid rate of growth. However it seems better to avoid reading into this line any specific historical reference which would differentiate it from the lines which immediately precede it and with which it is so intimately connected.

Cara deum suboles, magnum Iovis incrementum (49) I take to mean 'beloved offspring of the gods, mighty scion of Jupiter'.[90] There is no evidence that Antonius at this time identified himself with Jupiter. But he was proud of his descent from Hercules, son of Jupiter;[91] and any child of Antonius could be described as *Iovis incrementum* as a result. *Cara deum suboles* may be taken generally or as referring to the divinities associated with the child's parents, Hercules, Mars (god of the Octavii) and Venus (Antonius' mother was a Julia and Octavia was brought into connection with Venus when her brother became Julius Caesar Octavianus). A further possibility may be suggested tentatively. At the end of his life Julius Caesar was probably identified as *Iuppiter Iulius.*[92] Antonius was chosen to be his *flamen*, but was not inaugurated until the peace of Brundisium in 40 BC.[93] It seems possible therefore that, when the expected *puer* of a marriage designed to unite the heirs of Caesar is called *magnum Iovis incrementum*, there is a deliberate reference to Caesar himself, as *Iuppiter Iulius.*

The last four lines (60-63) provide a more substantial indication of the child's parentage. As already noticed these lines bear a striking resemblance to Catullus 61, 209ff., and Statius *Silvae* 1,2,266ff. But in spite of the close similarity of Vergil to Catullus here, it seems better to see the similarity as due to both poets employing the same epithalamic topos.[94] This would also explain the similarities to Statius. Vergil has transferred the insistence on speed (*brevi*, Catullus 61,204; *heia age* ... *properate*, Statius *Silvae* 1,2,266) to the child (*incipe* ... *incipe*). This is natural since he does not address the parents directly.[95] With Statius Vergil shares a direct address to the *puer* coupled with a reference to the ten months of pregnancy. With Catullus he shares the reference to the laughter of the child.

The scholiast comments on the last line: *proinde nobilibus pueris editis in atrio domus Iunoni lectus, Herculi mensa ponebatur.*[96] He sees a reference to the *genethlioi*[97] and this suggests that Vergil is subtly alluding to the Roman version of a standard epithalamic topos. But this does not explain Vergil's emphasis on laughter, the obliqueness of the expression[98] or the reason for recalling in the last line the earlier passage, *ille deum vitam accipiet divisque videbit/permixtos heroas et ipse videbitur illis* (15f.). The laughter of the child, when taken in connection with this prediction and with the description of the miracles that will attend his birth (18ff.),[99] suggests the divine or miraculous nature of the child.[100] But comparison with the passages of Catullus, Statius and others leads us to expect a reference to what the child has inherited from his mother. If the mother is indeed Octavia, then that is surely what we have. As the sister of the new Iulius Caesar Octavianus she may be assumed to enjoy the special protection of Venus, divine ancestress of the Iulii.[101] Venus-Aphrodite is regularly φιλομμειδής – *ridens* or the subject of the verbs *ridere*, μειδάω, γελάω.[102] So too Caesar claimed that his *flos aetatis* came from Venus,[103] and Nonnus makes his Beroe laugh at birth to show herself a true daughter of Venus (*Dionysiaca* 41,212).

If this is true, then we would also expect an allusion to the father. I have followed most scholars in reading *parenti* and in this context this must mean father (cf. *patriis virtutibus*, 17; *facta parentis*, 26). We have already seen that there is probably a reference on one level to Hercules in the final line. But the whole line can easily be seen as a reference to Hercules who shared the banquets of the gods and took as his wife the goddess Hebe.[104] So the child is urged to smile at his father and show himself a second Hercules, who was αἰὲν ἄδακρυς.[105] Antonius made much of his descent from Hercules via Anton in his propaganda, on his coins and in his style of dress.[106] As the child will be a second Hercules, so he will be the true son of his father Antonius.

That this line of argument is correct is confirmed by a comparison with Theocritus *Idyll* 17.[107] In this encomium of Ptolemy Philadephus, Theocritus begins with the parents, Lagus and Berenice, and then goes on to describe the wonderful events that marked Ptolemy's birth on Cos. Lagus is shown in heaven with his ancestors, one of whom is Heracles. Theocritus then devotes fourteen lines to a description of Heracles enjoying the banquets of the gods, in the company of other heroes and the gods themselves, before being led off to the bed-chamber of Hebe, his divine bride. The final line of our poem and lines 15f., which are followed by the miraculous events that will mark the birth of the *puer*, allude to just this scene. Ptolemy Philadelphus is descended on his father's side from

37

Heracles.[108] His mother, Berenice, though not a direct descendant of Aphrodite, is described at length as enjoying the special favour of that goddess.[109] Vergil's *puer*, if he is the child of Antonius and Octavia, is of exactly the same lineage, descended from Heracles on his father's side and from a mother who, though not a direct descendant of Venus, enjoyed her special favour.

None of these clues is strong enough to show that Vergil was relying on it to identify the child. But Vergil's audience, given the date and the occasion of the poem and the fact that Pollio himself was not about to become a father,[110] could hardly fail to think of the wedding of Antonius and Octavia and their expected offspring. Once they did, they could hardly have failed to recognise these subtle allusions to the child and his parents. Moreover, if the child was the expected child of M. Antonius, this provides an obvious reason why its identity was so soon forgotten.[111] Not only was it in fact a girl, but it was the child of the man who lost the struggle for world leadership at Actium and who was, in the following decades, either studiously forgotten or maliciously denigrated.

4.   C. Asinius Pollio, Consul and the Wedding of Antonius and Octavia
It is now possible to see the problem that faced Vergil when he wrote *Eclogue* 4. There is no evidence beyond the uncritical deductions of the scholiasts from allegorical interpretations of *Eclogues* 1 and 9 that Vergil owed any debt or allegiance to Octavian or Maecenas when he wrote this poem: neither is named or honoured in the *Eclogues*.[112] Nor is there any reason to imagine Vergil as a follower of Antonius. His inseparable friend Varius Rufus had criticised Antonius' behaviour after Caesar's death.[113] But Pollio certainly was a loyal supporter of Antonius; and in a poem written in Pollio's honour that is what counts. Vergil was associated with Philodemus and the Epicurean community at Naples. Most of them fought on the side of the Republicans at Philippi; afterwards many went over to Antonius, not Octavian. These people were among Vergil's first readers, the audience he had in mind as he wrote.[114]

But to praise Pollio at this moment was not easy. To trace Pollio's career would have been impossible since some reference to his battles with Octavian would have been inevitable or strikingly obvious by its absence. There was no room for reference to Pollio's 'great and glorious' deeds in the north Adriatic performed when preparing for Antonius' return and renewal of war.[115] That would have been inconsistent with the current theme of reconciliation, the new concord. It was possible to look only at the present and the future. Pollio's consulship was remarkable for only one thing, the removal of the threat of civil war through the reconciliation of the two triumvirs. Yet Pollio's role even here was not unique: he, Maecenas and L. Cocceius Nerva had all been involved and the most important of the negotiators was Nerva.[116] Pollio's consulship was only a symptom, not a cause, of the new era of peace. The important figures were not, in the present political situation, the consuls, but the triumvirs: the future lay in their hands. However to mention either of these men by name would be to detract from the glory of Pollio. The Republic might be finished; but the Empire had not yet begun, with its different concept of the role of the consuls.[117]

Vergil's task, then, was plain. He must honour and praise his friend and patron on achieving the consulship. He must emphasise the glory of his consulship while not straining the credulity of his audience by pretending that the triumvirs do not count.[118] Their part must be brought in, but not in such a way as to detract from Pollio. This is of course the function of the *puer*. The wedding of Antonius and Octavia was the act which guaranteed the lasting nature of the reconciliation and the one action that offered itself to the poet for celebration. Moreover since it was the outcome of the marriage, the lasting *concordia*, that was significant, it is the *concordia* on which attention is focused, not the bridal pair or the wedding ceremony. Again, the latter themes would have detracted from Pollio's glory. But to base the poem vaguely on ideas of *concordia* and a new age would have entailed making poetry out of abstract notions and would still make it appear that Pollio was being given credit for something achieved in fact by others. Hence the *puer*: he is not named or identified, so he is no threat to the consul's glory. Yet his identity is clear enough for those who have eyes to see; and so the truth of the situation is not distorted. The expected child and the new age of concord are both the outcome of the marriage.

5. The *Puer* and the *Saeculum*

The connection between the birth and the development of the *puer* and those of the new *saeculum* is intimate, but has been interpreted in a variety of ways. Many have insisted that the idea of such a connection is Jewish, not Graeco-Roman, and have considered that the *puer* must be the Messiah:[119] Vergil would have learned of him directly from Jewish connections of Pollio and Antonius,[120] or indirectly through the Sibylline oracles.[121] The Sibylline oracles, as they exist today, are obviously permeated with Judaism, but it is not certain that those known to Vergil were. The scholiasts do not tell us that the *Cumaeum carmen* was

Messianic; but it is most improbable that they knew this specific prophecy at all.[122] There is certainly no indication in *Aeneid* 6 that Vergil thought Eastern or Jewish ideas characteristic of a Cumaean Sibyl; and the only way it seems possible for such ideas to be reflected in this poem is through their having had a general influence on the late Republican concept of a *saeculum* as a result of Rome's contacts with the East during the first century.[123]

The concept of a *saeculum* is basically Etruscan; and its place in the religious and political thought of the forties BC has been recently explained by S. Weinstock.[124] Since it is important to an understanding of our poem it is worth repeating some of his basic points here. The *saeculum* was originally the longest span of human life from birth to death.[125] When used to measure periods of history, a start was made from the founding of a city. A *saeculum* ended with the death of the oldest man of the generation whose births had coincided with the foundation of the city; and then a new *saeculum*, measured in the same way, began. The oldest man — the man of the *saeculum* — whose life was taken as the measure of the age, would seem to have been important only for his longevity; and who he was could only be decided in retrospect. In 249 BC, as a result of consulting a Sibylline oracle, centennial games were introduced at Rome. They were repeated, three years late, in 146 BC. These were the *ludi Tarentini*, which were also called *ludi saeculares*; and, in association with the introduction of these games, the *saeculum* became fixed at a period of one hundred or one hundred and ten years. The result however is curious, since the concept of the man of the *saeculum* becomes more, not less, important. The deaths of the oldest men of their generation were still recorded in connection with the change of *saecula*. But a new and powerful idea of the man of the *saeculum* arose, according to which the man of the *saeculum* was a man of superhuman and semi-divine qualities and a man of destiny. In the first century it seems that Pompey,[126] Cicero,[127] Caesar, even P. Cornelius Lentulus Sura (*cos.* 71 BC)[128] and later, of course, Augustus[129] all claimed to be such a man.

The idea that one *saeculum* was ending and another beginning was current at the end of the forties. No games had been held in either 49 or 46 BC; but they must have been expected in the near future.[130] The relevant portents were recorded in the books of the *haruspices*. M. Peperna (*cos.*92 BC), the last man of his generation, died in 49 BC.[131] The comet which appeared in 44 BC was said by a Vulcanius, a *haruspex*, to mark the end of the ninth and beginning of the tenth *saeculum.*[132] He too was perhaps claimed as the last man of his generation, for he promptly died.[133] In 43 BC the same claim appears to have been made for an unnamed *haruspex*, who announced that the age of kings was returning and all would be slaves, and then died.[134] The coins tell the same story in more optimistic terms.[135]

Most of our evidence suggests that the ending of a *saeculum* was viewed with dread. So in 65 BC the *haruspices* declared that not just the *saeculum* but the existence of Rome was at an end unless the gods intervened.[136] In 66 BC Cicero had suggested that the gods had intervened by sending Pompey. His language is sufficiently close to that of our poem to merit quotation: Everyone, he says (*De Imperio* 41f.), *Cn. Pompeium sicut aliquem non ex hac urbe missum, sed de caelo delapsum intuentur*; and he seems *ad omnia nostrae memoriae bella conficienda divino quodam consilio natus*. It seems likely that the birth-omen of Caesar, announcing his mastery of the world, was devised for a similar purpose.[137]

Seen against this background, more of the characteristics of the *puer* become significant than they do in attempts to relate the idea of the *puer* and the new age to other theories of world ages.[138] It is with his birth that one age will end and another begin (8f.), he will be heaven-sent (*caelo demittitur*, 7 cf.49), he will be a king and master of the world (*reget . . . orbem*, 17), marvellous omens announce and accompany his birth (50ff.,18ff.) and it is clearly implied that under his rule war will cease (35ff.). These current ideas about a new *saeculum* and the man of the new *saeculum* seem to have been emotional and vague and, so far as we know, they had not received extended literary treatment before Vergil. That is why Vergil attempts to associate them with other views of a sequence of ages. *Ultima Cumaei . . .carminis aetas* alludes to the ideas of the Sibylline prophecy in which there were, as in Etruscan lore,[139] a sequence of ten ages[140] — an idea obviously not exploited in this poem. It is unknown whether Servius' information that each age was characterised by a metal and that the divine ruler of the tenth was Sol is based on anything other than the references to iron and gold in lines 8f. and to Apollo in line 10.[141] In *magnus ab integro . . .ordo* (5) the reference to current political and religious thought is followed by a glancing allusion to the theory[142] of the *Magnus Annus*. But the necessary destruction of the world by fire or flood is omitted and the idea is assimilated to current saecular theory by the words *saeclorum nascitur*. From the philosophic we pass to the literary tradition of Hesiod and Aratus. The *virgo* points to Aratus.[143]

The characterisation of the best age as that of Cronos-Saturn[144] and the idea that the new generation is heaven-sent[145] and that the characterising metals of the present age and the best age are iron and gold point to Hesiod.[146] But again this tradition has been assimilated to the current idea of a new *saeculum* with its man of destiny in order to lend it depth and resonance. The distinctive ideas of this tradition, that there are four or five ages and that the world moves ever away from its perfect beginning, have nothing to do with Vergil's controlling idea. So this introductory passage reaches its climax with an unmistakable reference to the idea of a new *saeculum* associated with the birth of a miraculous child presided over by Lucina and Apollo.

This same pattern is repeated in the description of the new *saeculum* (26ff.). Vergil draws various details from the commonplaces of descriptions of happier times in Hesiod, Aratus and Lucretius. Hesiod's description in the *Works and Days* of the Golden Age (109ff.), the Heroic Age (156ff.) and life in a just state (225ff.) provided a repository of themes and ideas for subsequent descriptions of such ages.[147] Vergil's description of the new age in *Eclogue* 4 belongs to this tradition and shows in addition some similarities to the descriptions of Aratus (*Phaenomena* 100ff.)[148] and to Lucretius' account of the life of early man (5,933ff.).[149] However it is not useful to think in terms of specific allusions or imitations. Vergil's Golden Age is rather a composite, redolent of all the descriptions of such an age likely to be remembered.[150] But he has turned the idea round: for while those happy ages all lay in the distant past, his will come in the near future.

The final detail of the description, the sheep that change colour in the fields, comes from no description of a Golden Age but from an Etruscan prophecy. The passage is preserved by Macrobius (*Saturnalia* 3,7,2) who quotes this passage and adds:

> traditur autem in libris Etruscorum, si hoc animal insolito colore fuerit inductum, portendi imperatori rerum omnium felicitatem. est super hoc liber Tarquitii transcriptus ex Ostentario Tusco. ibi reperitur: "purpureo aureove colore ovis ariesve si aspergetur principi ordinis et generis summa cum felicitate largitatem auget, genus progeniem propagat in claritate laetioremque efficit." huius modi igitur statum imperatori in transitu vaticinatur.

Vergil has taken over this picturesque bucolic portent, brightened it up a little and made it a permanent feature of his Golden Age, for the happiness it portends will be always present then. The joyful exuberance of this idea is enhanced by the addition of a specious rationalisation. It is through the food they eat that the flocks will change their colour — a neat combination of wit and *doctrina*. By bringing his description of the new age to a climax on this motif, Vergil has successfully linked his purely literary and composite picture with the political and religious speculation of his time.[151]

That ideas about the *saeculum* do provide the most appropriate background against which to see *Eclogue* 4 is confirmed by the descriptions of new Golden Ages associated with Augustus, Caligula,[152] Nero,[153] Domitian[154] and Honorius.[155] *Eclogue* 4 has clearly influenced these later descriptions and was drawn upon by later writers just because they understood the nature of the poem. That political and religious propaganda also provided a source independent of Vergil for these later descriptions is shown by the strikingly similar ideas reflected in inscriptions.[156]

6.   Silvae Sint Consule Dignae

Now that the poem has been established more firmly in its historical context, and its relevance to the addressee, to the historical situation in which it was composed and designed to be first read, and to current political and religious ideas about a new *saeculum* explored as far as the available evidence allows, it is time to turn to a different line of approach. Attempts to identify the genre of the poem have been many and various.[157] It has been called a genethliakon,[158] an epithalamium,[159] an epibaterion,[160] a basilikon.[161] But this is to ignore Vergil's clear identification of the genre in *silvae sint consule dignae* (3), as was seen by Norden and Carcopino, who called the poem a Konsulatsgedicht,[162] une de ces pièces 'consulaires'.[163] The poem might be entitled *consulatus, de consulatu C. Asinii Pollionis* or *panegyricus dictus C. Asinio Pollioni consuli.*[164]

To become consul was to reach the pinnacle of one's career, to be surpassed only by winning a triumph. For a *novus homo*, like Cicero or Pollio, the achievement was so much the greater. It was a time to be congratulated by friends and family, for making speeches and prayers: it was a time of great ceremonial. I know of no evidence that this occasion was made the subject of epideictic exercises and there are no rhetorical prescriptions for such speeches, but it is hardly improbable that they did exist.[165] Cicero's *Ad Familiares* contain many examples of letters of congratulation on appointment to various positions, including some to newly elected consuls;[166] Pindar wrote in honour of Aristagoras of Tenedos when he was elected president of the council (*prytanis*) and in honour of Hieron when he took the title Aetnaean; Tibullus wrote poems for Messalla when he was granted a triumph and for his son Messallinus on his appointment as one of the quindecimvirs; Statius wrote a poem for Crispinus when he was made military tribune.[167] The custom of writing poems in honour of such occasions was clearly well established. All these poems are encomiastic and use encomiastic topoi; but they are distinguished by the nature of the appointment and they concentrate on the sentiments suitable to each occasion and office. No complete poems in honour of consuls survive which are earlier than or even contemporary with our poem. But at least one such famous poem existed, the *De Consulatu* of Cicero;[168] and the Greek poet Archias began a poem on Cicero's consulship.[169]

Cicero was doubtless not the only man so honoured. It is probable that Philodemus wrote his treatise *On the Good King according to Homer* in honour of L. Calpurnius Piso's becoming consul in 58 BC.[170] But even without these works it is clear that no Roman in the mid-first century BC could have been unaware of the things customarily said on the occasion of a man becoming consul or of the sentiments appropriate to the occasion.[171] We have to glean our knowledge of these from later works; but this is unlikely to be misleading in view of the traditional nature of the material, the ceremonial nature of the occasion and the traditional glory and functions of the office itself, since all this makes for conservatism. In what follows I shall call these traditional elements the topoi of the genre and the genre itself the *laudatio consulis* (praise of a consul) in the interests of brevity.

The topoi of the genre can be established on the basis of the following members of the genre: Cicero *De Consulatu Frr.* 10-18 (Morel); Ovid *Ex Ponto* 4,4 (for Sextus Pompeius *cos.* AD 14); 4,9 (for P. Pomponius Graecinus *cos.suff.* AD 16 and his brother L. Pomponius Flaccus *cos.des.* AD 17); Statius *Silvae* 4,1 (for Domitian *cos.* 17 AD 95); Sidonius Apollinaris 1;2 (both for Anthemius); Claudian 1 (for Probinus and Olybrius); 6; 7 (both for Honorius *cos.* 3); 8 (for Honorius *cos.* 4); 16; 17 (both for Manlius Theodorus); 21-24 (for Stilicho); 27; 28 (both for Honorius *cos.* 6).[172] These topoi can sometimes be confirmed by their presence in the prayers of Ausonius 'written' on the day before he took up the consulship (*Opuscula* 3,5; 6 (Peiper)) and in Ovid's conversation with

Janus (*Fasti* 1,63-294). These examples of the genre are very different from each other in time and character and some general observations are in order. Cicero's poem was in three books and so at least comparable in length to the poems of Sidonius and Claudian. It was however different from the other members of the genre in so far as it was autobiographical and retrospective or historical, while the poems of Claudian and Sidonius are prospective. This latter distinction must have been lessened by the fact that prophecy and prediction apparently played a large part in Cicero's poem. Whether or not this feature of Cicero's poem indicates that prophecy was already strongly associated with the genre, this point is obviously of significance for *Eclogue* 4.[173] The poems of Ovid and Statius are distinguished from the other members of the genre by being much briefer.[174] This brevity is achieved by omission or severe compression of the encomium of the consul.

The primary elements which characterise the genre can be simply stated. They comprise the speaker (A1); the addressee who is a consul (A2); an encomiastic celebration of the consulship (A3). In addition, an analysis of all members of the genre yields the following list of topoi or secondary elements.

B1 The relationship of the speaker to the consul and an explanation of why he is singing his praises: Ovid *Ex Ponto* 4,4,1ff.; 9,1ff.; (75ff.); Statius *Silvae* 4,1,17ff. (Janus speaks); Claudian uses separate *praefationes* (6; 16; 23; 27) as does Sidonius (1).[175]

B2 Emphasis on the beginning of a new year: Statius *Silvae* 4,1,1ff.; Sidonius 2,8ff.; Claudian 1,1ff.; (266ff.); 7,1ff.; 8,1ff.; Ovid *Ex Ponto* 4,4,3; Ausonius 3,6,1ff. (Peiper).

B2a This is sometimes coupled with references to Janus: Ovid *Ex Ponto* 4,4,23; Statius *Silvae* 4,1,13ff.; or to the (new-born) sun:[176] Statius *Silvae* 4,1,3; Claudian 1,1-3; 268; 7,9; cf. Ausonius 3,5 (Peiper) (refrain): *Iane veni, novus anne veni, renovate veni sol.*

B2b The beginning of the year is a time to think of peace not war: Statius *Silvae* 4,1,13ff.; Claudian 8,6ff.; 22,1ff.; cf. Ovid *Fasti* 1,67f.: *(Iane) dexter ades ducibus quorum secura labore/otia terra ferax, otia pontus habet*; 121-4: *cum libuit Pacem placidis emittere tectis,/libera perpetuas ambulat illa vias:/sanguine letifero totus miscebitur orbis/ni teneant rigidae condita bella serae*; 287f.: *Iane, fac aeternos pacem pacisque ministros,/neve suum, praesta, deserat auctor opus.*;[177] Ausonius 3,5,24 (Peiper).

B2c It is also a time to think of renewal, rebirth and the return of *saecula*: Statius *Silvae* 4,1,3: *sole novo*; Claudian 1,1f.: *Sol qui...volvis...redeuntia saecula*; cf. Cicero *Fr.* 11 (Morel); Ovid *Fasti* 1,149ff.; Ausonius 3,5;6 (Peiper).

B3 The new year is to be a particularly happy one: Ovid *Ex Ponto* 4,4,18; (4,9,55ff.); Statius *Silvae* 4,1,1ff.; Claudian 1,266f.; 24,1ff.; 28,12ff.; cf. Cicero *Fr.* 17 (Morel): *o fortunatam natam me consule Romam.*

B3a It will begin a new age: Statius *Silvae* 4,1,17f.: *salve, magne parens mundi, qui saecula mecum/instaurare paras* (Janus is speaking); 35: *mecum altera saecula condes.*

B3b It will see the return of former glory, of *Iustitia*, of the Golden Age: Statius *Silvae* 4,1,17ff.; Sidonius 2 (100f.); 524ff.; Claudian (7,184ff.); 8,613ff.; 17,113ff. (Manlius Theodorus, not an emperor); 22, 311ff.; 441ff.; 24,89ff.

B4 The consul himself is praised: Ovid *Ex Ponto* 4,9,75ff.; Statius *Silvae* 4,1 (briefly and indirectly, though implicitly throughout). This may be expanded into a full encomium drawing on all the topics: ancestors, parents, homeland, birth, upbringing and education, virtues, deeds in war, deeds in peace. So Sidonius 2; Claudian 1; 7; 8; 17; 21; 22; 24; 28.[178]

B5 The ceremonial of inauguration:[179] Ovid *Ex Ponto* 4,4,24ff.; 4,9,23ff.; Statius *Silvae* 4,1,1ff.; Sidonius 2,544ff.; Claudian 1,226ff.; 17,270ff.; 24,1ff.; 240ff.; cf. Cicero *Fr.*11, 13ff. (Morel); Ausonius 3,5,1ff. (Peiper).

B6 The good omens for a prosperous year: Statius *Silvae* 4,1,23f.; Claudian 1,205ff.; 28,12ff.[180]

B6a This is usually part of the description of the universal joy felt by gods and denizens of the empire: Ovid *Ex Ponto* 4,9,17ff.; Statius *Silvae* 4,1,5ff.; 34f.; 45f.; Claudian 1,226ff.; 236ff.; 17,270ff.; 22,360ff.; 421ff.; 24,202ff.; 28,611ff.

B7 A prophecy or prediction concerning the course the year is to take and the glorious deeds to be performed: Cicero *Frr.* 11;13 (Morel); Statius *Silvae* 4,1,37ff.; Claudian 1,268ff. (the unfolding seasons); 7,189ff.; 8,638ff.; 22,336ff.; 397ff.; cf. Ovid *Ex Ponto* 4,4,45ff.; 4,9,41ff.; Ausonius 3,5;6 (Peiper).

B8 A command to the year to begin, to the consul to enter office:

Sidonius 2,1ff.; 544ff.; Claudian 1,266ff.; 7,1ff.; 17,270ff.; 28,640ff.; cf. Ausonius 3,5 (Peiper) (refrain).[181]

This list of conventional topoi helps us to understand more or less precisely the type of material which would have occurred to Vergil as he began to compose a poem in honour of a consul and which would have been evoked in the mind of his audience when they read the phrase *silvae sint consule dignae* (3). It is now possible to see how Vergil has played against these expectations. Much of the material of the topical list has been drawn from Claudian, a late writer. The conservatism guaranteed by the ceremonial and traditional nature of the occasion has already been mentioned. In addition we should recall that in the encomia of consuls embedded in his poems Claudian clearly reflects the precepts of the rhetoricians. These precepts were deduced, from at least the time of Aristotle's *Poetics,* from analysis of earlier examples. In the case of such traditional material there can be no objection to using late writings to illuminate works of a much earlier date.[182]

Vergil begins with three lines of introduction. He here acknowledges the greatness of the task that faces him (*paulo maiora canamus*); promises a Theocritean song through the invocation of *Sicelides Musae*; and clearly indicates the occasion of his song: it is to honour a consul. The appeal to Callimachean poetics in his acknowledgement that not everyone likes his type of poetry is clearly intended as a compliment to the good taste and poetic sensibilities of the addressee. Moreover the fact that it was Pollio who first encouraged Vergil to be the Roman Theocritus would make it clear that the invocation of the Theocritean Muses is intended to reveal the poet's relationship to the addressee. It is noteworthy that Vergil achieves originality and challenges the attention of his reader by the economy and subtlety with which he communicates this information. The economy and the subtlety are possible only because these prefatory topics[183] are conventional (B1).[184]

At line 11 Vergil returns to the consul. He predicts (B7) that the glorious age (*decus hoc aevi*, 11) will begin in Pollio's consulship. The return of the Golden Age with the consulship of Pollio clearly distinguishes his consulship from all previous consulships and marks its special glory (B3). The prediction continues with the information that under Pollio's leadership civil war will cease and the earth will be freed from its perpetual dread (B7). *Te duce* is vague and our lack of detailed evidence makes it impossible to be sure to what Vergil refers. It may be an attempt to bring in a reference to Pollio's military virtues.[185] From the moment he entered office it may have been widely known that his next assignment would be the pro-consulship of Macedonia, where he would be training troops as a prelude to the Parthian campaign. It is at least possible that Pollio was expected to take part in the Parthian campaign;[186] and of course the defeat of the Parthians was often seen as the means by which the Romans would atone for the sin of civil wars.[187] There is however an alternative explanation: Dio (48,32) tells us that after the treaty of Brundisium the festival that had been vowed for the completion of the war against the assassins was celebrated by the consuls. Unhappily it is not clear from his account whether he means the *ordinarii* or the *suffecti*. But if Pollio was one of these consuls it would be natural to relate these lines to this action and to see his expiation of the *scelus* as a religious, not a military, act. Again, the vagueness may be designed to allow both references.

Obviously Vergil has omitted all mention of the beginning of a new year (B2), since Asinius Pollio entered office not on the first of January but some time in September. Similarly the topos is omitted by Ovid in his poem for P. Pomponius Graecinus, the suffect consul for AD 16. In place of this he has made Pollio's consulship mark not the beginning of another new year but the beginning of a new *saeculum* − the new *saeculum* of which there had been so much talk both during Caesar's dictatorship and immediately after his death.[188] In making this simple but brilliantly effective substitution he could draw on the associated topoi: the beginning of a new year conventionally evoked thoughts of renewal of the ages (B2b, B3a) and rebirth (B2a).[189] In choosing to give the new *saeculum* the character of a restored Golden Age, Vergil could rely upon the conventional ideas associated with the entry of the new consul to office, namely hopes for peace instead of war (B2b) and for the restoration of Rome to her former greatness (B3b).[190] This seems to have been how Cicero presented his consulship, with himself in the role of saviour. What is apparently new in Vergil is not so much the association of Pollio's consulship with a new age as three other factors: the strong emphasis which the idea is given; the detailed description of the Golden Age itself; and its association with the *puer* as the saviour king rather than with Pollio himself. Cicero's attempts to portray himself as the saviour of Rome had brought ridicule upon him.[191] Vergil avoids stretching the credulity of his audience and running the same risk for his patron.

A conventional picture of the unfolding seasons of the year is given by Claudian 1,269-274:

> prima tibi procedat hiems non frigore torpens,
> non canas vestita nives, non aspera ventis
> sed tepido calefacta Noto; ver inde serenum
> protinus et liquidi clementior aura Favoni
> pratis te croceis pingat; te messibus aestas
> induat autumnusque madentibus ambiat uvis.

The careful sequence *prima hiems, ver inde, aestas, autumnus* and the second person address to the year are noteworthy. Vergil has presented in place of something like this prophecy (B7) a description of the stages in the development of the new *saeculum* and of the *puer* with whom it is indissolubly linked. Here too is the deliberate sequence *at tibi prima* (18), *at simul* (26), *hinc ubi iam firmata virum te fecerit aetas* (37); and the agricultural imagery also recalls the conventional description of the seasons. It is the introduction of the child that is really novel and stimulating, for this adds a new dimension of human interest and, since the child's identity is not revealed unambiguously, of mystery.

As the *Parcae* close the prophecy, the focus of attention is less the new *saeculum* itself or the consul who will inaugurate it than the child. Vergil deliberately exploits this fact. If the command *adgredere o magnos . . . honores* (48) were addressed to Pollio, it would, in view of the topoi of the genre (B5, B8) and of the apparent allusion in it to the *cursus honorum*, cause little surprise. But Vergil addresses the command triumphantly to the child, as is revealed in the next line. So in the following lines it is not the consul who is commanded to behold (*aspice . . . aspice*, 50, 52) the good omens and the universal rejoicing (B6a) but the child. It is worth quoting Statius: *aspicis ut templis nitor, altior aris/ignis et ipsa meae tepeant tibi sidera brumae?* (*Silvae* 4,1,23f. – Janus speaking); *tunc omnes patuere dei laetoque dederunt/signa polo, longamque tibi, dux magne, iuventam/annuit atque suos promisit Iuppiter annos* (*Silvae* 4,1,45-7).

In the next section Vergil expresses a wish that he may one day *tua dicere facta* (54). This topos, in which the poet, near the end of an encomium, talks of himself and his poetry, is common in encomia of all types: in the *Homeric Hymns* and the *Hymns* of Callimachus;[192] in the *Odes* of Pindar and Theocritus' encomium of Ptolemy, *Idyll* 17.[193] But again the normal practice is to promise a song to the addressee of the poem. So Pindar hopes to sing of future victories for Hippocleas (*Pythian* 10,55ff. (Sn.–Mae.)), Vergil to sing of Pollio (*Eclogue* 8,9f.), Tibullus of Messallinus (2,5,113ff.). The topos occurs in two members of the genre *laudatio consulis*: Sidonius (2,540ff.) promises Anthemius a panegyric and Claudian hopes that he will be able to sing the epithalamium at Honorius' wedding.[194] Again the child has appropriated a topic which we would expect to have been attached to Pollio.

The final lines are, as noted above, an epithalamic topos, not a topos of the *laudatio consulis*. But the inclusion of this topic is made easier by its similarities to two of the more conventional endings for a *laudatio consulis*. There are clear syntactical and formal similarities between the repeated *incipe* and the command to the year to begin and the command to the consul to enter office (B8) as found in Claudian 1,268f.: *o...felix... annus,/incipe quadrifidum Phoebi torquere laborem*, and Sidonius 2,547f.: *perge, pater patriae, felix atque omine fausto/captivos vincture novos absolve vetustos*. In view of the intimate relationship of the child and the *saeculum* and of Vergil's substitution of the *saeculum* for the new year as the period inaugurated by the consul, this conventional background is significant. Moreover, in poems in praise of consuls where there is a conventional encomium of the consul, a closing topos could be a reference to a son and heir.[195] What must have been a conventional thought is preserved in Claudian 17,336-340:

> accipiat patris exemplum tribuatque nepoti
> filius et coeptis ne desit fascibus heres.
> decurrat trabeata domus tradatque secures
> mutua posteritas servatoque ordine fati
> Manlia continuo numeretur consule proles.

A very similar use of the same topos is found towards the end of Tibullus' poem for Messalla *triumphator*, 1,7,55f.: *at tibi succrescat proles, quae facta parentis/augeat et circa stet veneranda senem*. The expectation of either of these conventional endings would obviously make the introduction of the epithalamic topos at the end of *Eclogue* 4 so much easier.

In this section an attempt has been made to elucidate the poem in the light of the conventions of the genre *laudatio consulis*. The indication of the poet's relationship to the consul, the emphasis on the beginning not of a new year but of a new *saeculum*, the explicit praises of the consul, the prophetic description of the new age and the character of the new age, all these can be more easily understood when seen as simple variations on the commonplaces of the genre. The playful sophistication whereby the *puer* rather than the consul becomes the focus of attention in the latter part of the poem should not be misunderstood. Cicero's claim to be a saviour and

50

his assertion that his consulship marked the beginning of a new and glorious age for Rome can hardly have been more extravagant than Vergil's claims for Pollio. Yet the ridicule which Cicero had invited by his extravagant and incredible claims provided a terrible warning. By introducing the *puer* as the saviour king, unborn and not explicitly identified, Vergil avoids running the same risk. It was obvious in 40 BC that the dawning of a wholly unexpected new era of peace had less to do with Pollio than with the agreement reached by Octavian and Antonius, symbolised by the marriage of the latter to Octavia.[196] To introduce either of these men directly would have been to risk overshadowing Pollio. The device of focusing attention on the child, clearly intended as the future offspring of that marriage, enabled Vergil not to violate historical truth to the point of incredibility by claiming too much for Pollio. Without violating the truth, Pollio's consulship is highly praised in such a way that Rome's consul is not overshadowed by another: an unborn child, however miraculous, poses less threat than one of the triumvirs. It is an ingenious solution to a most difficult problem.

The device of embedding praises of one man in an encomium of another is quite often employed. But the other man is usually a son of the addressee. So, for example, Pindar includes in a poem written in honour of Hieron praises of his son Deinomenes (*Pythian* 1); and in a poem for Xenocrates of Acragas he praises his son Thrasybulus (*Pythian* 6). The achievements of the son are clearly intended to redound to the credit of the father.[197] No wonder the scholiasts were drawn into believing that the *puer* of *Eclogue* 4 was a child of Pollio. But it is also clear that praises of non-relatives could also be included. For example, Propertius, in his *recusatio* to Maecenas (3,9) includes praise of Augustus. Propertius obviously does not intend to detract from the glory of Maecenas when he praises Augustus in his *recusatio* to Maecenas. Rather he intends the association to reflect credit on his patron by reminding his reader that, although Maecenas does not hold public office, he is, because of his friendship with Augustus, an important and powerful man. This poem of Propertius causes no difficulty because the relationship of Maecenas and Augustus is such a well-known historical fact. In the case of *Eclogue* 4 failure to appreciate the historical relationship between Pollio and the child has led the majority of scholars to concentrate on the unborn child at the expense of the addressee of the poem, the consul Pollio. Another parallel is worth mentioning. The formal similarities of Tibullus 1,7 to *Eclogue* 4 have already been noted. In three respects the *puer* of *Eclogue* 4 resembles the Osiris of Tibullus 1,7. Both are benefactors to mankind and the providers of material prosperity; neither of them is a living, historical person. Osiris is a god; and the *puer* is at once an unborn child and envisaged as possessing semi-divine or heroic features. Finally, it is clear that Osiris and the *puer* are each intended to enhance, rather than detract from, the glory of the dedicatee of their respective poems, Messalla and Pollio. Indeed ancient poets often combine hymns to gods with praises for this very purpose: Callimachus combines a hymn to Zeus with praise to Ptolemy (*Hymn* 1); Vergil combines a hymn to the *Indigetes* with praise of Augustus (*Georgics* 1,498ff.); Tibullus combines a hymn to Apollo with praise of Messallinus (2,5); and Propertius combines a hymn to Apollo with praise of Augustus (4,6). In view of this technique, Vergil may have deliberately given the *puer* divine characteristics in order to capitalise on the analogy with this traditional pattern and to help the reader to understand that Pollio, not the *puer*, is the *laudandus* in *Eclogue* 4.

At any event it is evident that special historical circumstances could always give rise to the unusual. So Pindar in a poem written in praise of Arcesilas of Cyrene (*Pythian* 4) includes praises of Damophilas, an exile who had commissioned the poem hoping to secure his return. Claudian writing in praise of the consul Honorius includes praises of Stilicho (8,432ff.; 28,426ff.). The shift of attention from the consul in *Eclogue* 4 to the child is, then, more apparent than real. The sole significance of the child is his association with the new age. But the glory of that age reflects credit on Pollio whose consulship marks its beginning.

It would be a mistake to regard Pollio's consulship as of little importance. The entry into office of a Roman consul was clearly analogous to the accession of a Hellenistic king. The analogy would not be lost on Vergil's Roman readers since the practices of Hellenistic rulers had been topical during Caesar's dictatorship. In particular, it is worth noting that the custom of treating the accession day of a Hellenistic ruler as his second birthday had probably been discussed at Rome in connection with Julius Caesar.[198] This association of accession days and birthdays provides an additional conventional basis for the combination of Pollio's entry to the consulship with the birth of the child.

7.   *Eclogue* 4, Theocritus *Idyll* 17 and the Basilikon.[199]

It has long been recognised that *Eclogue* 4 is an imitation of *Idyll* 17.[200] This is in itself important, since it means that those who follow Servius in believing this poem to be 'non-pastoral' are wrong.[201] For Vergil, ignorant of the later development of pastoral and the definitions of modern critics, pastoral could only mean poems written in the manner of Theocritus and his imitators.[202] Unfortunately we do not know under what title Vergil knew the poems of Theocritus, or what he called his own poems.[203] However, Calpurnius Siculus, Vergil's successor, makes extensive use of *Eclogue* 4 and clearly did not consider it an alien intruder into the collection.[204]

Any reader would come to this *Eclogue* with the expectation that it would be, like all its predecessors, an imitation of Theocritus. When he meets the invitation to the *Sicelides Musae* to join the poet in singing rather more grand songs (*paulo maiora canamus*) this expectation is heightened and refined: it will not be a rustic or urban mime. When he learns that the poem is to be *silvae consule dignae* his attention is directed towards the two poems which Theocritus had written for Hellenistic kings, *Idyll* 16 for Hieron II of Syracuse and *Idyll* 17 for Ptolemy Philadelphus of Egypt. The Romans were accustomed to think of their consuls as the equivalents of Hellenistic kings; and this association must have been all the more apparent to any Roman at the time of Caesar or immediately afterwards.[205]

The opening lines of *Eclogue* 4 pose some minor problems. In line 2, *non omnis arbusta iuvant humilesque myricae*, Vergil characterises his Theocritean verse as shrubs, a Hellenistic topos.[206] In the next line he says: *si canimus silvas, silvae sint consule dignae*: if we are singing of woods, that is, composing Theocritean song, let the woods, that is, the material, be worthy of the consul. This play on the meaning of *silva*, as the raw material with which a writer works, depends upon the analogy of the Greek word ὕλη, which is often used in this sense.[207] This play on words is much clearer when we remember the simile of the woodcutter (ὑλατόμος) on Mount Ida wondering where to start in Theocritus *Idyll* 17,9f., which is based on the same idea. Further, we have already noted that Vergil's lines implicitly compliment the poetic discrimination of Pollio and refer to Pollio's patronage of the poet. Again a similar compliment is paid by Theocritus to Ptolemy at *Idyll* 17,112-116:

> Nor has any man ever come for the contests of Dionysus, any
> man who is skilled at striking up a clear song, to whom he has
> not given a gift worthy of his skill. And these mouthpieces of
> the Muses sing Ptolemy in return for his benefactions.

In both cases Vergil is clearly relying on our recognition of the conventions of prefatory material and also of the Theocritean passages, to convey much more than he actually says. But the striking parallel in form, content and function is with the opening of *Idyll* 17,1-4:

Ἐκ Διὸς ἀρχώμεσϑα καὶ ἐς Δία λήγετε Μοῖσαι
ἀϑανάτων τὸν ἄριστον, ἐπὴν† ἀείδωμεν ἀοιδαῖς·
ἀνδρῶν δ᾽ αὖ Πτολεμαῖος ἐνὶ πρώτοισι λεγέσϑω
καὶ πύματος καὶ μέσσος· ὃ γὰρ προφερέστατος ἀνδρῶν.

(From Zeus let us begin and do you, Muses, end with Zeus, the best of immortals, (whenever we sing songs(?)).[208] And of men, in turn, let Ptolemy be mentioned at the beginning and last and in the middle. For he is the most excellent of men). It is fairly clear that Vergil is alluding to these lines in *Eclogue* 4,1-3 from the parallels ἀρχώμεσϑα ... Μοῖσαι and *Musae... canamus*, ἐπὴν† ἀείδωμεν, λεγέσϑω and *si canimus* and *sint*. As we shall see, it is typical of the relationship between the two poems that Vergil should have altered this model by working in topics from other passages in the same poem.

In the previous section we saw that many of the topoi of the *laudatio consulis* were transferred from the consul to the child. Likewise the encomium for Pollio, traditional in the genre,[209] and which we are also encouraged to expect by the opening allusion to *Idyll* 17, does not materialise. It is the *puer*, not Pollio, who plays the role of Theocritus' Ptolemy. We have already seen that one important function of this parallelism is to provide a substantial clue to the identity of the child. The prediction (15f.) *ille deum vitam accipiet divisque videbit/permixtos heroas et ipse videbitur illis* together with the last line of the poem (63) *nec deus hunc mensa dea nec dignata cubili est* combine to suggest Hercules, ancestor of the Antonii, as he is depicted at length in Theocritus *Idyll* 17. But here we are chiefly concerned with another aspect of the child. He will be a king (*reget... orbem*, 17) as Ptolemy was, and, whether or not *magnum Iovis incrementum* is an allusion to the title *Iuppiter Iulius* adopted by Caesar, as a king the child will enjoy the special protection of Jupiter or Zeus.[210] So in Theocritus *Idyll* 17, 73-76:

Zeus the son of Cronos has kings who deserve our reverence in his care and he is the greatest whom Zeus loves when he is first born. Much prosperity attends him, he rules over much land, much sea.

These lines are perhaps alluded to by Vergil in 49-51 where the mention of Jupiter is followed by a sign of Jupiter's approval and a division of the *mundus* into land, sea and sky.[211] On this level at least the

54

significance of the line is simple enough.

The description of Herakles forms in Theocritus part of the section on parents and ancestors. The whole section is followed, as recommended by rhetoricians,[212] by a description of the birth of Ptolemy and the attendant miracles (64ff.). Theocritus compares the birth of Ptolemy, implicitly and explicitly, with the birth of Apollo. Vergil handles the material differently to produce similar results. He does not imitate the description in *Idyll* 17 in any detail. But there are two points of interest. Firstly, when Vergil describes the miracles that attend the birth of the *puer* as commonplaces of the *aurea aetas*, he may be intending a sort of conceptual pun. For when Theocritus uses the comparison to the birth of Apollo, he is alluding to the description of the birth of the god in Callimachus *Hymn* 4, 260ff.[213] The most striking feature of the Callimachean description is that everything on Delos is turned to gold. It seems at least possible that Vergil is intending to display his deep understanding of the Theocritean allusion through an implicit conceptual pun. Secondly, Vergil contrives to retain a Theocritean colouring for his description. So *ipsae lacte domum referent distenta capellae/ubera* (21f.) is reminiscent of πολλάκι ταὶ ὄιες ποτὶ τωὔλιον αὐταὶ ἀπῆνθον, Theocritus *Idyll* 11,12 (often his sheep came back of their own accord to the fold); *nec magnos metuent armenta leones* (22) of ἔσται δὴ τοῦτ' ἆμαρ ὁπηνίκα νεβρὸν ἐν εὐνᾶ/καρχαρόδων σίνεσθαι ἰδὼν λύκος οὐκ ἐθελήσει, Theocritus *Idyll* 24,86f. (And that will be the day when the jagged toothed wolf seeing the fawn in its lair will refuse to harm it); *errantis hederas passim cum baccare* (19) of κισσὸς ἐλιχρύσῳ κεκονιμένος · ἁ δὲ κατ' αὐτόν/καρπῷ ἕλιξ εἰλεῖται ἀγαλλομένα κροκόεντι, Theocritus *Idyll* 1,30f. (ivy spotted with yellow clusters: and down along it winds the tendril rejoicing in its yellow fruit). But his purpose is clearly just to make the passage sound Theocritean.[214]

Approaches to Vergil's imitation of Theocritus on a purely verbal level are often unhelpful. The imitation of *Idyll* 17 in *Eclogue* 4 is, rather, conceptual and works on a number of levels. Vergil has clearly envisaged his *puer* as a Roman analogue of Ptolemy as portrayed in *Idyll* 17. The *puer* will rule the earth in peace (17): *pacatumque reget. . .orbem*. The same is true of Ptolemy (*Idyll* 17,85): τῶν πάντων Πτολεμαῖος ἀγήνωρ ἐμβασιλεύει (of all this the heroic Ptolemy is king); λαοὶ δ' ἔργα περιστέλλουσιν ἕκηλοι κτλ, 17,97ff. (and people go about their business in peace etc.). The *virtutes* that make this possible for Vergil's *puer* are the father's: *patriis virtutibus* (17). So Theocritus begins his section on the

55

ancestors of Ptolemy (*Idyll* 17,13) ἐκ πατέρων οἷος μὲν ἔην τελέσαι μέγα ἔργον (because of his ancestors he (Ptolemy son of Lagos) was one who could execute a great deed) and emphasises Ptolemy's likeness to his father when he was born (17,63f.): ὁ δὲ πατρὶ ἐοικώς/παῖς ἀγαπητὸς ἔγεντο (he was born the very image of his father, a beloved boy-child). Again, Vergil's description of the child enjoying the company of the gods and heroes (15-17) is reminiscent of Theocritus' description of Ptolemy's father (*Idyll* 17,16f.): τῆνον καὶ μακάρεσσι πατὴρ ὁμότιμον ἔθηκεν/ἀθανάτοις (the father made him of equal honour even with the blessed immortals). The description of Ptolemy's mother's labour (*Idyll* 17,60ff.), with its reference to 'Eileithuia, loosener of girdles' who 'gave kindly assistance' (εὐμενέοισα παρίστατο) is recalled in Vergil's prayer *tu modo nascenti puero . . .casta fave Lucina* (8-10).

Awareness of the Theocritean model helps to remove an old problem in *Eclogue* 4,17: *pacatumque reget patriis virtutibus orbem*. The question is whether *patriis* means 'of his father/ancestors' or 'inherited from his father'; and whether *patriis virtutibus* goes with *pacatum* or *reget*. The line may most simply be taken as a compressed version of Theocritus *Idyll* 17,104f.: the people of Egypt enjoy peace (97ff.) because Ptolemy, a new 'Achilles',[215] protects them and ᾧ ἐπίπαγχυ μέλει πατρώια πάντα φυλάσσεω/οἷ' ἀγαθῷ βασιλῆι, τὰ δὲ κτεατίζεται αὐτός (he is very much concerned to safeguard all he has from his father, as a good king should be concerned, and other possessions he himself acquires). The *puer*, then, will rule what his father has conquered with his *virtutes*. This he will rule with the *virtutes* he has inherited. He will also complete the conquests of his father and rule those too, a true son of his father. Such compression is typical of imitative writing,[216] but there is compensation in the economy, the suggestiveness and the challenge to the reader.

However, an approach to the relationship between the two poems based on a generic analysis will reveal how deep and intimate the relationship actually is. In a poem belonging to the genre *laudatio consulis*, as we have seen, an encomium of the consul might have been expected. In *Eclogue* 4 we find instead an encomium of the *puer*. This was clearly recognised by Servius who remarks (*ad* 18): *rhetorice digesta laudatio: non enim inprovide in principio universa consumpsit, sed paulatim fecit laudem cum aetate procedere*. Since the *puer* will be a king, the relevant type of *laudatio* is the basilikon. Vergil, then, has included in his praises of the consul Pollio an encomium of the child which is exactly analogous to the encomium of Ptolemy in Theocritus *Idyll* 17, which is also a basilikon.

Vergil's poem is written deliberately to recall but also to rival or to surpass his model; and the relationship between the two poems results in an elaborate generic game.

Another aspect of Vergil's handling of generic material in *Eclogue* 4 deserves attention since it has considerable implications for the understanding of how the Roman poets took over Greek genres. It has often been noted in this paper that the Roman consul is the equivalent of the βασιλεύς. *Eclogue* 4 is a *laudatio consulis* which includes a basilikon. Vergil seems therefore to be playing on the equivalence of the consul and the βασιλεύς in order to establish that the *laudatio consulis* is the Roman equivalent of the basilikon. This technique of including the Greek equivalent within the Romanised genre is another feature of *Eclogue* 4 that can be paralleled from Tibullus 1,7. There the hymn to Osiris-Bacchus seems to be intended as a dithyramb and it is included within the Roman version of a dithyramb, that is within the triumph-poem.[217] That Vergil intended his reader to appreciate this play between the Roman and Greek versions of the same genre is confirmed by two considerations. Firstly, within *Eclogue* 4 Vergil alerts us to the equivalence of the consul and the βασιλεύς by two devices: he models *Eclogue* 4 on Theocritus *Idyll* 17 and therefore leads us to expect the consul Pollio to be cast in the role of the βασιλεύς Ptolemy; and he employs, as a generic sophistication, the omission of a major topos, the encomium of the consul (B4), with the result that the included basilikon is felt to be a substitute for this topos; and this device again draws attention to the analogous characters of the consul and the βασιλεύς. Secondly, Claudian's poems of the genre *laudatio consulis* are well-known as Romanised versions of the basilikon and indeed they have often been considered simply as basilika.[218] It is important to understand this aspect of Vergil's technique in *Eclogue* 4, since it provides a general framework for considering his manipulation of generic material within this poem and confirms as valid the view that throughout *Eclogue* 4 Vergil is deliberately manipulating topoi derived from Theocritus *Idyll* 17 *qua* basilikon.

The basilikon begins at line 18 immediately after the generic signal in *reget...orbem* (17)[219] and it occupies the entire prophecy which was delivered by the *Parcae* (47). The device of prophecy, which as we have already seen was a regular feature in the *laudatio consulis*, was an important and regular feature of the basilikon also.[220] Prophecy was a favourite Hellenistic mode of composition[221] and Vergil makes full use of his opportunity.

Quintilian says (*Institutio Oratoria* 3,7,11) that in praising a man one should include those things *quae responsis vel auguriis futuram claritatem promiserint.*[222] In *Eclogue* 4 the prophecy begins with the birth of the child and the miracles that will attend it. The details are interesting: *cunabula* (23) is the spot where the baby lies, its cradle;[223] *munuscula* is the most appropriate word[224] for the presents given by Tellus who here plays the role assigned to Cos in Theocritus and Delos in Callimachus *Hymn* 4,260ff. That these events all take place in the immediate vicinity of the child is confirmed by the repeated *tibi* (18,23); and *passim* (19) and *vulgo* (25) must mean simply 'all round you', not 'all over the world'.[225] Each of the gifts is relevant to the child. The significance of the ivy, the *colocasia* and the *acanthus* can, perhaps, no longer be established with certainty. But the following points seem relevant. The *hedera* is the plant of Dionysus and the *colocasia* and *acanthus* have Egyptian associations.[226] These hints at Dionysus, conqueror of Asia, may be no more than allusions to an encomiastic commonplace.[227] However, there might be a further hint here at the identity of the child's father, a question raised by *patriis* in line 17. After Philippi, Antonius had been hailed as Dionysus the Beneficent and Bringer of Joy at Ephesus, but whether this association was known in Italy is unclear. It must be remembered though that the only coins struck by Antonius to mark his association with Dionysus carry on the back the head of Octavia, not of Cleopatra.[228] The particular combination of Hercules, Dionysus and Achilles (36) inevitably recalls Alexander, the obvious model for Antonius as he prepared for his Parthian campaigns. In view of the associations of these plants with the East[229] there is a further possibility that they were in the *Cumaeum carmen* as the signs by which the new saviour would be known. The *baccar* is easier. It was a plant with apotropaic qualities and so the natural equivalent of the *bulla* given to Roman children on the day of their birth to ward off the evil eye. It is connected with *hedera* also at *Eclogue* 7,25ff. and it seems likely that in both cases Vergil is suggesting a connection between *baccar* and *Bacchus.*[230] The goats with their hanging udders will provide food for the child and are therefore kept safe.[231] The flowers and the exotic *Assyrium amomum* are simply to delight the child;[232] and the snake and poisonous plant are destroyed to keep him from harm. It is inevitable that we think of the parallel motifs in Horace's description of his own childhood, especially *Odes* 3,4,17-20: *ut tuto ab atris corpore viperis/dormirem et ursis, ut premerer sacra/lauroque conlataque myrto,/non sine dis animosus infans.* But the miracles that are associated with the birth of the child are

58

also intended, as the rhetoricians suggest, and as is explicit in Theocritus *Idyll* 17,73ff., to presage the future. All the details here are commonplaces of descriptions of the Golden Age.[233] Thus they predict in themselves that under the rule of this king the Golden Age will return; and it is probably because Vergil wanted them to have this additional function that he diverges so far from his Theocritean model. But the relationship of the child to the Heroic Age and Golden Age in the following sections seems at first sight puzzling. The child does nothing, except read; and yet at line 54 Vergil promises that one day he will sing of his *facta*.

The connection between a new ruler and the return of a 'Golden Age' is well established[234] and we need here only mention the case of Augustus. In *Aeneid* 6,791-5 Vergil says:

> hic vir, hic est, tibi quem promitti saepius audis,
> Augustus Caesar, divi genus, aurea condet
> saecula qui rursus Latio regnata per arva
> Saturno quondam, super et Garamantas et Indos
> proferet imperium.

To Vergil in the twenties the man of the new *saeculum*, so often promised, had turned out to be Augustus. The return of the Golden Age is here connected with the celebration of saecular games (*condet saecula*) and world-wide conquest, especially conquest of the East. The role that Vergil had predicted for the *puer* in *Eclogue* 4 was fulfilled in fact by Augustus. But this is not the private hope and vision of one man but of a whole generation: the reign of Augustus was celebrated in comparable terms on inscriptions throughout the empire.[235] After Actium Augustus was acclaimed as the man of the new *saeculum* and the new age was to be one of peace, happiness and prosperity. In view of the saecular portent with which Vergil ends his prophecy, it is worth recalling the description of the age of Augustus in Horace's *Carmen Saeculare* which employs the same generic material as Vergil's description of his new age: *fertilis frugum pecorisque tellus/spicea donet Cererem corona;/nutriant fetus et aquae salubres/et Iovis aurae* (*Carmen Saeculare* 29ff.). Moreover, both poems contain references to the *Parcae*; and Horace's lines — *vosque veraces cecinisse Parcae/quod semel dictum stabilisque rerum/terminus servet* (*Carmen Saeculare* 25ff.) — are reminiscent of Vergil's line — *concordes stabili fatorum numine Parcae* (*Eclogue* 4,47). Horace's new age belongs to Augustus, as he puts it at *Odes* 4,15,4f.: *tua, Caesar, aetas fruges et agris rettulit uberes*. The age of Augustus became an important concept. So the citizens of Narbo celebrated the day of his birth: *qua die eum saeculi felicitas orbi terrarum rectorem edidit*; and the day he first entered the consulship: *qua die primum imperium orbis terrarum auspicatus est.*[236] In *Eclogue* 4 the day of entry to the consulship and the birthday are divided between Pollio and the *puer*. The relationship of the *puer* to his *aetas* is clearly thought of in the same way as the relationship of Augustus to his *aetas*.

The way in which a ruler influences his age is rarely explained. The normal relationship is simply temporal: while this man is ruler, the world enjoys these blessings.[237] When more explicit statements are made, it seems that the character of the ruler is reflected in the character of the age. Some wit said of Tiberius:[238]

> asper et immitis, breviter vis omnia dicam?
> dispeream, si te mater amare potest . . .
> aurea mutasti Saturni saecula, Caesar;
> incolumi nam te ferrea semper erunt.

> (Suetonius *Tiberius* 59)

No wonder Vergil is anxious that his *puer* should begin life with laughter (60-63)! At other times the blessings seem to be provided by the gods since they approve of the ruler. Especially relevant here is Callimachus, who in the *Hymn to Zeus* (77-95) explains the material prosperity to be enjoyed under Ptolemy as the reward from Zeus for his ἀρετή and δικαιοσύνη.[239] Or they may be brought about by the divinity, the *numen*, of the ruler himself, as Calpurnius Siculus says of Nero: *illius ut primum senserunt numina terrae,/coepit et uberior sulcis fallentibus olim/luxuriare seges . . . (Eclogue* 4,112-4).[240] In whatever way the relationship between the ruler and his age is defined, it is clear that whatever happens under his rule is his responsibility and can properly be called his *facta*. Vergil has not simply synchronised the development of the child and the development of the *saeculum* out of some private whim.

The parallels noted between the *puer* and Augustus are striking and suggestive. Both are seen as the men of a new *saeculum*; for both it will be an *aurea aetas* and mark a return of *Saturnia regna*; both are compared to Hercules and Dionysus, Augustus explicitly, the *puer* implicitly; both will rule the world and under both the world will be pacified.[241] The idea of the *aurea saecula* of Augustus is intimately connected with the celebration of the saecular games and the successful completion of the conquest of the East. It was suggested above that even if the new Trojan war (*Eclogue* 4,35f.) could not refer to Antonius' imminent Parthian campaign, it must refer by a simple allegory[242] to some future Eastern conquests. This Eastern war checks the development of the new age which will not reach perfection until it is successfully completed. Now, while it is undeniable that *Eclogue* 4 deeply influenced the way writers thought of the *aurea aetas* of Augustus and later Emperors, it cannot be responsible for all the details. We must assume that this nexus of ideas originally centred on Julius Caesar.[243] He was to be the man of the new *saeculum*; the blessings of his rule as portrayed in Cicero's *Pro Marcello* are close to those of Augustus' rule as portrayed by Velleius Paterculus;[244] he apparently planned to inaugurate the new *saeculum* after the successful completion of the Parthian campaign. In 40 BC Vergil predicts that his *puer* will play the role that Caesar was to have played; in the twenties he, like Horace, saw Augustus as Caesar's successor in this role. This is made certain by one important point. Whether or not the *puer* is the expected child of Antonius and Octavia, offspring of the marriage designed to unite the Caesarian faction and so the true successor of Caesar, whether or not *magnum Iovis incrementum* (49) contains an allusion to Caesar as *Iuppiter Iulius*, the phrase *pacatumque reget...orbem* (17) must refer to Caesar's claim to be *dominus orbis terrarum*. For Caesar's claim, though foreshadowed by Pompey, was an innovation at Rome. In the Republic only *Roma*, the Roman people, could be said to rule the world, not an individual man.[245]

The realisation that Vergil is here making use of current beliefs about a new ruler and a new *saeculum* is important and not irrelevant to this section of the poem as a basilikon. For Vergil is here modernising and Romanising a traditional topic of the basilikon, the praise of conditions under a good king. The idea goes back to an important passage in Homer, *Odyssey* 19,108-114:

> For your fame goes up to broad heaven as does the fame of
> some blameless king, who, a god-fearing man, and lord among
> many powerful men, upholds justice, and the black earth bears
> wheat and barley and the trees are heavy with fruit and the
> flocks bear young without ceasing and the sea provides fish as
> a result of his good leadership and the people prosper under
> him.

The same topos appears in Hesiod *Works and Days* 225-237[246] almost immediately after his description of the five ages (*Works and Days* 106-201). This juxtaposition is of obvious relevance to *Eclogue* 4, where the descriptions of the Heroic Age and the Golden Age derive ultimately from Hesiod. What distinguishes Hesiod's version of this topos from that of Homer is the absence of seafaring and the assimilation of material from his description of the Golden Age. The Homeric passage was taken as the basis for the lists of topoi in the rhetoricians and the seafaring topos appears to be derived from the reference in Homer to the sea providing fish.

This Homeric passage was frequently quoted and discussed in treatises on kingship, including Philodemus *On the Good King according to Homer*.[247] In *Fr.* 4 Philodemus is distinguishing the βασιλεύς from the τύραννος and in his description of the material prosperity of a people under a good king he quotes *Odyssey* 19,109-14. In columns 11 and 12 he emphasises that 'τὸ ζηλότυπον (jealous rivalry) should be banished' and that 'the result of this unity (ἡ ὁμόνοια, *concordia*) is material prosperity, such as that of Phaeacia and Ithaca; Homer really believes that good harvests go with a benevolent and just ruler'. 'The connection between τὸ ζηλότυπον and στάσις may betray an outsider's comment on the struggles of the nobility.' These teachings of Philodemus must have seemed strikingly relevant to any Roman late in 40 BC: the jealous rivalry of Antonius and Octavian had nearly destroyed Rome; but now there was *concordia* and *pax*. When Vergil, in his description of the material prosperity to be enjoyed under the new ruler, thought of this Homeric topos, it seems at least possible that he thought of it in connection with the interpretation of his teacher Philodemus.[248] In one sense they both faced the same problem; and it is worth quoting a final observation of Oswyn Murray: 'The naturalisation of kingship theory in Rome through the mediation of Homer shows a touch of genius; a dangerous topic has been rendered harmless' (p.178). *Mutatis mutandis* the same is true of Vergil's description of his future king.

The Homeric passage was from an early date schematised by the rhetoricians and it is reflected in Theocritus *Idyll* 16, in the prayers for prosperity under Hieron, a passage in which the agricultural imagery is retained. It is also reflected in *Idyll* 17, where it occupies most of the poem after the scene describing the birth of Ptolemy. But in *Idyll* 17, in contrast to *Eclogue* 4, the agricultural imagery is largely absent.[249] The rhetorical schematisation of this topos, which is reflected in Cicero's *Pro Marcello* on the rule of Caesar, in Horace *Odes* 4,5,[250] in inscriptions[251] and in the 'panegyrics' of Velleius Paterculus on the rule of Augustus and Tiberius,[252] is preserved by Menander. Something very like it must have been well known to Vergil; and I quote the parts most relevant to our poem:

> You will speak of the fruitful seasons, the prosperity of the cities and say that the markets are full of produce ... that the land is farmed in peace, the sea is sailed without danger ... we do not dread barbarians, we do not dread enemies and we are more securely fortified by the arms of the king than cities by their walls ... And what greater boon ought they (the cities) to ask of the gods than that the king be safe? For rains in season and the produce of the sea and abundant harvests of fruit are our good fortune because of the justice of the king. That is why in exchange for all this we, the cities and tribes and people and races, crown him, hymn his praises ... After this you will utter a prayer asking god that the reign may last a very long time, that his kingdom may be handed on to his sons, that it may be handed down to their offspring.

Rhetores Graeci 3,377,10ff. (Spengel)

Bearing in mind these various considerations we can now reconsider the final sections of the prophecy.

After the description of the child's birth Menander prescribes a section περὶ φύσεως and on the beauty of the child. This topic Servius believed was implicit in the gift of the *baccar*: '*per quod pulchrum indicat puerum*'. Then Menander prescribes a new section: ἐξῆς δὲ κεφάλαιόν ἐστιν ἡ ἀνατροφή (3,371,17f. (Spengel) (and next is a section (on) the upbringing). In lines 26f. Vergil recalls, apparently, such a rhetorical formula; and in accordance with the rhetorical prescription, the second section of his prophecy is devoted to the rearing and education of the child.[253] As the child studies and attempts to emulate the heroes of whom he reads, the *saeculum* comes to reflect the Heroic Age — as described by Hesiod. There are some features of the Golden Age in this Heroic Age and new, Heroic, wars. The object of the child's study, which has clearly fired his imagination and shaped his character, becomes the reality of this new age, because it is his age and reflects his character.

But there is a further interesting aspect of this description. Even at this stage the world enjoys the blessings of the good king. Agriculture flourishes (33); the harvests are good (28); the seas are sailed; the cities are protected by their walls (32f.); and there will be new and doubtless victorious wars of conquest. Conventionally it is exactly these things which are adduced to proclaim the material prosperity enjoyed by the subjects of a good king. Yet here they are made to represent a state of affairs short of perfection, a result of some original sin. It is not possible that *priscae vestigia fraudis* (31) refers to the same thing as the *sceleris vestigia nostri*, the crime of civil strife. These will have long been removed by Pollio. Vergil may rather have in mind the *fraus* of Laomedon, whose failure to honour his pledge led to the destruction of Troy.[254] But the precise reference matters less than that Vergil, by the introduction of this thought, has made the conventional description of the material prosperity to be enjoyed under a good leader correspond merely to a halfway stage in the development of the new *saeculum* towards its full perfection.

The third and final section of the prophecy again begins with a clear allusion to the generic pattern: cf. ἀκολουθεῖ τοίνυν τοῖς ἐπιτηδεύμασι λοιπὸν ὁ περὶ τῶν πράξεων λογός (Menander 3,372,12f. (Spengel)) (then after the education comes the next section on deeds). The *adulescens* of the previous section has now mastered *virtus* and become a *vir.* [255] The Roman concept of *virtus*[256] has been substituted for Menander's δικαιοσύνη; and it is through this that the material prosperity to be enjoyed under the new saviour king reaches its perfection. There will be no more sailing, no trade, no agriculture. In so returning to Hesiod's description of life under just rulers with its absence of seafaring,[257] Vergil has produced a witty modification of the conventional topoi. This is especially apparent since in Theocritus *Idyll* 17 the topoi occur in their conventional form: agricultural at lines 77-81, walled cities at 82ff., seafaring and trade at 90ff. and 95ff.; Ptolemy's heroic wars are also emphasised, especially in 93f. and 102f., as is his great wealth at 95 and 104ff. The absence of these blessings of civilisation means not a diminution of prosperity and happiness but an increase. The multi-coloured sheep that graze in the fields will be, as was noted above, a constant sign of the continuing *felicitas* of the ruler and his people. If the wit of Vergil's adaptation of conventional topoi in this section is recognised, then the transition to this image can be seen as part of a gradual crescendo, rather than a sudden toppling over into bathos.

Vergil's relationship to Theocritus *Idyll* 17 is now much clearer. He has recognised that poem for what it is, a basilikon. Perhaps prompted by the agricultural imagery of *Idyll* 16 he has produced his own version of a basilikon, consciously using the precepts of the rhetoricians such as those preserved in Menander, but with acute awareness of the origins of the topoi in Homer and Hesiod, and of their treatment by Theocritus. This rhetorical framework has been adapted to reflect the current belief in the imminence of a new *saeculum* and a new ruler, cast in the self-image fostered and promulgated by Julius Caesar, whose successor the child will be. At the same time Vergil is able to recall the popular teachings of Philodemus and his modifications of Hellenistic kingship theory for the Roman political situation.

The remainder of the poem has already been discussed with reference to the overall genre, the *laudatio consulis*. Since some of the topoi are applied to the child, not the consul, (so continuing the intellectual playfulness just noted) they must now be considered in relation to the basilikon.

Menander says that all the people of the empire crown the king in return for the prosperity he guarantees them. It is to this topos that Vergil alludes in his command *adgredere o magnos... honores*(48). The belief that kings enjoyed the protection of Zeus (Theocritus *Idyll* 17,73f., see above) and Menander's prescription that we should pray to Zeus for the safety of the king are reflected in the phrase *magnum Iovis incrementum* (49) and in the omens of assent that follow. The universal approval emphasised by Menander is there too in *laetentur...omnia* (52). These topoi are connected with ideas of the fame and rewards that the ruler will win, and are discussed at the end of Philodemus' pamphlet. The idea of rewards for the new king is referred to in the final line of the poem (63): *nec deus hunc mensa dea nec dignata cubili est,* as well as in line 15: *ille deum vitam accipiet.* The fame of the king is secured by song (cf. ὑμνοῦμεν in Menander 3,377,26) and the significance of song in this context is referred to in Theocritus *Idyll* 17, 115-17: 'And the mouthpieces of the Muses sing of Ptolemy in return for his benefactions. What could be finer for a prosperous man than to win noble fame among men?' The importance of the μάντις, bard or philosopher, to the ruler also formed the subject of the penultimate section of Philodemus' treatise. It is this topos which occurs in Vergil's wish that he may one day sing of the *facta* of the *puer.* But even this personal seal, a sphragis, conceals an encomiastic motif. For Vergil's prayer that he should live a long time (53), *longae maneat pars ultima vitae*, is a subtle adaptation of the conventional prayer in Menander that the king should live a long time. The one implies the other.

The employment of the sphragis as a closing element is normal, as already noted, in encomia of all kinds.[258] But the subject matter here (53-7) also appears to be a conscious adaptation of the material which Menander recommends for use in a second prologue of the basilikon. Epilogue and prologue material is, of course, completely interchangeable. Menander makes the following recommendation (3,369,5ff. (Spengel)):

> Therefore just as we appease god by hymns celebrating his praises, so too we win over kings by speeches. Whenever you are seeking for amplification, you will take ideas for your second proem either from the mighty voice of Homer, saying that your theme needs nothing less than that; or take Orpheus, son of Calliope or even the Muses themselves, saying that even they would scarcely have been able to speak on the theme as it deserves, but that nonetheless there is nothing to stop us from trying as best we can!

The function of the sphragis is now clear: it emphasises the virtues and achievements of the future king and encourages him with thoughts of future songs. Vergil the neoteric, the Callimachean, is not proposing to become an epic poet. It is simply that because his subject will be greater and better than those of Orpheus and Linus, therefore his song will be better than theirs![259] Again a conventional topos has been modified wittily. As though to confirm this interpretation and to prevent misunderstanding, Vergil has made the style of this passage markedly bucolic or Theocritean, rather than epic, in its balances and parallelism. The introduction of Pan serves the same end, for he is a god often associated with bucolic poetry.[260] Moreover lines 58f. appear to be a variation on a theme from Moschus[261] *Lament for Bion* 55f.:

> Πανὶ φέρω τὸ μέλισμα; τάχ᾽ ἂν καὶ κεῖνος ἐρεῖσαι
> τὸ στόμα δειμαίνοι, μὴ δεύτερα σεῖο φέρηται.

(Shall I take your musical instrument to Pan? Perhaps even he would fear to put his lips to it, lest he should take second place to you). For in both passages there is a reference to a contest.

It is also noteworthy that Vergil, in a way characteristic of his reworking of *Idyll* 17, expands the topos of a future song which is treated so briefly by Theocritus (lines 135ff.) and does so with material drawn from exactly the same prologue commonplaces on which Theocritus drew in *Idyll* 17, 5-8: 'The heroes, who were in former times born of demigods, found skilled poets when they had performed fine deeds. But may I, who am skilled at singing fine things, hymn Ptolemy: hymns are the reward even for the immortals themselves.' The train of thought in Vergil and the relation of the sphragis to the rest of the poem is clear only when we remember the conventional background and the significance of the topos as it is presented here in Theocritus.[262]

The two final sections of *Eclogue* 4, lines 53-63, comprise a reworking and amplification of all the topoi treated by Theocritus at the end of *Idyll* 17, and not only of the promise of a future song (*Idyll* 17,135-137): 'Fare well, lord Ptolemy: and I shall make mention of you as much as of the other demigods, and, I think, I shall utter words not to be rejected by future generations: only ask Zeus for virtue.' The salutation to Ptolemy here is conventional in epilogues of hymns and in basilika.[263] If the king is well the people will enjoy prosperity. That this is what Theocritus intends is made clear by the reference to ἀρετή: like the *virtus* of the *puer* in *Eclogue* 4, ἀρετή is the guarantee and the source of the material prosperity.[264] Alternatives to the greeting χαῖρε, (fare well), are commands indicating 'come' or 'accept this gift', or some form of γελάω (laugh). So Vergil's command to the child *incipe*. . . *risu cognoscere matrem*. . . *incipe* (60ff.) is, in a sense, simply a substitution of one conventional leave-taking for another; and its significance is basically the same as that of the χαῖρε in Theocritus. If the child laughs, this will provide a good omen for the start of the new age, a guarantee of future happiness.

The χαῖρε topos has been further modified by being conflated with material taken from an earlier passage in *Idyll* 17. In 121-34, the lines preceding the epilogue, Theocritus deals with the honours Ptolemy has paid to his mother and his father, and with the marriage of Ptolemy to his sister; finally he closes on an epithalamic topos, the reference to the marriage of Zeus and Hera.[265] These themes have been elegantly combined with the χαῖρε topos in Vergil *Eclogue* 4. The child is to smile at his mother and at his father (*matrem*, 60; *parenti*, 62); his own future marriage is 'predicted' (*dea*. . .*dignata cubili est*, 63); and the last four lines are in themselves an epithalamic topos.

In the closing sequence, then, Vergil continues to rework his Theocritean model but less radically than in the central prophecy. None the less the basic techniques remain the same. He looks through the Theocritean poem, as it were, to its rhetorical skeleton, and then he picks out various topoi and produces his own version in order to 'rival' Theocritus. The topoi which Theocritus handles at length tend to be compressed by Vergil, those which Theocritus touches on briefly are expanded, often through the addition of related material from elsewhere in *Idyll* 17. In the central portion of the poem, however, Vergil's approach is more radical. He is still making use of his awareness of the generic identity of *Idyll* 17 to produce a 'rival' basilikon for a king who will surpass Ptolemy in the benefits he will bestow. Traditional Golden Age descriptions from Hesiod and his imitators are conflated with the description of life under a just and virtuous ruler to produce a much more 'pastoral' basilikon than Theocritus *Idyll* 17. This tendency of Vergil to revert, so to speak, to a bucolic norm is also evidenced by his treatment of the Simaetha *Idyll* (2) in *Eclogue* 8.[266]

When Vergil imagines his future king, however, the way in which he conceives of him is the only way open to a Roman living in 40 BC: that is, he sees him as a new Julius Caesar, someone more than a man but less than a god, and above all, the man of the new *saeculum*. The connection with the new *saeculum* is essential. For this is the link with the *laudandus* Pollio, who, as consul, will inaugurate the new age which will for ever be dated as beginning *Pollione consule*.

8. *Eclogue* 4, Catullus 64 and the Epithalamium

While the relationship of *Eclogue* 4 to its Theocritean model has been largely ignored or played down by scholars, its relationship with Catullus 64 has been widely acknowledged and studied in detail.[267] That Vergil is imitating Catullus was recognised by Macrobius (*Saturnalia* 6,1,41), who drew attention to the similarity of *Eclogue* 4,46f.: *'talia saecla' suis dixerunt 'currite' fusis/concordes stabili fatorum numine Parcae*, and Catullus 64,326f., the refrain in the song of the Fates: *sed vos, quae fata sequuntur/currite ducentes subtegmina, currite, fusi*. But Vergil is combining imitation of this refrain with allusion to two other passages which introduce and close the prophecy – Catullus 64,321f.: *talia divino fuderunt carmine fata/carmine perfidiae quod post nulla arguet aetas;* and 382f.: *talia praefantes quondam felicia Pelei/carmina divino cecinerunt pectore Parcae*. When Catullus made the *Parcae* sing of Achilles at the wedding of Peleus and Thetis, he was, if not innovating,[268] at least choosing an unusual variant of the story, for that task is usually given to another.[269] But reference to the lot of a man decided by the Fates at his birth is not unusual and comparison with Tibullus 1,7,1-4 is illuminating:

> Hunc cecinere diem Parcae fatalia nentes
> stamina, non ulli dissolvenda deo,
> hunc fore, Aquitanas posset qui fundere gentes
> quem tremeret forti milite victus Atax.

The application of the motif here in Tibullus and elsewhere[270] suggests that this is another topos that Vergil has diverted from the consul to the child.

However the relationship between the two poems rests on more than this striking detail. There are other general similarities: *Eclogue* 4 and the song of the Fates in Catullus 64 are almost identical in length and structure; both contain a prophecy concerning the life of an unborn child which occupies thirty-eight lines in Catullus, twenty lines in Vergil. Vergil has a further fifteen lines concerned directly with the child. This similarity is reinforced by a Catullan colouring which Vergil creates in this poem by his borrowing of metrical patterns[271] and of words and phrases[272] from Catullus 64.

This sustained allusion to Catullus 64 has a most important function within *Eclogue* 4. The occasion of the prophecy in Vergil is not made explicit beyond the fact that it is associated with Pollio's consulship. In Catullus it is delivered unambiguously at the wedding of Peleus and Thetis. Taken together, these facts inform us that the prophecy in *Eclogue* 4 was given at the wedding of Octavia and Antonius.[273] Just as Vergil used the allusion to Theocritus *Idyll* 17 to give a clue to the identity of the child, so here he uses the allusion to Catullus 64 to give a clue to the occasion of the prophecy. By this means Vergil again emphasises the connection, which he has not made explicit, between the child, the new age he ushers in, and the consul Pollio, and obviates the necessity for reference to the triumvirs.

That the wedding was the occasion when the *Parcae* delivered their prophecy is confirmed by the epithet *concordes*.[274] The theme of *concordia* or ὁμόνοια was important in epithalamia and treatises on marriage;[275] and it was considered one of the greatest blessings of marriage. In an epithalamic poem or speech a prophecy of the future joys of *concordia* which the bridal pair would enjoy was expected,[276] and in Catullus 64 the word is actually found in the song of the *Parcae*, immediately before the introduction of Achilles (334-6):

> nulla domus tales umquam contexit amores,
> nullus amor tali coniunxit foedere amantes,
> qualis adest Thetidi, qualis concordia Peleo.

But the marriage of Octavia and Antonius was not only, or even primarily, a private affair; and it was natural to think of the blessings of marriage which normally affected only the bridal pair as extending to all men.[277] Such an extension is not the invention of Vergil. Men were delighted because 'they thought that ὁμόνοια between these men (Antonius and Octavian) meant εἰρήνη for themselves': so Dio summarises the reactions to the wedding alliance (48,31,2). For twenty years before, the idea of *concordia* had been in vogue as a religious, philosophical and political concept, since the need for concord among the great was so pressing and obvious.[278] The renewal of the first triumvirate in 55 BC, the establishment of the second in 43 BC, and its renewal in 40 BC, were all marked with propaganda on the theme of *concordia* and *pax*, reflected in statues and coins bearing the symbols of the *caduceus* and clasped hands. On each occasion there was a dynastic marriage. The link, then, between marital concord, political concord and universal peace was commonplace in the propaganda of the late republic. Vergil capitalises on this background and celebrates not the marriage itself but the consequences and significance of the marriage. As though to underline this point, Vergil's only other piece of sustained imitation of Catullus 64 in this *Eclogue* is in the description of the Golden Age which will be the result of the marriage. In lines 40f.: *non rastros patietur humus, non vinea falcem/robustus quoque iam tauris iuga solvet arator*, Vergil alludes to Catullus 64, 38-42:

> rura colit nemo, mollescunt colla iuvencis
> non humilis curvis purgatur vinea rastris,
> non glebam prono convellit vomere taurus,
> non falx attenuat frondatorum arboris umbram,
> squalida desertis rubigo infertur aratris.

This passage describes the immediate result of the marriage of Peleus and Thetis, a brief return of the Golden Age to Thessalia.[279] The point in *Eclogue* 4 is exactly the same: the new *saeculum* will be a new Golden Age, an age of *concordia* and *pax*. But in Vergil it will come more slowly and be enjoyed not just locally and for the duration of the wedding, but universally and without end.

In this connection a further observation can be made. It was shown above that Vergil created his picture of the final perfection to be reached in the new age by wittily modifying or negating the signs of material prosperity that traditionally characterised the reign of a good king. The final result of course is a greater degree of blissful prosperity, not a lesser. But the same blessings were also traditionally the blessings conferred by marriage on mankind, and as such they were topical in epithalamia.[280] Thus Vergil's new age stems from two causes: its material prosperity is due to the reign of a good king; but it is also the result of the marriage of Antonius and Octavia. This latter connection is not difficult or abstruse, for it was traditional to associate the theme of marital *concordia* with the idea of children; and the procreation of children was the reason for marriage in Roman eyes. It was precisely through the children that marriage guaranteed the future existence of the race, the safety of the state, and the salvation and prosperity of the home and family.[281]

So far we have examined the similarity between *Eclogue* 4 and Catullus 64. The relationship between the two poems is similar to that between *Eclogue* 4 and Theocritus *Idyll* 17. The allusion is established by a striking parallel; the poet takes over a general colouring from the model; and he manipulates specific topoi, making use of their status as topoi within the relevant genre as well as their particular function within the model. We must now consider the deliberate contrast Vergil has created with Catullus 64.[282]

The *Parcae* in Vergil (*Eclogue* 4,46f.) remain mysterious powers not minutely visualised but kindly, harmonious and reliable. In Catullus 64, 303ff. they are described at length as balding, ancient hags, the wool of fate sticking to their wizened lips. The contrast must be deliberate and reflects the contrast between the different sequences of the ages decreed in the two poems.

Catullus 64 begins with the first ship, the Argo, setting sail. It is the beginning of the Heroic Age: implicitly therefore it is the end of the Golden Age, and Golden Age features appear only briefly and paradoxically in connection with the wedding of Peleus and Thetis. This wedding marks the beginning of the new, Heroic, age, just as the wedding of Antonius and Octavia marks the beginning of a new age for Vergil in *Eclogue* 4. The Heroic Age in Catullus 64 is not perfect, but nonetheless it is infinitely preferable to the age in which Catullus lives. The Ariadne-Theseus episode does recount a series of betrayals of family and friends; but there is also bravery in Theseus' initial exploit, punishment for each betrayal, and reward for Ariadne in her marriage to Dionysus. In the same way it is implicit that Achilles, although he is the cause of much suffering and death, fights bravely against the enemies of his country and secures fame for himself and for his family. Catullus ends with an account

71

of the horrors of his own Iron Age, an awesome and grotesque contrast that makes the Heroic Age seem glorious by comparison. It is precisely these three ages, the Golden, the Heroic and the modern age of Iron, that appear in reverse order in the prophecy of *Eclogue* 4. Vergil does not make use of the five ages of Hesiod, the ten of the Sibylline oracle, or the great year of the philosophers.

Catullus introduces his catalogue of crime and corruption at the end of 64 (398f.): *sed postquam tellus scelere est imbuta nefando/iustitiamque omnes cupida de mente fugarunt.* It is this catalogue that is evoked by Vergil in *Eclogue* 4, 13f.: *te duce, si qua manent sceleris vestigia nostri,/ inrita perpetua solvent formidine terras.* But in Vergil the new age is dawning: *iam redit et virgo* (6). Vergil portrays the development of this age as passing through a heroic period characterised, exactly as in Catullus 64, by the Argo, by Achilles, and by imperfection (*pauca tamen suberunt priscae vestigia fraudis*, 31). From this he passes to the perfection of the new age, described in terms which deliberately recall Catullus' description of the joy which the marriage of Peleus and Thetis brings to Thessalia (see above). Vergil imagines his new age as the perfect antithesis to the modern age in Catullus 64; and in lines 15f. he plays the optimism of his Theocritean model[283] against the pessimism of his Catullan model. For these lines, *ille deum vitam accipiet, divisque videbit/permixtos heroas et ipse videbitur illis,* which echo Theocritus *Idyll* 17,20ff., also allude to Catullus 64,384-6:

> praesentes namque ante domos invisere castas
> heroum, et sese mortali ostendere coetu,
> caelicolae nondum spreta pietate solebant.

and *per contrariam* to 405-8:

> omnia fanda nefanda malo permixta furore
> iustificam nobis mentem avertere deorum.
> quare nec talis dignantur visere coetus,
> nec se contingi patiuntur lumine claro.

The same blend of Theocritus' description of Herakles and Catullus 64,405ff. can be felt when Vergil reverts to this theme at the end of his poem (63): *nec deus hunc mensa, dea nec dignata cubili est.*

More striking however is the contrast between the *puer* of *Eclogue* 4 and Achilles in Catullus 64, a contrast which is highlighted by the parallel structure of the prophecies concerning them in each poem. Catullus begins with a brief mention of the birth (*nascetur*, 338) and the training (340f. –

stag-hunting) of Achilles. He then deals with Achilles' deeds in war (343-360), his death (362), and the honours paid to him after his death (363-370). Vergil has expanded the topoi treated briefly by Catullus, the birth and the training of the *puer*; he substitutes deeds of peace for Achilles' deeds in war; and, most importantly, he has omitted any mention of the death of the *puer*. The result is a deliberate and balanced contrast to the figure of Achilles in Catullus 64, a contrast which Vergil may be emphasising by dissociating the *puer* and Achilles within his own poem (36): *et iterum ad Troiam magnus mittetur Achilles*[284]. In a sense Vergil is simply reverting to the norm. Prophecies, which were at home in the *laudatio consulis* and in the basilikon, were also regularly used in epithalamia (see above). We are told by Menander[285] that the orator should say that the bridal pair will have dreams that will foretell the birth of children, lifelong concord, increased prosperity and so on. Ps.-Dionysius says, in a lacunose passage, that there should be a prophecy concerning the children, predicting success in their studies.[285] The kind of vague prophecies that could be expected are found in two poems of Statius written to congratulate friends on the birth of a son: in *Silvae* 4,7 and 4,8 we find vague promises of success and glory, emphasis on the happiness the children will bring to their parents, and stress on how they will take after their parents. Ps.-Dionysius even prescribes a prediction of the future marriage of the child.[286] Vergil's prophecy is clearly modelled on this normal epithalamic type, except that he is concerned with what the child will mean to all men, not just to his parents, the bridal pair.

Seen against this background the emphasis on death in Catullus' account of Achilles' life is especially horrific and incongruous. Death and funerals are the very antithesis of weddings and birth, and ancient writers never seem to tire of playing on this fact.[287] But in life too, contact with death was carefully avoided on occasions celebrating births and weddings.[288] It is therefore striking that in Catullus 64 the account of Achilles' deeds in war is undermined by the unexpected reference to the perjury of Pelops rather than to that of Laomedon (346), and by the fact that the losses he inflicts on the enemy are represented by mothers lamenting for their sons (349).[289] Achilles' own death is mentioned without elaboration, but the honours that glorify him after his death are particularly sinister.[290] Not only does the sacrifice of Polyxena recall the sacrifice of Iphigenia in Lucretius *De Rerum Natura* 1, 80-101 and the moral condemnation expressed there (*tantum religio potuit suadere malorum*, 101); but also it inevitably recalls the purpose of Polyxena's sacrifice. This was to send her as a wife to Achilles in the underworld; it is thus a perversion of the epithalamic topos of the future marriage of the child, and it provides another point of contact with the sacrifice of Iphigenia, who came to Aulis expecting to marry Achilles. These grim aspects of Achilles' life do not mean that Catullus saw the Heroic Age as no better than the present one.[291] But, as Achilles typifies the Heroic Age, it too is imperfect. Vergil alludes to this conception of the Heroic Age when he prefaces his description of it with *pauca tamen suberunt priscae vestigia fraudis* (31); and in the development of the new *saeculum*, the Heroic Age is succeeded by the Golden Age, a deliberate and complete contrast to the present age as described by Catullus. The contrast between the *puer* of *Eclogue* 4 and Achilles in Catullus 64 therefore reasserts the traditional topoi of epithalamic prophecies, such as the birth and growth of children, and the harmonious concord, the material prosperity and the happiness which children assure; and it allows their full significance to be realised.

It was suggested above that Vergil's conception of the material prosperity that the *puer* will bring may have been influenced by the treatise of Philodemus *On the Good King according to Homer*. It is worth noting that to Philodemus (column 9,14ff.)[292] Achilles exemplified τὸ ζηλότυπον, the cause of στάσις and civil war: he was not just warlike (πολεμικός) but a lover of war (φιλοπόλεμος) and of strife. It is precisely as a contrast to this that unity and concord are praised, and the material prosperity enjoyed under a good ruler is illustrated. It seems too much for coincidence when Vergil depicts the future child of Antonius and Octavia, the very essence and guarantor of the *concordia* that now exists, as a contrast to the Achilles of Catullus.

But although the prophecy which concerns the birth, development and significance of a child is clearly of a type we might expect to find in an epithalamium, *Eclogue* 4 is not an epithalamium. There is no wedding ceremony, no bridal pair, no marriage gods. The poem remains a *laudatio consulis*. The expected encomium of the consul, which would have been a Roman version of the genre basilikon, does not occur. But the prophecy concerning the child who will be a king takes its place. The substitution is facilitated by the fact that prophecy plays an important role in both genres. The occasion of the prophecy, revealed only implicitly by allusion to Catullus and confirmed by the epithet *concordes* given to the *Parcae*, was the wedding of Antonius and Octavia.

The importance of recognising the epithalamic topos at the end of *Eclogue* 4 (60-63) has already been noted: the laughter is the child's gift from Venus *via* Octavia; and his becoming a new Hercules indicates that he is a true son of his father Antonius. Again the absorption[293] of this topos is made easier by two factors: by the presence in the *laudatio consulis* of the command to take up office and begin the auspicious year; and by the topoi employed by Theocritus at the close of his basilikon, *Idyll* 17, the command χαῖρε, the references to Ptolemy's parents, and the allusion to Ptolemy's own marriage. Similarly the prayer to the birth goddess Lucina (*Eclogue* 4,8-10) might be considered as an epithalamic topos[294] that has been absorbed into the *laudatio consulis* even though it occurred in Theocritus *Idyll* 17. Moreover, at Rome, the moon and the sun were contemporary symbols for the beginning of a new *saeculum*[295] and the fact that Apollo and his sister will favour the birth of the *puer* is another point of contrast to Catullus 64, where these gods are conspicuously absent from the wedding of Peleus and Thetis.[296] While all these considerations seem relevant, the topos as it occurs, in the form of a prayer for a future birth, would doubtless be most at home in an epithalamium.

It is also worth noting that most of the other topoi of the poem would not have been out of place in an epithalamium. The emphasis on the significance of the moment (4-10);[297] the explicit praises of C. Asinius Pollio, who was the matchmaker, the friend of the groom, the consul of the year, and surely an important wedding guest (11-14);[298] the universal joy and excitement (48-52);[299] the promise of a future song for the child (53-59);[300] all these could have been found in an epithalamium written for the wedding of Antonius and Octavia. It is not surprising that this is the case: the epithalamium and the *laudatio consulis* are, after all, epideictic genres which both celebrate special occasions of a highly ceremonial nature. But Vergil may be exploiting the fact that his readers would have seen such combinations of ambivalent material in epithalamic contexts to enable him to import a specifically epithalamic topos at the end of his *laudatio consulis*. These topoi retain only sufficient reminders of their epithalamic nature to remind the reader obliquely of the event which made Pollio's consulship glorious. In this way Vergil secures attention for Pollio while writing in full accord with the truth. It is a delicate balance superbly maintained.

9. *Eclogue* 4, Horace *Epode* 16 and the *Sibylline Oracles*

Two traditional approaches to the study of *Eclogue* 4 have been largely ignored in this article. I have said nothing about Horace *Epode* 16 and little about the *Sibylline Oracles*. For the sake of completeness I shall deal with these now.

There can be no doubt that *Eclogue* 4 and Horace *Epode* 16 are closely related. But I consider *Epode* 16 as largely irrelevant to a study of *Eclogue* 4 since I am convinced that it was written as an answer to *Eclogue* 4 when it became apparent that the peace secured by Brundisium was only fleeting.[301] The *Eclogues* were published in 39 BC,[302] the *Epodes* in 30 BC, and consequently the onus of proof lies with those who wish to place *Epode* 16 before *Eclogue* 4. There is no evidence that Horace was an intimate of Vergil before the *Eclogues* were published. These are general considerations: but the argument from verbal similarities, though not conclusive, tends to confirm this view, since similarities in *Epode* 16 to *Eclogue* 4 are combined with reminiscences of other *Eclogues*.[303] It is more likely that this would have happened if Horace had the whole collection in mind as he wrote, rather than that Vergil kept announces that a new age of peace, prosperity and happiness is about to begin. Horace begins by announcing that: *altera iam teritur bellis civilibus aetas* (*Epode* 16,1). This second age is to see the destruction, not the salvation, of Rome. Vergil's optimistic interpretation of the new age has therefore proved to be ill founded, the old fears well justified. Those who want to find the Golden Age existence that Vergil had promised must leave Rome and sail to the Isles of the Blessed set aside for the *melior pars*, as they had been set aside for the heroes in Hesiod's account of the Heroic Age. This seems a natural way to read *Epode* 16. But if Vergil were replying to Horace, instead of Horace answering Vergil, we should surely expect some more explicit indication in *Eclogue* 4 that Rome was not to fall by her own hand, that there was no need to sail away to enjoy the Golden Age, since it was coming to Italy to be enjoyed by all. That would not be a natural or obvious way to read *Eclogue* 4.

To know whether Vergil is making any extensive use of a Sibylline Oracle is quite a different problem. If *ultima Cumaei venit iam carminis aetas* (*Eclogue* 4,4) is to be taken as an allusion to a specific prophecy, then we can only conclude that it is now no longer extant. Of the extant *Sibylline Oracles* only the third is early enough to have been used by Vergil. The most recent extensive study of that poem states emphatically:[304] 'La dâte qui nous paraît la meilleure est celle de 42 avant notre ère ...Il est certain que la 4e *Églogue* de Virgile ou la 16e *Épode* d'Horace ne doit rien à la Sibylle, mais ces trois oeuvres expriment également une aspiration à l'âge d'or profonde et universelle qui leur donne à toutes une qualité d'accent particulièrement émouvante.' It would not be surprising however if there had been a Sibylline Oracle which announced the coming of a new saviour king and a new Golden Age. Nor would it be surprising if this had been associated at Rome with the idea of the dawn of a new *saeculum*. The Etruscan theory of *saecula* had long been associated with the Centennial Games which had first been introduced as the result of consulting a Sibylline Oracle (see above). Moreover Sibylline prophecies played an important role in the later celebration of the *Ludi Saeculares* in 17 BC and subsequently.[305] A general allusion to a current prophecy seems probable.[306] But the only indications of a more specific debt are in the Eastern associations of some of the miraculous events that will attend the child's birth, the *baccar*, the *colocasia* and the *Assyrium amomum* (19-25); and in the often remarked but vague similarities to the prophecy of Isaiah. I quote only the more striking passages for comparison: 'The wolf shall dwell with the lamb and the leopard shall lie with the kid and the calf and the young lion and the fatling together and a little child shall lead them' (*Isaiah* 11,6); 'The sucking child shall play on the hole of the asp and the weaned child shall put his hand on the basilisk's den' (*Isaiah* 11,8). Perhaps some Sibylline prophet had used these details to indicate the signs by which the new saviour would be recognised; perhaps they had even in some way been connected in the prophecy with Antonius, who was hailed as 'Dionysus the Benefactor and Bringer of Joy' in the East after Philippi (Plutarch *Antonius* 24). But this can only be speculation and leads nowhere, even if it is worth being aware of the possibility.

A final aspect of this question however deserves more consideration than it has received. It is possible that Vergil wrote his prophecy in a style that was intended to be reminiscent of the style of the Sibylline prophecies. R.G. Austin long ago[307] pointed out that *at tibi* (18) and *at simul* (26) recall the ἀλλά and αὐτάρ which the Sibyls used to mark the different stages of their prophecies; that the assonance, rhyme and anaphora so characteristic of *Eclogue* 4 are also noticeable stylistic features in the Sibylline prophecies; and that the tendency to make the sense units coincide with the end of the lines is another feature common to *Eclogue* 4 and the Sibylline prophecies.[308] Moreover, the reminiscences of Hesiod that colour our poem are also a marked feature of the *Sibylline Oracles*.[309] It seems then that Vergil is exploiting the stylistic similarities of the *Sibylline Oracles*, the poems of Theocritus, and Catullus 64, in order to impose a unified tone and a stylistic consistency on the diverse materials that have gone into the making of his poem. Beyond this point we can only speculate. But it is perhaps worth noting that the extant

Sibylline Oracles associate the coming of a new age of peace, prosperity and happiness with the birth of the Messiah, just as Vergil's new age is associated with his very Roman *puer*. On the other hand, in the *Sibylline Oracles* Rome will be destroyed as a prelude to this new age, and fears of Rome's destruction as the present *saeculum* ended were certainly widespread in the late Republic. If this idea was also found in the *Sibylline Oracles* known to Vergil and his audience, then Vergil is clearly making a deliberate point when he makes it plain, after announcing the arrival of the *ultima aetas* of the Sibyl, that Rome has survived, that the Roman world will enjoy the new peace and prosperity, and that the Messiah will be, in effect, a Roman.

Before turning from this tantalising subject it is worth quoting two of the passages from the third book of the *Sibylline Oracles*, which are in some respects so close but in others so far from *Eclogue* 4:310

Ἥξει ἐπ᾽ ἀνθρώπους μεγάλη κρίσις ἠδὲ καὶ ἀρχή,
γῆ γὰρ παγγενέτειρα βροτοῖς δώσει τὸν ἄριστον
καρπὸν ἀπειρέσιον σίτου οἴνου καὶ ἐλαίου
αὐτὰρ ἀπ᾽ οὐρανόθεν μέλιτος γλυκεροῦ ποτὸν ἡδὺ
δένδρεά τ᾽ ἀκροδρύων καρπὸν καὶ πίονα μῆλα
καὶ βόας ἔκ τ᾽ ὀίων ἄρνας αἰγῶν τε χιμάρους
πηγάς τε ῥήξει γλυκερὰς λευκοῖο γάλακτος
πλήρεις δ᾽ αὖτε πόλεις ἀγαθῶν καὶ πίονες ἀγροὶ
ἔσσοντ᾽· οὐδὲ μάχαιρα κατὰ χθονὸς οὐδὲ κυδοιμός·
οὐδὲ βαρὺ στενάχουσα σαλεύσεται οὐκέτι γαῖα·
οὐ πόλεμος οὐδ᾽ αὖτε κατὰ χθονὸς αὐχμὸς ἔτ᾽ ἔσται,
οὐ λιμὸς καρπῶν τε κακορρέκτειρα χάλαζα·
ἀλλὰ μὲν εἰρήνη μεγάλη κατὰ γαῖαν ἅπασαν,
καὶ βασιλεὺς βασιλῆι φίλος μέχρι τέρματος ἔσται
αἰῶνος, κοινόν τε νόμον κατὰ γαῖαν ἅπασαν
ἀνθρώποις τελέσειεν ἐν οὐρανῷ ἀστερόεντι
ἀθάνατος, ὅσα πέπρακται δειλοῖσι βροτοῖσιν.
Αὐτὸς γὰρ μόνος ἐστὶ θεὸς κοὐκ ἔστιν ἔτ᾽ ἄλλος·
αὐτὸς καὶ πυρὶ φλέξειεν χαλεπῶν μένος ἀνδρῶν.

Oracula Sibyllina 3,743-61.

(A great judgement and rule will come upon men, for earth, begetter of all things, will give to mortals the best of harvests without stint, of wheat and wine and olive-oil and pleasant draughts of heavenly honey and the fruit of

78

orchard trees, and fat sheep and cattle and from the sheep lambs and from the goats kids and she will cause to gush forth sweet streams of white milk and in turn cities and rich fields will abound with good things. There will be on the earth neither sword nor din of battle: the earth will no longer totter and groan deeply. Nor will there be war, nor will there be upon the earth drought or famine or crop-destroying hail. But a great peace will be upon the whole earth and king will be friend of king to the end of time and in the starry heavens god will make a common law for men over the whole earth for whatever is done by wretched mortals. For he alone is god and there is no other besides and he will burn in fire the power of evil men.)

Εὐφράνθητι, κόρη, καὶ ἀγάλλεο· σοὶ γὰρ ἔδωκεν
εὐφροσύνην αἰῶνος, ὃς οὐρανὸν ἔκτισε καὶ γῆν.
Ἐν σοὶ δ' οἰκήσει· σοὶ δ' ἔσσεται ἀθάνατον φῶς·
ἠδὲ λύκοι τε καὶ ἄρνες ἐν οὔρεσιν ἄμμιγ' ἔδονται
χόρτον, παρδάλιές τ' ἐρίφοις ἅμα βοσκήσονται·
ἄρκτοι σὺν μόσχοις νομάδες αὐλισθήσονται·
σαρκοβόρος τε λέων φάγεται ἄχυρον παρὰ φάτνῃ
ὡς βοῦς· καὶ παῖδες μάλα νήπιοι ἐν δεσμοῖσιν
ἄξουσιν· πηρὸν γὰρ ἐπὶ χθονὶ θῆρα ποιήσει.
Σὺν βρέφεσίν τε δράκοντες ἅμ' ἀσπίσι κοιμήσονται
κοὐκ ἀδικήσουσιν· χεὶρ γὰρ θεοῦ ἔσσετ' ἐπ' αὐτούς.

Oracula Sibyllina 3,785-95.

(Rejoice, maiden, and exult, for he has given you immortal joy, he who made heaven and earth. And he will dwell in you: and he will be an eternal light for you. And wolves and lambs mixed up together will graze the grass on the mountains and leopards will graze together with deer; wandering bears will be folded with calves and the flesh-eating lion will eat chaff beside the manger like an ox; and very tiny children will drive them in harness: for he will make the wild beast harmless upon the earth. Serpents and asps will sleep with new-born babes and not hurt them. For the hand of god will be over them.)

The difference between the Jewish tones of the Sibyl and the Graeco-Roman tones of Vergil are striking and obvious. But the similarity of the message and of the physical details of the earthly paradise is no less remarkable just because of this. Stylistic similarities are worth noting. Both Vergil and the Sibyl, of course, use future tenses and imperatives, and both give the overall impression of composing line upon line, paragraph upon paragraph. But small details are also of interest. The first sentence quoted (743-51) should be compared with *Eclogue* 4,4-10:

> ultima Cumaei venit iam carminis aetas:
> magnus ab integro saeclorum nascitur ordo.
> iam redit et virgo, redeunt Saturnia regna
> iam nova progenies caelo demittitur alto.
> tu modo nascenti puero quo ferrea primum
> desinet ac toto surget gens aurea mundo,
> casta fave Lucina: tuus iam regnat Apollo.

In both the sheer sound effect is of great importance in creating the tone of excitement. Compare, for example, the effect of μεγάλη, ἠδὲ, ἀρχή, γῆ; τὸν ἄριστον καρπὸν ἀπειφέσιον; σίτου, οἴνου ἐλαίου; δένδρεα, ἀκροδρύων; βόας, ἄρνας, πηγάς; οἴων, αἰγῶν; πλήρεις, πόλεις with the effect of the alliteration on *m, n, c* and *r* that runs through Vergil's lines, and the assonance of *integro, ordo, virgo, caelo, alto, modo, puero quo, tcto, mundo, Apollo*. Or compare the sound effects of γῆ γὰρ παγγενέτειρα or γλυκερὰς λευκοῖο γάλακτος with *Cumaei venit iam carminis* or *ab integro saeclorum nascitur ordo* or *surget gens*. Both writers employ repetition: καπρόν (745,747), πίονα (747) πίονες (750), γλυκεροῦ (746) γλυκεράς (749); cf. *nascitur* (5) *nascenti* (8), *redit, redeunt* (6), *regna* (6) *regnat* (10), *tu* (8) *tuus* (10), reinforced by the near repetitions *progenies* (7) *gens* (9), *ferrea* (8) *aurea* (9). The movement of Vergil's passage is articulated by the repeated *iam* as the Sibyl in lines 751-4 uses οὐδέ, οὐκέτι, οὐ or σοὶ in lines 785-87. In Vergil too the device is frequently used: *te* (11-14); *ille* (15f.); *quae, alter, altera* (32-5); *nec, non* (38-42). Repetitions at the beginnings of lines, *ipsae* (21-23), *occidet* (24,25), *aspice* (50,51), *Pan etiam Arcadia* (58,59), and *incipe parve puer* (60,62), find parallels in αὐτός (760-761), εὐφράνθητι (785), εὐφροσύνην (786); while the effect of ἔδονται, βοσκήσονται, αὐλισθήσονται, κομήσονται (788-90, 794) is similar to that of *arista, uva, mella, fraudis, cingere muris, infindere sulcos* at the end of lines 28-33, or *incrementum, mundum, profundum* at 49-51 or *referent distenta, magnos metuent armenta, blandos fundent* at 21-23.

There is little point in extending this analysis but it should perhaps be emphasised that the style of this passage from the Sibyl is not atypical; nor is it chosen primarily to illustrate the style of *Eclogue* 4, but for its content. All the features of the *Eclogue* discussed here can be paralleled endlessly from the remaining *Sibylline Oracles*. I think it must be fair to conclude that Vergil is deliberately using a prophetic style designed to be reminiscent of the *Sibylline Oracles*. It is entirely consistent with this view that the child, despite many clues to his identity, remains anonymous and that the detailed description of the future predicts happiness and prosperity without being precise as to what will happen and when it will happen in terms of the Roman historical situation.311

10. Some Remarks on Style

What makes *Eclogue* 4 a great poem and of perennial and immediate appeal is, perhaps above all else, its emotion and pure excitement. The emotion it conveys, that of relief, of the overwhelming incredulous joy, which accompanies the passing of a crisis and the glimpse of a better tomorrow, is an extremely difficult one to handle in words. The choice of details used to characterise the new age makes a large contribution to establishing the emotional tone. On the one hand, they are familiar to us from countless appearances in Golden Age descriptions. Yet they are so fantastic that there is never a question of believing that they will really happen. It is the mood that is important, the feeling that anything might happen.

The emotional vigour of the poem is balanced by a careful symmetry. The structure may be simply analysed: three lines of preface are followed by two sets of seven lines, the central prophecy of twenty-eight lines, a further two sets of seven lines and a closing set of four lines 'completing' the three-line preface. This effect of symmetry and balance is strengthened by the structure of the prophecy, which comprises three sections: the Golden Age elements of the first (the birth) and the third (manhood) lend a balance to the whole. All this creates an impression of stately grandeur and controlled formality highly appropriate to the ceremonial nature of the theme and the importance of the prophecy. It is supported apparently by the stichic nature of the writing and the general avoidance of enjambement, by the formal artistry of the arrangement of nouns and their adjectives within the lines, and by the formality of the sentence structures, with their careful anaphora. Nonetheless the dominant tone of the poem is not simply one of stately and ceremonial magnificence. For set against these stylistic features are others that move the poem forward and create a sense of underlying agitation and excitement.

The basic structure of the poem is more complex than it first appears. The first two seven line sections, 4-10 and 11-17, subdivide regularly into blocks of four and three lines, the longer preceding the

81

shorter. The corresponding later sections, 46-52 and 53-59, divide less formally into two plus two plus three lines and two plus three plus two lines. Within the prophecy also the divisions are less regular: it has three sections of eight, eleven and nine lines, and again within these sections the divisions are irregular: 5 (=3+2) +3 (=1+2); 5 (=2+3) +6 (=3+3); 5 (=3+2) +4. The apparent formality of the word patterning within the lines is also more varied than a first glance might suggest. Even lines 28-30, which appear on the surface to be so similar, differ subtly from each other:

> molli paulatim flavescet campus arista
> incultisque rubens pendebit sentibus uva
> et durae quercus sudabunt roscida mella.

These lines may be represented as b c C A B; b a C B A; a A C b B. Exactly the same is true of the apparently ordered sentence structure of 32-5:

> quae temptare Thetim ratibus, quae cingere muris
> oppida, quae iubeant telluri infindere sulcos;
> alter erit tum Tiphys et altera quae vehat Argo
> delectos heroas, erunt etiam altera bella.

There are, effectively, two overlapping patterns of anaphora of *quae* and *alter*. In 32-33 the first colon has the relative followed by infinitive, accusative and ablative; the second repeats the sequence, but reverses the order of ablative and accusative; the third separates the relative from the infinitive and accusative by interposing the controlling verb *iubeant* and the unexpected dative *telluri*. 34f. are linked to what precedes by the assonance of the Greek names *Thetis* and *Tiphys* and the *quae* which picks up the anaphora aurally but not grammatically; the *alter* of the first colon becomes *altera* in the second, and *altera* is repeated in the third, but in a different metrical position; *erit tum* is omitted in the second member and becomes *erunt etiam* in the third, heading the colon. The whole poem can easily be analysed in similar terms; and even though it is possible only to discuss the mechanics of the writing, it is clear that the balanced symmetrical calm is constantly in danger of being disrupted by these shifting undercurrents. This is what creates the impression of barely controlled emotion underlying the formal grandeur.

Equally important is the constant forward movement of the poem, which contradicts the static qualities of the concentric blocks of sense. Here the devices of anaphora and repetition, of alliteration and assonance, already noted as features of the *Sibylline Oracles*, play an important role. But while these various types of repetition are a most important device for securing the headlong forward movement of the poem, there is another feature, also important but less susceptible of analysis. Each of the main sections of the poem ends on a line which caps or at least summarises the emotional heights reached in that section and which then provides the starting point for the subsequent section. So the preface ends upon the paradoxical line: *si canimus silvas, silvae sint consule dignae* (3). The first main section of the frame culminates in the emotional prayer to Lucina and the second in the impossible vision: *pacatumque reget patriis virtutibus orbem* (17). Within the prophecy itself we have the exotic flourish in: *Assyrium vulgo nascetur amomum* (25) and the climax of: *atque iterum ad Troicm magnus mittetur Achilles* (36). The final section of the prophecy and the first section of the frame end with lines that summarise the preceding lines: *sponte sua sandyx pascentis vestiet agnos* (45); and, more clearly: *aspice, venturo laetentur ut omnia saeclo* (52). The effect of these two summary lines is to check briefly the mounting extravagance as the emotional excitement reaches its peak.

The emotion culminates in lines 53-59 where the poet excitedly predicts what the new age will mean to him as a poet. As it reaches this peak the heavy parallelism serves to steady and control the surge of excitement as the poem nears its end. In 55-57:

non me carminibus vincet nec Thracius Orpheus
nec Linus, huic mater quamvis atque huic pater adsit,
Orphei Calliopea, Lino formosus Apollo

the movement of the sentence is controlled by the repetitions *non, nec, nec; Orpheus, Orphei; Linus, Lino* and by the emphatic parallelism of *huic mater, huic pater* and the corresponding *Orphei Calliopea, Lino . . . Apollo*. This is only slightly offset by the inexact correspondence of *quamvis* to *adsit* and the fact that in the first phrase *Orpheus* has an adjective, while *Linus* has not, and in the third *Apollo* is given an adjective but not *Calliopea.*

Having steadied the mounting excitement the final control is achieved through the amusing verbal play of 58f.:

Pan etiam, Arcadia mecum si iudice certet,
Pan etiam Arcadia dicat se iudice victum,

where the parallelism is so exact as to be almost confusing. The final lines close gently with the homely note reinforced by the balance of *incipe, parve puer* (60, 62) and the repeated *matrem* (60), *matri* (61); *risu* (60), *risere* (62); *nec deus, dea nec* (63).

11. Conclusions

Eclogue 4 is an immensely rich, complex and sophisticated poem. But its underlying 'message' may be expressed simply: the worst is over, destruction has been avoided, and this moment is a turning point; the future will be a time of prosperity and happiness. In spite of all the sophisticated intellectual games, this simple message is never obscured.

One point deserves emphasis. Even at this date, when there is no worthwhile evidence that Vergil had been associated closely with Julius Caesar or with either of his successors, Octavian or Antonius, Vergil envisages the future happiness and prosperity of Rome as depending on one man, a sole ruler. Later Vergil joined the circle of Maecenas (probably early in 38 BC) and was able to see Octavian, the future Augustus, as the one man who could fulfil the role he had formulated earlier, in this *Eclogue*. If this view of the situation is correct, then it helps to explain why Vergil should have abandoned Pollio for Maecenas. It also encourages the belief that Vergil was one of those instrumental in defining the image which Octavian had to present in order to fulfil the needs and desires of a whole generation of Romans: Vergil, that is, was not merely a paid hack or mouthpiece for the propaganda of the regime. But however much hindsight endorses this view of Vergil as a serious political thinker and as one genuinely concerned with the fate of Rome, it would be a mistake to take the 'sole ruler' theme as the main message of *Eclogue* 4. Such a view would be incompatible with the declared function of the poem — to honour the consulship of Pollio. It is not however inappropriate to remark on the tact, the intellectual honesty and the avoidance of shallow opportunism which Vergil exhibits in fulfilling his task. Not even for a moment does he suggest that Pollio might fulfil the role of 'sole ruler'.

The infinite variety and endless fascination of this poem perhaps lies more in the combination of its various elements than in any one aspect. It is an occasional poem; but because it concentrates on the emotions of the occasion rather than on historical facts it transcends the moment to become of universal and perennial interest. If a critic insists that a poem should contain within itself all that is necessary for understanding it, he would judge *Eclogue* 4 a failure. It has manifestly not failed as a poem, if we judge from the interest shown in it over two thousand years. The difficulties that do arise add to the interest and fascination: they offer no real obstacle to enjoyment or understanding when the poem is seen against its appropriate historical and literary background and provided that the critic is willing to make an effort of historical imagination.

NOTES

1. I am much indebted to Francis Cairns for his advice and comment on the final draft of this paper and to James N. O'Sullivan for checking the translations from Greek: the responsibility for all remaining errors is mine. This paper is a revised and expanded version of my seminar text, which was also used for papers given to the University of Durham and to a C.A./A.R.L.T. Conference.

2. The notes concentrate on primary sources and such secondary works as will not be found in Vergilian bibliographies. A survey of recent work on *Ecl.* 4 can be found in *CW* 68 (1974), with reference to earlier bibliographies. See also P. Felix *A Bibliography of Vergil* (Philologica 5) Roma (1975).

   The following abbreviations are used:

   T.R.S. Broughton *Magistrates of the Roman Republic*, volume 2 (Philological Monographs published by the American Philological Association no. 15) Cleveland (1952) — Broughton *MRR*

   F. Cairns *Generic Composition in Greek and Roman Poetry* Edinburgh (1972) — Cairns *GC*

   M.H. Crawford *Roman Republican Coinage* Cambridge (1974) — Crawford *RRC*

   B. Gatz *Weltalter, goldene Zeit und sinnverwandte Vorstellungen* (Spudasmata 16) Hildesheim (1967) — Gatz *Weltalter*

   R.G.M. Nisbet and M. Hubbard *A Commentary on Horace : Odes Book 1* Oxford (1970) — N -H

   R. Syme *The Roman Revolution* Oxford (1939) — Syme *RR*

   S. Weinstock *Divus Julius* Oxford (1971) — Weinstock *DJ*

   G. Williams *Tradition and Originality in Roman Poetry* Oxford (1968) — Williams *TORP*

3. Jerome (*Chronicle ad* A.D. 4/5) says he died at the age of eighty. Cf. Tacitus *Dial.* 17;34 and Seneca *Contr.* 4, *praef.* 2.

4. Catullus 12, 6–9.

5. Cicero (*Ad Fam.* 1,6,1) refers to Pollio going to Cilicia (February 56 BC).

6. Cinna *Frr.* 1–5 (Morel); Iulius Hyginus wrote a commentary on this poem.

7. *Ecl.* 3,86; cf. Pliny *Ep.* 5,3,5 and 7,4,4 for *nova carmina; Ecl.* 8,10; Hor. *Od.* 2,1,9–12; *Serm.* 1,10,42; Tacitus *Dial.* 21 for tragedies; fragment in Morel *FPL* p.99.

8. Cicero *Ad Fam.* 10,31–33.

9. *Ecl.* 8,11–12: *accipe iussis carmina coepta tuis.* The view of G. Bowersock (*HSCP* 75 (1971) pp.73ff.), accepted by W.V. Clausen (*HSCP* 76 (1972) pp.201ff.) and E.A. Schmidt (*Zur Chronologie der Eklogen* Heidelberg (1975) I intend to show is untenable in a future paper.

10. *Ecl.* 3,84ff.

11. For Parthenius and Latin poets see W.V. Clausen *GRBS* 5 (1964) pp.181ff.; N.B. Crowther *Mnem.* 29 (1976) pp.65ff.

12. See Broughton *MRR* p.238.

13. The standard work is J. André *La vie et l'oeuvre d'Asinius Pollio* Paris (1949).

14. Seneca *Contr.* 7,4,7; Cic. *Ad Att.* 4,15,4; 4,16,5. But see Shackleton Bailey *ad loc.*

15. [Cic.] *Ad Fam.* 10,31. Naturally it must be remembered that Pollio is writing to Cicero. The letters from Pollio are discussed by M. Gelzer *Chiron* 2 (1972) pp.297ff.

16. Without much success: see Broughton *MRR* p.327. Velleius Paterculus however calls it a *clarissimum bellum* (2,73,2).

17. *Asinius autem Pollio firmus proposito et Iulianis partibus fidus, Pompeianis adversus, uterque* (i.e. with Plancus) *exercitus tradidere Antonio.* (Vell.Pat. 2,63,3).

18. Vell.Pat. 2,76,2.

19. The fullest references to sources for the following account are in Broughton *MRR*, with a succinct narrative. I note only disagreements.

20. Even in these years this must be counted a special honour. The normal age was forty-two.

21. This was contested by Antonius' supporters (Appian *BC* 5,22); Dio (4o,12,5) confuses the claim with historical reality.

22. Servius Auct. preserves the truth (*ad Ecl.* 6,64): *fugatoque Asinio Pollione, ab Augusto Alfenum Varum legatum substitutum, qui Transpadanae provinciae et agris dividendis praeesset.*

23. Apart from the guesses of the scholiasts. The eighteen cities promised to the veterans were all in Italy; Cisalpina was not. Pollio's role there was a more military one, as the other sources indicate. See Broughton's weak attempt to defend the tradition (*MRR* p.377f., cp. p.372).

24. I accept *Catalepton* 8 as genuine testimony.

25. *Eclogue* 3 must belong to this year. I intend to discuss the chronology of the *Eclogues* in a future paper.

26. The scholiasts report that Vergil began the *Eclogues* at twenty-eight i.e. 42 BC (Asconius Pedianus *apud* Probus p.329H) and say they were begun at the insistence of Pollio. Asinius Gallus was probably born in 41 BC (Servius Auct. *ad Ecl.* 4, 11: *Pollione consule designato*). Both of these facts, with the absence of evidence to the contrary, suggest Pollio had a sabbatical in 42 BC. L. Antonius celebrated a triumph *ex Alpibus* when he entered the consulship in 41 BC. He may, then, have been Pollio's predecessor in Cisalpina, but it may have been granted for some battle fought in 43 BC (Cic. *Ad Fam.* 10,33,4: *L. Antonium Alpes occupasse).*

27. Macrobius *Sat.* 2,4,21: *at ego taceo: non est enim facile in eum scribere qui potest proscribere.* Cf. Martial 11,12.

28. Appian *BC* 5,35;50;64; Vell.Pat. 2,76,2; Macrobius *Sat.* 1,11,22.

29. Appian *BC* 5,64.

30. It is possible to overstate Pollio's opposition to Augustus in the twenties (Seneca *Contr.* 4, *praef.* 5); but I am unconvinced by the recent attempt completely to overthrow Syme's view (in *RR*) of Pollio's relations with Augustus in A.B. Bosworth *Historia* 21 (1972) pp.441ff.

31. Pliny *N.H.* 28,19: *hinc Theocriti apud Graecos, Catulli apud nos proximeque Vergilii incantamentorum amatoria imitatio.* But see J. Granarolo *Lustrum* 17 (1973-74) pp.50ff.

32. D.O. Ross *Backgrounds to Augustan Poetry* Cambridge (1975) pp.21ff., 115f.; cf. E.A. Schmidt *Poetische Reflexion* München (1972) p.168, who also compares Prop. 2,1,3f.

33. *nondum etiam Ascraeos norunt mea carmina fontis,/sed modo Permessi flumine lavit Amor;* cf. *Ecl.* 6,64f.: *tum canit errantem Permessi ad flumina Gallum/Aonas in montis ut duxerit una sororum.*

34. The idea was developed by H.W. Garrod *CR* 22 (1908) pp.150f.; J. Hubaux *Les thèmes bucoliques dans la poésie latine* Brussels (1930) pp.73f.; M. Desport *L'incantation virgilienne* Bordeaux (1952).

35. See A. Momigliano *JRS* 31 (1941) pp.151f.

36. Most recently by L. Berkowitz *CSCA* 5 (1972) pp.21ff.

37. Pollio's exact title in Cisalpina is unknown.

38. So, correctly, J. Carcopino *Virgile et le mystère de la IVᵉ Églogue* Paris (1930) esp. pp.124ff.

39. Vergil does not say the child will be born in the consulship of Pollio; only that the *magni menses* will begin to unfold. The real beginning of the new *saeculum* must date from the child's conception, not his birth (see below). Some horoscopes are known to have been cast from the time of conception (W.W. Tarn *JRS* 22 (1932) p.157 with references) so this is clearly not impossible.

40. The date is provided by an inscription on the base of a restored *signum concordiae* erected at Casinum on 12 October 40 BC (*CIL* 10,5159). It seems to me that this is likely to have been erected weeks rather than days after the signing of the treaty (as Carcopino suggests p.123).

41. Dio says (48,32,1) that the consuls were removed καίπερ ἐπ' ἐξόδῳ ἤδη τοῦ ἔτους ὄντος even though the *suffecti* would hold office καὶ ἐπ' ὀλίγας ἡμέρας. If Pollio sailed with his legions it would probably not have been after the end of October. If not he could have left much later: Cicero made the same crossing, in the other direction, from Corcyra to Italy late in November 50 BC (*Ad Fam.* 16,7). I should add that I believe *Ecl.* 8,6f. to refer to Pollio's activities early in 40 BC (cf. Broughton *MRR* p.378).

42. Vell.Pat. 2,76,3: *adventus deinde in Italiam Antonii apparatusque contra eum Caesaris habuit belli metum, sed pax circa Brundisium composita.*

43. Syme *RR* p.218; Crawford *RRC* pp.496 (continuation of a theme of Caesarian coinage); 507f.; especially Nos 494: 32,33,39a, 41,42,44).

44. See further below.

45. Asconius Pedianus quoted below.

46. This argument was put to me forcefully by Professor H.D. Jocelyn.

47. For details and bibliography see M. Geymonat *P. Vergilii Maronis Opera* Paravia (1973) p.23. Add R.D. Williams *CPh.* 71 (1976) pp.119ff.

48. Most scholars read *parenti* and understand 'mother'. My reasons for preferring 'father' are given below – but it does not affect the argument here.

49. See K.J. Dover *Theocritus: Select Poems* Basingstoke and London (1971) pp.xlvff. for a useful summary; also R. Gimm *De Vergilii stilo bucolico* Leipzig (1910); U. Ott *Die Kunst des Gegensatzes in Theokrits Hirtengedichten* Hildesheim (1969).

50. An alternative would be to suppose that Vergil has so vividly imagined the child (cf. Catullus 61,209ff.) that he talks as if the pregnancy were over. But I cannot find a parallel to such a use of a perfect with an imperative: the tense is always future perfect (hence the corruption?). The strongest argument against the future perfect here is that it would not balance *dignata est* (63).

51. Cf., e.g., Sen. *Med.* 150ff.: *Sile ... manda ... pertulit ... potuit.*

52. See further below.

53. Not the short-lived child born in AD 73 (Suet. *Dom.* 3). See K. Scott *The Imperial Cult under the Flavians* Stuttgart (1936) pp.74ff.

54. Ps.-Dion. 2,266,4ff. (Usener-Radermacher); Menander 3,407,14ff.; 411,15ff. (Spengel).

55. For a full list of candidates see Berkowitz *op.cit.* (n.36) p.21 and K. Büchner

P. *Vergilius Maro* Stuttgart (1966) pp.190ff. The view that the *puer* is some Eastern deity, which is stated most fully by E. Norden *Die Geburt des Kindes* Leipzig (1924) and often repeated with variations, was persuasively demolished by G. Jachmann *Annali della Scuola Normale Superiore di Pisa* 21 (1952) pp.13ff. The poem is a Latin poem for an Italian audience by an Italian in connection with the consulship of a specific man. No other argument is necessary.

56.   This vital point is too often neglected. No child conceived after Pollio became consul would have been born in his consulship. The only moment that it is appropriate for a poet to speak of conception is in connection with a wedding. See below.

57.   The other candidate known to Servius is Augustus, inevitably. Philargyrius likewise thinks of Christ.

58.   The most important paper assuming the *puer* to be Pollio's is that of F. Marx *Neue Jahrb.* 1 (1898) pp.105ff. E. Norden *op.cit.* (n.55) was most influential in his rebuttal of the idea and in this was followed by G. Jachmann. The idea is not yet dead however.

59.   He was consul in 8 BC. If born in 41 then he was, like his father, only 35. But *Pollione consule designato* could refer to any time after November 43. The remark is important as an indication of Asinius Gallus' ambitions to succeed Augustus (Tac. *Ann.* 1,13,2).

60.   See especially R. Syme *CQ* 31 (1937) pp.39ff. Detailed criticism of his views I reserve to a later date. I agree that Saloninus was never a son of Pollio. The corollary, that Pollio either took time off in the Perusine war or had his wife with him, is unthinkable.

61.   It was popular before Norden's book and was reinstated by Jachmann.

62.   *Eclogue* 1 is quite different. Even Servius could see that Meliboeus' speech was critical (*ad* 70); cf. Servius Auct. *ad Georg.* 4,564.

63.   On Octavian see above. Scribonia was the sister of Sextus' father-in-law. On the marriage see Dio 48,16,1ff. Pollio had fought with Caesar against Pompey, against Sextus in Spain, joined Antonius out of hatred for the *Pompeiani*. When the triumvirs had become reconciled to Sextus in 39 BC Pollio withdrew his support, apparently to the annoyance of Antonius (Vell.Pat. 2,76,2) and even at Actium remained neutral (*id.* 2,86,3). I venture to think that this is more than a coincidence.

64.   This is, of course, not new, and is accepted by most historians and many modern critics.

65.   Appian *BC* 5,64.

66.   Vell.Pat. 2,86,3.

67.   Dio 48,31,2: ἐπὶ ταῖς τοῦ Ἀντωνίου καὶ τοῦ Καίσαρος καταλλαγαῖς, ὡς καὶ σφετέρας εἰρήνης τῆς ἐκείνων ὁμονοίας οὔσης, ἥσθησαν. (They were pleased at the reconciliation of Antonius and Caesar, for they thought that harmony between them meant peace for themselves). Cf. Vell.Pat. 2,76,2.

68.   L. Antonius claimed to be fighting for just this (Appian *BC* 5,43).

69.   Dio 48,31,3f. accepts that Octavia was pregnant when she married Antonius. But Marcellus, her son by her previous marriage, was born in 42 BC at the latest. Prop.3,18,15 cannot be wrong on this point. Perhaps Vergil's reference to the ten months that will elapse before the *puer* is born is designed to obviate just these slanders. I owe this ingenious suggestion to Professor D.A. West. For the truth see Plut. *Ant.* 31.

70.   For the various celebrations see especially Dio 48,31,3–5 (the *ovatio*, the wedding, spectacles); 32,3f. (*Aqua Iulia*; the games vowed for the war against Caesar's assassins; unhappily it is not clear which set of consuls celebrated them).

71. See E. Gabba *HSCP* 75 (1971) pp.139ff. for recent discussion and bibliography.

72. Dio 48,5ff.; Appian *BC* 5,12ff. See Broughton *MRR* for details.

73. Suet. *Aug.* 15; Sen. *De Clem.* 1,11,1; Dio 48,14,4. The official version is in Appian *BC* 5,48f.; cf. Vell.Pat. 2,74,4. See Weinstock *DJ* pp.398ff. *Trecenti* is of course vague, but there is no need to doubt the story. All that matters here is that it was widely believed.

74. It is not known when Pollio's colleague, Cn. Domitius Calvinus, entered office.

75. Weinstock *DJ* pp.329, 399 n.12.

76. Weinstock *DJ* pp.261ff.

77. Above, n.67.

78. Appian *BC* 5,58; cf. Weinstock *DJ* pp.186ff.

79. See Weinstock *DJ* p.196 for the connection between Parthian Wars and a new *saeculum*.

80. Servius *ad loc.* is the first of many to make the connection.

81. See Crawford *RRC* pp.740ff.

82. Servius *ad Ecl.* 4,4; 10: *Sol* as the god of the tenth and final age of Sibylline prophecy.

83. Crawford *RRC* pp.511; 737 n.1; 740.

84. See especially Himerius 9,3 (Colonna); Menander Rhetor 400,7ff.; Claud. *Epith.Praef.* 16, all referring to the wedding of Peleus and Thetis. Also e.g. Stat. *Silv.* 1,2,16.

85. Theocr. *Id.* 18,50ff.; Sen. *Med.* 61ff.; Stat. *Silv.* 1,2,269; cf. Himerius 9,21 (Colonna).

86. Cf. n.84; add Cat. 64,299ff.

87. So, recently, e.g. G. Williams in *Quality and Pleasure in Latin Poetry* Cambridge (1974) pp.37, 40; C. Hardie in *The Ancient Historian and his Materials* Farnborough (1975) p.114. See too W.W. Tarn *JRS* 22 (1932) p.155.

88. E.g. Herod. 1,1ff., where the voyage of the Argo is also mentioned.

89. Himerius 9,16 (Colonna) referring to Sappho. But the comparison with Achilles is an encomiastic topos found in many genres.

90. The alternative is to make this line the equivalent of *Aen.* 9,642 (Apollo to Ascanius): *dis genite et geniture deos*. But the singular and most specific *Iovis* is decisive against this view. The line was not so taken by the author of the *Ciris* (398) who applies it to the Tyndaridae; cf. *Aen.* 8,301 (Hercules): *salve, vera Iovis proles, decus addite divis.*

91. See especially Plut. *Ant.* 4,2; 36,7; 60,5; Crawford *RRC* p.510; no.494. On such genealogies see now T.P. Wiseman *GR* 21 (1974) pp.153ff.

92. See Weinstock *DJ* pp.287ff.; C. Habicht in *Le culte des souverains dans l'empire romain* Geneva (1972) pp.52f. for bibliography. The evidence (Dio 44,6,4 and Cic. *Phil.* 2,110) leaves some doubt as to whether he was called *Iuppiter Iulius*. Add also *JRS* 65 (1975) p.149 (E. Rawson) and pp.174f. (J. Noth). I have now found that this suggestion was anticipated by H. Wagenvoort *Studies in Roman Literature, Culture and Religion* Leiden (1956) p.29, but he thought the child was Octavian.

93. Plut. *Ant.* 33,1. So Weinstock *DJ* pp.307,392,399,401; L.R. Taylor *The Divinity of the Roman Emperor* Connecticut (1931) p.118. But Broughton *MRR* p.390 dates this to 39 BC without comment.

94. Ps.–Dion. 2,266,4ff.; 2,271,21ff. (Usener-Radermacher); Theocr. *Id.* 18,50ff.; cf. Sidonius 11,131ff.; Aristoph. *Pax* 1324; Himerius 9,21 (Colonna). See P.Fedeli *Il carme 61 di Catullo* Freiburg (1972) pp.113ff.; A.L. Wheeler *AJP* 51 (1930) p.215 for discussion and bibliography.

95. Such formal sophistication does not basically affect the identity of the topos. See Cairns *GC* index *s.v.* 'formal sophistication'.

96. W. Warde Fowler in *Virgil's Messianic Eclogue* London (1907) pp.75ff.

97. So Stat. *Silv.* 1,2,269; Sen. *Med.* 61; Himerius 9,21 (Colonna).

98. *dea nec dignata cubili est* certainly suggests a different kind of relationship from acceptance by a goddess of childbirth.

99. The parallels clearly show that this is the correct interpretation of this passage. Cf. e.g. [Hom.] *Hymn* 3,61ff.; Callim. *Hymn* 4,260ff.; Theogn. 5ff.; and esp. Theocr. *Id.* 17,58ff. The Golden Age does not begin, regress, then finally come. See below.

100. For smiling children see esp. D.R. Stuart *CPh.* 17 (1921) p.218.

101. Weinstock *DJ* pp.15ff.

102. See A.S. Pease on *Aen.* 4,128, esp. [Hom.] *Hymn* 5,49: ἡδὺ γελοιήσασα φιλομμειδὴς ᾿Αφροδίτη (sweetly-smiling, laughter-loving Aphrodite).

103. Suet. *Caes.* 49,3; Weinstock *DJ* pp.15ff.

104. See Hom. *Od.* 11,601ff.; Pind. *Nem.* 1,105ff. (Sn.-Mae.).

105. Theocr. *Id.* 24,31; Tarn *op.cit.*(n.87)p.156 n.1 quoting ὁ[δ᾿ εἰς ἐμὲ μειδιάασκε from a Herakles poem.

106. Above, n.91.

107. The relevance of *Id.* 17 to *Ecl.* 4 was first noticed by R.T. Kerlin *AJP* 29 (1908) pp.449ff.

108. Theocr. *Id.* 17,24ff.

109. *Ibid.* 34ff.

110 It is not clear how Vergil's readers would be expected to know this anyway.

111. I.e. by the time Asinius Gallus was able to make his claim.

112. Naturally this depends on one's interpretation of *Ecl.* 1. In comparison with the explicitness of Vergil's encomia of Maecenas and Octavian in the *Georgics* and the *Aeneid* and with those of Horace and Propertius, Vergil's attitude to Octavian in *Ecl.* 1 is ambiguous and unenthusiastic.

113. *Frr.* 1ff. (Morel). The interpretation depends on the similarity with Cic. *Phil.* 2,92; 97 etc. See Norden on *Aen.* 6,621f.

114. A. Momigliano *JRS* 31 (1941) pp.151ff.

115. *Pollio Asinius ... diu retenta in potestate Antonii Venetia, magnis speciosisque rebus circa Altinum aliasque eius regionis urbes editis* (Vell.Pat. 2,76,2).

116. Appian *BC* 5,60ff.

117. As exhibited, for example, in Pliny's *Panegyric* and the *gratiarum actiones* of the *Panegyrici Latini.*

118. Menander 3,368,3ff. (Spengel); 398,1ff.: 'For if you mention qualities of a kind that he does not have, everybody will know that none of these is appropriate to him and, besides, you will seem to be untrustworthy; and you will make yourself an object of suspicion with regard to the rest of what you say as a result of this and you will make the audience unreceptive to the speech. For it is necessary always to fall in with what is acknowledged'. Cf. Cairns GC. pp. 105ff.

119. E.g. J.B. Mayor *Virgil's Messianic Eclogue* London (1907) pp.87ff.

120. The connection between the ratification of Antonius' protégé, Herod, as king of Judaea and Pollio's consulship was given new life by F. Marx *Neue Jahrb.* I (1898) pp.124ff. But it is not certain that this happened before Pollio left for Macedonia.

121. See esp. A. Kurfess *ZRGG* 3 (1951) pp.253ff. W.W. Tarn (*JRS* 22 (1932) pp.135ff.) attempts to relate *Eclogue* 4 to the *despoina* prophecy in *Or.Sib.* 3,350ff. which he believes to belong to the propaganda of Cleopatra. This type of approach seems to reveal the most probable nature of the link between *Eclogue* 4 and the *Cumaeum carmen*. Tarn's interpretation of this prophecy has not convinced everyone. See, for basic bibliography, P.M. Fraser *Ptolemaic Alexandria* Oxford (1972) vol.2 pp.989f. n.17; 994 n.231; 1116 n.14. See further below.

122. Augustus burned two thousand prophecies in 12 BC and also sifted out the *libri Sibyllini* (Suet. *Aug.* 31; Tac. *Ann.* 6,12). These could only be consulted at the command of the Senate and were destroyed in the time of Stilicho (Rut. Namat. 2,52) at the end of the fourth century.

123. Cf. Weinstock *DJ* p.192.

124. Weinstock *DJ* pp.191ff. Some of the important primary sources will be given below.

125. Censorinus *De Die Nat.* 17.

126. Cic. *De Imp.* 41; 42.

127. Cic. *Cat.* 3,26.

128. Cic. *Cat.* 3,9; 4,2.

129. Verg. *Aen.* 1,286ff.; 6,789ff.; Hor. *Od.* 1,2; 4,15 etc.

130. Weinstock *DJ* pp.181ff.

131. Dio 41,14,5.

132. Servius Auct. *ad Ecl.* 9,'6.

133. So Weinstock *DJ* p.195.

134. Appian *BC* 4,4,15.

135. Crawford *RRC* pp.511,737,740, cf.743.

136. Cic. *Cat.* 3,19; cf. Plut. *Sulla* 7,7.

137. Weinstock *DJ* pp.21,194f.

138. A convenient survey of all such theories with discussion of *Eclogue* 4 can be found in Gatz *Weltalter* esp. pp. 87ff.

139. See the incidents related in nn.131, 132, 134.

140. See Servius *ad Ecl.* 4,4; Gatz *Weltalter* pp.79ff.

141. See above n.122. It is not clear that the ancients knew ten metals (Gatz *Weltalter* p.84; Juvenal 13,28). Cf. H.J. Rose *The Eclogues of Virgil* Berkeley (1942) pp.171ff.

142. The *Magnus Annus* is not of course confined to Stoicism, and occurs in Pythagoreanism.

143. Arat. *Phaen.* 100ff.; cf. Hes. *Op.* 225ff.

144. Hes. *Op.* 111.

145. Hes. *Op.* 110; 128; 144; 158.

146. Hes. *Op.* 109; 176.

147. Cf. *Ecl.* 4,15ff. and Hes. *Op.* 112; 115; *Ecl.* 4,39 and Hes. *Op.* 118; *Ecl.* 4,36 and Hes. *Op.* 156ff.; *Ecl.* 4,28 and Hes. *Op.* 172f.

148. Cf. *Ecl.* 4,38f. and Arat. *Phaen.* 110–13.

149. Cf. *Ecl.* 4,40ff. and Lucr. *DRN* 5,933ff.

150. See Gatz *Weltalter*; Ov. *Met.* 1,89ff., with Bömer's commentary (Heidelberg (1969) pp.48f.).

151. The portent may have been a saecular portent. For *felicitas* cf. *ILS* 112 (Narbo), on an *ara* erected on Augustus' birthday: *qua die eum saeculi felicitas orbi terrarum rectorem edidit.* For *felicitas* and Caesar see Weinstock *DJ* pp.112ff. Coins bearing the *cornucopia*, symbol of *felicitas*, were struck in 40 BC (Crawford *RRC* nos. 520,525, and pp.527, 529).

152. Philo *Leg. ad Gaium* 8ff., esp.13, where the early days of his principate are compared to life under Kronos.

153. Sen. *Apocol.* 4,9ff.; Calp.Sic. *Ecl.* 1,40ff.

154. E.g. Stat. *Silv.* 1,6,39; Mart. 5,19,1f.; 8,55,1f.; F. Sauter *Der römische Kaiserkult bei Martial und Statius* Stuttgart-Berlin (1934) pp.19ff.

155. Claud. *In Ruf.* 1,51ff.; 357ff. (385f.: *sed sponte rubebunt attonito pastore greges)*; cf. *De Cos. Stil.* 2,333ff.; 446ff.

156. *ILS* 112 (Narbo); *Inscr. in Brit. Mus.* 894 (Halicarnassus); Ditt. *OGIS* 458.

157. In what follows familiarity with the methods and concepts set out in F. Cairns *Generic Composition in Greek and Roman Poetry* Edinburgh (1972) is presupposed. My debt to this book is great and gladly acknowledged.

158. F. Marx *Neue Jahrb.* 1 (1898) pp.105ff.

159. D.A. Slater *CR* 26 (1912) pp.114ff.; W.W. Tarn *JRS* 22 (1932) pp.135ff.; H.J. Mette *Rh.M* 116 (1973) pp.71ff. Cf. G. Williams in *Quality and Pleasure in Latin Poetry* Cambridge (1975) pp.44f.; *TORP* pp.274ff.

160. E. Pfeiffer *Vergils Bukolika* Stuttgart (1933) pp.68ff. This is the genre that F. Cairns has called the prosphonetikon (*GC* pp.18ff.).

161. R. Kukula *Römische Säkularpoesie* Leipzig (1911) pp.72ff.

162. E. Norden *Die Geburt des Kindes* Leipzig (1924) p.7.

163. J. Carcopino *Virgile et le mystère de la IVe Eglogue* (1930) p.124.

164. See the titles preserved in the MSS of Statius, Sidonius and Claudian.

165. Cf. Menander 3,422f. (Spengel) on the *stephanotikos logos*.

166. See, e.g., Cic. *Ad Fam.* 15, 7-13.

167. Pind. *Nem.* 11; *Pyth.* 1; Tib. 1,7; 2,5; Stat. *Silv.* 5,2.

168. For the fragments see W. Morel *FPL* pp.68ff. and for the fame of the poem see the testimonia collected by him. For the influence of this poem see G.B. Townend in *Cicero* (ed. T.A. Dorey) London (1964) pp.118ff.; contrast A. Cameron *Claudian: Poetry and Propaganda in the Court of Honorius* Oxford (1970) p.254. See also J. Soubiran *Cicero: Aratea* Paris (1972) pp.27ff.; 69ff. The title of his poem is uncertain.

169. Cic. *Pro Arch.* 28. The poem was never finished.

170. See O. Murray *JRS* 55 (1965) pp.161ff. I am not dissuaded by the reservations of Weinstock *DJ* pp.182,198f. See also A.J. Woodman *CQ* 25 (1975) pp.273f.

171. For the traditional nature of the occasion see Cic. *De Leg. Agr.* 2,1ff. The opening of the speech to the senate is unfortunately lost.

172. In view of the large number of examples from Claudian it is important to distinguish the topical from the propagandist elements. See Cameron *op.cit.* (n.168).

173. *Ad Att.* 2,3,4 is a prophecy of future glory by the Muse Calliope; *De Div.* 1,72 concerns the omens predicting the crisis of 63 BC. The relevance to *Ecl.* 4 was noted by O. Crusius *Rh.M* 51 (1896) p.556. Cf. the prophecy of Janus in Stat. *Silv.* 4,1.

174. Ov. *Ex Pont.* 4,4 has 50 lines; 4,9 has 137 lines; Stat. *Silv.* 4,1 has 47 lines.

175. This topic occurs in many epideictic genres. Cf. Menander 3,399,23ff. (Spengel) on the epithalamium; Cairns *GC* p.168 for triumph poems.

176. Martial (9,42) prays to Apollo for a consulship for Stella. But that may be because Stella was a poet. It is possible that the enigmatic half-line *tuus iam regnat Apollo* (*Ecl.* 4,10) may allude to this topic.

177. Martial gives Janus the epithet *pacificus* (8,66,11). Cf. Cic. *Fr.* 17 (Morel): *cedant arma togae, concedat laurea linguae* (v.1. *laudi*).

178. For Claudian see esp. L.B. Struthers *HSCP* 30 (1919) pp.49ff.; A. Cameron *Claudian* pp.30ff.; 253ff.

179. Of course the point of the inauguration ceremony was to secure the favour of the gods and this topic is closely related to the next.

180. Cf. the omen announcing Cicero's consulship reported by Servius *ad Ecl.* 8,105: *hoc* (the leaping flame) *uxori Ciceronis dicitur contigisse, cum post peractum sacrificium libare vellet in cinerem: quae flamma eodem anno consulem futurum ostendit eius maritum, sicut Cicero in suo testatur poemate.* Cf. Dio 37,35,4 ;Plut. *Cic.* 20,1f.; S. Weinstock *DJ* p.21.

181. Cf. Stat. *Silv.* 5,2,175ff. where Crispinus is commanded to take up the office of military tribune (*vade... vade*). Since Crispinus was to serve abroad this poem is cast as an encomiastic propemptikon.

182. See on this important point Cairns *GC* pp.105ff., who analyses Theocr. *Id* 17 in the light of Menander's prescription for a basilikon and establishes 'the general reliability of Menander as a witness for the state of generic patterns many centuries before he lived'.

183. These topics are treated at length in the *praefationes* of Claudian.

184. Throughout this section the letter in parenthesis refers to the letter given to the topos in the preceding analysis.

185. See Ovid *Ex Pont.* 4,9,75ff.; and e.g. Claudian 7,68ff.; 21 *passim.*

186. Antonius was apparently surprised and dismayed when Pollio abandoned his active career after his triumph (Vell.Pat. 2,76,3; 86,3).

187. Hor. *Od.* 1,2,29ff. and N–H *ad loc.*

188. See above and Weinstock *DJ* pp.191ff.

189. Cf. Mart. 8,8,1f.: *Iane ... renoves voltu saecula longa tuo.*

190. Ov. *Fast.* 1,191–288 emphasises the connection of Janus and Saturn.

191. See the testimonia in Morel *FPL* 16–21, pp.72f.

192. See E.L. Bundy *CSCA* 5 (1972) pp.39ff.

193. Theocr. *Id.* 17,135ff. For Pindar see E. Thummer *Pindar:die Isthmischen Gedichte* Heidelberg (1968) I pp.82ff.

194. Claud. 8,650f.: *o mihi si liceat thalamis intendere carmen/connubiale tuis; si te iam dicere patrem!*

195. This is a regular topic in the basilikon: Menander 3,377,29f. (Spengel). See below.

196. See Weinstock *DJ* pp.192f.; F. Cairns *Eranos* 69 (1971) pp.84ff. The new *saeculum* could have been an age of civil war in which Rome would be destroyed.

197. Quint. *Inst. Or.* 3,7,18: *adferunt laudem liberi parentibus.*

198. Weinstock *DJ* pp.188ff.

199. This section especially has benefited from discussion of the underlying principles with Francis and Sandra Cairns.

200. The suggestion was first made by R.T. Kerlan *AJP* 29 (1908) pp.449ff. and developed by R. Kukula *Romische Säkularpoesie* Leipzig (1911) pp.68ff. The idea was largely ignored until G. Williams revived it in *TORP* pp.274ff.; *Quality and Pleasure in Latin Poetry* Cambridge (1974) pp.39f.

201. Servius *ad Ecl.* 4,1: *nam licet haec ecloga discedat a bucolico carmine, tamen inserit ei aliqua apta operi.*

202. See E.A. Schmidt *Poetische Reflexion: Vergils Bukolik* München (1972) pp.9ff.

203. Schmidt *op.cit.* (n.202) pp.36ff.

204. Calpurnius *Ecl.* 1; 4. Cf. *Einsiedeln Eclogues* (1); 2.

205. On this see now E. Rawson *JRS* 65 (1975) pp.148ff. for discussion and further bibliography.

206. See C. Griffiths *PVS* 9 (1969-70) pp.1ff., a most stimulating paper. She draws attention to Nicander *Ther.* 612ff. where *myricae* are linked with Apollo and said to have prophetic powers. Obviously then the plant has been especially chosen for this poem because of its associations both with prophecy and with Theocritus (*Id.* 1,13 etc.).

207. When Cicero uses *silva* in this sense he feels bound to qualify it by *quasi: Or.* 3,12; 50,139.

208. None of the alternative readings alters the sense, which is confirmed by the scholiast *ad loc.* Cf. *Id.* 16, 1–4.

209. See topos B5 in the analysis of the genre above. Claudian 7 (*III cos.Hon.*), 10: *quem primo a limine vitae* introduces the birth omens that show he will be a divine ruler (*te nascente*, 18); 39: *mox ubi firmasti recto vestigia gressu* introduces the ἀνατροφή (*facta tui numerabat avi*, 52; *hos tibi virtutum stimulos, haec semina laudum,/haec exempla dabat. non ocius hausit Achilles/semiferi praecepta senis,* 59ff.).

210. See N–H on Hor. *Od.* 1,12,50.

211. See N–H on Hor. *Od.* 1,12,15.

212. Menander 3,370,28ff. (Spengel). For Theocr. *Id.* 17 as a basilikon see Cairns *GC* pp.100ff. Throughout this section I have made free use of his perceptive analysis. There is a fine discussion of Theocr. *Id.* 16 and 17 in W. Meincke *Untersuchungen zu den Enkomiastischen Gedichten Theokrits* Kiel (1965).

213. See also [Hom.] *Hymn* 3,61ff., and esp. cp. *ridenti* (20) and *blandos . . . flores* (23) with 'and the earth laughed underneath (her)' (117); and 'then with gold all Delos blossomed, just as does a mountain-top with woodland flowers' (135ff.). See also Theognis 5–10 and cp. *Assyrium vulgo nascetur amomum (Ecl.* 4,25) with 'all Delos was filled without limit with ambrosial perfume and huge earth laughed' (8f.). Both passages describe the birth of Apollo. See addendum.

214. No more can be said of the reminiscences of Theocr. *Id.* 1,13 at *Ecl.* 4,2; 12,16 at 4,9; 13,17f. at 34ff.; or 24,1 at 4,61 (Ἡρακλέα δεκάμηνον); 24,105f. at 4,57 (Λίνος . . . υἱὸς Ἀπόλλωνος). It is however worth noting that the last two come from the *Herakliskos*, a poem in which there is an extensive prophecy concerning the life of Herakles. See S. Posch *Beobachtungen zur Theokritnachwirkung bei Vergil* Innsbruck-München (1969) for tables of Theocritean reminiscences.

215. Gow notes that Theocr. *Id.* 17,103 is an allusion to Hom. *Il.* 16,141, a description of Achilles, with whom Ptolemy, successor of Alexander, is thus implicitly compared.

216. See A.G. Lee *Allusion, Parody and Imitation* Hull (1971).

217. See Cairns *GC* pp.168 and 95ff.

218. See above, n.178.

219. See Cairns *GC* p.25.

220. See E. Norden *Rh.M* 54 (1899) pp.466ff. (=*Kleine Schriften zum klassischen Altertum* Berlin (1966) pp.422ff.).

221. See W. Kroll *Studien zum Verstandnis der römischen Literatur* Stuttgart 2nd. ed. (1964) pp.220ff.; R. Heinze *Virgils epische Technik* Stuttgart 5th. ed. (1965) (= 3rd. ed. 1915) pp.394ff.; N–H on Hor. *Od.* 1,15.

222. See also Menander 3,371,3ff. (Spengel) and with εἴ τι σύμβολον γέγοψε περὶ τὸν τόκον ἢ κατὰ γῆν ἢ κατ᾽ οὐρανὸν ἢ κατὰ θάλασσαν cf. *Ecl.* 4,50f.; Suet. *Aug.* 94; Cic. *De Div.* 1,36,79; Weinstock *DJ* pp.19ff.

223. But bearing in mind the setting of the parallel passages on the birth of Apollo and Ptolemy, Servius is probably quite right to comment: *cunabula lectuli in quibus infantes iacere consuerunt: vel loca, in quibus nascuntur, quasi cynabula: nam κύεω est graece niti.*

224. So Servius *ad loc.* Cf. Hor. *Epist.* 1,7,17: *non invisa feres pueris munuscula parvis.*

225. G. Jachmann *Die vierte Ekloge Vergils* (n.55) pp.16ff. did a grave disservice to the poem in arguing in this influential paper that Vergil presents from the first a fully developed Golden Age. Cf. Claudian *Carm. Min.* 30,70ff. (birth of Serena).

226. See Servius *ad loc.*

227. See Norden (n.220) on *Aen.* 6,791ff. where Augustus is compared in turn to Hercules and Dionysus. Norden analyses this passage as a basilikon.

228. Plut. *Ant.* 24 (41 BC). For Antonius and Dionysus see L.R. Taylor *Divinity of the Roman Emperor* Middletown (1931) pp.100ff. In view of Vergil's use of Theocritus *Id.* 17 it is worth noting her comment that Dionysus had been 'thought of as incarnate in Alexander and after him in the Ptolemaic and Attalid kings' (p.108); the coins on which the heads of Antonius and Octavia appear 'recall the issues of the Ptolemies and their powerful wives' (p.122). See also W.W. Tarn *JRS* 22 (1932) pp.149ff.

229. So also *Assyrium amomum* (25).

230. See Servius *ad Ecl.* 4,18ff. and 7,25ff. Bacchus, of course, would be relevant in different aspects to each passage.

231. Cf. Call. *Hymn* 4,274: Delos finishes speaking and the child γλυκὺν ἔσπασε μαζόν (a detail omitted by Theocritus). The goats are reminiscent of Amaltheia, which suckled Zeus: see e.g. Call. *Hymn* 1,47f., a poem which ends with praises of Ptolemy Philadelphus.

232. See n.213.

233. See Jachmann *op.cit.* (n.55); Gatz *Weltalter* pp.227 *s.v. Ecl.* 4; 229ff. (*loci communes*); F. Bömer on Ovid *Met.* 1,89ff. (Heidelberg (1969) pp.47ff.).

234. See Gatz *Weltalter* pp.134ff. Vergil is the first to speak of an actual return of a Golden Age, as far as we know, but others had compared life under various rulers to life under Kronos.

235. See N–H on Hor. *Od.* 1,2,43.

236. *ILS* 112. See Weinstock *DJ* pp.196f., 206ff., 217ff.

237. Cf. *Ecl*: 4,8f. *nascenti puero quo ferrea* etc. For the ablative cf. *incolumi Caesare* (Hor. *Od*. 4,5,27).

238. These lines probably do not belong to the same poem, but shed light on each other and on *Ecl*. 4,60–63.

239. Cf. Aesch. *Suppl*. 625ff.; Eur. *Alc*. 568ff. I owe these references to Mr. E. Whittle. Callimachus obviously has in mind the topos of prosperity under a good king discussed below.

240. This is a self-conscious return to the more mystical belief found in Hom. *Od*. 19,108ff., on which see Stanford's note. Calpurnius of course has our poem in mind and is giving his own interpretation of the relationship.

241. *pacatum* (17). There is a useful discussion of *pax* in Weinstock *DJ* p.267 and A.J. Woodman *CQ* 25 (1975) p.292 (with bibliography).

242. Cf. *Aen*. 6,89: *alius Latio iam partus Achilles*.

243. Weinstock *DJ* pp.196f.

244. See e.g. Cic. *Pro Marc*. 23; Vell.Pat. 2,89.

245. Weinstock *DJ* pp.50ff.

246. It must be from this passage that *Iustitia/* Δίκη becomes associated with the Golden Age.

247. In what follows I draw on O. Murrary *JRS* 55 (1965) pp.161ff., an excellent article. The quotations are taken from pp.169 and 177. A. Momigliano *JRS* 31 (1941) pp.152f. first attached political significance to the pamphlet and assigned it to the period of Caesar's dictatorship. P. Grimal *REL* 44 (1966) pp.254ff. also argues for a Caesarian date. For a Roman view of kingship see Cic. *De Rep*. 1,55ff. and *passim.*

248. It is noteworthy that Philodemus discussed the 'Life under Kronos' in his *De Pietate* with reference to Hesiod among others (see Gatz *Weltalter* pp.114f.).

249. Cairns *GC* pp.100ff.

250. Esp. *Od*. 4,5,17ff. See Cairns *GC* p.114.

251. *IBM* 4,1,894, 9f.: εἰρηνεύουσι μὲν γὰρ γῆ καὶ θάλαττα, πόλεις δὲ ἀνθοῦσιν εὐνομίᾳ ὁμονοίᾳ τε καὶ εὐετηρίᾳ . . .

252. Vell.Pat. 2,89; 126. See the splendid paper of A.J. Woodman *CQ* 25 (1975) pp.290ff.

253. See n.209.

254. Verg. *Georg*. 1,498ff.; cf. Cic. *Pro Marc*. 18.

255. *firmata aetas* is almost a technical term. See *OLD s.v. firmo*.

256. But note the stress on ἀρετή at Call. *Hymn* 1,93–5 and Theocr. *Id*. 17,137.

257. The absence of sea-faring and the stress on self-sufficiency is peculiar to Hesiod: contrast Hor. *Od*. 4,5,19: *pacatum volitant per mare navitae* etc. The bees in the oaks (*Op*. 233) perhaps suggested *durae quercus sudabunt roscida mella* (29) and the sheep heavy with fleeces, as distinct from being fecund, as in Homer, might have suggested the introduction of the saecular portent (42ff.).

258. Cf. E.L. Bundy *CSCA* 5 (1972) pp.77ff.

259. Servius *ad loc.*: *non sibi arrogat sed hoc dicit: tanta est materia tuae laudis, ut etiam humile ingenium in ea supra omnes possit excellere.*

260. Theocr. *Id*. 1,3: μετὰ Πᾶνα τὸ δεύτερον ἄθλον ἀποισῇ is in fact the line which establishes the link and which is inverted here. In the same poem Pan's Arcadian homeland is referred to (123ff.).

261. *Ecl*. 4,1 is perhaps also an allusion to the *Lament for Bion* refrain and Bion is called the Doric Orpheus at 1.18. In some MSS the *Lament* is attributed to Theocritus.

262. See Cairns *GC* pp.105f.

263. See E.L. Bundy *CSCA* 5 (1972) pp.49ff. for what follows. For the 'hymnic pattern' in *Ecl*. 4 see E.W. Leach *Vergil's Eclogues: Landscapes of Experience* Ithaca and London (1974) pp.229f. and *Arethusa* 4 (1971) pp.171f. On hymns see Cairns *GC* pp.91f.

264. See Call. *Hymn* 1,93ff.

265. For marriages of the gods see Menander 3,401,4ff. (Spengel). For Zeus and Hera see Ps.–Dion. 2,262,2ff. (Usener-Radermacher).

266. See F. Muecke *AUMLA* 44 (1975) pp.169ff.

267. While Vergil's debt to Catullus 64 for specific phrases had always been recognised, the importance of Catullus as a model was first emphasised by D.A. Slater *CR* 20 (1912) pp.114ff. Modern studies of *Ecl*. 4 which concentrate on this aspect of the poem are: K. Büchner *P. Vergilius Maro, der Dichter der Römer* Stuttgart (1961) pp.186ff.; L. Herrmann *Les Masques et les Visages dans les Bucoliques de Virgile* Brussels (1930) pp.58ff.; F. Klingner *Virgil* Zürich and Stuttgart (1967) pp.68ff.; E. Linkomies *Arctos* 1 (1930) pp.168ff.; M.C.J. Putnam *Virgil's Pastoral Art* Princeton (1970) pp.136ff.; Williams *TORP* pp.274ff.

268. See W. Kroll *Catull* Stuttgart (reprint) (1968) *ad loc.*; J.C. Bramble *PCPh.S* 196 (1970) pp.27ff.

269. Apollo, the Muses or Chiron. For details see the commentators on Cat. 64.

270. [Tibullus] 4,5,3f.; cf. Ov. *Trist*. 5,3,25 and K.F. Smith on Tib. 1,7,1ff.

271. See G.E. Duckworth *TAPA* 95 (1964) pp.17ff. and the bibliography cited there.

272. The similarities that have been noted are: *Ecl*. 4,5 – Cat. 64,22; 4,6 – 64,398; 4,7 – 64,23; 4,11 – 64,25;323; 4,13 – 64,295;397; 4,14 – 64,59; 4,15f. – 64,384ff.; 405ff.; 4,17 – 64,357; 323ff.; 4,18 – 64,103; 4,26 – 64,51; 4,27 – 64,348; 4,28 – 64,353f.; 4,30 – 64,106; 4,35 – 64,4ff.; 78; 4,38 – 64,1; 4,40f. – 64,38ff.; 4,42ff. – 64,318ff. (*lana, vellera, Parcae*); 4,52 – 64,22ff.; 4,54 – 64,348. Some of these are much more compelling than others but the cumulative effect is important. See L. Herrmann *op.cit.* (n.267) pp.62ff.; W. Berg *Early Virgil* London (1974) pp.208f. The information is repeated for convenience and completeness.

273. See Williams *TORP* p.282.

274. Also used of *Parcae* in the epithalamium of Sidonius Apollinaris 15,201.

275. For a survey of some relevant material see K. Gaiser *Für und Wider die Ehe* München (1974). For *concordia* see A.L. Wheeler *AJP* 51 (1930) pp.214f.; P. Fedeli *Il carme 61 di Catullo* Freiburg (1972) pp.119ff. (with bibliography on the epithalamium).

276. Menander 3,407,14ff.; 411,15ff. (Spengel); Ps.–Dion. 6,266,4ff. (Usener-Radermacher).

277. Cf. *Pan.Lat*. 6(7),1;13.

278. For what follows see Weinstock *DJ* pp.260ff. The foundation of the second triumvirate was marked by the marriage of Octavian to Claudia, step-daughter of M. Antonius. See Syme *RR* p.189; Crawford *RRC* p.510.

279. See esp. G. Pasquali *St.Ital.Filol.Class*. 1 (1920) pp.17f.; J.C. Bramble *PCPh.S* 196 (1970) pp.38ff.

280. Menander 3,401,21ff. (Spengel); Libanius 8,560,13ff. (Foerster); Himerius 9,9; cf. 9,6 (Colonna); cf. Cat.61,66ff.; Licinius Calvus *Fr*. 6 (Morel); P. Fedeli *op.cit.* (n.275) pp.50ff.

281. See e.g. Ps.–Dion. 6,262,11 – 263,18 (Usener-Radermacher); Menander 3,401,16ff.; A.L. Wheeler *AJP* 51 (1930) pp.211f.

282. The interpretation of Catullus 64 is problematic. The best discussion of the darker aspects of the poem is J.C. Bramble *PCPh.S* 196 (1970) pp.22ff. An important statement of the opposite view is given by G. Giangrande *Ant.Cl.* 41 (1972) pp.123ff. D.P. Harmon *Latomus* 32 (1973) pp.311ff. presents a compromise view rather similar to my own.

283. Theocr. *Id.* 17,16–33.

284. This seems more likely than the other views of the significance of Achilles discussed above.

285. See n.276 above.

286. Ps.–Dion. 6,271,21ff. (Usener-Radermacher).

287. See J.C. Bramble *PCPh.S* 196 (1970) p.31 n.2. Note esp. Pind. *Pyth.* 3,100ff. (Sn.-Mae.).

288. Weddings were avoided in the month of May when the Lemuria was celebrated. For death and birthdays see F. Cairns *Hermes* 99 (1971) pp.150ff.

289. Contrast Theocr. *Id.* 16,85ff. where the context is very different.

290. See Quint. *Inst. Or.* 3,7,17.

291. The contrast at the end of the poem is too explicit to be ignored.

292. O. Murray *JRS* 55 (1965) p.169.

293. On 'absorption' and 'inclusion' see Cairns *GC* pp.88ff., 158ff.

294. See e.g. Theocr. *Id.* 18,50ff.; Stat. *Silv.* 1,2,269; Sen. *Med.* 61ff.; Himerius 9,21 (Colonna).

295. Cf. Hor. *Carm.Saec.* 1ff.; Crawford *RRC* p.511.

296. Cat. 64,299f.

297. Menander 3,408,8ff. (Spengel); A.L. Wheeler *AJP* 51 (1930) p.216.

298. Ps.–Dion. 6,270,18ff. (Usener-Radermacher); Menander 3,403,12ff. (Spengel); Claud. 10 (Epithalamium for Honorius and Maria), 295ff. (praise of Stilicho).

299. Ps.–Dion. 6,271,1ff. (Usener-Radermacher); Menander 3,409,8ff. (Spengel); *Pan. Lat.* 6(7),1; Claud. 12 (Fescennina).

300. Ps.–Dion. 6,271,23f. (Usener-Radermacher); Himerius 9,21 (Colonna).

301. The latest full discussion of *Epod.* 16 is D. Ableitinger-Grunberger *Der Junge Horaz unde die Politik* Heidelberg (1971) with useful bibliography. She dates *Epod.* 16 to 38 BC.

302. I intend to publish my views on the date of the *Eclogues* in the near future.

303. See, most recently, H. Hierche *Les Épodes d'Horace (Collection Latomus* 136) Brussels (1974) pp.152f. Cf. *Epod.* 16,1 – *Ecl.* 4,4; 16,9ff. – 1,70f.; 16,33 – 4,22; 16,43ff. – 4,28ff.; 39f.; 16,49f. – 2,42; 3,30; 4,21; 16,52 – 4,24; 16,61 – 1,50; 16,57 – 4,34. Some of these parallels are less compelling than others, but the accumulative effect is impressive. There are no reminiscences from *Eclogues* later than 4.

304. V. Nikiprowetzky *La Troisième Sibylle (Études Juives* 9) Paris (1970) p.217.

305. Note esp. Hor. *Carm.Saec.* 5: *quo Sibyllini monuere versus.* See also G. Pighi *De Ludis Saecularibus Populi Romani Quiritium* Milan (1941) for the evidence.

306. See A. Kurfess *ZRGG* (1951) pp.253ff. for the latest discussion.

307. R.G. Austin *CQ* 21 (1927) pp.100ff.

308. Eleven of the eighty-six paragraphs of *Or. Sib.* 3 begin with ἀλλά, including the major new section at line 97; three begin with αὐτάρ, three with ὁππότε,

καὶ τότε. The first, second and fourth sections have 51–52 per cent of lines marked in Nikiprowetzky's text with punctuation and this rises to 61 per cent in the third section. In *Ecl.* 4 71 per cent of lines are thus end-stopped. This is only of course a rough guide. Note also that Hesiod introduces three of his five ages with αὐτὰρ ἐπεὶ (*Op.* 121;140;156); cf. *Op.* 169c;174.

309. The evidence is collected in an appendix to the edition of the *Oracula Sibyllina* by A. Rzach (1891).

310. The parallels are noted as early as Lactantius *De Ira* 22m–23; *Divin. Inst.* 7,24.

311. The importance of considering *Eclogue* 4 as a prophecy was impressed upon me by C. Macleod and J.G. Howie.

[Addendum to n.213]

A very similar technique to that used by Vergil is employed by Persius (5,161ff.) in his imitation of Horace (*Sat.* 2,3,259ff.). The scholiast notes that Persius inserts the name Davus from the Menandrian orginal into Horace's imitation of Terence *Eunuchus*. See M. Coffey *Roman Satire* London (1976) pp.115; 240 n.96.

STRUCTURE AND MEANING IN VERGIL'S *AENEID*

by

E.L. HARRISON
(University of Leeds)

The purpose of this paper is to suggest that a greater sensitivity to Vergil's employment of formal correspondence in the design of the *Aeneid* could help us to solve some of the problems of interpretation which the work still undoubtedly presents. It will be concerned in particular with Vergil's use of two related elements to point some significant development which they frame, with the second usually, though not necessarily, echoing the first in ring composition of the simplest kind. Such echoes are common enough in any writing, whether prose or verse, that aspires to some degree of artistic shaping; but Vergil's use of them in the *Aeneid* seems so pronounced as to offer us useful guidance that we ought not to neglect.

We can approach our topic by focusing attention on Dido, gradually increasing the amount of text enclosed by each frame. At the start of Book Four Dido makes it abundantly clear to her sister Anna that she is in love with Aeneas (9-23). But having done so she at once takes a solemn vow to continue preserving her chastity as a widow, a form of chastity that enjoyed a special respect in Roman society because it embodied the ideal of the *univira*,[1] the widow who combined the virtue of continence with that of unbroken loyalty to her dead husband:

> "sed mihi vel tellus optem prius ima dehiscat
> vel pater omnipotens abigat me fulmine ad umbras,
> pallentis umbras Erebo noctemque profundam,
> ante, pudor, quam te violo aut tua iura resolvo"

$$(4, 24\text{-}27)$$

But Anna knows only too well what kind of reply Dido yearns to hear, and she at once obliges by producing a series of cogent reasons, first personal then political, explaining why Dido should abandon her resolution and marry Aeneas (31-49); and a mere twenty-eight lines after Dido's solemn vow the poet tells us that Anna's argument has disposed of the ideal it embraced: *His dictis impenso animum flammavit amore/spemque dedit dubiae menti solvitque pudorem* (54f.). This short sequence enclosed by *pudor* and *pudorem* comprises a crucial part of the Dido story: mentally the queen has already surrendered herself to Aeneas, and henceforward her physical surrender when the opportunity arises is

101

clearly inevitable. But her words also contain the first element in another frame that looks beyond the perjury thus committed to the divine retribution that will ultimately overtake it. For in her oath Dido calls on Jupiter to destroy her with his lightning should she fail to preserve her *pudor*: *"vel pater omnipotens abigat me fulmine ad umbras"* (25); and in due course Vergil suggests by his imagery that Jupiter's lightning-stroke has indeed found its mark. For what really destroys Dido finally is Aeneas' departure from Carthage, which comes about on the orders of Jupiter himself, transmitted to the hero by Mercury (223-37; 265-76); and when Aeneas draws his sword to cut the cable that ties him to Carthage, it flashes like a stroke of lightning (*ensem fulmineum*, 579f.).

No doubt some readers of Vergil will less readily accept such an interpretation than others; so here let me cite a comparable arrangement involving Dido's opposite number in the second half of the epic, Turnus. In Book Twelve a truce is arranged under which Aeneas and Turnus are to decide the issue of the war in a duel, and Latinus invokes Jupiter's *fulmen* against any violators of the sworn agreement (200). Aeneas displays great courage in seeking to preserve the truce (311-17). But Turnus not only incites his people to violate it by his suddenly assumed air of pathetic helplessness (219-21), but also revels in violating it himself once he knows that Aeneas has been removed from the battlefield by a treacherous arrow-shot (324-82). Again the poet's imagery suggests that once Jupiter's *fulmen* has been solemnly invoked it will find its mark where there is need, and again Aeneas is the agent of the god's retribution. For immediately before the actual death-blow that disposes of Turnus, Aeneas brings him low with a cast of his spear; and the din it makes as it speeds towards its target is greater than that of any *fulmen* (922).

If we return to Book Four as a whole we again find it framed, this time by the poet's striking use of the term *vulnus*, which Austin and others have noted.[2] At line 2, *vulnus alit venis*, it is the figurative wound of Roman love poetry. But there is nothing figurative about *infixum stridit sub pectore vulnus* at the end of the book (689): for now it is the death-wound Dido has inflicted on herself with Aeneas' sword. Vergil could scarcely have indicated the formal unity of the book more vividly than by framing it with these two wounds, and letting Dido pass from one to the other in the course of it.

Finally there is a remarkable frame that encloses the whole of the action at Carthage, from the beginning of Book One to the end of Book Four. At the start Juno prevails on Aeolus, keeper of the winds, to create havoc on the grand scale with a storm at sea; at the end she sends Iris to bring peace at last to the dying queen. The antithesis is pointed by the repetition of the term *luctari*. At 1, 53 it is the *luctantis ventos* that Juno's agent releases, the boisterous winds that struggle violently to burst out of their prison-house; and the release only multiplies their violence. But at 4, 695 it is Dido's *luctantem animam*, her struggling soul, that Iris sets free; and when this leaves its prison-house its struggles finally come to an end.

If we leave Dido and consider the *Aeneid* generally we find comparable framing elements round other books. Book Six begins and ends with a picture of Trojan ships at anchor first at Cumae (1-5) then at Caieta (900f.). Book Eight begins with a sneer from Aeneas' enemies that he has brought with him his defeated household gods (11), but in the climax of its closing episode his greatest descendant appears on a magic shield leading those same gods to victory at the battle of Actium (679). Book Nine begins with the goddess Juno sending Iris to persuade Turnus to attack the Trojan camp in Aeneas' absence (1-15), and ends with Jupiter sending that same divine messenger to ensure that Turnus withdraws and Juno stops supporting him (801-5). There is a similarly antithetical frame round Book Twelve, where Turnus declares at the start that he will vindicate the Italians from the charge of cowardice by despatching Aeneas with his sword (16), but in the end himself succumbs to the sword of Aeneas (950).

Moreover there are comparable frames round the whole work, of which I should like to cite two, one on a divine, the other on a human level, both involving developments of fundamental importance in the epic action. In the first Juno delivers an impassioned monologue complaining that the Trojans have been allowed to frustrate all her attempts at destroying them, even though she is queen of the gods (1, 37-49); and her closing words are: *"et quisquam numen Iunonis adorat?/praeterea aut supplex aris imponet honorem?"*(48f.). ("And does anyone worship the divinity of Juno? Will anyone hereafter humbly place sacrifices in my honour on my altars?"). The last word of that monologue (*honorem*) emphasizes that her chief concern is with cult that will enhance her prestige as a divinity; and she feels that this is now threatened. This concern remains with her throughout the epic; and at the conclusion she finally goes off happy because, in a speech that ends with that same word, Jupiter promises her that the future race of Romans will honour her with cult more than any other: *"nec gens ulla tuos aeque celebrabit honores"* (12,840).

That example illustrates how opposition to the Trojan destiny on a divine level is finally overcome. The other shows its defeat on a human level. The very first glimpse we have of Aeneas comes at the height of the storm that wrecks the ships off North Africa: *extemplo Aeneae solvuntur frigore membra* (1, 92). The terrifying onslaught of the storm has left Aeneas in a state of shock, and in the sudden chill produced by such a condition he has lost control of his limbs. Certainly by introducing his hero in such a fashion Vergil avoided any risk of anticlimax. At the end of the epic, however, the motif is transferred to his adversary, Turnus; and though the phrase is the same (*solvuntur frigore membra*, 12, 951), Turnus loses control of his limbs, not just in temporary shock, but in death.

There are of course variations of this framing technique, of which I should like to mention two, the first because it seems a remarkable example of Vergil's capacity for employing purely formal arrangements, the second because it exhibits a triple form that will become immediately relevant in another context. One of the many arrangements of the *Aeneid* involves a division into three groups, with the first four books referring to the tragedy of Dido, the middle four to the Roman destiny, and the last four to the tragedy of Turnus. Certainly Book Six, with its parade of Roman heroes of the future, and still more Book Eight, ending with Actium and the triple triumph, can be regarded as the most Augustan. In this respect, then, Vergil can be thought of as making his most drastic departure from the immediate epic action towards the end of the middle group of four books, and his most drastic return to it at the start of the last four, in other words, in Book Nine. The way in which he indicates this return is, if I am correct, quite remarkable. In an earlier juxtaposition of Augustan panegyric and immediate theme in *Georgics* 3, where Vergil passes from a preface promising at some length a poem in honour of Octavian to the treatment of the immediate theme, farm animals, there is a bridge passage:

> interea Dryadum silvas saltusque sequamur
> intactos, tua, Maecenas, haud mollia iussa:
> te sine nil altum mens incohat. en age, segnis
> rumpe moras!

Georgics 3, 40-43

(Meanwhile let me pursue the woods of the Dryads and the virgin glades, your uncompromising orders, Maecenas. Without you to prod me I get nothing worthwhile started. Come on now, an end to lazy delay!). The closing words are of course addressed to himself, not to his patron. Now in the *Aeneid* such a bridge-passage has no place, since the Augustan elements have been successfully integrated into the epic action. Nevertheless Vergil seems to have alluded somewhat abstrusely to the transition by framing Book Nine between two striking phrases taken from this brief *Georgics* passage: at 9, 13 *rumpe moras* is now used by Iris to urge Turnus to attack the Trojan ships, and at 9, 804 *haud mollia iussa* now refers to the uncompromising orders sent by Jupiter to Juno to put an end to her activities in the Trojan camp. Can this be a mere coincidence?

The second variation takes us to Book Five, where the frames assume the form of question and answer. I would suggest that in fact Book Five can be seen structurally in terms of three sets of these, arranged on a basis of ring composition. At the start of the book a terrible storm hits the Trojan fleet as it leaves Carthage, and Aeneas' helmsman, Palinurus, cries: "*heu, quianam tanti cinxerunt aethera nimbi?/quidve, pater Neptune, paras?*" (5, 13f.). ("Alas, why have such great clouds encircled the sky? What have you in store, Father Neptune?"). Father Neptune gives his answer to the question thus addressed to him in unexpected fashion at the end of the book: for what he has in store is in fact to send Somnus, god of sleep, to dash the helmsman from his post so that he is lost overboard, and it is with this incident that Book Five closes (854-60, cf. 814f.).

Inside that question and answer comes a similar arrangement at lines 95f. and 722-40. Aeneas is sacrificing at the tomb of Anchises, and as he does so calls on his dead father in four solemn lines (80-83). In immediate response to his prayer a snake appears, tastes the offerings, and then vanishes behind the tomb. It would be ludicrous to imagine that the snake in question represents anything other than the dead Anchises; and we might reasonably have expected the omniscient epic poet to say so in the narrative without further ado, and to go on indeed to depict Aeneas as coming to the same conclusion with his usual pious enthusiasm. But instead Vergil inserts a second question into the text by letting Aeneas wonder: *geniumne loci famulumne parentis/esse putet* (95f.) (whether he should deem it to be the local deity or his father's attendant spirit). In this somewhat contrived fashion, I take it, the question is raised at this early stage in the book as to whether the dead Anchises is really concerned with Aeneas and the Trojan destiny any longer. The answer comes at a critical point in the subsequent action (722-40), when an attack on the Trojan ships by his own womenfolk has left Aeneas in the depths of despair, and a nocturnal visit from his dead father fires him with fresh enthusiasm for his mission (746-48).

Finally inside that arrangement we have a third, yet again involving a supernatural context, and this time occurring in the course of the actual Funeral Games. There are five events, and appropriately enough it is the central one that contains it. At this point, the Boxing Match, Vergil shifts the emphasis in favour of the local people, his intention clearly being to acknowledge in his allusive fashion certain aspects of Sicily's destined role in Roman history. This development reaches its climax with Acestes' arrow-shot (519-40), but at this earlier stage it is manifested in two ways: Vergil lets the Sicilian boxer, Entellus, defeat his Trojan opponent, Dares, and he also brings into prominence the local deity, Eryx. In fact it is this latter move that provides our central question and answer. Eryx was originally a king of the region and a famous pugilist. After he had the misfortune to meet Hercules in combat, with the inevitable result, he was deified. Meanwhile his former protégé, Entellus, now an old man, feels unable to compete any longer as a boxer, and fails to respond to the challenge thrown out by the boastful Dares (375-85). Whereupon Acestes tries to egg him on: *"ubi nunc nobis deus ille magister/nequiquam memoratus Eryx?"* (391f.) ("Where now, pray, is that divine Eryx, whom you have idly referred to as your teacher?"). Entellus reacts by overwhelming the Trojan with a storm of blows which Vergil compares to a hailstorm striking a roof. In the end Aeneas is compelled to intervene to rescue his compatriot, his words as he does so supplying the answer to Acestes' teasing question: *"non viris alias conversaque numina sentis?/cede deo"* (466f.) ("Do you not realize his strength is of a different order, and that divine support has turned his way? Yield to the god".). Eryx is a *praesens deus* who has made his powerful presence felt on behalf of his former pupil in his hour of need.

This brings me to a passage where awareness of Vergil's framing tendency can help us to dispose of what I take to be a long-standing misinterpretation. Here again it is a triple structure that is involved. In Book Nine Nisus and Euryalus sally forth by night from the Trojan camp on a mission to Aeneas, who is absent in Etruria (314ff.). On their way they pass through the lines of the besieging enemy, killing several of them without much difficulty because they are strewn about the place in a drunken sleep (324ff.). As they are leaving, however, a strong enemy detachment of cavalry unexpectedly appears, returning from a mission to Latinus, and a helmet Euryalus has just taken from a corpse and placed on his head flashes in the moonlight, betraying their hurried departure, so that in the end both the Trojans are killed (367ff., cf. 365f.). The lines with which I am concerned come at the critical point in this development:

> et galea Euryalum sublustri noctis in umbra
> prodidit immemorem radiisque adversa refulsit.
> haud temere est visum, conclamat ab agmine Volcens:
> "state viri . . . .

(373-76)

The generally accepted translation is roughly as follows: And the helmet, in the glimmering shade of the night, betrayed the reckless Euryalus, and meeting the moon's rays, reflected them. It was not seen heedlessly: Volcens shouted from his column: "Halt, you men . . . . But there is a simple objection to this rendering which seems to me to rule it out: if the flashing helmet "was not seen heedlessly" one would surely have expected *visa* in the text, to agree with *galea*, rather than the neuter *visum*. Moreover if the arrangement at whose presence I have already hinted is valid, *haud temere est visum* (375) points, not forward to the purposive action of the enemy column, though that in itself certainly makes excellent sense, but backward to something quite different. This arrangement involves three corresponding pairs of elements in ring composition, as in the last case, but this time each second element, instead of answering a question put by the first, bears an ironical relationship to it. When Nisus first gets his idea for the disastrous enterprise he tells Euryalus: "*aut pugnam aut aliquid iamdudum invadere magnum/mens agitat mihi nec placida contenta quiete est*" (186f.). ("For a long time now my heart has been astir to embark on a battle or some mighty deed, and has been dissatisfied with quiet peace".). But Nisus' mighty deed only succeeds in taking him from the temporary peace of his fortified camp to the permanent peace of death: *tum super exanimum sese proiecit amicum/confossus placidaque ibi demum morte quievit* (444f.) (Then thus pierced through he flung himself over his lifeless friend, and at last found peace in quiet death.). That frame encloses the whole enterprise, and the ironical echo is surely unmistakable.

The second frame comes inside this frame and again comprises an utterance of Nisus followed by ironical narrative. When Nisus proposes the enterprise in the first place, he tells the assembled Trojan chiefs: "*locum insidiis conspeximus ipsi/qui patet in bivio portae quae proximo ponto*" (236f.). The essential feature here is the deceitful element contained in the term *insidiae*, an element it shares with *fraus*: in fact the two terms are often used synonymously. For it is a fundamental principle of the *Aeneid*, as it is of Livy's history, that deceit of any sort should be left to

107

foreigners:[3] in the *Aeneid* Greeks may employ it successfully, but not Trojans or Italians.[4] Indeed, as soon as Nisus begins to speak in such a fashion the ultimate failure of his enterprise is a foregone conclusion. To bring out Vergil's point here we can exaggerate the effect somewhat and translate: "We have ourselves spotted a place for our deceitful enterprise, one which leaves an opening at the gate nearest the sea". The ironical echo Comes later when the pair are surprised by the returning detachment and dash into a nearby wood (381ff.). For though Nisus gets away safely, he looks back only to discover that his companion has been captured, and that the element of deceit in the place where he now finds himself actually contributes to Euryalus' downfall: *ac videt Euryalum quem iam manus omnis/fraude loci et noctis, subito turbante tumultu,/oppressum rapit . . . .* (396-8).

Finally we have the inner pair, which in effect bring together the two sets of violent deaths, first those that Nisus and Euryalus inflict, and then those that they themselves suffer, which are implicit in the disastrous flash of moonlight that causes them: *tris iuxta famulos temere inter tela iacentis/armigerumque Remi premit . . . .* (329f.). (Nisus dispatched three attendants [i.e. of Rhamnes] who were lying beside him haphazardly among their weapons, and then Remus' armour-bearer.). There is thus no logic about the deaths of these Italians: they die simply because they have the bad luck to be lying in the path of the two bloodthirsty Trojans as they go on the rampage. But the second passage has a very different story to tell: *haud temere [sc. esse] est visum* (375) (it seemed to be no mere accident). The reason why the moon's intervention seems purposeful is not far to seek. For this whole operation has been presided over by that most sensitive of Olympians, the moon-goddess herself, Diana, whose mythology is rich in stories of the revenge she exacts from those who fail to pay her due deference. Certainly Nisus and Euryalus have both been guilty of that: there is not a trace of any prayer or vow to her before they set out, and what is worse, Euryalus in his moment of triumph fails to dedicate to her any of the plunder he takes. Indeed, there is unmistakable irony about the way in which she selects an item from this to serve as the medium for her revenge. It is relevant here to cite a comparable story told by Diodorus Siculus (4, 22, 3). There we hear of a hunter who, having killed a huge wild boar, dedicates its head to himself instead of Artemis, and then goes off to sleep under the tree where the offending trophy hangs. The aftermath is not hard to guess: the great head in due course falls down and kills him, and the danger involved in denying the gods their due is thus clearly illustrated. Euryalus' gesture in donning the plundered helmet and ignoring Diana is similar to the hunter's, and he suffers a similar, if more subtly devised, fate. Nisus does at last get round to acknowledging the goddess as *dea praesens* at 404ff., but by then it is too late: the offences have already been committed, and the inexorable process of divine retribution is already under way. If it is with Diana's help that Nisus proceeds to strike down two of Euryalus' captors with his spears, her intervention still serves merely to hasten the inevitable conclusion.

Here let me add a few supplementary points. Actual usage seems to support this interpretation: *non temere est* is idiomatic and regularly means "it is not accidental, there is a reason for it", whereas *non* or *haud temere* used adverbially seems to mean "not easily" rather than "to some purpose". Moreover *temere* occurs nowhere else in the *Aeneid*, but then twice in less than fifty lines, first positively, then negatively, which surely strengthens the case for seeing the occurrences as a pair, related to each other with that same touch of irony that characterises the relationship of the other two pairs. Finally there is a Lucretian echo that seems to endorse the view I have taken that Nisus and Euryalus are in effect the victims of Diana's anger. This earlier poet, in a famous passage vindicating Epicureanism from the charge of wickedness and transferring it to pagan religion instead, described how the Greeks, becalmed at Aulis by an angry Diana, sacrificed the young princess Iphigenia to the goddess to secure the winds they needed for the voyage to Troy. In a line heavy with irony he referred to her murderers as: *ductores Danaum delecti, prima virorum* (1, 86) (chosen leaders of the Greeks, foremost among heroes). Vergil now echoes that same line to describe the Trojan leaders who approve Nisus' plan and despatch him and Euryalus on their hare-brained escapade: *ductores Teucrum primi, delecta iuventus* (9, 226) (foremost leaders among the Trojans, chosen warriors). For by doing so they, no less than their Greek predecessors, are in effect partaking in a sacrifice to that same angry goddess.[5]

Finally let me cite an example at the end of the epic where formal correspondence can help us with a crucial passage which, I believe, tends to be misunderstood. At 12,793ff. Jupiter's patience finally snaps and he tells Juno to give up her support of Turnus once and for all. Almost five hundred lines earlier (318ff.) Aeneas was wounded as a result of Juno's machinations (cf.156ff.) yet Jupiter made no move then, though he now quite naturally includes that incident among his complaints (797). The obvious question arises, what event moves him to intervene so decisively now, if that one failed to do so? The answer is given quite clearly by

Vergil, but it has been paraphrased out of existence by translators from Dryden onwards, and neutralized by a long line of commentators who read unnecessary difficulties into his text. Turnus has a magic sword made, like Aeneas' weapons, by the god Vulcan. We learn at 12,735ff. that he entered the fray without it, taking his charioteer's sword instead, and that this one, being the work of a mere mortal, shattered when it met the divinely wrought armour of Aeneas. Whereupon Turnus' sister Juturna, obeying Juno's earlier orders, as Jupiter knows only too well, and taking advantage of a lull in the duel, rushed in and gave Turnus his magic sword back. It is this last development that has proved too much for Jupiter, for it was he himself who was responsible for Turnus taking the field without that magic sword in the first place, so that Juturna's action constitutes a piece of especially offensive defiance. No doubt employing Iris or Mercury for the purpose, since he always works through an intermediary, Jupiter snatched it from Turnus' possession prior to his leaving for the battlefield. Hence the god's indignant outburst at this new turn of events:

"mortalin decuit violari vulnere divum?
aut ensem (quid enim sine te Iuturna valeret?)
ereptum reddi Turno et vim crescere victis?"

(797-99)

("Was it fitting that a god should be profanely subjected to a wound inflicted by a mortal? Or that a sword (for what could Juturna have strength to do without your help?) snatched away [understand of course 'by me', since he is the speaker, and is so affronted by the interference] should be restored to Turnus?"). Maguiness comments, "As nobody had taken Turnus' sword from him, *ereptum* seems to be used loosely for 'missing' "[6]; and the commonest translation of the word, from Dryden onwards, is "lost". But *ereptum* should not be treated in such an arbitrary fashion: *rapere* is a violent term, and the compound form still more so. It means 'snatched away', and anything less expressive than that is inadequate.

Here another question inevitably arises: why is there such general agreement that nobody took the sword away if in fact Jupiter did, and if acceptance of that fact not only explains his intervention at this point, but also corresponds with what he actually says? The answer can be found by referring to the already mentioned flashback that occurs earlier, at 735ff. There, when Turnus' sword-blade shatters, the poet explains the background to this incident. Most of the detail is given in plain narrative and is beyond dispute. Turnus took his charioteer's sword instead of his

110

own; it was adequate for normal fighting; but it naturally failed when it met Aeneas' magic armour. But the poet qualifies the detail at the very beginning of the account by calling it *fama* (735) (report). In other words what he gives here represents what mere mortals make of immortal activity about which they are left in the dark; and according to this, but only according to this, Turnus left his magic sword behind through hastiness and grabbed the wrong one instead. On the other hand when we reach Jupiter's own account, but only then, we get the real truth behind what happened. In keeping with his general policy of promoting Turnus' destruction at the hands of Aeneas Jupiter in fact had Turnus' magic sword removed at the very moment when he most needed it, as he was about to take the field for the decisive duel. Once he had gone, of necessity taking an alternative sword instead, Jupiter obviously had the original restored, thus providing the basis for the popular version of what happened, i.e. it was there all the time, and Turnus merely grabbed the wrong one in his haste, and thus also making it possible for Juturna to recover the original later and take it to Turnus.

If I seem to have laboured a point of detail, it should be stressed that it is one involving the climax of the epic action, and deserves as much patience as we can give it. I have tried to show that Jupiter earlier had Turnus' sword snatched from him, and now tells us as much. This brings me at last to consideration of the frame that lends formal support to such an interpretation. For among the echoes that accumulate towards the end of the *Aeneid* are two of the reversing type that are especially striking, both of which take the reader back to Turnus' speech immediately after the metamorphosis of the Trojan ships in Book Nine. The first of these is well known: Turnus, conceding at last that the gods are against him, cries out: *"di me terrent et Iuppiter hostis"* (12, 895) ("It is the gods who terrify me, and a hostile Jupiter"), which in effect reverses his earlier cry: *"nil me fatalia terrent/si qua Phryges prae se iactant responsa deorum"* (9, 133f.). ("Any fateful responses of the gods the Trojans boast about hold no terrors for me"). A second, I suggest, now becomes clear and deserves equal recognition. Let me recall what is involved in that earlier passage. Vergil there fuses two Homeric motifs. He lets Turnus attack the Trojan ships with fire, as Hector attacked those of the Greeks in the *Iliad* (*Aeneid* 9, 69ff. cf. Homer *Iliad* 8, 212ff.); and he also imitates a passage in the *Odyssey* where Zeus allows Poseidon to punish the Phaeacians by turning to stone the ship in which they carried Odysseus on the last stage of his voyage to Ithaca (Homer *Odyssey* 13, 125ff.). Now however it is a question of Jupiter allowing the goddess Cybele to rescue from Turnus' attack ships that were made from her sacred pines, and to do so by transforming them miraculously into sea-nymphs (9, 77ff.). Just one further detail is worth stressing: when Jupiter made this concession to Cybele he gave his assent in its most solemn form, combining the oath by the river Styx and the nod that shakes Olympus (9, 104ff.). All we have to do next, I would suggest, is read Turnus' explanation of the event as he saw it, and imagine how Jupiter would naturally react to his words: *"Troianos haec monstra petunt, his Iuppiter ipse/auxilium solitum eripuit."* (9, 128f.). ("This miracle is aimed at the Trojans: it is from them that Jupiter has snatched away their accustomed support."). Such a perversion of Jupiter's real purpose demanded a reply, and we can now see, I suggest, that it received a suitably ironical one in the subsequent action. For Turnus himself proves to be the one who has his *auxilium solitum* snatched away by Jupiter, and the god picks the most critical moment to do it.

NOTES

1. See G. Williams *JRS* 48 (1958) pp.23ff.

2. R.G. Austin *P. Vergili Maronis Aeneidos Liber Quartus* Oxford (1955) *ad* 4, 689.

3. See E. Burck in *Rom und Karthago* (ed. J. Vogt) Leipzig (1945) p.321.

4. Contrast e.g. 2, 195ff. with 2,387ff. and 11,522ff.

5. As Jonathan Foster has kindly pointed out to me in correspondence, the above interpretation imparts a new and sinister ambivalence to Euryalus' words when he first hears of the projected enterprise: *"est hic, est animus lucis contemptor"* (9,205).

6. W.S. Maguinness *Aeneid Book Twelve* London (1953) *ad* 12,799.

HORACE *ODES* 1,37 AND PINDAR *DITHYRAMB* 2[1]

by

ALEX HARDIE

(Foreign and Commonwealth Office)

Horace *Odes* 1,37 is universally regarded as an expression of the poet's personal reactions to the death of Cleopatra, and as such it is thought to lie in some relationship with Alcaeus' poem on the death of the tyrant Myrsilus —*Fr.* 332(LP).[2] This paper attempts to show that the poem is not a monodic personal statement, but a choral dithyramb; that its literary debt is to Pindar; and that the occasion which inspired it was not the death of Cleopatra, but the *triplex triumphus* of Octavian.

1. *Odes* 1,37 as a Dithyramb

Odes 1,37 contains three general features which suggest that Horace consciously wrote it as a dithyramb, within an accepted ancient definition of the genre. First, it is a narrative poem: after an introductory stanza it describes, in chronological order, Cleopatra's hostile intentions before Actium and Roman responses to them (5-12); the defeat at Actium and Octavian's pursuit (12-21); the return to Egypt, the Roman invasion and the final suicide (21-32). The traditional lyric genre most closely associated with pure narrative was the dithyramb, and most extant poems classified by Alexandrian scholars as dithyrambs reveal a high narrative content.[3]

A late testimonium (ps.–Plutarch *De Musica* 10, discussing Xenocritus), which alludes to narrative content, reveals a second dithyrambic feature of *Odes* 1,37, namely its concentration on the heroic:[4] ἡρωικῶν γὰρ ὑποθέσεων πράγματα ἐχουσῶν ποιητὴν γεγονέναι φασὶν αὐτόν· διὸ καί τινας διθυράμβους καλεῖν αὐτοῦ τὰς ὑποθέσεις. This is not a full definition of the dithyramb, but a notice which, for present purposes, is rather more valuable: it implies that any narrative lyric poem with heroic themes was automatically classified by many critics as a dithyramb. Deeds of heroism and associated themes proliferate in extant examples of the genre.[5] Horace depicts Octavian in heroic colours; and, by introducing him only after the allusion to Actium and withdrawing him before the reference to the Alexandrian campaign, effectively presents him in isolation from the 'official' Roman naval and military effort. Octavian plays a solitary role in confrontation with the lone Cleopatra. The heroic effect is enhanced by the epic-style simile at 17ff., and by the designation of Cleopatra as *monstrum*(21), which suggests that her adversary is a

Hercules.[6]

The third feature of *Odes* 1,37 which suggests that it is a dithyramb is the motif of Dionysiac drinking which it contains as well as some less obvious Dionysiac material. The dithyramb was in origin associated exclusively with the worship of Dionysus.[7] Despite a later expansion of the scope of the genre, these origins were not forgotten, and Dionysiac themes (revels, birth legends, drunkenness, etc.) are well represented in surviving fragments.[8]

These general features suggest identification of the poem as a dithyramb and they direct the reader to look for more specific indicators: these are found in the obligatory drinking and dancing *pede libero* mentioned in lf., and will be considered in detail later.

2. Pindar *Dithyramb 2*

Horace concentrates on the person of Cleopatra, and adds unity to his narrative by his attention throughout to her changing state of mind and her reactions to events. It has been correctly suggested that Horace depicts the queen as a tragic figure.[9] There is nothing inherently strange about the tragic treatment of a defeated enemy: moralising historians favoured the tragic approach to the careers of fallen tyrants.[10] But it is odd that a dithyramb, a heroic narrative, should concentrate thus on the defeated adversary, to the seeming exclusion of the 'hero' himself We are justified in seeking a literary precedent for this central paradox, and the only extant dithyramb which was regarded by later critics as according 'tragic' treatment to the defeated adversary is Pindar *Dithyramb 2 – Frr.* 70b; *249a,b; 81 (Sn.–Mae.). This work can act as a useful commentary on *Odes* 1, 37 and detailed examination of the surviving fragments is necessary.

The poem opens with a strong antithesis between the 'old' and the 'new' dithyramb:

Π‌ρὶν μὲν ἕρπε σχοινοτένειά τ' ἀοιδὰ
  δι‌θυράμβων
καὶ τὸ σά‌ν κίβδηλον ἀνθρώποισιν ἀπὸ στομάτων,
διαπέπ[τ]α[νται . . . .] . . . . [
  κλοισι νεαι

(1–5)
4   διαπέπτα[νται δὲ νῦν ἱροῖς] πύλα[ι κύ]κλοισι   G –H

114

(Of old, the song of the dithyrambs, moving in a straight line, and the counterfeit 'san' crept from the lips to mankind. But now, new gates have flown open for the sacred circles of singers.) σχοινοτένεια is usually taken as a criticism of length,[11] but Pindar's metaphor is that of a stretched out rope, which suggests only 'straightness'. Aristotle used a related 'string' metaphor to describe old, unsophisticated, prose style:[12] τὴν δὲ λέξιν ἀνάγκη εἶναι ἢ εἰρομένην καὶ τῷ συνδέσμῳ μίαν, ὥσπερ αἱ ἐν τοῖς διθυράμβοις ἀναβολαί, ἢ κατεστραμμένην καὶ ὁμοίαν ταῖς τῶν ἀρχαίων ποιητῶν ἀντιστρόφοις. (Rhetoric 1409a, 25ff.). (Style must be either strung out and made one only by the connecting particle, like the rambling structure of the dithyramb, or periodic and analogous to the strophic structure used by the old poets.) We cannot press far Aristotle's comparison of the 'strung out' prose style to the rambling dithyramb, since he seems to be talking about the later dithyramb of his own age; but his distinction between the 'strung out' and the periodic style, and the analogies he tries to draw between the strung-out style and dithyrambic structure on the one hand and periodic style and strophic structure on the other may help to define Pindar's application of the term σχοινοτένεια. Pindar is criticising the older dithyramb as 'moving in a straight line' in style and narrative structure. His opening antithesis is therefore likely to be a discreet stylistic pointer to his own technical innovations, and, as a dithyrambic opening, it was almost certainly novel and arresting.

Pindar also describes the 'old' dithyramb in one set of terms and the 'new' dithyramb in completely different terms: the πύλαι νέαι (3) seem at first simply to imply correction of the old technical faults of style and sound, and to refer to the new scope created by those corrections. However, the following sentence, addressed to the chorus:

[. . . . ε]ἰδότες
οἵαν Βρομίου [τελε]τάν
καὶ παρὰ σκᾶ[πτ]ον Διὸς Οὐρανίδαι
ἐν μεγάροις ἵ̣στα̣ι̣ντι.

(5–8)

(. . . . knowing what kind of Dionysiac rites the gods institute even by the sceptre of Zeus.) suggests that the 'new gates' in fact refer to the opening up of new subject matter: the lacuna at the start is best filled by an imperative (for example, Maas's ἰαχεῖτ' or Puech's κελαδεῖτ'), a supplement which produces a type of asyndeton commonly used by Pindar to convey the nuance 'therefore'.[13] This nuance, together with the reference to the knowledge of the chorus concerning the conduct of mystic rites on Olympus, confirms that the 'new gates' opened for the chorus refer not to new techniques, or to new ways of telling an old story, but to new knowledge and subject matter. Pindar has therefore used implicit contrast in his antithesis, leaving the audience to deduce that the 'new' dithyramb incorporates technical improvements and that the subject matter of the 'old' dithyramb was more limited.

The second innovation, subject matter, is exemplified in the account of the revels on Olympus (6–18). Only then, in the transition passage which follows (18ff.), does Pindar implicitly explain how the 'new' dithyramb came about:

$$\text{ἐμὲ δ' ἐξαίρετο[ν}$$
$$\text{κάρυκα σοφῶν ἐπέων}$$
$$\text{Μοῖσ' ἀνέστασ' Ἑλλάδι κα[λ]λ[ιχόρῳ}$$

(23–25)

(The Muse has set me up to be her chosen herald of wise words to the fair dancing grounds of Greece.) Pindar does not claim originality by the customary direct statement of personal achievement, but implies it by stressing his uniquely favoured position as sole herald of the Muse. He has brought σοφὰ ἔπη to Greece and has imparted his knowledge to its choruses.[14] The statement constitutes the essential explanatory link between the two parts of the opening antithesis; and by delaying it thus, Pindar has further exemplified the originality of the 'new' stylistic technique (which, of course, is his personal achievement as κῆρυξ).

The whole passage should be compared with Aristophanes' claim, in the Parabasis of the *Peace* (739ff.), to have ennobled Comedy. The chorus first (739–747) describes and exemplifies the bad jokes, most with Heraclean associations,[15] which the lone Aristophanes has driven from the stage; lines 748–750 summarise his claim to have removed this vulgar rubbish and to have ennobled Comedy with elevated thought and language; finally (751–760), as an example of the new subject matter, the chorus describes Aristophanes' 'Heraclean' combat with the 'beast' Cleon. The whole passage is a complex parody of a particular type of heroic narrative, in which an individual and altruistic deed or achievement, with Heraclean associations, is prefaced by a picture of communal debasement or fear, and is followed by a corresponding picture of communal enlightenment and joy.[16]

There are certain points of correspondence between narratives of this type and Pindar's claim to have ennobled the dithyramb: the debasement of the old, pedestrian dithyramb (ἕρπε 1, κίβδηλον 3); the implication in ἀνθρώποισιν (3) that the debasement impinges on the human condition; the unusual emphasis on Pindar as sole herald;[17] the benefits which Pindar has passed on to the choruses of Greece.[18] If Pindar is adapting this type of narrative pattern — and the introduction to a narrative dithyramb about Heracles would be an appropriate place for it — then he has altered the conventional narrative order ('before', action, 'after') by juxtaposing the 'before' and 'after' elements and placing the action section last. But, while Aristophanes' parody of the narrative pattern suggests that it was very well known, particularly so, perhaps, in narrative dithyrambs, there is no direct evidence on the point, and it would be unwise to insist that Pindar did have it in mind.

Pindar's description of orgiastic revels on Olympus is unique in ancient literature. Lines 8—18 describe orgiastic music striking up in honour of the Phrygian *Magna Mater*; in response, torches kindle, the Naiads scream and set up a war dance, the thunderbolt breathes fire, the weapon of war is stirred, and the snakes on the aegis of Pallas hiss out. The dominant idea is the spread, from one source, of destructive madness and war. Much of Pindar's description seems to have been transferred to an Olympian setting from the ritual of the devotees of Cybele, in particular of the Curetes.[19] The passage is tightly constructed, the various responses to the orgiastic music being introduced by the thrice used ἐν δέ (10, 12, 15). Lines 19—23 coincide with the start of the *antistrophe* and lie outside the tight structure of the previous section. They are dominated by Dionysus and show a different side of orgiastic influence:

> ῥίμφα δ᾽ εἶσιν Ἄρτεμις οἰοπόλας
> ζεύξαισ᾽ ἐν ὀργαῖς
> Βακχίαις φῦλον λεόντων α[∪ ∪ – ∪ ∪ –
> ὁ δὲ κηλεῖται χορευοίσαισι κα[ὶ θη—
> ρῶν ἀγέλαις.

(19–23)

21 ἀ[γρότερον Βρομίῳ Bury, Schr.

(And the solitary Artemis comes swiftly, having yoked in Bacchic frenzy a wild pride of lions for Dionysus; and he is spellbound by herds of wild beasts which also dance.) Artemis' normal power over wild beasts is here rationalised as being Dionysiac; her swift journey is prompted not by the orgiastic music around the *Magna Mater*, but, assuming Bury's Βρομίῳ

(21) is correct, by Dionýsus. The theme has changed from the warlike response aroused by the *Magna Mater's* music to the taming and civilising influence of Dionysiac thraldom. Strabo believed that Pindar was pointing to the basic association of Greek and Phrygian orgiastic cult.[20] This is true, and is emphasised by the general designation of the revels as Βρομίου τελετάν (6), but in setting the insane and destructive influence of the *Magna Mater* against the civilising influence of Dionysus, Pindar is surely drawing a distinction between Greek and Phrygian cult in terms of the effects on those who came in contact with both. Horace, it will be argued, used this Pindaric distinction as the conceptual basis for his own contrast between Roman and oriental.

The narrative section of the dithyramb is almost entirely lost, but the outline of the subject matter, and of Pindar's treatment, can be reconstructed with some confidence. The poem was given a main and an alternative title by its Alexandrian editor: these are read by Grenfell-Hunt as ΘΡΑΣ[ ]ˊΗΡΑΚΛΗΣ ˊΗ ΚΕΡΒΕΡΟΣ ΘΗΒΑΙΟΙΣ where the first word is restored as Θρασύς. Snell, thinking that the poem narrated the entire story of Heracles' visit to the underworld, restored the first two words as Κ]ΑΤΑ[ΒΑΣΙΣ ΗΡΑΚΛΕΟΥ[Σ]. Considerations of letter spacing apart, this restoration, and Snell's thesis, is rendered unlikely by the existence of the alternative title, which suggests that Cerberus' role was central, and that his capture was not simply an episode in an extensive treatment of the entire saga. The restoration Θρασύς would point to the way Pindar treats Heracles in the poem: ϑράσος is the confident boldness of the Homeric hero which, in the fifth century, tips over into rash boldness and violence. It makes the hero go too far after he has accomplished his just aims and, for example, perpetrate atrocities on captured cities.[21]

One fragment, which, on metrical grounds, certainly belongs to this poem, establishes that Pindar's treatment of Heracles was as unfavourable as ϑρασύς would suggest:

$$- \cup - - - \; σὲ \; δ' \; ἐγὼ \; παρά \; μιν$$
$$αἰνέω \; μέν, \; Γηρυόνα, \; τὸ \; δὲ \; μὴ \; Δί$$
$$φίλτερον \; σιγῷμι \; πάμπαν \cdot - \cup - - |||$$

Fr. 81 (Sn.–Mae.).

(... I praise you, Geryon, as against him; but I would say nothing that displeases Zeus ....) The poet gives his own novel opinion; he actually criticises Heracles' conduct in the tenth labour (the cattle of Geryon) and

118

praises the monster. The explanation emerges in the source for the fragment, Aelius Aristides (*Oratio περὶ ῥητορικῆς* II p. 70 D), who continues, apparently paraphrasing Pindar: οὐ γὰρ εἰκός, φησίν, ἁρπαζομένων τῶν ὄντων καθῆσθαι παρ' ἑστίᾳ καὶ κακὸν εἶναι. Rather than play the coward, Geryon stoutly resisted the unjust removal of his property by the mighty Heracles. The allusion to the Geryon episode, and the paradoxical verdict, seem to have been introduced by Pindar as a brief apostrophe in order to point the moral and to assist in the understanding of the main theme, Heracles' defeat of Cerberus. Pindar later returned to his criticism of Heracles in the poem which starts νόμος ὁ πάντων βασιλεύς (*Fr.* 169 (Sn.-Mae.)). A new portion of this poem, *Fr.* 169,6ff. (Sn.-Mae.) = *p.Oxy.* XXVI,2450 col.2 and col.3, shows the hero using appalling savagery in the eighth labour, the mares of Diomedes (20ff.), and there too Pindar alludes to Geryon to point the moral (4ff.).[22]

The evidence for the later view of Pindar's treatment of Cerberus as 'tragic' is found in Tertullian:

Hercules nunc populum capite praefert, nunc oleastrum nunc apium. habes tragoediam Cerberi, habes Pindarum atque Callimachum qui et Apollinem numerat interfecto Delphyne dracone lauream induisse qua supplicem.

De Corona 7

tragoedia Cerberi is not a normal way of referring to the twelfth labour; yet *habes* implies that the reader should be well acquainted with this abnormal term. Although it is not specifically stated, we must take the phrase as representing a well known view about the treatment imposed on the myth by Pindar. Given the alternative title Κέρβερος and Pindar's unfavourable portrayal of Heracles, we must, with Turyn, refer Tertullian's notice to *Dithyramb* 2.

It is most unlikely that Pindar himself regarded his treatment of Cerberus as a *tragoedia*; it is the later interpretation of *Dithyramb* 2 as a *tragoedia* which primarily concerns us.[23] A possible indication of the background of Pindar's treatment and of the origins of the later interpretation is contained in accounts of the Cerberus–Heracles encounter where the beast offers little resistance to the hero, and is terrified from the start. The best example occurs at Seneca *Hercules Furens* 791ff.: *ut propior stetit/Iovis natus, antro sedit incertus canis/leviterque timuit.*[24] It is possible that Pindar, drawing on some such version of the encounter, has rationalised in Dionysiac terms Heracles' ability to subdue and terrify Cerberus by his presence alone. Pindar gives

119

prominence in the introduction to the Dionysiac power over wild beasts; he rationalises Artemis' powers in Dionysiac terms; and it is also relevant that Dionysus himself subdued Cerberus by his presence alone.[25] It is a fair assumption, therefore, that Pindar's Cerberus, in thrall to a 'Dionysiac' Heracles, was incapable of resisting him. The poet's incidental praise of Geryon's resistance indicates his particular interest in the two monsters' reactions to attack, and he may be contrasting Geryon's robustness with Cerberus' helpless timidity. But Heracles will still have used savage and unnecessary violence on the helpless Cerberus: this is the point of the title Θρασὺς Ἡρακλῆς, and the notion is supported by the persuasive parallels which Ostwald finds between *Dithyramb* 2 and Pindar's treatment of Heracles' attack on Diomedes in *Fr.* 169 (Sn.-Mae.).[26]

The humiliation of an already defeated tyrant, no matter how dreadful his previous conduct, is a pitiable and 'tragic' spectacle. Tragedians, of course, were sensitive to the point and could employ a range of devices, usually involving chorus reaction, to forestall a sympathetic reaction, if this was appropriate, or, conversely, to excite pity. As a 'tragic' figure, Cerberus will have been analogous to Euripides' Pentheus: Cerberus is reduced from monstrous power and tyrannical status – Pindar gives him not three but a hundred heads[27] to enhance his traditional dreadfulness – to powerlessness in the face of the 'Dionysiac' Heracles and thence to pitiable humiliation at the hands of his θρασύς persecutor. There are two points at issue in the poem: the immoderate use of violence by the hero, and the reactions of the adversary to the presence of a superior power.

3. The Interpretation of *Odes* 1,37

> Nunc est bibendum, nunc pede libero
> pulsanda tellus, nunc Saliaribus
>   ornare pulvinar deorum
>   tempus erat dapibus, sodales.
>
> antehac nefas depromere Caecubum
> cellis avitis, dum . . .

The conventional interpretation of this passage is as follows: the occasion is the arrival of the news of Cleopatra's death, this being indicated by the similarity of *nunc est bibendum* to the opening words of Alcaeus' poem on the death of the tyrant Myrsilus, νῦν χρῆ μεθύσθην –*Fr.*332(LP). Horace in essence says to his drinking companions (*sodales*) 'Now (at last[28]) we can celebrate; it was wrong to do so before this moment, while Cleopatra was threatening Rome.' He envisages part 'Greek' and part Roman celebrations – Greek symposiastic drinking and uninhibited dancing, and a Roman *lectisternium*.

It is not clear, in this mixture of religious and secular, public and private celebration, who is to do what, and why. Radical reinterpretation is necessary in order to give a coherent context and purpose to the poem. One point which ought to be self-evident can be made as a preliminary. This is that the *sodales*, and they alone, are to perform the activities indicated in the first stanza; this will be confirmed below, but it may be noted here that if this were not the case, the direct address to them, combined as it is with the gerund *bibendum* (1) and the gerundive *pulsanda* (2), would have no point whatsoever.

The first task is to establish the nature of the contrast between the three *nunc* clauses and the *antehac* clause. *antehac*, unqualified, may mean either 'hitherto', i.e. 'up to this point in time; or merely 'once', 'aforetimes'.[29] Commentators here give it the former sense, thus producing a sharp and precisely defined temporal distinction between it and the *nunc* clauses. On this supposition a contrast must be intended between a religious embargo on a celebratory symposium with drinking of Caecuban, which has been observed up to this moment, and a new-found freedom to carouse; the natural paraphrase is: 'Now at last we may celebrate in carousal; . . . hitherto, this was sinful'. But the gerund *est bibendum* suggests not freedom to drink, but obligation to drink, and the correct translation is: 'Now, there must be drinking; . . . once, it was sinful to carouse', with the punctuation as shown.

Moreover it is necessary to translate *antehac* as 'once'. The word is given temporal reference not by the preceding *nunc* clauses, but by the following *dum* clause, which explains when it was sinful to carouse and why. It was wrong because – and so long as – the queen threatened the destruction of the Capitol; and we later learn that those insane ambitions ended at Actium (*sed minuit furorem*, 12) so that *dum . . . parabat* refers only to the period before the battle. In *Odes* 1,37 Horace describes events, namely the pursuit of Cleopatra and the Alexandrian campaign, which took place a considerable time after Actium. Cleopatra presented no threat to the *imperium* after Actium, and no threat of any kind after Octavian's pursuit. The time described in *dum . . . parabat* is therefore well in the past. It is not the time coming immediately before *nunc*. If it were objected that this interpretation uses later sections of the ode to explain earlier ones, it could be answered that this is a legitimate procedure with Horatian odes and that in any case lines 5-32 constitute a single period.[30]

To sum up: *antehac nefas* (*erat* understood), qualified as it is by the contents of the *dum* clause, stands in opposition to *sed minuit* and not to the *nunc* clauses of the first stanza. *antehac nefas* has no application to the period between Actium and the present time, and it must therefore be translated 'Once, it was sinful'. The words *antehac nefas* etc. take us back to the very start of the narrative, and in fact refer to the conventional 'before' situation in what will be seen to be a modified version of the narrative scheme discussed in §2. Two consequences follow from what has been said: first, *nefas depromere* must refer to the cessation of normal symposiastic drinking at the start of the conflict, and not to the postponement of a supposed special celebratory symposium until the present time. Second, the temporal distinction between 'now' and 'once' is quite different from that between 'now' and 'hitherto': the three cases of *nunc* no longer carry the nuance 'at last', and the natural emphasis is in fact transferred on to the second or third words of the clause which they introduce. This is where the real area of contrast lies: Horace intends a contrast between a religious obligation not to drink observed before Actium, and an obligation, presumably religious, to drink now. It is therefore unlikely that *est bibendum* refers to symposiastic carousal. It is true that Alcaeus' νῦν χρῆ μεθύσθην does refer to a symposium, but one at which the normal obligations of conduct are paradoxically reversed: the drinkers are to get roaring drunk[31] and are to celebrate a man's death in a manner deliberately intended to offend normal standards of conduct on such occasions.[32] That is an index of Alcaeus' hatred for Myrsilus. There is no drunkenness in Horace's first stanza, nor any unseemly celebrations of an enemy's death; if there is any reminiscence of Alcaeus, it serves only to highlight the propriety of the *sodales*' conduct.

If the adjective *Saliaribus* be left aside for the moment then lines 2-4 (*nunc Saliaribus/ornare pulvinar deorum/tempus erat dapibus*) can clearly be seen to refer to the *lectisternium*, a ceremony not to be confused with the *supplicatio*. The *lectisternium* was normally performed in times of danger, but very occasionally on a *festus dies*. [33] Images of the gods were placed on their respective couches (*pulvinaria*) in front of which the *VIIviri Epulonum* set a sacrificial meal. Horace's singular *pulvinar* is difficult, but may be explained by metrical exigency. *ornare* translates the formulaic Greek κοσμεῖν which is regularly used in descriptions of Greek sacred banquets, but which is applied not to the κλίνη (the *pulvinar*) but to preparation of the table (τράπεζα) holding the food.[34] The Greek table decoration has no ritual or formulaic Roman equivalent. By importing a Greek formula into the equivalent Roman ceremony, Horace introduces a nuance of literary 'unreality' and 'timelessness' to his allusion to an actual Roman event.

The syntactical departure from the gerund and gerundive of the first two *nunc* clauses indicates clearly that prescription has been abandoned. With the removal of the nuance 'at last' from *nunc, tempus* need not be taken in a strict temporal sense and may be translated 'fitting time', 'appropriate occasion'. The imperfect *erat* derives from the Greek use of imperfects of verbs denoting propriety, obligation etc., to express what ought to be, but is not.[35] The construction need not throw undue emphasis on the negation of the desired state of events, but may simply make clear that the speaker is talking in hypothetical terms. *tempus erat* does not always carry this force in Latin, but here the combination with *nunc* is decisive: compare *Ars Poetica* 19 (on the inappropriate use of purple patches), *sed nunc non erat his locus* (where *locus* also means καιρός); the purple patches ought not to be there, but they are.[36]

We may now turn to the adjective *Saliaribus* (2). At *Odes* 1,37, 2ff., the speaker suggests that the nature of the occasion is such that it would be appropriate to celebrate a *lectisternium* using Salian food. Yet the speaker does not expect his suggestion that the gargantuan Salian *cenae* should be introduced into the different ritual context of sacred *dapes* to be taken literally and seriously; rather he is making a comment on the nature of the occasion, namely that it is worthy of celebration on this scale. The 'Salian *lectisternium*' is an imaginary concept designed to comment on the extraordinary religious obligations arising from the present occasion, and the significance of the activities which will actually take place, the drinking and the dancing. Normal ritual response is inadequate, and these activities, the religious purpose of which is now confirmed, are to be performed in an attempt to fulfill the abnormal obligations. Since the third *nunc* clause comments on the nature and purpose of the activities described in the first two, it should not be assumed that the polysyllabic *Saliaribus* is used simply in its derivative sense 'very lavish'; it also directs us to the contemporary functions of the Salian *collegium*, the significance of which will be discussed in §4. As we shall see there, it is the *Salii* who are the *sodales* singing this choral dithyramb and not the *VIIviri Epulonum*, even though the Salian speaker is talking not of Salian banquets but of the *lectisternium* of the *VIIviri*.

The religious drinking and dancing are the adjuncts to the delivery of a choral dithyramb by the *sodales*. The literary association of drinking and dithyramb performance is as old as Archilochus (*Fr.*77D): ὡς Διωνύσοι' ἄνακτος καλὸν ἐξάρξαι μέλος/οἶδα διθύραμβον οἴνῳ συγκεραυνωθεὶς φρένας. *pede libero* suggests the wild foot movements of the dithyrambic dance[37] but it also alludes to the traditional view of the dithyramb as 'unmetrical'.[38] The best parallel for the latter allusion is Persius *Satire* 1, 13: *scribimus inclusi, numeros ille, hic pede liber*. Lines 5f. (*antehac nefas depromere Caecubum/cellis avitis*) support the thesis that the ode is imagined by Horace as a choral ode and that Horace's normal lyric *persona* is absent. The lines refer, as we have seen, to the suspension of normal symposia during the period before Actium; but Caecuban was the finest wine, the drinkers had houses with *cellae*, and the houses were ancestral (*avitis*). The drinkers are well born and wealthy Romans, with whom Horace would not number himself; nor would he refer to his own symposia in this way.[39] The *sodales* speak as a group (note the plural *cellis*), they are noble Romans, and they 'unconsciously' reveal their status by automatically referring to normal symposia in terms of *cellae* and Caecuban.

Although the use of the plural vocative in self address by the full chorus is found in Pindar, as is the use of an opening gerund with its suggestion of absolute duty,[40] the first stanza, with its imperative statements addressed to the *sodales*, is probably to be attributed to a chorus leader in the traditional role of *exarchōn* of the dithyrambic chorus.[41] His introductory suggestions and scene-setting occupy one sentence and one stanza; the full chorus then responds with the single period which constitutes the remainder of the poem. For the same movement in tragedy, compare Euripides *Hercules Furens* 760f., where the *coryphaeus* probably speaks alone to the chorus:[42] γέροντες, οὐκέτ᾽ ἐστι δυσσεβὴς ἀνήρ./ σιγᾷ μέλαθρα· πρὸς χοροὺς τραπώμεθα. The chorus responds with a delighted song (764ff.).

In *Odes* 1,37 we do not yet know the occasion of the dithyramb, the identity of the singers, or the nature of the extraordinary event which has rendered normal ritual response inadequate. The main narrative answers these questions. The following exposition of the narrative attempts to show how Horace combines 'tragic' and 'heroic' themes. The structure of the poem is designed to accommodate this combination, and the narrative moves to and fro between distinct 'tragic' and 'heroic' sections, via short bridge passages which appear to continue what precedes, but which in fact properly belong with what follows. It will also be argued that Horace introduces concealed 'Dionysiac' references throughout the poem. In isolation, some of the words concerned could not plausibly be given such force, but taken together, in the context of a dithyramb, they do constitute a continuous motif, which helps to give the poem conceptual unity.[43]

Antehac (5) introduces a recollection of the *sodales'* reactions to the threats of Cleopatra: it takes us back to the very start of the story, and functions as what was described in the second section as the 'before' situation in a particular type of heroic narrative. The conventional 'before' situation is one of communal fear or debasement in the face of a particularly dreadful threat or oppression; the *sodales'* unconventional reaction, pious abstinence from pleasure, immediately characterises them favourably. The clause *dum Capitolio/regina dementis ruinas/funus et imperio parabat* (6ff.) explains when and why it was wrong to hold symposia; but it also belongs equally with what follows, and acts as a bridge between the 'before' picture of the heroic narrative and the first tragic passage. The summary of Cleopatra's planned aggression against Rome gives us two hints for the interpretation of the woman and her character: she was a *regina*, a woman and an oriental queen, and her intentions merit the epithet *dementis*. The third stanza supplies some of the background to these hints: *contaminato cum grege turpium/morbo virorum, quidlibet impotens/sperare fortunaque dulci/ebria* (9ff.). The description of the followers as eunuchs contrasts with *regina* (*virorum* is ironic) and characterises the nature of the monarchy. The keynote is corruption. The flock of perverts and eunuchs in the service of an oriental queen recalls the effeminate and mutilated devotees of Cybele, and in this context the collective noun *grex*, denoting the mindless and indiscriminate group in the thrall of its mistress, pinpoints the reference; compare (with Nisbet-Hubbard *ad loc.*) Martial 3, 91, 2: *semiviro Cybeles cum grege.*[44] Horace suggests that Cleopatra has the same effect on her followers as does Cybele: she corrupts them. *contaminato* should carry full verbal weight, and be read as 'corrupted', rather than 'corrupt'. *turpium morbo* refers primarily to sexual perversion[45] but the nuance of infectious corruption is also present. Livy's vocabulary in his account of the Bacchanalian scandals is relevant to the thesis that Horace is talking about a special kind of infection. E.g. 39, 9: *huius mali labes ex Etruria Romam, velut contagione morbi, penetravit*; 39, 15: *primum igitur mulierum magna pars est et is fons mali huiusce fuit: deinde simillimi feminis mares, stuprati et constupratores*; 39, 15: ⟨The gods . . .⟩ *suum numen sceleribus libidinibusque contaminari indigne ferebant.* Pentheus regarded ordinary Dionysiac enthusiasm as an infection which could be passed on by physical contact.[46] Pindar's account of the spread, from the music of the *Magna Mater*, of noise and madness and the stirring of weapons of destruction and war, is a good literary representation of the 'infectiousness' correctly ascribed to orgiastic ritual and influence.

The description of the court, coming after the threat of *funus imperio* is laughable; effeminates were *imbelles* and the Roman reader would appreciate that the military threat presented by them was limited.[47] *quidlibet . . . ebria* confirms that the venture was 'tragically' doomed to failure. The progress of the tyrant who experiences success, is carried away by it, loses self control and entertains delusory ambitions, particularly of foreign conquest, is standard. Cleopatra is the tragic tyrant who will suffer reversal and fall, and the key words *sperare* (ἐλπίς) and *fortuna* (τύχη) scarcely require illustration.[48] The best parallel is Polybius' account of the 'tragic' end of Philip V: intoxicated by fortune as a punishment for past excesses, he conceived a war of aggression against Rome, which, since Rome was under divine protection, was bound ultimately to fail. The domestic policies which, according to Polybius, he undertook in preparation for the military adventure, provoked discord which extended, with 'tragic' results, to his own household.[49] Similarly, Cleopatra's aggression was bound to fail, partly through the inadequacy of a retinue corrupted by herself, and partly, perhaps, because of Roman attention to religious observance in the face of a threat to the most sacred place in the city. In any case, the *ruinae* simply cannot happen: they are the irrational fantasy of a sick mind, hence *dementis*. The transfer of the adjective from intender to intention is meant to emphasise the insanity and hopelessness of the entire enterprise. It is notable also − and this aspect will be referred to again later − that Horace gives life to the hackneyed metaphor *ebria* and draws out its drinking connotations with *dulci*, suggesting the actual taste of Cleopatra's good fortune.

Swift and inevitable military reverse removed thoughts of *ruinae:sed minuit furorem/vix una sospes navis ab ignibus* (12f.). *sed* indicates the extent to which the *furor* was diminished: it is adversative to the main verb which precedes, *nefas (erat)*, as qualified by the *dum* clause. Defeat removed her hopeless and insane ambitions to conquer Rome, the product of her *furor*, but it did nothing more. *ignibus* deliberately exaggerates the role of fireships at Actium. but fire was a type of τὸ δύσμαχον, the irresistible force, and it suggests the inevitability of defeat. As a weapon in war, it was particularly associated with Dionysus.[50] *vix una* is also an exaggeration, but it prepares for the 'heroic' confrontation between the lone Caesar and the lone Cleopatra which follows.

Horace concentrates on Cleopatra's mental response to the defeat. The syntactically parallel clause which follows (*mentemque . . . Caesar*, 14ff.) continues the account of her mental progression, but it acts as a bridge back to the heroic narrative and summarises what was achieved during Caesar's pursuit. The achievement is placed first and the intention

126

behind the pursuit last; the intention, *daret ut catenis/fatale monstrum* (20f.), may conveniently be considered first. *monstrum*, like its Greek equivalent, τέρας[51], can refer to monsters, and here it certainly alludes to legendary beasts of the type which Hercules cleared from the earth.[52] An Erymanthian Boar, or any such beast, could justly be called a *fatale monstrum* which had to be removed, because its very presence brought terror and destruction and made civilised life impossible. Cleopatra's powers of physical destruction had now been eliminated but, according to Horace, she was corrupted by oriental orgiastic influence (*mentemque lymphatam*, 14, see below) and she passed on her corruption and madness to those about her, with disastrous results. She was, in essence, infectious, and that is why Caesar had to pursue her after the overwhelming victory at Actium.

The suggestion that *catenis* refers to the Roman triumph and so by implication to Cleopatra's ultimate execution and that Caesar's main aim in pursuing Cleopatra was to ensure her participation in his triumph is probably incorrect, since Cleopatra evaded the triumph. It is inconceivable that Horace should imply any failure on the part of Octavian. It is much more likely that Horace is alluding to the live capture, by Hercules, of certain legendary *monstra*; the hero was given the task of capturing the Erymanthian Boar alive, and in one version he hauled Cerberus out of Hades bound in adamantine *catenae*.[53] The word does not allude to Cleopatra's ultimate fate, had she been captured, but conveys the idea of live restraint. Dionysus bound his mad victims in chains, and it may be noted that close restraint was an ancient treatment for madness, although the word regularly used for the bonds is *vincula*, not *catenae*.[54] Caesar's action was risky, in that it would mean coming to grips with an infectious *monstrum*; altruistic in that Cleopatra presented no direct threat to Italy after Actium; and moderate, in that there is no suggestion of the butchery of the adversary.

mentemque lymphatam Mareotico/redegit in veros timores/Caesar (14ff.) describes what was actually achieved during the pursuit, and must therefore be compared carefully with the intention. *lymphatam*, used in all periods of Latin literature specifically to denote orgiastic frenzy, is here combined with *Mareotico* in an arresting oxymoron[55] which confirms that Horace intended an orgiastic connotation. The specification of the Egyptian wine takes the idea a stage further: just as he exploits the drinking metaphor in *ebria* to comment on Cleopatra's mental state, so in this phrase Horace uses the consumption of oriental wine to suggest the admission into her mind of oriental orgiastic frenzy. *lymphatam* may also

127

refer to panic, or irrational terror, with or without Dionysiac asso-
ciations,[56] and Horace may wish to suggest Dionysus' power to inject
panic in enemy troops.[57] Caesar took this state of mind and reduced it to
veros timores. Why does Horace use the plural when the singular would
have scanned equally well, and what is the force of *veros*? The plural
timores is so uncommon as to suggest derivation from the much
commoner Greek plural φόβοι,[58] which is often used of irrational fears and
fantasies arising from an abnormal psychological condition and may also
be used of divinely inspired fear.[59] Of itself, therefore, *timores* may
denote a special kind of fear, abnormally induced and with irrational
associations; as such, it looks back to *lymphatam* and highlights the
'irrational terror' aspect of its meaning. *veros* is to be regarded as the
paradoxical qualification of *timores* and the pointer to the true contrast
between it and *lymphatam*: Cleopatra's insane and frenzied terror becomes
fear of something real and substantial, of a greater power. Merely by
coming close to the queen, (*remis adurgens*, 17), Caesar has replaced
irrational terror by rational fear and madness by sanity. That was an
extraordinary and, as *timores* hints, a superhuman, achievement, which
requires explanation. We have seen that Dionysus could induce fear and
tameness by his presence alone and that Heracles, for example, may have
been invested with special 'Dionysiac' powers by Pindar. The reduction to
sanity is a different idea, and may derive from the curative function to
which all orgiastic cults, including that of Dionysus, laid claim.[60] The
most relevant parallel is *Orphic Hymn* 39, 1ff., where the Corybantic
daemon is called φόβων ἀποπαύστορα δεινῶν. If the notion that Horace
should invest Octavian with exotic Dionysiac functions seems odd, it
should be remembered that he is writing a dithyramb, in origin a cult song
for Dionysus, and that it is an artificial literary exercise. Caesar had
intended to capture and restrain the mad Cleopatra by conventional means
(*catenis*) but in the event he induced sanity and consequently removed the
essential danger of orgiastic infection by superhuman powers and without
having to catch the adversary. The achievement was thus greater than the
projected action.

The double simile at lines 17ff. assists the portrayal of Caesar as
'ancient hero', and the first part, the hawk and the doves, derives from the
conventional epic simile first found at *Iliad* 22, 139ff., where it is used to
describe Achilles' pursuit of the fleeing Hector. The second part, the hare
and the hunter, seems to have no parallel in extant epic, although the hare
itself is found as the prey of dogs (*Iliad* 10, 361) and of the eagle (*Iliad* 22,
310). The hare, like the *columba*, was proverbial in antiquity for its
cowering timidity (LSJ *s.v.* λαγώς). The literary associations of the animal

are clear from a reference, at Aeschylus *Eumenides* 25f., to the death of
Pentheus: . . . Βάκχαις ἐστρατήγησεν θεός,/λαγὼ δίκην Πενθεῖ
καταρράψας μόρον· The Horatian *lepus* would find no cover in the open,
snow-covered plains described in line 19, and even its proverbial swiftness
is offset by the speed (*citus* 18) of the *venator*; it is therefore particularly
easy prey. The Aeschylean parallel might suggest that Horace wishes to
present Cleopatra as a tragic figure to be pitied. This is not the case.
Horace erases any suggestion of pity or sympathy in his description of the
real situation which follows the simile, *daret ut catenis fatale monstrum*
(20f.). It is the reader's task to determine the relationship between simile
and 'reality' and the way in which each deepens the meaning of the other.
Just as *volantem* (16) prepares for the first, hawk and doves, part of the
simile, so the allusion in *daret . . . monstrum* to the heroic hunting and
capture of *monstra* is a throwback to the second, hunting, part of the
simile. Horace intends the reader to consider the two hunting passages
together and to reconcile the apparently conflicting pictures which they
present. The real point is that when this *fatale monstrum* was hunted by
Caesar, she assumed the status of a scared hare to a swift hunter, and was
easy prey. A confrontation which, in prospect, seemed likely to be a
conventional epic struggle between hero and beast, became, by virtue of
the hero's special powers and of the beast's reactions to them, very unepic
and unheroic.

Horace may be reinforcing this point by the incongruous use of
Haemoniae (20): hunting in Thessaly is conventionally associated with
lions, bears and boars, not with hares. Indeed, if we are meant to see a
direct allusion to Achilles' pursuit of Hector in the hawk and doves simile,
citus venator probably refers to the early life as a hunter of the
swift-footed Achilles in Chiron's Thessalian home. Pindar, the earliest
source for Chiron's guardianship, stresses Achilles' reliance on his swiftness
when hunting (*Nemean* 3, 41ff.). Horace may, therefore, be saying in
effect 'it was as if Achilles was hunting hares'. The hawk was the fastest of
all birds (*Iliad* 22, 139) and the simile emphasises the speed of the hunter;
the implication is that Caesar could have caught Cleopatra if he had so
wished, and as he had originally intended. The fact that Cleopatra was
reduced to the status of a timid hare, and did not need to be captured,
revealed Caesar's special powers, and the fact that Caesar did not press on
to catch this 'easy prey' revealed his restraint in action as well as in
intention.[61]

To return, finally, to the sympathetic nuance present in *molles
columbas* and *leporem*, both creatures are only pitiable insofar as they
normally face inevitable and violent death from a powerful pursuer which

terrifies them. Cleopatra was not butchered, and is not to be pitied. But by introducing the doves and the hare into the simile, Horace briefly manipulates the reader's sympathies, and gives him a preliminary guideline for the interpretation of Cleopatra's final fall.

The first stanza of the final section acts as a bridge back from the heroic to the tragic narrative, continuing the voyage to Alexandria from Cleopatra's point of view. Horace claims that she had two alternatives: to go into obscure exile, or to return to Alexandria and face death. The choice between death and exile is one commonly presented to tragic figures, particularly after a return to sanity; and death by suicide is normally considered the superior and preferable alternative.[62] The fact that she had a choice must affect the interpretation of *generosius/perire quaerens* (21f.): if *generosius* is taken with *perire* alone, the implication is that death was certain, and only the manner of it a matter of choice. This produces the logically absurd paraphrase 'seeking a more noble manner for her certain death ... she rejected the safety of exile'. Moreover, on this reading, *generosius* is made to contrast with *catenis*, which, however, we found to mean not 'the triumph — followed by death' but 'live restraint'. *generosius* should in fact be taken with *quaerens* (for the separation of adverb from participle, compare *Satires* 1, 9, 8: *misere discedere quaerens*); the absence of fear and the rejection of exile then follow quite naturally (*nec muliebriter/expavit ensem nec latentis/classe cita reparavit oras,* 22ff.), and the contrast is between the fearlessness with which she seeks death and the *timores* she felt in the face of Caesar. The contrast throws into relief the latter's superhuman powers. The transferred epithet *latentis* (23) suggests 'skulking', a suitable posture in exile had the queen been a 'maenad' still. The fact that she now rejects such 'skulking' is another pointer to her regained sanity.[63] *nec muliebriter* (22) characterises the sane Cleopatra as a tragic woman without the instinctive feminine reactions: she is a figure in the grim Medea mould, who has the emotional reactions of a man, and who feels no regrets for the ruination, through her own agency, of all around her. She is *ferox invictaque.*[64] We see the Roman *ensis* through her sane eyes and feel no pity at the remorseless advance of the military machine, since the queen herself is not distressed. This, together with her new, grim stature, prepares us for the culmination of the tragedy:

> ausa et iacentem visere regiam
> vultu sereno, fortis et asperas
>   tractare serpentis, ut atrum
>   corpore combiberet venenum,
>
> deliberata morte ferocior   (25-9)

The deliberate action *visere*, the reaction denoted in *vultu sereno*, and the suggestion of fixed purpose after mature consideration which is present in the *ut* clause and *deliberata*, all reinforce the picture of a new and awesome sanity. *iacentem regiam* ironically completes the picture of political and military downfall: the *regina* who had planned *ruinae* for the Capitol, the *pignus imperii*, now sees the *regia*, the symbol of her own monarchical rule, 'flattened'. There are three further, 'Dionysiac', ironies in the stanza. *iacentem* is a historical inaccuracy, but Dionysus always dealt thus with the palaces of tyrants.[65] The irony of *tractare serpentis*, where *asperas* is carefully introduced to convey the sensation of touch, is that snake-handling with impunity was an integral feature of much orgiastic cult.[66] The most obvious irony is *corpore combiberet:* previously, Cleopatra's mind had been polluted, in metaphorical terms, by drinking; now she poisons her body by 'drinking in' the corrupting black venom.[67]

As a *regina*, Cleopatra suffered a complete reverse, which hardly distressed her. But she was not personally humiliated, and her driving motivation was pride, the wish to avoid humiliation: *saevis Liburnis scilicet invidens/privata deduci superbo/non humilis mulier triumpho* (30ff.). *scilicet* introduces the chorus' conjectural reconstruction of Cleopatra's thoughts in an attempt to explain the suicide, and these may be paraphrased thus: 'Why should I, who have lost my monarchy, allow myself to be taken, on the ships which did the damage, to be humiliated personally in the official triumph for their victories?' *scilicet* may also strike a sarcastic note, pointing to the irony of *privata* which, used of a queen whose *regnum* no longer exists, may allude to the denial to the *privatus* of any formal role in the business of *Res Publica*. The terminology of Augustus' references to his triumphs at *Res Gestae* 4, 3 is relevant: *in triumphis meis ducti sunt ante currum meum reges aut regum liberi novem*. The chorus suggests that as a *privata* Cleopatra has no place in a Roman triumph.

Complex cause and effect is at work. The lone Caesar reduced Cleopatra to sanity, thus removing the real danger; when sane, she was *ferocior*, a Medea type. She was thus led to exercise the prerogative of the rational tragic figure, to choose death rather than exile and suicide rather than humiliation. The suicide was tragic and ironic, but it did avoid personal humiliation, and we may feel awe, but not pity. We also see the Alexandrian campaign, which destroyed the very symbol of her monarchy, through her sane and uncaring eyes, and we feel no pity for that either. Caesar's' heroic action led ultimately to Cleopatra's absence from his

131

triumph, and the official Roman campaign, whereby she became a *privata*, rendered her absence appropriate. Horace has distinguished the *regina* from the individual woman, and has dissociated Caesar as 'hero' from the conventional military effort. These elements, woven into the separate sections of tragic and heroic narrative, are brought together and made to interact at the end of the poem.

4. The Occasion of *Odes* 1, 37

It has always been assumed that the occasion which inspired *Odes* 1, 37 was the death of Cleopatra. This is inherently unlikely, since it would imply that Cleopatra was enough of a danger to mankind and Rome after the pursuit for her death to be worth celebrating, and would thus suggest that Caesar had achieved nothing by his heroic pursuit. In the terms in which this poem presents the situation Cleopatra's death was a matter of indifference to Rome. This is emphasised by the representation of her departure for exile as a practical alternative to death. The real occasion is pinpointed by the last word, *triumpho*, which brings us back to present time and to the situation in the first stanza. Octavian celebrated a *triplex triumphus* in August 29 BC for the Actian, Alexandrian and Illyrican campaigns; two of these campaigns are mentioned in the poem, and they are recalled at the end in *saevis Liburnis* (30). In truth, Octavian was deeply annoyed that Cleopatra escaped his triumph,[68] but the internal logic of Horace's poem accounts for her absence in a way which brings credit to Octavian while it simultaneously points to the constitutional appositeness of her absence (see above § 3).

One reason for singing a dithyramb on this occasion was Caesar's performance of a heroic deed and the fact that the powers he revealed were 'Dionysiac'. However, a close etymological relationship, widely accepted in antiquity, existed between the word *triumphus* and the Dionysiac cult title Θρίαμβος, hence also between *triumphus* and διθύραμβος.[69] But *triumpho* is not simply another 'Dionysiac' reference; it has recently been argued in this connection that when Roman poets wrote poems celebrating triumphs, they regarded them as dithyrambs, and that this conflation is one example of the process by which poems for purely Roman occasions were associated with traditional Greek genres.[70] No triumph poem earlier than *Odes* 1, 37 has yet been identified, and Horace may have been the first to have made literary capital out of the *triumphus/Θρίαμβος/διθύραμβος* relationship.[71] If so, then he was probably particularly conscious of what he was doing, namely associating a real occasion in Roman public life with the traditional Greek response to a

132

heroic deed, the coming of a victor, etc., the dithyramb, in order to produce a wholly literary celebration of the occasion of Octavian's *triplex triumphus* with little real basis in the occasion itself. The literary unreality of the celebration of a real Roman occasion is important for the interpretation of *Saliaribus* (2).

In a poem written for Octavian's triumph in 29 BC, *Saliaribus* would direct the reader to the inclusion, by a Senatorial decree of the same year, of Octavian's name in the *Carmen Saliare*.[72] This, the only quasi-divine honour which Augustus later mentioned in the *Res Gestae*, placed him on a level with the gods in whose hands lay the safety of the Roman state in war.[73] Vergil alludes to this honour in his account of the origins of the observances at the *Ara Maxima* in honour of Hercules (*Aeneid* 8, 280ff.). Evander recounts to Aeneas, in a heroic narrative of the type discussed above, the story of Hercules' conquest of the *monstrum* Cacus; a sacrificial feast is prepared and two choruses of Salians enter, *qui carmine laudes/Herculeas et facta ferunt* (287f.). This hymn to Hercules summarises the traditional labours, alludes to Hercules' elevation to divine status (301) and then proceeds to the main element, the Cacus encounter. The meaning of the Salian hymn in relation to Octavian's triumph is made clear through their collocation in *Aeneid* 8, and the attempts made by scholars to draw parallels between Hercules and Octavian as θεοὶ ἐπιφανεῖς are certainly correct in substance.[74]

Horace's chorus comprises a group of noble Romans gathered together to observe religious obligations; *sodales* is to be read not as 'drinking companions' but as the designation of members of a religious *sodalitas*. Two arguments would support identification of the *sodalitas* as the *collegium* of Salian priests. The first arises from the re-definition of the contrast between the *nunc* clauses and the time denoted by *antehac*, and the conclusion that the natural emphasis and the area of contrast falls on the second and third words of the *nunc* clauses: in the second *nunc* clause, the emphasis falls on *pede libero*, on the lack of rhythm of the dance to be performed now; there may, therefore, be implicit contrast between this rhythmless dance and another rhythmical, dance performed during the period before Actium in response to Cleopatra's threats, that is, the heavy triple-beat *tripudium* of the Salian priests.[75] Second, Horace might be drawing on the common view of the Salians as the Roman 'equivalent' of the Greek Curetes: Pindar's orgiastic revels are for the most part the ritual of the Curetes writ large, and Strabo adduces the Pindaric passage in his discussion of them.[76] Since the Curetes were the attendants of Cybele, who could better praise the superhuman Caesar, conqueror of an oriental, orgiastic queen, in the year 29 BC, than their Roman counterparts, the Salian priests? Horace has distanced the rites to be performed from the real observances of Roman religion, and his *lectisternium* is a notional literary conflation of Greek and Roman elements. He has associated his celebration of a real event, the *triumphus*, with the traditional Greek dithyrambic response to analogous situations; and we need not be surprised that he has taken another element from the real world of 29 BC, the Salian *collegium*, and put his literary celebration into its collective mouth.

The dithyramb is sung in honour not of Dionysus, but of Octavian. He stands revealed as a Herculean θεὸς ἐπιφανής, as more than human and much more than a *triumphator*, and the revelation has rendered normal religious observance inadequate, thus prompting the Salians' unprecedented dithyramb. This is how Horace represents in literary terms the quasi-divine honours bestowed on Octavian by the Senate and through the agency of the Salian priests in 29 BC. The association of Octavian with Dionysus need not occasion surprise, despite Antony's much publicised identification of himself as a new Dionysus: the story was circulated that the god had deserted Antony for Octavian at Alexandria.[77] Dionysus himself had a connection of long standing with *Italia*.[78] Moreover, Alexander the Great had fostered the notion of himself as the successor in world conquest of his legendary ancestors Dionysus and Heracles, and Pompey's studied imitation of the king drew Roman attention to the two figures as models for a living general.[79]

4. *Dithyramb* 2 as a Model for *Odes* 1, 37

Several general Pindaric features can be observed in *Odes* 1, 37 before its particular debt to *Dithyramb* 2 is considered. After the introductory stanza, the poem consists of a single period which, *monte decurrens velut amnis*, runs for twenty-eight lines; Horace employs majestic periods elsewhere when he wishes to recall Pindar; but here, the technique is taken to an extreme of *audacitas*, which the poet may have thought particularly suitable for a Pindaricising dithyramb. Horace's swift moving and unified narrative of the complex events of 31/30 BC is achieved by selection of detail: he concentrates almost completely on Cleopatra's internal reactions, and the battles at Actium and Alexandria are made to seem almost mere events within Cleopatra's mind (the former battle is despatched in one line, the latter in one word). The model and the essential literary precedent for this artistic telescoping of events was supplied by Greek choral lyric and by Pindar above all. In lines 14-21, the summary at the beginning of the account of the pursuit of what was achieved therein, the amplification on how it was achieved, and the return, by implication, to the beginning in the concluding *ut* clause, all this is modelled on Pindaric technique.[80] Syndikus has commented on the Pindaric origin of the important link words *sed* (12) and *quae* (21).[81]

It is a technical borrowing which supplies the first direct link between *Odes* 1, 37 and Pindar *Dithyramb* 2: Pindar's opening antithesis, with implicit contrast between its two parts, was probably a revolutionary start to a dithyramb and an important stylistic pointer to his innovations in narrative technique. Horace too has opened his dithyramb with an antithesis, contrasting past and present in different terms. In Horace's case the antithesis comprises the juxtaposed 'before' and 'after' sections of a heroic narrative, the 'action' section being placed third; it is less certain that Pindar is adapting the heroic narrative pattern in the same way. As a signpost to direct imitation, this technical borrowing is not obvious; but it did not have to be. By composing a choral dithyramb, Horace invited the reader to go back to the accepted classical master of the genre, Pindar, and to look hard in the Alexandrian edition of the *Dithyrambs* for a possible model.

The essential clue, however, to Horace's use of *Dithyramb* 2 as the direct model for *Odes* 1, 37 is twofold: first, Horace's unambiguous designation of Cleopatra as a *monstrum*, which brings her into comparison with Cerberus; and second, his implication that Caesar, the 'ancient hero' who set out to enchain her, is a Hercules. Onto this hero/adversary relationship, Horace has grafted characterisations which correspond with Pindar's novel contrast between the influence of the Phrygian *Magna Mater* and the Greek Dionysus: Cleopatra becomes the oriental queen associated with eastern orgiastic cult and its effects, the insane arouser of war, while Caesar is the tamer of the beast. Pindar rationalises Artemis' powers in Dionysiac terms, and may have done the same for Heracles; Caesar's power to reduce Cleopatra to fear and sanity is clearly superhuman, relating closely to the powers of Dionysus and the effects claimed for his rites. On the other hand, the 'official' Roman weapons of war, so tersely described in *ignibus* (13) and *ensem* (23) might be derived, with conscious irony, from the destructive weapons stirred by the Cybele-worship in the Pindaric revels – πῦρ (16) and ἔγχος (17).

Horace almost certainly took the idea of a 'tragic' dithyramb from a current view of *Dithyramb* 2. But whereas Pindar's Cerberus may have been a Pentheus figure, pitiably humiliated, Cleopatra, a Medea figure, is ultimately neither humiliated nor pitiable. Her fearful reaction to the

'Dionysiac' Caesar is similar to that of Cerberus to Heracles, but she is permitted to go on to face an army which did not frighten her. Pindar discredited his hero, probably by making him use excessive violence on an already tamed and fearful beast; Caesar leaves Cleopatra alone, enabling her to exercise rational choice and to reveal grim personal stature. The difference lies in the different uses to which the two heroes put their superhuman powers, and the contrast between Pindar's Heracles and the Caesar of *Odes* 1, 37 will not have been lost on the reader.

The reconstruction of *Dithyramb* 2 given in §2 was conjectural; yet there are points of correspondence between it and *Odes* 1, 37 which are fundamental, and are unlikely to be coincidental. The Pindaric poem, with its concern about the use and abuse of heroic power and about the reactions of a weaker adversary, its contrast between oriental and 'civilised', its association of Heracles and Dionysus and its extrapolation from the ritual of the Curetes, was a well chosen model which fitted both the occasion being celebrated and the extraordinary honours given to Octavian in 29 BC. Yet, and this was Horace's chief concern, it permitted, within its innovatory framework, much conceptual remodelling directed towards the greater glory of Octavian.

In many ways, the poem is the opposite of what it seems: instead of a personal, monodic reaction to the death of Cleopatra, modelled on the drunken and indecorous celebration of Alcaeus, we have a Pindaricising dithyramb, concerned with more elevated themes and written for the *adventus* at his official triumph of a θεὸς ἐπιφανής. The poem reflects contemporary propaganda, but its real import is so concealed as to scotch any suggestion that the poet is acting as a propagandist in the normal sense of the word. Horace does not seek to persuade or to mould opinions; his purpose is to use contemporary events, transposed into universal 'literary' terms, in order to suggest that literature of the highest order, in the classical tradition of Pindar, could be produced in association with the regime and under the inspiration of its exploits. The propaganda lies in the literary achievement itself and in the creation of a complex poem of lasting merit.

NOTES

1. I am grateful to Professor Francis Cairns, Mr. J.G. Howie and Mr. Oliver Taplin for valuable advice and suggestions on this paper; responsibility for its conclusions is, of course, mine alone.

2. Literature on the poem is listed in R.G.M. Nisbet and M. Hubbard *A Commentary on Horace: Odes I* Oxford (1970), (henceforth N–H) p.406 and H.P. Syndikus *Die Lyrik des Horaz* Darmstadt (1973) I pp.331ff.

3. For Alexandrian classification of the dithyramb see A.E. Harvey *CQ* N.S. 5 (1955) pp.173f.

4. See R. Jebb *Bacchylides The Poems and Fragments* Cambridge (1905) repr. Hildesheim (1967) p.39 for helpful remarks on this testimonium.

5. See Francis Cairns *Generic Composition in Greek and Roman Poetry* Edinburgh (1972) p.97 and the examples cited there.

6. J.V. Luce *CQ* N.S. 13 (1963) p.254.

7. A. Pickard-Cambridge *Dithyramb Tragedy and Comedy* 2nd. ed. revised T.B.L. Webster Oxford (1962) pp.1ff.

8. Bacch. 18,42ff. (Sn.–Mae.); Pind. *Frr.* 72, 73, *74, 70b, 70c, 85 (Sn.–Mae.); Prat. *Fr.* 708 (PMG).

9. Luce *art.cit.* p.257. Kiessling-Heinze comment (on line 7): 'Er sieht die Königin wie eine μαινάς der tragischen Bühne'. This is correct.

10. F.W. Walbank *BICS* 2 (1955) pp.4ff.

11. The parallels adduced by Grenfell-Hunt (*p. Oxy.* XIII No. 1604) and C.M. Bowra *Pindar* Oxford (1964) p.195 in support of this translation are all from late rhetoricians. *LSJ s.v.* is much closer, with 'moving straight forward'.

12. I am grateful to Mr. J.G. Howie for pointing out this parallel.

13. See L. Dissen's *Excursus de Asyndeto apud Pindarum* in his *Pindari Carmina cum Fragmentis* 2nd. ed. Gotha (1843).

14. With the important word εἰδότες (5), compare *Paean* 6, 54 = *Fr.* 52f, 54(Sn.-Mae.) (of the Muses); *Ol.* 2,86 (of the poet); Theogn. 769ff.

15. 'Greedy Heracles' jokes are removed (741f.) and A. 'frees the slaves' from jokes about beatings which 'invade their backs' causing havoc (i.e. like a legendary monster, 743ff.)

16. The perfect example occurs at Lucr. *DRN* 1,62-79 (the overthrow of 'the beast' *religio* by the 'Herculean' Epicurus); cf. also Verg. *Aen.* 8,193-267.

17. Bowra (*op.cit.* p.6) rightly comments on the uniqueness of this claim.

18. With the dative κύκλοισι of the group which benefits from an altruistic act, cf. Ar. *Peace* 749.

19. Note the ῥόμβοι τυπάνων (9), the torches (10f. and cf. Eur. *Cret. Fr.* 472,13f.), and the war-cries (ἀλαλαί, 13, see *LSJ s.v.*) and the warlike nuance in the body movements ῥιψαύχενι/σὺν κλόνῳ (13f.).

20. Strabo 10, 3, 13. . . . φησι (sc. Pindar) σοὶ μὲν κατάρχει (8) . . . . πεύκαις (11) τὴν κοινωνίαν τῶν περὶ τὸν Διόνυσον ἀποδειχθέντων νομίμων παρὰ τοῖς Ἕλλησι καὶ τῶν παρὰ τοῖς Φρυξὶ περὶ τὴν μάτερα τῶν θεῶν συνοικειῶν ἀλλήλοις.

21. Well illustrated by Aesch. *Agam.* 764ff.: φιλεῖ δὲ τίκτειν "Υβρις/ . . . "Υβρω . . . ἄμαχον ἀπόλεμον ἀνίερον,/Θράσος . . .

22. See Martin Ostwald *HSCP* 69 (1965) pp.109ff. (now reprinted in *Pindaros und Bakchylides* ed.W.C. Calder III and J. Stern, *Wege der Forschung* cxxiv Darmstadt (1970) pp.194ff.) for discussion of the unfavourable treatment of Heracles there and in *Dithyramb* 2, with interesting parallels.

23. Cf. Prop. 3, 17, 39f. (a promise to sing a dithyramb): *haec ego non humili referam memoranda coturno/qualis Pindarico spiritus ore tonat*, where *coturno* might be a specific reference to a dithyramb believed to be 'tragic'.

24. Cf. also Verg. *Aen.* 8,296f.

25. Cf. e.g. Hor. *Od.* 2, 19, 29ff.

26. See above n.22.

27. Schol. ABT *ad* Hom. *Il.* 8, 368: Πίνδαρος ... ἑκατόν ... ἔχειν αὐτὸν κεφαλάς φησιν; cf. Hor. *Od.* 2, 13, 34: *belua centiceps.*

28. E. Fraenkel *Horace* Oxford (1957) p. 159 sees a possible allusion to the anxious opening of *Epod.* 9.

29. Cf. *OLD s.v.*

30. Fraenkel *op.cit.* p.427 n.1; semicolons should not appear before *sed* (12) and *quae* (21).

31. The opening words are powerfully reinforced by †καὶ τινα† πὲρ βίαν πώνην (1f.) which places deliberate emphasis on the drunkenness.

32. Syndikus *op.cit.* I pp.331f.

33. *RE s.v. lectisternium*; the only celebration on a *festus dies* recorded by Livy is that at 29, 14, 14 (the entry into Rome of the *Magna Mater* in 204 BC).

34. *I.G.* II,949: [ἱεροφάν]της [ἀνέγραψ εν] τοὺς ἐπιφθ[έντας τήν τε] κλίνην στρῶσαι τῷ [Πλούτωνι καὶ τὴν] τράπεζαν κοσμῆσα[ι; *I.G.* II², 676,13f.: ἐπεμελήθησα[ν] δὲ καὶ τῆς στρώσεως τῆς κλί]νης καὶ τῆς κ[οσ]μή[σεως τῆς τράπεζας]. Cf. also *I.G.* II,948 (*S.I.G.³* 1022); Xen. *Cyrop.* 8, 2, 6.

35. Goodwin *Syntax of the Moods and Tenses of the Greek Verb* §§ 415ff.; Barrett on Eur. *Hipp.* 618f.

36. The function of the imperfect *erat* here has been variously explained (cf. e.g. Brink *ad loc.*; Fraenkel *op.cit.* p.324 n.3) but the Greek usage seems the most satisfactory parallel.

37. For wild foot movements cf. Prat. *Fr.* 708, 14 (PMG) (a dithyramb): ἄδε σοι δεξιᾶς καὶ ποδὸς διαρριφά·

38. Cf. Hor. *Od.* 4, 2, 11f. (of Pindar's *Dithyrambs*): *numerisque fertur/lege solutis.*

39. At *Epod.* 9, 1ff., H. implies that the celebratory Caecuban will be from Maecenas' house; his normal wine is mediocre (*Od.* 1, 9, 7; 1, 20, 1 and N-H *ad loc.*).

40. Self-address: *Paean* 6,121f.=*Fr.* 52f,121f.(Sn.-Mae.): ⟨ἰὴ⟩ ἰῆτε, νῦν, μέτρα παιηό-/ν]ων ἰῆιτε], νεόιιψ. Gerund: *Ol.* 2, 5f.: Θήρωνα ... γεγωνητέον.

41. See Pickard-Cambridge *op.cit.* index *s.v. exarchōn*; also Fraenkel *op.cit.* p.403 on chorus directions, and Francis Cairns *AJP* 92 (1971) pp.440ff. on chorus direction in the *Odes.*

42. See Wilamowitz's general introduction to this ode.

43. The principle behind this discussion is concisely formulated in the context of sustained metaphor by Francis Cairns *CQ* N.S. 24 (1974) p.97.

44. For the use of the Greek ἀγέλη in the related context of maenads see Eur. *Bacch.* 1022f.

45. Cf. Cat. 57,6: *morbosi pariter.*

46. Eur. *Bacch.* 343ff. with Dodds *ad loc.*, noting that all forms of pollution were held to be transmissable by touch.

47. Cf. e.g. Livy 39, 15: *hoc sacramento initiatos iuvenes milites faciendos censetis, Quirites*? (during the Bacchanalian scandal).

48. See, most conveniently, F.M. Cornford *Thucydides Mythistoricus* London (1907) pp.221ff. For delusions of power under Dionysiac madness see Eur. *Bacch.* 945f. with Dodds *ad loc.*

49. On Polybius' treatment cf. F.W. Walbank *JHS* 58 (1938) pp.55ff.

50. *Irresistible fire:* see Dodds on Eur. *Bacch.* 778; *Weapon of Dionysus:* Eur. *Bacch.* 622ff.; cf. Naev. *Trag.* 50f. (Ribbeck); Soph. *Ant.* 966; 1126ff.; Nonnus *Dionys.* 23, 255ff.

51. Fraenkel *op.cit.* p.160.

52. Luce *art.cit.* p.254; N-H *ad loc.*

53. Ov. *Met.* 7,412; Sen. *HF* 808; cf. 816.

54. Celsus 3, 18, 21: *ubi perperam aliquid dixit aut fecit fame, vinculis, plagis coercendus est;* cf. Ov. *Am.* 1, 7, 1f. Dionysus bound his mad victims in chains: cf. Soph. *Ant.* 955ff. The live capture of beasts was a great feat and Dionysus was praised for his capture of a live tiger, *qui vivus capi adhuc non potuit* (Varro *LL* 5,100); cf. Verg. *Aen.* 6,804f.

55. *Oxymoron:* see N-H *ad loc.*; *lymphatam:* cf. Pacuv. *Trag.* 422 (Ribbeck); Cat. 64,254f.; Verg. *Aen* 7,377; Sen. *Med.* 382ff.

56. N-H *ad loc.*

57. Eur. *Bacch.* 302ff. and Dodds *ad loc.*

58. I am grateful to Professor Cairns for this suggestion.

59. See esp. E.R. Dodds *The Greeks and the Irrational* Berkeley (1951) pp.76ff., with notes, quoting Aristides Quintilianus (who may draw on Theophrastus) on the tendency of ἐνθουσιασμοί to produce δεισιδειμονίας τε καὶ ἀλόγους ψόβους (*De Mus.* p.42 Jahn).

60. Dodds *ibid.*, quoting an important statement by Varro, which shows that the curative function of Dionysiac ritual was known at this time (*ap.* Serv. *ad* Verg. *Georg.* 1,166): *Liberi patris sacra ad purgationem animae pertinebant.*

61. Fred C. Mench Jr. *AJP* 93 (1972) pp.314ff. notes that literary hawks catch their prey, but entirely misses the point.

62. See Stanford's helpful note on tragic suicide at App. E to his edition of Sophocles *Ajax.*

63. For skulking maenads see Plaut. *Bacch.* 53ff. Pi.: . . . *Bacchas metuo et bacchanal tuom . . . mala tu es bestia, nam huic aetati non conducit, mulier, latebrosus locus.* For the tendency of *furiosi* to seek out deserted places, Francis Cairns *CQ* N.S. 24 (1974) p.107.

64. See Brink on *Ars. Poet.* 123 for the stock (dry eyed) Medea type; for Medea's disinterest in the ruination of all around her, Sen. *Med.* 426ff. Tragic ladies reacting like men, Aesch. *Agam.* 10f.: ὧδε γὰρ κρατεῖ/γυναικὸς ἀνδρόβουλον ἐλπίζον κέαρ.

65; Dionysus destroyed the palaces of Pentheus and Lycurgus. That the destruction of Cleopatra's palace is a historical inaccuracy is not a problem for us: it was accepted in 'tragic' historiography that details might be falsified. See F.W. Walbank *JHS* 58 (1938) pp.56ff.

66. Eur. *Bacch.* 101ff. and Dodds *ad loc.*; esp. Naev. *Trag.* 21 (Ribbeck): *iubatos angues inlaesae gerunt;* Ov. *Met.* 4,483.

67. For the nuance of corruption in *atrum venenum* see Austin on Verg. *Aen.* 2,221.

68. Plut. *Ant.* 86,4.

69. H.S. Versnel *Triumphus* Leiden (1970) pp.11ff.

70. Cairns *op.cit.* n.5 above pp.95ff.

71. *Ibid.* p.286 for identified examples.

72. *Res Gestae* 10, 1.

73. Dio 51, 20, 1: ἔς τε τοὺς ὕμνους αὐτὸν ἐξ ἴσου τοῖς θεοῖς ἐσγράφεσθαι; L.R. Taylor *The Divinity of the Roman Emperor* Am. Phil. Ass., Philological Monographs 1 Middletown (Conn.) (1931) pp.151, 236.

74. See H. Schnepf *Gymn.* 66 (1959) pp.250ff. and H. Bellen *Rh.M* 106 (1963) pp.23ff. (on *adventus dei*).

75. The *tripudium*, danced by the Salians at the start and end of the 'campaigning season', was felt to relate to dances in honour of Cybele (also called *tripudia* cf. Cat. 63,26), whence an interesting parallel at Ov. *Fast.* 6,329f. (dances at a feast for Cybele): *pars bracchia nectit/et viridem celeri ter pede pulsat humum.*

76. See n.20; for Salians and Curetes, Dion.Hal. 2, 70, 4.

77. Plut. *Ant.* 75.

78. Soph. *Ant.* 1117f.: (Dionysus) κλυτὰν ὃς ἀμφέπεις/'Ιταλίαν.

79. S. Weinstock *Divus Julius* Oxford (1971) p. 37.

80. Compare esp. the structure of Pind. *Pyth.* 3, 5-46, and see R.W.B. Burton *Pindar's Pythian Odes* Oxford (1962) pp.81f. See further Syndikus *op.cit.* I pp.333f.

81. *Ibid.*

PROPERTIUS 4,1

by

C.W. MACLEOD
(Christ Church, Oxford)

The unity and coherence of Propertius 4,1 are still debated. It also poses the reader another and larger question: what an Augustan poet may mean when he considers the different possibilities open to him as a writer, when he states a programme and refuses alternatives, and in particular when he indicates his relation to Callimachus' aesthetic. That question in its turn leads us to ask how the writer's character as more or less a Callimachean is connected with his character as the poet of love and as the poet of Rome, the *vates*. The claim of this paper is that Propertius 4,1 is a well-knit whole, and thus represents these three *personae* as significantly related aspects of one person. In what follows I go through the poem bit by bit in an attempt to illustrate this thesis.

At the beginning of 4,1 Propertius is playing the guide (*xenagos*) to a visitor to Rome, the *hospes* (*xenos*) of line 1.[1] This fiction prepares us for a book containing *aitia* because the guide, in pointing out the sights, naturally goes back to the origins of buildings or cults or customs, and contrasts the present with the past appearance of the city. This device of Propertius' recalls Catullus 4. That piece too is addressed to *hospites* (1), visitors to the poet's home for whom he is playing the guide; it too goes back to a past, which includes the boat's origin, contrasting it with the present (*sed haec prius fuere* . . ., 25); and in explaining how the boat and its owner came to settle by the lake it corresponds to lines 39-56 in Propertius' poem. The later writer, then, transfers what Catullus does with a possession of his own to the imperial city and a public theme; but as we shall see, there is also something of the personal quality of Catullus' poem in his successor's. Rome's past and present are intimately connected with Propertius' future, as the story of Catullus' boat is also part of his own life-story.

More obviously part of the background to our poem are Tibullus 2,5 and *Aeneid* 8,[2] where Evander is the guide who tells how his people came to settle where they are and how one of their cults came into being. The correspondence between Propertius 4,1 and these poems is more than external. In all three places there is a certain conflict of feeling: on the one hand nostalgia for the old, rustic simplicity, on the other admiration for the splendours of present-day Rome, esp ̀cially those for which Augustus was responsible.[3] With this goes a dual view of Roman history: there is a deep cleft between the ancient and the modern, and yet the new is also a glorious development or recreation of the old. The theme of continuity with the past and such a two-sided treatment of it are typical of Augustan poetry. They are found already in Vergil *Eclogue* 1, which pours contemporary history into a bucolic mould. The poem set Tityrus, who can rejoin a blamelessly happy past and remain on his own land, against Meliboeus, who can look forward only to a wretched and homeless future. This contrast is summed up in two lines which exactly correspond in metre and syntax, the solemn pronouncement of the *iuvenis* and the embittered exclamation of Meliboeus: *pascite ut ante boves, pueri, summittite tauros* (45) and *insere nunc, Meliboee, piros, pone ordine vites!* (73).

Continuity with the past is also an important theme in the *Aeneid*, where again it is handled dialectically. On the one hand, it is the god's will that Aeneas should not refound Troy; and he must turn his back on any dream of recreating his own city.[4] On the other hand, it is still Troy's gods he carried to Latium; and the arrival in Italy is a return to the homeland of Dardanus, the founder of Troy itself.[5] In Augustan poetry as a whole, when the guilt and corruption of Rome or its parent city, Troy, is stressed, there is the sense that the old values may be lost for good (Propertius 3,13; Horace *Odes* 3,6) or that the present must break with the past (*Odes* 3,3); at the same time that break, represented by the new age or its leader, Augustus, and his family, often renews the virtues of some ideal past, mythical (*Eclogue* 4; *Epode* 16) or historical (*Odes* 1,12; 4,4; *Aeneid* 6,777ff.; 8,626ff.). In the *Georgics* such continuity is represented by rural life (1,493-7), which is both happy leisure, like that of the Golden Age, and honest toil, like that of the old Romans (2,458ff.). Here, then, as the poet of Rome, Propertius takes up the theme of the city's history in the spirit of his great contemporaries.

This line of argument is summed up in 37f.: the Roman who 'would not think his stock's nurse was a she-wolf' has as good as lost contact with his past. These words are ambiguous, as the whole section is. The she-wolf — still less if she was a metaphorical one (see Livy 1,4,7) — is not a glorious ancestor; at the same time she belongs to a past admirable in its very primitiveness.[6] At 39 the poem enters a new stage as Propertius turns to the story of Rome's foundation. Such stories (*ktiseis*) find a place in Callimachus' *Aetia — Fr.* 43(Pf.); cf. *Hymn* 2, 65ff. — as in Tibullus 2,5 and *Aeneid* 8; and it is proper that a book of Roman *aitia* should begin with the *aition* of Rome itself. A fixed characteristic of *ktiseis* is the account of the oracles which led to the foundation:[7] so here, in lines 49-54. The emphasis, as in Tibullus 2,5, is on how the omens were good and the prophecies ratified. This happy note is reinforced by Propertius' treatment of the theme *recidiva Pergama.*[8] Commonly in Augustan poetry Troy, hated by the gods, is a guilty part of Rome's past; so that Rome should be distinct from Troy is essential.[9] But here we learn that the escape of Aeneas and his companions was a sign of divine favour. Furthermore, Aeneas is fused with Augustus in 46f.: the emperor at Actium receives 'the arms of resurgent Troy'[10] from Venus, just as in *Aeneid* 8 Aeneas received from her in Latium the arms which portrayed Augustus' victory at Actium; and *Ilia tellus vivet* (53f.) is a joyful prediction. No doubt this changed view is in the spirit of the new age instituted by the *Ludi Saeculares* in 17 BC: indeed in the *Carmen Saeculare* (41f.) Horace speaks of Troy as *ardentem sine fraude* and Aeneas as *castus*; and in both places Aeneas' safe escape from Troy is a good omen for Rome. Rome there and in our poem represents more the renewal of an ideal Troy than the break with a guilty one.[11] Similarly, the murder of Remus, an archetype of Rome's sin in Horace *Epode* 7,17-20, is here (49f.) treated as merely a sacrifice which guaranteed the well-being of the city[12] and was even, it seems, ordained by the Sibyl. Lines 55f. round off this section by recalling, but without any of their gloomier implications, 37f. Now the she-wolf's milk has made Rome's walls grow and its fortunes prosper: the past is active and beneficent in the present.

At line 57 the poet enters his own poem. He does so by means of a complex symbolism. A sustained comparison is made between Propertius the writer describing the foundation of Rome and the foundation of Rome itself; and so the poet metaphorically takes on the roles of founder (*ktistēs* and prophet (*mantis, vates*). First, the poet as 'founder': in 57 Propertius writes: *moenia namque pio coner disponere versu. Disponere* here has two of its senses, one relating to building[13] and one to poetry.[14] In particular, the placing of walls is one of the first acts of the founder of a city and regularly mentioned in *ktiseis*[15]. Thus the religious ceremony evoked by lines 67f. should be compared to the sacrifices of a founder:[16] the request for a well-omened silence is suitable both to the sacred action[17] and to the inspired poem.[18] In 67 the words *surgit opus* refer both to Propertius' work and, by extension, to the city;[19] they echo *resurgentis Troiae* (47), *creverunt moenia* (56) above. The symbolism is elaborated by 65f.: *scandentis quisquis cernit de vallibus arces/ingenio muros aestimet ille meo!* Strictly speaking, Propertius is referring to the hill-towns of Umbria,[20] but again the language is meant to suggest a city being built and Propertius as the builder. That city is Rome, the subject of Propertius' work; it is also Propertius' work itself.

The symbolism here is bold but it boils down to two notions familiar in ancient poetry. (1) The poet is described as doing what he describes being done.[21] Particularly relevant parallels are Ovid *Fasti* 1,663ff. and 4,731ff., where the writer imagines himself present giving instructions for the conduct of the festival whose origin he is recording. (2) Poetry is compared to building: see Rothstein *ad loc.* and e.g. Pindar *Olympian* 6,1ff.; *Pythian* 6,5ff.; Horace *Odes* 3,30. This metaphor is also embodied in the usage of Latin *condere*, 'found' (a city) and 'write' (verse), which Propertius applies to his own work in line 74. Furthermore, Propertius had already made an analogy between the growth of Rome and the growth of his poetry in 3,9, 49ff.:

celsaque Romanis decerpta Palatia tauris
    ordiar et caeso moenia firma Remo,
eductosque pares silvestri ex ubere reges,
crescet et ingenium sub tua iussa meum. . . .

Next, the poet as 'prophet': the founding of cities is accompanied by oracles and omens such a Propertius records in 41-54; and in 39ff. the poet speaks in the past tense as an oracle would in the future. In particular, *melius* corresponds to the λῶιον of oracular responses.[22] The prophet also has a role in foundations scarcely less important than the founder's, one which Horace adopts in *Epode* 16;[23] and as a priest he is naturally associated with ceremonies like that of lines 67f. in our poem. So while Propertius' prophecies in lines 57ff. literally concern his own work, metaphorically he is identified with the founding prophet or priest, as he is with the founder. Here again what Propertius says of himself and his own work echoes what he said of Rome: *iam bene spondebant tunc omina* (41), *date candida, cives, omina* (67f.); *pios* (44), *pio* (57).

Now in writing a book with *aitia* in it Propertius is apparently being the faithful Callimachean; that is implicit in line 69 and explicit in line 64. Again, in rejecting Ennius (61), he follows Callimachus' refusal to imitate Homer. But this is not a consistent position. When he writes (62f.), *mi folia ex hedera porrige, Bacche, tua,/ut nostris tumefacta superbiat Umbria libris*, this is to reverse the sentiments and imagery of Callimachus *Epigram* 7:

Ἦλθε Θεαίτητος καθαρὴν ὁδόν· εἰ δ᾽ ἐπὶ κισσὸν
    τὸν τεὸν οὐχ αὕτη, Βάκχε, κέλευθος ἄγει,
ἄλλων μὲν κήρυκες ἐπὶ βραχὺν οὔνομα καιρὸν
    φθέγξονται, κείνου δ᾽ Ἑλλὰς ἀεὶ σοφίην.

So too Propertius himself in 3,17 sees Bacchus and the poetry he would inspire (21-40) in contrast to his own normal manner as a love-poet;[24] and *tumefacta* implies, at least on the principle *quod facit ab eo quod fit,*[25] that Propertius' books have the quality of *tumor,*[26] the epic or tragic bombast the Alexandrian spurned as he spurned the tragedian's ivy crown. As in 3,1,[27] the language Propertius uses to speak of his future renown is in deliberately striking contrast to his Callimachean programme. And it is the roles of founder and prophet which embody this grandiose, and so un-Callimachean, streak: as 'founder', Propertius makes a comparison between his own poetry and the great city; as 'prophet', he looks forward to a great future (like the city's) for his poetry.

This clash of Callimachean and un-Callimachean in Propertius' programme is designed and significant. The *aitia* in the book which follows are in essence antiquarian and Alexandrian poems. Even poem 6, which touches on Actium, studiously avoids actual description of the battle and openly turns away from its martial theme in line 69: to this extent Propertius is not taking the master's name in vain. At the same time, the origins of Rome's gods or cults or customs belong with the origins of Rome itself; and that in its turn naturally leads to a theme for 'prophecy', how the city grew from its past to its present, much as the *aition* in poem 6 leads to the treatment of Augustus' wars. As an antiquarian, a 'guide', the poet expresses in lines 1-38 some nostalgia for olden times; but with the opening of a prophetic perspective, the tone changes to one of triumph and grandeur. Thus the poet's wavering between modes is one and the same thing as the Roman's mixture of feelings about his city, its past and its present.

At line 71 the astrologer Horos breaks in. His abrupt appearance with its command to stop (*quo ruis . . .?*) recalls the tragic *deus ex machina:*[28] besides, e.g., Euripides *Iphigenia in Tauris* 1435 and *Helen* 1642, compare [Plato] *Clitopho* 407a:

ἐγὼ γὰρ, ὦ Σώκρατες, σοι συγγιγνόμενος πολλάκις ἐξεπληττόμην ἀκούων, καί μοι ἐδόκεις παρὰ τοὺς ἄλλους ἀνθρώπους κάλλιστα λέγειν, ὁπότε ἐπιτιμῶν τοῖς ἀνθρώποις, ὥσπερ ἐπὶ μηχανῆς τραγικῆς θεός, ὕμνεις λέγων· "Ποῖ φέρεσθε, ὤνθρωποι; . . . "

But there is something divine about him in a more important respect; he corresponds to the Apollo of Callimachus' *Aetia* prologue, copied by Vergil in *Eclogue* 6, Horace in *Odes* 4,15 and Propertius himself in 3,3, in preventing the poet from taking a wrong course. But at this point it becomes necessary to examine the objections to the unity of the poem, which are usefully formulated by Sandbach in *CQ* 12 (1962) pp. 266-71.

(1)   Sandbach observes that despite Horos' injunctions, Propertius does in this book write *aitia*. But the purpose of this is to introduce a book which contains both poems about origins (2; 4; 6; 9) and poems about love (3; 5; 7; 8). The diversity of its themes and inspiration is here presented in the form of a dramatic clash. This is a device which can be found elsewhere in Propertius and in Latin poetry.[29] It may also be relevant that the *aitia* and the love poems in this book are not quite the same as the alternatives hinted at here. Propertius does not again take the role of the 'prophet' as he does for a while in 4,1; he remains the antiquarian. Nor is he the elegiac lover faithfully devoted to one woman.[30] To that extent, then, the book might be seen as less a combination of the two genres than a kind of compromise between them.

(2)   Sandbach rightly says that *dicere fata* must mean 'foretell the future'; and that is not what Propertius was envisaging in line 69. But, as we saw, Propertius has been in two senses the prophet: literally the prophet concerning his own work, metaphorically the founding prophet of his city. Sandbach further objects that in the metaphor of spinning at line 72 the threads must be those of fate, not poetry; and that Propertius could hardly be saying of the *fata populi Romani* something as derogatory as what he says there. But Propertius is there speaking of a poem of his own, a poem which includes *dicere fata*: the choice of metaphor applicable both to verse and to the fates is highly appropriate.[31] Further, that such a poem would have to contain ill-omened events becomes clear at lines 109-18 (of which more below); it also becomes clear there that they affect not Rome or Troy, but their Greek enemies. Nor is the past tense of *condita sunt* an objection. In line 69 Propertius uses a future tense of his aetiological work; but in 67 it 'is rising', and this kind of anticipatory present is particularly associated with prophetic utterances.[32] Thus in *Eclogue* 4,60-3 Vergil encourages the child who was barely conceived at the beginning of the poem to smile at its mother; or Propertius in 3,1, 9-12 sees himself enjoying the triumph which results from the fame of the work he was praying Callimachus and Philetas to inspire just before. In any case, in 4,1,39-56 Propertius has prophesied about Rome and himself.[33] That is why the lyre is mentioned in line 72, rather than the elegist's *tibia*. Propertius, in so far as he is prophesying, would naturally ask inspiration from Apollo, the prophet god, whose speciality the lyre is:[34] Apollo is hostile and unwilling because his instrument would have been misused, and also because he himself, as we learn later, told Propertius not to write such poetry.

(3)   Sandbach argues that if Horos is warning Propertius he will not achieve his programme, it is strange that no more reference is made to

146

antiquarian verse; and that when the astrologer commands *at tu finge elegos* (135), he cannot be distinguishing love-elegy from learned elegy, because the distinction is not one that Roman poets are accustomed to make. But in fact that distinction can be made. Catullus in poem 35 addresses the piece to Caecilius as *poetae tenero*: this means his friend has become a love-poet[35] and thus abandoned, as what follows reveals, his learned poem on the Magna Mater. In Vergil *Eclogue* 10,50-69, the elegist Gallus is dragged by love away from the Euphorionic through the Theocritean mode down to complete surrender to his passion; being a lover and a love-poet is here not only contrasted with being a learned poet but also, where Vergil takes leave of the bucolic genre, seen as equivalent to abandoning poetry altogether (cf. Horace *Epode* 11,1). And Propertius himself in 3,2,1f. sets the straight love-poetry he is writing in that poem against the Callimachean aspirations of 3,1: *carminis interea nostri redeamus in orbem:/ gaudeat in solito tacta puella sono.*[36] Furthermore, *elegi* are peculiarly associated with the subject of love.[37] If Apollo's warning in lines 135-46 seems directed against war, that is because at that point in Propertius' life a soldier's career or martial poetry was the natural alternative to love and love-poetry; but the god's words apply no less to any kind of writing which is not the lover's. And the poem Propertius risked writing would have included, as lines 45-8 indicate, bellicose material.

Lines 71-150, then, can and must be considered part of the same poem as lines 1-70.

Horos' speech may be divided into two main sections. In the first (71-118) he establishes his credibility in the manner of his kind: Rothstein compares Cicero *Ad Familiares* 6,6,7:[38]

quoniam, ut augures et astrologi solent, ego quoque augur publicus ex meis superioribus praedictis constitui apud te auctoritatem augurii et divinationis meae, debebit habere fidem nostra praedictio.

He does so partly by a general commendation of astrology, partly by examples of his own success in it: the word *fides* recurs emphatically four times over (80; 92; 98; 108).[39] The second section turns to Propertius. Horos gives a brief account of the poet's past, which further confirms his prestige as an astrologer;[40] he ends with a warning about the future, in lines 135-46, which includes a record of Apollo's warning in the past.[41] This section is comparable to a horoscope. For the tracing of a whole life, compare O. Neugebauer and H.B. van Hoesen *Greek Horoscopes* Philadelphia (1959) [*GH*], No. 95 or *AP* 14,124 (Metrodorus). For the

147

warning at the end, compare *GH* No. − 3, 15-17: εχει κινδυνους φυλαττου εως ημερω μ̄ χαρω του αρεως or *AP* 11,365 (Agathias) which parodies the pronouncements of astrologers:

"Εἴπερ ἐπομβρηϑῇ τὸ ἀρούριον, ὅσσον ἀπόχρη
μηδέ τιν᾽ ὑλαίην τέξεται ἀνϑοσύνην . . .
ἐσϑλόν σοι τὸ ϑέρος μαντεύομαι, εὖ δ᾽ ἀποκόψεις
τὰς σταχύας· μούνας δείδιϑι τὰς ἀκρίδας."

In other words Horos conflates *genethlialogia* (plotting the course of a man's life from the position of the stars at his birth) with the system of *katarchai* (times propitious or otherwise for an undertaking), a combination common in ancient astrology.[42] However, Propertius treats these forms very freely. The *genethlialogia* is merely an account of the poet's past life, not a prediction of his future based on the stars; and lines 147-51 are a strange *katarchē* because rather than saying 'avoid such-and-such under Cancer', it says 'do anything you like, but beware of Cancer'. This suggests what one might have expected anyway, that Propertius' introduction of Horos need not imply he actually believed in astrology or even thought his readers did: Horos' significance is poetic.

Now, as we saw, the astrologer corresponds to the god Apollo in Callimachus; and more relevant to Propertius than his strictly astrological talk is his claim to interpret the will of the gods. This he makes in each of the two stories he tells to demonstrate his powers: *vetante deo* (90); *Iunonis facito votum impetrabile* (101). There he represents a deity who forbids going to war and one who favours a courtesan: this perhaps corresponds to Apollo's encouraging Propertius to be a soldier in love as opposed to a real soldier. At all events, in 133ff. Horos speaks for the god. In all this he contrasts with Propertius. The poet too had claimed to be the mouthpiece of Apollo (73f.) and to foretell the future. Horos outdoes him on both counts, because his knowledge of the poet's past enables him to scotch Propertius' 'prophecies' about the city and himself. He is, then, a truer *vates*; and Propertius' genre of love-poetry is a *fallax opus* (135) by contrast with the truth-telling of the astrologer.[43] At the same time, by this means Propertius works a *sphragis*, a miniature autobiography like that of 1,22, into his opening poem.[44]

The function of Horos in the poem may be further explored by considering more correspondences between its two halves.

(1) Lines 109-18 are a kind of answer to 39-56. Propertius told of the happy prophecies of the Sibyl and Cassandra, and he identifies his own poem with them. Horos discredits all prophets who are not astrologers by

reference to Calchas and counters the happy fate of the Trojans and its accompanying prophecies with the woes of the Greeks and theirs. In this the poet makes a significant connection and contrast out of material more loosely combined in Lycophron's *Alexandra* (1226-80 and 373-86; 387-408). The implication is that in dealing with Rome's past Propertius would have to be a prophet of gloom as well as of gladness, to reveal how Cassandra was raped as well as what she foretold, to report impious words and deeds as well as pious ones (44 and 57; 109-18). This brings out the darker side of the theme of Rome's foundation: the crime and suffering behind it. This is what Vergil does in the *Aeneid* as a whole, not least in Diomede's account of the Greeks' *nostoi* (11,252-77). And Propertius himself, likewise in contexts where he is rejecting the theme of Roman history, indicates the grim background to Augustus' triumph in 2,1,27;29 and 3,9,55f.

(2)— In lines 119-50 we have an account of the poet's past which, as the speaker sees it, should condition his whole future. In 39-70 we have the growth of Rome into something new and greater than its rustic past, which includes the poet's rising to a new and greater theme. And in both places an utterance normally couched in the future, a prophecy or a horoscope, is transposed into the past tense: in particular, we have both in 53f. and 117f. an imperative, the former Propertius', the latter Horos', vividly projected back into the past.[45] Horos, then, breaks the correspondence between poet and city: by the same token he restores the connection between the Callimachean and the lover which Propertius commonly states (e.g. 2,1,39ff.; 2,34,31ff.; 3,3,47ff.; 3,9,43ff.). Hence Apollo, whom he represents in 133ff., is both the Callimachean god and the instigator of love-poetry: this contrasts with Propertius' attempt to exploit him as a prophetic god, condemned in 73f. Indeed Horos' character is exactly analogous to the one the elegist normally adopts. His work is private and not concerned with the city, past or present; and his choice of life is consistent, as he says Propertius' should be. In this he embodies the spirit of Callimachus' *Aetia* prologue which both rejects grand themes and asserts that the poet is faithfully sticking by what Apollo told him at the very beginning of his career. He may also be recalling Callimachus *Epigram* 1,12;16 (Pf.), τὴν κατὰ σαυτὸν ἔλα, which Propertius himself echoes in defending his preference for love and love-poetry in 2,1,46: *qua pote quisque in ea conterat arte diem*. Other features of Horos which are reminiscent of the Alexandrian master are his preference for his own style of divination (103-8), as exclusive as Callimachus' poetry which walks 'unfrequented paths' (cf. esp. *Fr.* 1,25-8;

149

Epigram 28 (Pf.)) and his claim to speak the truth with authority: compare *Fr.*512 (Pf.), ἀμάρτυρον οὐδὲν ἀείδω, and Theocritus *Idyll* 7,43f.:[46]

> "τάν τοι", ἔφα, "κορύναν δωρύττομαι οὕνεκεν ἐσσι
> πᾶν ἐπ᾿ ἀλαθείᾳ πεπλασμένον ἐκ Διὸς ἔρνος".

Propertius' own Vertumnus makes a similar claim in 4,2,19f.

In short, both what Horos recommends and what he is are one version of Propertius' character and aims as a poet. But the astrologer's function is not only to state and embody part of a poetic programme. He also reveals the inescapable power of love over the man and the suffering behind the splendours of his country. So the clash between Propertius and Horos is a way of uniting the diverse consciousness of the artist, the lover and the citizen in one context; and the extreme artifice of the poem is an attempt to do justice to contrasting roles and feelings such as any individual in his real life has.

It remains to consider the meaning of Horos' last words. It was suggested above that they are a deliberately eccentric form of astrological advice; and the concluding *time* corresponds to the δείδιθι of Agathias' epigram or the φυλάττου of the horoscope quoted there. Further, lines 147-9 present a common motif of love-poetry, which appears elsewhere in Propertius (3,16,11ff.), the true lover's immunity to all evil.[47] This would naturally imply that what the poet has to fear in line 150 concerns him as a lover. Now it was believed that Cancer made those born under it variable or many-sided. Thus Trimalchio boasts in Petronius *Satyricon* 39,8: *in cancro ego natus sum: ideo multis pedibus sto* . . .[48] The lover, then, must fear Cancer, because it would cause him to abandon that devotion to his one woman which characterizes the elegist: compare *una puella* above (140) and other places in Propertius (e.g. 2,1,47f.; 2,25). And that faithfulness is often closely linked with his character as a Callimachean poet.[49] A pleasing feature of this interpretation of the line is that it makes *octipedis* do more than merely cover the one part of the crab's anatomy as *terga* does the other; and granted that Horos' warning applied to the lover and the poet at once, then the echo of 72, *non . . . a dextro . . . colo*, in 150, *terga sinistra,*[50] not only makes a neat ring-composition for his speech, but also indicates the intimate connection between those two aspects of it. The advice of these lines, like other things in Horos' speech, makes no sense as astrology; but that is no excuse for denying that they do as poetry. And while there is surely a wry humour in Propertius' being trumped by an astrologer, the irony would be ruined if Horos were meant to be no more than a boastful dummy.[51]

NOTES

1. Cf. A. Dieterich *RhM* 55 (1900) p.191, though Call. *Fr.*392 (Pf.) does not belong here.

2. For details, see W. Wimmel *Kallimachos in Rom* Wiesbaden (1960) pp.280f.

3. Cf. Dieterich *art.cit.* pp.191ff.

4. *Aen.* 3,493-505; 4,340-7; 5,613-40; 704-30; 12,819-40.

5. *Aen.* 1,5f.; 7,205-11; 240-2.

6. *Putet*, the better attested reading, thus makes good sense.

7. Cf. esp. Tib. 2,5,39ff.; Verg. *Aen* 8,333-6. In general A.S. Pease *CPh.* 12 (1917) pp.1ff.; Benno Schmid *Studien zu den griechischen Ktisissagen* (Diss. Fribourg-en-Suisse, 1947).

8. *Aen.* 4,344; 7,322; 10,58.

9. See note 4 above and e.g. Verg. *Georg.* 1.50lf.; *Aen.* 6, 62-5; Hor. *Od.* 3,3,18ff.

10. J.L. Marr *CQ* 20 (1970) p.161, objects to the anaphora *arma* .... *arma*, where the first use of the same word has a literal, the second a figurative meaning. But this is classified by rhetoricians as a form of *paronomasia*; and Propertius employs much the same kind of figure in 4,8,16. See further D.R. Shackleton Bailey *Propertiana* Cambridge (1956) p.254; Hdt. 1,45,3; Plat. *Laws* 909b; Hermogenes p.342,19ff. (ed. H. Rabe); Sen. *Ep.* 94,74; 101,14. The *variatio* (the same sense in different words) of *vexit... portans* is in elegant counterpoint to the *paronomasia* (the same word in different senses) of *arma...arma*.

11. Prop. 4,1,47: *resurgentis... Troiae*, recalls Verg. *Aen.* 1,206: *illic fas regna resurgere Troiae*. But what in the *Aeneid* is a dream of Aeneas', due to be corrected by events (see 12,819-40), is in Propertius boldly said to be realised in Augustus' time. See also Ov. *Fast.*1,523 and Bömer *ad loc.*

12. Cf. Prop. 3,9,50; Florus 1,1,8. Note also Bömer on Ov. *Fast.* 4,809.

13. See *TLL* V(1) 1422,44ff.

14. E.g. Lucr. *DRN* 3,420.

15. Call. *Fr.*43,60 (Pf.); Livy 1,7,3; Ov. *Fast.* 4,811; Vitr. 1,5.

16. Cf. e.g. Livy 1,7,3.

17. Cf. Hor. *Od.* 3,1,1ff.; Prop. 4,6,1ff.

18. Cf. Hor. *Od.* 2,13,29f.

19. Cf. Call. *Fr.*43,63 (Pf.) πύργον ἐ[γειρόμεν]ον.

20. 'L'immagine properziana esprime efficacemente la caratteristica di molti paesi umbri, disposti a gradinate sulle colline' (Fedeli *ad loc.*).

21. Cf. K.-H. on Hor. *Sat.* 1,10,36; R. Kassel *RhM* 109 (1966) pp.8-10; F. Cairns *CQ* 21 (1971) p.207 n.1.

22. H. Parke and D. Wormell *The Delphic Oracle* II Oxford (1956) pp.25, 42, 154, 189; Hdt. 4,156,2. Similarly in enquiries to the oracle: see D.R. Shackleton Bailey *op.cit.* p.218; H. Parke *The Oracles of Zeus* Oxford (1967) pp.263, 267-70.

23. Cf. F. Cairns *Generic Composition in Greek and Roman Poetry* Edinburgh (1972) pp.183-5.

24. Bacchus inspires Propertius the love-poet in 2,30,38; 3,2,9; 4,6,76. But in 3,17 he is clearly cast in quite a different role, as a refuge from love.

25. Cf. W. Stroh *Die römische Liebeselegie als werbende Dichtung* Amsterdam (1971) p.19 n.37; *CQ* 23 (1973) p.301 n.1.

26. See Call. *Frr.*192,12f.; 215 (Pf.). Also Hor. *A.P.*94;97 and Brink *ad locc.*; Prop. 2,30,18 with Cairns *art.cit.* pp.206-12 on lines 19-22 there.

27. See F. Quadlbauer *PhiloL* 112 (1968) pp.96-9,110-2.

28. If Horos makes a sudden entry here, that removes a problem posed by lines 121-6, 'the fact that ... the astrologer, to prove his powers, tells the poet he comes from Umbria, a fact of which Propertius himself had already informed him in 63-6' (Butler and Barber). Horos has not been present during 1-70; all that he knows he knows as a *vates*. And as Butler and Barber point out, he also specifies which Umbrian town the poet comes from. We are not required to wonder what becomes of the *hospes* at line 71 or before.

29. See *CQ* 13 (1973) pp.306,309.

30. Cf. W. Suerbaum *RhM* 107 (1964) p.357.

31. The comparison of spinning and poetry is embodied in the usage of the Latin word *deducere*: see *TLL* V (1) 282,55-76 with 279,69-76.

32. Cf. Kühner-Gerth II (1) 382,5(a).

33. Thus the present tense of *cantans*, if that is the right reading in 73, is quite appropriate. Furthermore, in lyric an expressed intention or command to praise or invoke someone can be equivalent to praising or invoking them: cf. Pind. *Ol.*2,1–4; 6,87; Hor. *Od.* 1,12,13ff.; Aristoph. *Lys.* 1279-90; 1316-20.

34. See Tib. 2,5,1ff.; for the poet as mouthpiece of the god, see Prop.4,1,133 (a deliberate echo); 2,1,3; Theocr. *Id.* 16,29 with Gow and Dover *ad loc.*

35. For this implication of *tenero* cf. *CQ* 23 (1973) p.301 n.4; further e.g. Ov. *Am.* 3,15,1; *AA* 1.7; 2,273; *Tr.* 3,3,73.

36. For other contrasts of love and learning, see *CQ* 23 (1973) p.306. n.1.

37. See Plaut. *Merc.* 409; Domitius Marsus *Fr.*7 (Morel); Ov. *Am.* 1,1,1ff.; *Rem. Am.* 379ff.; *Fast.*2,3ff.

38. Cf. Aesch. *Agam.* 1196f. and Fraenkel *ad loc.*

39. I take lines 87f. to be misplaced or interpolated with Passerat and many editors. Acute objections are levelled at lines 85f. by Marr *art.cit.* pp.164f.: possibly they should be deleted. The words *fallitur auro Iuppiter* (81f.) I put in parenthesis, with Tyrrell and Barber; for the parenthesis after *et*, cf. Hor. *Ep.* 1,6,22. They allude to a scurrilous version of the story of Zeus and Danaë in which the god becomes a golden shower as a bribe; cf. Hor. *Od.* 3,16,8 (with K.–H. *ad loc.*): *converso in pretium deo*. Propertius seems to echo the wording of that passage in *nunc pretium fecere deos* as he echoes its meaning in *fallitur auro Iuppiter*, which should be translated 'Jupiter disguises himself as gold' (cf. 4,5,14). A pointed argument *a fortiori*, then: how easy for men to make the planets, like the gods, 'a means of gain' (cf. Shackleton Bailey *op.cit.* p.221), when the supreme god himself actually takes on the appearance of money. That *Iovis* is used of the planet just after *Iuppiter* of the god effectively reinforces this thought. It is likewise reinforced if *fallitur auro* carries also the meaning 'is seduced by gold': for the use of *fallere*, see note 43 below; for the idea, Pl. *Rep.* 390e and Stallbaum *ad loc.*

40. Rothstein on line 119 compares *Petron. Sat.* 76; Aesch. *PV* 824ff. Paley aptly compares line 122 with Aesch. *Ag.* 1194.

41. I take Apollo's words to stretch from 135-46, with Heimreich. *Nunc* in 147 harks back to *tum* in 133 and indicates that Horos is drawing his own conclusion for the present from the god's advice in the past; and clearly line 150 (and hence at least lines 147-50 too) must be spoken directly by the astrologer.

42. Cf. A. Bouché-Leclercq *L'astrologie grecque* Paris (1899) pp.487-516.

43. As Lachmann saw (cf. Butler and Barber), love-poetry is also 'deceptive' because it teaches the lover 'i mille modi delle amorose frodi'. See also Stroh *op. cit.* p.107 n.169. But Propertius will be the one who is deceived (146) — which suggests the further sense for *fallax* of 'treacherous'. i.e. to the writer (cf. Rothstein on line 135), and strengthens the warning of Horos and Apollo.

44. Cf. Rothstein on line 119.

45. For the punctuation of 47ff. I follow Paley: a full stop after 47, an exclamation mark after 48, and 53f. not in inverted commas (i.e. as Propertius' words, not Cassandra's). *Ad Priami . . . caput* I take to mean 'addressed to Priam' (for the syntax, cf. Housman on Lucan 9,299); the phrase alludes to Lycophron's *Alexandra* 1226ff.

46. The claim to speak truth, like the whole episode in Theocritus, looks back to Hesiod (*Theog.* 28), both a divinely inspired *vates* and the master of the Alexandrians.

47. Cf. Tib. 1,2,25ff. and Smith *ad loc.*; Hor. *Od.* 1,22 and N.–H. on it.

48. Cf. Vettius Valens p.9,2ff. (ed. W. Kroll).

49. Cf. Cairns *art. cit.* pp.212f. and also Prop.2,23,1f. The model for this connection is Call. *Epig.* 28(Pf.). I cannot believe, then, that Stroh. *op.cit.* pp.106f. is right to see Callimachean πολυείδεια as flouted here: that would contradict the whole drift of Horos' injunctions.

50. The echo is noticed by G.P. Goold *HSCPh.* 71 (1966) p.92. Needless to say, it cannot be used, as he uses it, to show that lines 71-150 are a separate poem.

51. I am indebted for helpful criticism and suggestions to Professor Francis Cairns, Mr. A.S. Hollis and Mr. P.J. Parsons.

HORACE AND THE PARTHIANS

by

ROBIN SEAGER

(University of Liverpool)

The basic theme of the conquest of Parthia appears in Horace's poetry under several guises. The conquest may be seen as expiation for the civil wars, as a legacy left to Augustus by Caesar, as part of the overall prospect of world conquest, or as belated revenge for the defeat at Carrhae. In the poems of the thirties and twenties these aspects of the Parthian theme are variously combined, and the weight assigned to them varies greatly from poem to poem. Horace's desire for a Parthian war remains constant, but finds expression on widely different emotional levels, ranging from confident prayer (*Odes* 1,2) or prophecy (*Odes* 1,12) to passionate appeal to men (*Epode* 7) or gods (*Odes* 1,35). But despite his eagerness he firmly disowns the notion of a conquest undertaken for the wrong motives, a position implicit in *Odes* 1,29 and expressly stated in the rejection of economic imperialism in *Odes* 3,3.

Horace's fear that Augustus would not respond to the demand for a Parthian war is reflected in certain more problematical poems, such as *Odes* 2,9, which labours the point that the conquest has been long awaited, and *Odes* 2,13, where he remarks in passing that a Roman soldier is unlikely to meet his death in the course of a Parthian war. But *Odes* 3,4,37-40 should be read as an assertion that Augustus has abandoned conquests only temporarily, while he and the legions recover their strength, not as a declaration of lasting peace. Horace's standpoint receives its fullest exposition in *Odes* 3,5, which is both a promise that Augustus will win divinity by completing the task that Caesar left unfinished and avenging the disaster at Carrhae, and a challenge to him to do so.

In his later work Horace abandons his dream of conquest and accepts that freedom from external threats is sufficient cause for satisfaction, but his acknowledgement of Augustus' accomplishment is usually grudging. There is no pretence that Parthia has been conquered in *Odes* 4,5, the *Carmen Saeculare,* or *Epistles* 2,1. Only in *Odes* 4,14 and 4,15, and *Epistles* 1,12 and 1,18, are the recovery of the standards and the diplomatic detente with Parthia presented in language appropriate to a military victory and therefore consistent with Augustus' own systematic misrepresentation of the nature of his achievement.

155

The element of impatience and discontent in Horace's treatment of the Parthian question should serve as a warning against seeing him as simply an Augustan propagandist, recommending policies dictated by his patron. Even if Augustus' aim was a Parthian war, Horace's injunctions merely called attention to the fact that he was failing to bring it to fruition. But the extent to which Horace emerges as a critic of Augustus depends first on whether Augustus ever really wanted or intended to conquer Parthia, secondly on whether Horace was privy to Augustus' designs, whatever in fact they were. The answer to the first question is probably negative, but the second admits of no confident response. Therefore Horace's poems should not be used as evidence for the content of Augustus' foreign policy, since Horace himself may not have known what that policy was, while decision whether Horace was a critic of Augustus' policy or only of his performance must remain arbitrary.

PASTOR AND PASTORAL IN MEDIEVAL LATIN POETRY

by

P.G. WALSH
(University of Glasgow)

The study of any genre of poetry in Medieval Latin almost invariably necessitates the investigation of the influence of two great formative traditions. On the one side stands the magisterial authority of the Latin Classics; for Pastoral, the seminal work is Vergil's *Eclogues*, flanked by Calpurnius Siculus and Nemesianus. The Greeks play no direct role in the story, because in the West a knowledge of Greek became an exceptional attainment after the era of Boethius and Cassiodorus. Students with a Classical training experience severe cultural shocks when they find even the greatest Western minds of the Middle Ages guilty of elementary howlers, as when Thomas Aquinas derives *apeirokalia*, 'ignorance of the beautiful', from *a-*, *pur*, and *kalos* and translates it: *sine bono igne*, 'lacking good fire' (*Summa Theologiae* 2a2ae 135, 2). Clearly a Theocritus had no place on Western desks in the High Middle Ages. Of course, some Theocritean influence is mediated through Vergil, the master of creative imitation, but the Classical thrust begins with Vergil himself. The second great formative impulse comes from the Bible, from the agricultural imagery of Old and New Testaments. Of particular importance are *Isaiah* and the *Psalms, Luke* 2 and above all *John* 10, where Christ proclaims: *ego sum pastor bonus. pastor bonus animam suam dat pro ovibus suis* etc.

The unifying theme of this paper is the truism that the Christian sense of *pastor* successfully insinuates itself into the Classical literary mode. From the fourth to the thirteenth centuries Pastoral poetry was being written by men consciously aware of the fruitful possibilities inherent in exploiting the convergence of '*pastor Vergilianus*' and '*pastor Christianus*'. It need not and does not follow that every medieval poem written in the Pastoral genre will have conscious echoes of the biblical *pastor*. But the image of *ego sum pastor bonus* was so constantly before the mind of the Christian versifier that its exclusion was always the outcome of a conscious decision.

Vergilian Pastoral exercised a potent influence on Christian writers once Christianity had come of age intellectually in the later fourth century. It is worth asking why this should have been so. The obvious answer is that Christians regarded Vergil's *Eclogues* not as a form of literary escapism but as a *satura* of Classical values. The poet's reflexions on the contrast between the fortunes of individuals in *Eclogue* 1, the political optimism of *Eclogue* 4, the apotheosis of Daphnis in *Eclogue* 5, the exploration into the meanings of myth and science in *Eclogue* 6, the distillation of the poetic vision of Theocritus in *Eclogues* 2 and 8, represent the ordering of Vergil's own experience as authentic witness of Classical values. Christians reacted to the *Eclogues* as they reacted to Classical letters in general. It is well-known that in the fourth century Christians took opposing views of the value of Classical poetry and philosophy, with some ecclesiastical leaders defending them and others condemning them. Some, like Jerome, were almost schizoid, taking different attitudes at different times — contrast his twenty-second letter with his seventieth. When in a grimmer moment Jerome described all Classical poetry as the food of devils (*daemonum cibus est carmina poetarum*), one of the illustrations which he offers is bucolic poetry, *amatoria bucolicorum versuum verba* (*Epistula* 21, 13, 9).

But there was a more fruitful Christian approach, which was to baptise Pastoral. By the close of the fourth century, the Good Shepherd theme was being diffused in scriptural commentaries, in sermons, in devotional epistles, in Church art, and in poetry. We may illustrate this last from a poem by Prudentius:

> ille ovem morbo residem, gregique
> perditam sano, male dissipantem
> vellus adfixis vepribus per hirtae
>   devia silvae,
>
> impiger pastor revocat lupisque
> gestat exclusis humeros gravatus,
> inde purgatam revehens aprico
>   reddit ovili.

Cathemerinon 8, 33-40

(The sheep, sluggish with disease and lost to the sound herd as it foully sheds its fleece through the trackless regions of the shaggy wood when the brambles engage it, the energetic shepherd summons back. He drives off the wolves and with shoulders drooping bears it off. He cleans it, carries it back, and restores it to the sunny sheepfold.)

Other Christian poets go further, attempting not merely to introduce Christian themes to Classical measures but even to baptise the Vergilian Arcadia and the Vergilian shepherds. A striking example from the late fourth century is a poem by an Aquitanian friend of Paulinus of Nola, Endelechius. His friendship with Paulinus is noteworthy. Paulinus' chief importance as a Christian poet is as a Christianiser of Classical genres such as the epithalamion, epikedion, propemptikon, protreptikon, and natalicium.[1] Endelechius' poem embodies a different technique. He takes over Vergil's shepherds, and in 33 elegant asclepiadic stanzas they recite a Christian message. The three characters are Aegon, who is mentioned as a shepherd in Vergil *Eclogues* 3 and 5; Tityrus, the name of the shepherd in Vergil *Eclogue* 1 who receives his freedom from Augustus; and Bucolus, whose name shows that he is the personification of the genre.[2] The poem begins with a dialogue between Aegon and Bucolus, with Aegon asking the cause of Bucolus' grief:

A.   quidnam solivagus, Bucole, tristia
       demissis graviter luminibus gemis?
       cur manant lacrimis largifluis genae?
          fac ut norit amans tui . . .

B.   scis, Aegon, gregibus quam fuerim potens
       ut totis pecudes fluminibus vagae
       complerint etiam concava vallium
          campos et iuga montium . . .

Riese Anth. Lat. 893, 1- 4, 9-12

(A.   Why, Bucolus, do you wander alone, and heavily lament your griefs with downcast eyes? Why do your cheeks flow with copious tears? Inform one who loves you . . .

B.   Aegon, you know how rich I was in flocks, how my cattle wandering by the whole length of rivers filled also the hollow valleys, the plains, the mountain-ridges . . .)

But now, says Bucolus, the herds which have taken him a lifetime to amass have been lost in the space of two days. Aegon in reply mentions that the disease has spread from Pannonia and Illyricum into the territory of the Belgae, and from there into their own country. It is therefore clear that the *mise-en-scène* of the poem is Gaul. Bucolus embarks on a graphic description of the disease and its effect on the flocks; the whole passage is inspired by Vergil's celebrated account of the plague of Noricum in *Georgics* 2.

But now the third shepherd appears. His flock has not been ravaged by the plague. When Bucolus asks what god has saved him from the calamity, Tityrus explains:

> signum quod perhibent esse crucis dei,
> magnis qui colitur solus in urbibus
> Christus, perpetui gloria numinis
> cuius filius unicus

> hoc signum mediis frontibus additum
> cunctarum pecudum certa salus fuit.
> sic vero deus hoc nomine praepotens
> salvator vocitatus est.

105-112

(T.   It was what they call the sign of the cross, of the God who alone is worshipped in the great cities. It was Christ, the glory of the enduring godhead whose sole son he is.

This sign, implanted on the middle of their foreheads, was the undoubted salvation of all the flocks. So the god who is powerful under this name was repeatedly hailed as saviour.)

Tityrus now tells Bucolus that he too can pray to the Christian god. But faith alone will be his resource; the plague cannot be repelled by the slaughter of cattle, by pagan sacrifice, but rather by the sacrifice of a pure heart. Bucolus and Aegon are immediately converted:

> B.   haec si certa probas, Tityre, nil moror
> quin veris famuler religionibus . . .

> A.   et me consiliis iungite prosperis.

121f., 129

(B.   If you demonstrate that this is certain, Tityrus, I do not hesitate to serve the true religion.

A.   Enlist me too in your happy designs.)

The purpose of this poem is obvious. The intention of invading and capturing Vergil's Arcadia is explicit. All three Vergilian shepherds become Christians after observing the mighty works of God, the God whose concern is men and their cattle. To what sort of audience is the poem addressed? The elegance of the metrical scheme is a pointer; though the subject is a rustic one, the audience is not. Like the poems of his friend Paulinus of Nola (whose *Carmen* 18 is a conspicuous example of the theme of divine care for rustics and their oxen, mediated through St Felix), Endelechius' poem is written for those savants who can appreciate the elegance of the verses and the reminiscences of Vergil. We may describe it as didactic Bucolic, poetry in the service of evangelism.

Here, then, at the end of the fourth century Tityrus is the *pastor Christianus* who gathers Bucolus and Aegon into the flock of Christ. By the Carolingian age the reading of Classical literature is directed towards the formation of the Christian; it is a medium of instruction preparing Christians for a proper understanding of the Latin of the Bible, the Latin of the Fathers, the Latin of the Liturgy. It is fascinating to observe how popular Vergilian Pastoral becomes in this role. We think at once of Alcuin and his cuckoo-poems, but there is a further exploitation of the genre at Liège by the Irish poet Sedulius Scottus, and in the same era we can point to a very different type of Pastoral, the *Ecloga Theoduli*. Though the three versifiers have different aims, they are at one in sharing the Christian milieu which makes their different compositions more than Vergilian pastiche.

We know that at the court of Charlemagne leading cultural figures had Classical soubriquets. Alcuin himself was Flaccus, Angilbert was Homer; others had the names of Vergilian shepherds — Damoetas, Menalcas, Thyrsis. In Alcuin's poems the content is closely related to his life as teacher and pastor. The 'lament for the cuckoo' is an obvious example. Two characters, Menalcas and Daphnis, lament for their lost cuckoo; Vergil *Eclogue* 5, in which Menalcas and Mopsus lament the death of Daphnis, has provided the inspiration. Though no edition prints the poem in alternating couplets, it is clearly a dialogue in which Daphnis echoes, or sings a variation on, the themes suggested by Menalcas:

> M.   plangamus cuculum, Dafnin dulcissime, nostrum,
>   quem subito rapuit saeva noverca suis.
>
> D.   plangamus pariter querulosis vocibus illum;
>   incipe tu senior, quaeso, Menalca, prior.
>
> M.   heu, cuculus nobis fuerat cantare suetus,
>   quae te nunc rapuit hora nefanda tuis?
>
> D.   heu, cuculus, cuculus, qua te regione reliqui
>   infelix nobis illa dies fuerat.
>
> M.   omne genus hominum, volucrum, simul atque ferarum
>   conveniat nostrum quaerere nunc cuculum.
>
> D.   omne genus hominum cuculum complangat ubique;
>   perditus est cuculus, heu, perit, ecce, meus . . .

E. Dümmler *Poetae Latini Aevi Carolini* I, ii,269, 1-12

(M. Sweetest Daphnis, let us bewail our cuckoo, whom a savage stepmother has suddenly snatched from us.

D. Yes, let us bewail him together with words of complaint. I beg you as the older, Menalcas, to begin first.

M. What unutterable hour has now snatched you from your own, poor cuckoo which used to sing for us?

D. Poor cuckoo, poor cuckoo, that was an unhappy day for us wherever I abandoned you.

M. Let every race of men and birds and beasts gather now to seek our cuckoo.

D. Let every race of men lament our cuckoo everywhere. My cuckoo, alas, is lost and dead.)

And so the poem continues for about fifty lines. This cuckoo, as we know from Alcuin *Epistula* 65, is a defecting pupil called Dodo; Daphnis, as *Epistula* 133 indicates, is a cherished pupil of Alcuin, addressed there as *fili carissime*. So it is clear that in this poem Menalcas is none other than Alcuin himself.

The poem is a dialogue between master and pupil, perhaps a school exercise, and certainly invested with touches of appropriate joking, as when Menalcas expresses the fear that his cuckoo has been drowned in the waves of Bacchus: *heu mihi, si cuculum Bacchus dimersit in undis* (17). But for our purposes the main significance of this poem lies in the fact that Menalcas is an ecclesiastical *pastor* exercising a pastoral anxiety about his cuckoo who has strayed — the most magnificent of mixed metaphors.

A rather similar deployment of pastoral verses can be observed about the same period at Liège, but in the atmosphere not of the school but of the episcopal court. Sedulius Scottus provides himself with the *persona* of Tityrus and casts his patron, bishop Hartgar, in the role of Daphnis:

> Daphnis amoenus adest pastor bonus atque beatus;
> Tityre, plaude manu; Daphnis amoenus adest.

> L. Traube *P.L.A.C.* III, ii, 10, 5f.

and again:

> Tityrus in silvis ego tristis mente remansi.
> absens pastor erat, nulla quiesque fuit.

> ii, 2, 1f.

Here the *pastor* is the bishop, and the familiar ambivalence between the ecclesiastical and the Vergilian senses is once again in evidence.[3]

Our third Carolingian example is quite different. Here we have Vergilian Pastoral deployed not to describe the life of the school or the court, but for the apologetic purpose of contrasting pagan and Christian religious visions. The *Ecloga Theoduli* has been hesitantly attributed to Gottschalk because Theodulus (God's slave) is the Greek form of the German name.[4] The poem is written in Leonine, or internally rhyming, hexameters which demonstrate the learned technique of the author. The poem is a dialogue between the shepherd Pseustis (Falsehood) and the shepherdess Alithia (Truth). Pseustis hails from Athens and Alithia is of the seed of David. Under the presidency of Fronesis (Wisdom) the two rustic figures conduct their poetic controversy in quatrains. It is the old dispute renewed: what has Athens to do with Jerusalem? The Athenian Pseustis recounts the falsehoods of Classical myth, and Alithia rejoins with the truths of sacred Scripture. A reading of the poem thus permitted the Christian student to win some acquaintance with pagan mythology whilst at the same time learning to distinguish between the falsehood of pagan *fabula* and the truth of Hebraic *historia.*[5] We are to note that the deployment of the Vergilian Arcadia has been extended to the allegorical plane, with symbolic figures disputing the merits of Christianity and Classical humanism.

The *Ecloga Theoduli* had immense influence on medieval education, and we have constantly to bear in mind how deeply this and other 'religious' Pastoral affected the twelfth-century poets. We must of course take account of secular influences, not only Classical poetry but also the vernacular compositions especially from Provence. But the student of twelfth-century Pastoral will do well to keep in mind not only Vergilian and contemporary attitudes but also Christian exemplars. The lesson can usefully be learned by study of examples of two types of Pastoral, the first a traditional 'Vergilian' eclogue of M. Valerius, and the second a Pastourelle which appears in the *Carmina Burana.*

The mysterious M. Valerius has been well served by recent editors, first by Paul Lehmann in 1946 and second by Franco Munari, whose second edition (*M. Valerio, Bucoliche* Florence 1970), a most impressive work of scholarship, contains full details of earlier work on these poems. Munari does not however discuss the possibility that these poems may have a twelfth-century connotation. The standard view is that of Raby (*S.L.P.* II, p.88) that Valerius 'sang, without obvious references to his

163

medieval surroundings, the loves and contests of imaginary shepherds'. This view makes Valerius an earlier-day Sannazaro, who in his native city of Naples wrote *Piscatorial Eclogues* which are essentially Vergilian pastiche.[6] I think that Valerius' four *Eclogues* faithfully reflect Vergil's own procedure, in the sense that he mingles poems which reflect contemporary social issues with others of a more literary kind.

Munari has demonstrated that each of the four poems of Valerius has a Vergilian model, and the first is based on Vergil *Eclogue* 1, a composition in the form of a dialogue between Tityrus, happy as he lounges in the shade because Augustus has restored his lands, and Meliboeus, an unhappy *pastor* who has lost his lands and must now emigrate; the theme of the poem is the twosidedness of human fortune. In the poetic dialogue of Valerius, Cidnus and Ladon are the protagonists. These are names of rivers in Cilicia and Arcadia, and so learnedly personify the rustic life. Cidnus lies in the heat like Vergil's Tityrus, while Ladon labours on, expressing surprise that Cidnus neglects his sheep. Cidnus explains that it is not idleness that induces his neglect; believe me, he says, if I had any care remaining for myself my first thought would be for my flock: *nam michi si qua mei, credas, modo cura maneret,/esset prima gregis* (12f.). Ladon concedes that in the past Cidnus was always diligent, but he is resentful that other *pastores* and he himself are having to tend Cidnus' flock. This non-classical motif should alert us to the possible symbolism of the poem.

Cidnus explains that it is not the sun's heat but a more complex flame which he is enduring. The passion of love so besieges his mind that no anxiety for his flock or its *salus* remains: (*sed ferit interno non simplex flamma calore* (29); *nec michi cura gregis superest nec cura salutis* (31). The word *salus* introduces the familiar medieval ambiguity with its two senses of temporal health or safety and of eternal salvation. Ladon is dismayed by the news, and reacts sharply: *non sic notus eras. procul hoc, procul effice crimen* (33); *quin age, iam te redde gregi* (35). But why should a shepherd's love-passion be a *crimen*, a serious sin,[7] and why should it keep him away from his flock? This odd 'either-or' emphasis is re-echoed when Cidnus replies defensively that for long his only pleasure has been to take joy in his flock: *dudum, care Ladon, Cidno fuit una voluptas/de gregibus gaudere suis* (43f.). He now reveals who the lady is. She is no fit mate for a Vergilian shepherd; she lives in a house as big as a city: *scis, reor, hunc collem Lauros ubi dicimus Altas* (50); *hoc domus in colle est nostra, puto, non minor urbe,/et tamen hoc melius, domina quod Sistide gaudet* (53f.). So Sistis is a high-born lady living in a castle, or a

164

nun in a convent. The whole relationship begins to remind us of one or other of the set pieces of courtly love as described by Andreas Capellanus. Ladon is distressed, and calls the liaison a *nefas: ast nunc vince nefas ut vir* . . . (77); *ha, dolor et facinus! mens ergo permanet ista/nec te pastorum revocat privata voluptas* (82f.). But this reminder of the 'private pleasure' of *pastores* fails to bring his fellow-shepherd back from his infatuation.

It should now be clear that the theme of the poem is a motif frequent in twelfth-century poetry, the cleric crossed in love and neglecting his duties. Hence the collective farming by shepherds who take in each other's sheep. Hence the ambivalent reference to *salus*, the health and salvation of the flock. Hence the *crimen* and the *nefas* of a love-liaison not permitted to the ecclesiastical *pastor*. What then is the *privata voluptas*? The phrase might mean 'deprivation of pleasure', but as Cidnus has earlier said that his sole pleasure had been joy in his flock, the phrase must refer to the consolations which pastors find in their celibate calling.[8]

Just as the traditional form of Pastoral may explore the contemporary concerns of a Christian society, so also may the great innovatory form of Pastoral in the twelfth century, the Pastourelle. This is no place to discuss the controversies surrounding its origin, but since there is no earlier Latin form from which it directly evolves, the probability is that it begins in Latin through imitation of the vernacular at a time when the Provençal poem has already attained a stylised form. In essence the Pastourelle is a brief dialogue in which a gallant tries to seduce a shepherdess, sometimes successfully, sometimes with honourable failure, and sometimes with ignominy. The poem usually begins with the description of a *locus amoenus*, in which the gallant or the girl sits under a shady tree flanked by a rippling river, cooled by a pleasant breeze, and charmed by bright flowers and twittering birds. The other participant appears, and the badinage begins. E. Piguet in his book *L'évolution de la pastourelle du XIIe siècle à nos jours* Basle (1927) has classified the patterns in the vernacular versions. One popular sub-theme is the wolf-motif. As the gallant engages the *pastorella* in conversation, a wolf seizes one of her sheep, and she promises the gallant her favours if he rescues it. On his triumphant return, she breaks her promise and summons Robin her rustic fiancé. In another variant she sends Robin after the wolf, and enjoys the gallant's attentions in his absence.

What is of the greatest interest in the Latin Pastourelle is the attempt to baptise the genre, just as Endelechius had baptised the Vergilian form. Such Christianising was attempted in the vernacular; one finds it also in mixed French-Latin poems. Raby (*S.L.P.* II, p.334) provides a good example of this mixed type:

> L'autr'ier matin el mois de mai,
> > regis divini munere,
> que par un matin me levai
> > mundum proponens fugere,
> en un plesant pre m'en entrai
> > psalmos intendens psallere,
> la mere Dieu ilec trouvai
> > iam lucis orto sidere . . .

Further stanzas follow in which the beauty of the Virgin Mary is described. The couple then converse in religious sentiments appropriate to such a sacred encounter.

We need not therefore be surprised to find Latin Pastourelles with such a religious dimension, and we should scrutinise apparently secular poems, which on the surface appear to follow one of the Provençal patterns, for deeper content. For example, there is a Pastourelle in the *Carmina Burana* in which one of these patterns is superimposed on a theological scheme of the Redemption.

> lucis orto sidere
> exit virgo propere
> > facie vernali,
> oves iussa regere
> > baculo pastorali.

> 'cur salutas virginem
> que non novit hominem
> > ex quo fuit nata?
> sciat Deus, neminem
> > inveni per haec prata.'

> sol effundens radium
> dat calorem nimium.
> > virgo speciosa
> solem vitat noxium
> > sub arbore frondosa.

> forte lupus aderat,
> quem fames expulerat
> > gutturis avari.
> ove rapta properat
> > cupiens saturari.

> dum procedo paululum,
> lingue solvo vinculum;
> > 'salve, rege digna!
> audi, queso, servulum,
> > esto michi benigna!'

> dum puella cerneret
> quod sic ovem perderet,
> > pleno clamat ore:
> 'si quis ovem redderet,
> > me gaudeat uxore!'

mox ut vocem audio,
denudato gladio
lupus immolatur.
ovis ab exitio
redempta reportatur.

C.B. 157

(At the rise of the morning star, a maiden with the bloom of spring emerges, bidden to govern the sheep with shepherding crook.

The sun pours out its rays, affording excessive heat. The beautiful maiden avoids the harmful sun beneath a shady tree.

Advancing a step or two, I loose my tongue's bonds: 'Hail, one worthy of a king, please listen to your poor servant, and be kind to me.'

'Why do you greet a maiden who knows no man since the day she was born? God must know: no man have I found in these meadows.'

It chanced that a wolf lurked near, driven by the hunger of its greedy maw. Grabbing a sheep it hastened off, wishing to fill its belly.

When the girl saw that she was losing the sheep in this way, she cried at the top of her voice: 'If anyone restores my sheep, I'll make him happy as his wife!'

As soon as I heard this, I unsheathed my sword. The wolf was sacrificed. The sheep was brought back, redeemed from death.)

At one level the poem can be interpreted as a secular lyric exploiting the wolf-motif so popular in the vernacular Pastourelle. The promise of marriage, should the gallant succeed in saving the sheep, is a regular feature. But the poet does not describe the end of the affair, whether acceptance of the knight or the revoking of the marriage-promise. The treatment centres upon the idealised shepherdess, the virgin who promises marriage to the man who saves the sheep. As we examine the language in which she is described, we become aware of a sustained biblical and liturgical evocation contriving to depict her as a Virgin Mary. In stanza 2 she is described as *virgo speciosa*. The twelfth-century reader would think at once of *Song of Songs* 2, 13: *surge, amica mea, speciosa mea, et veni*. In stanza 3 the gallant in his reverential address uses the phrase *salve, rege digna*. The words surely evoke *Salve Regina*, one of the oldest Marian antiphons traditionally ascribed to Herman the Cripple, and a popular hymn in twelfth-century devotion. The shepherdess replies that she knows no man; the phrase she uses, *que non novit hominem*, reminds the reader of Mary's reply to Gabriel at the Annunciation (*Luke* 1, 34). How can this be, she asks, *quoniam virum non cognosco*?

Thus far we are justified in assuming that the poet invests his *pastorella* with evocations of the Virgin Mary. Now it is of the greatest importance for the interpretation of the poem to realise that such evocation is regularly applied also to the *persona* of the Church, for Mary is adduced as a 'type' of the *ecclesia.*[9] And just as the *pastorella* is a composite of Mary and the Church, so the gallant can be visualised as the redeeming Christ who is the bridegroom of the Church and at the same time the celibate priest whose vocation demands that he be an *alter Christus*. The sheep is a human soul, the wolf Satan.

The image of the wolf for the devil, the sheep for mankind, the shepherd for Christ the *pastor bonus* was familiar to every Latin reader in the twelfth century. We have seen that it is grounded in the Bible, from which it passes into countless Christian meditations. The first example that comes to mind is *Crux benedicta nitet*, the splendid composition of Venantius Fortunatus composed in Merovingian Gaul:

> crux benedicta nitet, Dominus qua carne pependit
> atque cruore suo vulnera nostra lavat,
> mitis amore pio pro nobis victima factus,
> traxit ab ore lupi qua sacer agnus oves . . .

MGH Auct. Antiquiss. IV, i, 2, 1

(The blessed cross shines forth on which the Lord hung in the flesh and washed our wounds with his blood. With devoted love he became for us a gentle victim. On that cross the consecrated lamb snatched his sheep from the mouth of the wolf . . .)

Familiar with such Christian allegory as this, twelfth-century readers of *Lucis orto sidere* could not have failed to detect the deeper implication of the poem.

A detailed analysis reinforces the Christian interpretation. The poem begins with the evocation of a celebrated Christian hymn, *Iam lucis orto sidere*, the importance of which is signalled by A.S. Walpole in his edition *Early Latin Hymns* (Cambridge 1922), no. 81. Moreover, we note that the *pastorella* has been ordered to rule the flock with the pastoral rod; a much more ecclesiastical picture now presents itself. After the *virgo speciosa* has settled herself beneath a shady tree, the gallant addresses her with a prayer, *Salve, rege digna*. It is the celibate cleric saluting the Church his future bride. In reply the Church, invested with the *persona* of Mary, proclaims that she has found no man in those fields, no *pastor* to be her husband. One of her flock is seized by the wolf who is the devil. She proclaims that she will wed the man who saves it. The gallant, assuming the *persona* of Christ, despatches the devil and redeems the sheep. The pastoral encounter is one in which the celibate priest proves his fitness to become wed to the Church by rescuing a soul from the clutches of the devil.

A final caveat. I do not suggest that such a deeper interpretation is regularly to be found in medieval Pastoral. But since the composers of such poetry are often clerics, the reader must keep his mind open to the possibility of the double sense of *pastor*, Vergilian and Christian.

NOTES

1. For the study of the genre-approach in Classical poetry, see Francis Cairns *Generic Composition in Greek and Roman Poetry* Edinburgh (1972). For its adaptation by Paulinus, see R.P.H. Green *The Poetry of Paulinus of Nola* Brussels (1971), and the present writer's Introduction to his translation *The Poems of St Paulinus of Nola (Ancient Christian Writers* Vol.40) Paramus, N.J. (1975)

2. There is a good analysis of the poem in W. Schmid 'Tityrus Christianus' *Rh.M.* (1953) pp.101ff.

3. There is a good discussion of Sedulius' Pastoral poetry in Raby *S.L.P.* I pp.243ff.

4. On the problem of authorship, see the references in M. Manitius *Geschichte der lateinischen Literatur des Mittelalters* I Munich (1911) pp.570ff.

5. See now P. Demats *Fabula* Geneva (1973) ch. 1.

6. Text and translation in Jacopo Sannazaro *Arcadia and Piscatorial Eclogues* (translated by Ralph Nash) Detroit (1966).

7. On the meaning of *crimen*, see e.g. *Carm. Bur.* 88 Refl., *pecco sine crimine* ('I misbehave without sinning'), and cp. Ov. *Met.* 9, 24 (*crimen* as fornication).

8. *Ecl.* 1 is not an isolated example of Valerius' concern for contemporary events; *Ecl.* 2 will also repay attention from this aspect.

9. See H. Barré 'Marie et l'église du vénérable Bede à saint Albert le Grand' *Etudes Mariales* (1951) pp.117ff.

THE SEQUENCE – REFLECTIONS ON LITERATURE AND LITURGY[1]

by

S.F. RYLE

(University of Liverpool)

This paper will attempt to provide at least partial answers to three questions associated with the Sequence-form. What were the distinguishing characteristics of a Sequence? How did the form emerge? And what rules governed its construction?[2]

Sequences were composed over a period of some seven hundred years, from the early ninth century until the end of the Middle Ages. The earlier poems, those written before about 1100, present the most interesting problems. Their language, highly poetic and striking, largely derived from the new word-formations of the classical Silver Age and from late antiquity, is employed with a freedom and spontaneity scarcely ever achieved in any other field of Latin verse. And whereas later examples of the form tend increasingly to observe normal poetic conventions, with stanzas that display consistent metrical patterns (though their length may vary) and a dominant role given to rhyme, so that they come to resemble conventional hymns, the early sequences appear in general to be governed by virtually none of the rules of verse-construction: they employ neither recognisable patterns of stress, that is, 'metre' as it is conventionally understood, nor regular stanza-length, nor assonance or rhyme at the ends of lines or stanzas, except where all the stanzas, (apart in certain instances from the first) end in the vowel *–a*. In fact their organising principle is that of syllabic correspondence between parallel strophes. The strophes themselves are broken up into small units of varying length, often extremely short, which possess only one essential common element, namely that they contain one or more complete word. What factors brought a verse-form of this type into existence? The germ of the answer, and the essential starting-point for any examination of the development of sequence-writing, is provided by the *prooemium* to Notker Balbulus' *Liber Ymnorum*, which dates from between AD 881 and 887:[3]

(2)   Cum adhuc iuvenulus essem et melodiae longissimae, saepius memoriae commendatae, instabile corculum aufugerent, coepi tacitus mecum volvere, quonam modo eas potuerim colligare.

(3)   Interim vero contigit, ut presbyter quidam de Gimedia, nuper a Nordmannis vastata, veniret ad nos, antiphonarium suum deferens secum: in quo aliqui versus ad sequentias erant modulati, sed iam tunc nimium

vitiati. (4) Quorum ut visu delectatus, ita sum gustu amaricatus. (5) Ad imitationem tamen eorundem coepi scribere: *Laudes deo concinat orbis universus, qui gratis est redemptus,* et infra: *Coluber Adae deceptor.* (6) Quos cum magistro meo Isoni obtulissem, ille studio meo congratulatus imperitiaeque compassus, quae placuerunt laudavit, quae autem minus, emendare curavit dicens: Singuli (*v.l.* singulae) motus cantilenae singulas syllabas debent habere. (7) Quod ego audiens, ea quidem quae in *ia* veniebant, ad liquidum correxi: quae vero in *le* vel *lu,* quasi inpossibilia vel attemptare neglexi, çum et illud postea usu facillimum deprehenderim, (8) ut testes sunt '*Dominus in Syna*' et '*Mater*'. Hocque modo instructus, secunda mox vice dictavi: *Psallat ecclesia mater illibata.*

(9)   Quos versiculos cum magistro meo Marcello praesentarem, ille gaudio repletus in rotulas eos congessit; et pueris cantandos aliis alios insinuavit. (10) Cumque mihi dixisset, ut in libellum compactos alicui primorum illos pro munere offerrem, ego pudore retractus numquam ad hoc cogi poteram.

((2)   When I was still only a boy, and my dizzy brain was incapable of retaining very long melodies (though I committed them to memory often enough), I began silently to consider how I might be able to master them.

(3)   But in the meantime a certain priest from Jumièges, which had recently been sacked by the Northmen, happened to arrive at our abbey, bringing with him his antiphonary. It contained some verses which had been set to *melismata* [of the *Alleluia*], but even then they were in an extremely bad state. (4) My delight on seeing them was offset by bitter disappointment when I tried them out. (5) Using them as a model, however, I began to compose *Laudes Deo concinat orbis universus, qui gratis est redemptus* and, further on, *Coluber Adae deceptor.* (6) When I showed these to my master Iso he congratulated me on my enthusiasm and showed consideration for my inexperience: he praised the things that were acceptable, but undertook the correction of those that fell short. 'A separate syllable' he said, 'should be attached to each movement of the vocal line.' (7) On hearing this I put right what I had set to *−ia*; as for *−le−* and *−lu−*, I thought them impossible and did not even attempt them, although later I found that even that task was perfectly simple with practice, (8) as '*Dominus in Syna*' and '*Mater*' reveal. With the benefit of this advice I shortly afterwards made a second attempt and composed *Psallat ecclesia mater illibata.*

(9)   I presented these verses to my master Marcellus [Moengal], who was overjoyed and copied them down in his notebooks, and entrusted them to

different boys to memorise and sing. (10) But when he said to me that I should collect them into a small volume and offer them to a distinguished person, I shrank from the suggestion in modesty and could never be prevailed upon to consent.)

Notker's *prooemium* stands as a *locus classicus* for students of the sequence as a result of two factors: the precise historical data that it contains – Jumièges was sacked by the Danes in 851, and other known facts about the characters mentioned tally in every case with the information that Notker gives – but more important, the brilliantly simple exposition of the essential features of the problem in their true order of significance.

At the root of Notker's troubles lay the difficulty of committing *melodiae longissimae* to memory. These melodies were attached to the word *Alleluia*, which prepared and rounded off a verse sung between the chanting of the two readings from Scripture at Mass. The *Alleluias* of Gregorian chant are relatively well known: they consist of a setting of the word itself with the first three syllables given fairly brief treatment – not more than half a dozen short notes to each separate syllable – followed by an extensive *melisma* on the final *–a*. This is followed by the singing of a verse to fairly elaborate music, ending with a *melisma* on the final word which usually has the same musical structure as that of the final syllable of the initial word *Alleluia*. At the conclusion of the verse the word *Alleluia* is repeated to the same melody as before.[4] These might reasonably be called *melodiae longae*, but hardly *longissimae*. Fortunately we possess examples of *melismata* to the *Alleluia* far more extensive than those of the standard Gregorian repertory. In the Ambrosian chant of Milan the second *Jubilus*, as the *melisma* on the final syllable of the *Alleluia* is known, is extended to enormous length.[5] The melodies that Notker and his contemporaries had to memorise were similar in extent to those of the Ambrosian *jubili*, with the difference that they were broken up into shorter and less flowing phrases.[6] It was in connexion with the *Alleluia-jubilus* that the term *sequentia* first came to be used. Amalar of Metz, archbishop of Lyon from 835 until 850 or 851, speaks of *haec iubilatio, quam cantores Sequentiam vocant,*[7] and in another work he mentions the practice of singing the Alleluia at Vespers during Easter week *cum omni supplemento et excellentia versuum et sequentiarum.*[8] Combining these texts with Notker's words *versus ad sequentias . . . . modulati*, we can see that the original significance of the term *sequentia* was purely musical, and that it only later came to be used of the words that were attached to the melodies. The name given to the literary compositions which the writers adapted to these pre-existing melodies was *prosa.*[9] Notker's evidence at least makes it clear that in the early sequences we are not dealing with some kind of Carolingian *vers libre*: in fact his teacher Iso (or Yso) was aware of what had clearly already become a convention, and was able to tell him that one syllable should be set to each note of the *melisma* – *singuli motus cantilenae singulas syllabas debent habere.* Thus in poems of sequence-form the structure of the stanzas is dictated by the melodic phrases to which they are set.

The priority of the music is therefore clear: the texts were composed to fit pre-existing melodies. From the literary point of view that might be regarded as a recipe for disaster. Only at the humblest level of inspiration can words be adapted to existing tunes. But the pioneer sequence-composers enjoyed an almost unparalleled degree of metrical licence. The musical phrases that dictated their word-groupings varied in length and imposed on them virtually no demands of regular word-stress: moreover the authors did alter the melodies to some extent, by making them less florid and giving them a more clearly-defined shape. The only restriction on their freedom in fitting the words to the musical phrases occurred at cadences; and the high proportion of stanzas and even of shorter units ending with words whose stress falls on the antepenultimate syllable is a notable feature.

Thus during the earliest period of sequence-writing the authors of the texts had to take into account only the external constraints imposed on them by the length of musical phrases. From the beginning they tried to emancipate the text from the melody, and, increasingly as time went on, to impose on it other forms of artistic discipline. The first organising principle that they chose to employ was that of parallelism or strophic responsion.

The practice of antiphonal chanting in Christian worship goes back to the earliest period, and derives from Jewish traditions. It originated in the Temple and was taken up by the synagogue after the destruction of Jerusalem. It is first mentioned in a specifically Christian context in the fourth century, but the word *antiphonos* occurs for the first time in a passage from Philo, describing the singing of hymns by a community of Jewish anchorites of both sexes in Egypt during the first century AD.[10] The most straightforward explanation of the younger Pliny's words in his famous letter to Trajan enquiring how the Christians should be dealt with, when he says of them *carmenque Christo quasi deo dicere secum invicem*, is to assume that he is referring to some kind of antiphonal hymn.[11] By the time Christianity became the established religion of the empire the chanting of psalms and hymns by alternate choirs had developed into standard liturgical practice. It no doubt owed something to the traditions of Greek choral lyric and tragedy; but it was also a pattern common to many forms of popular music-making. Moreover the very shape of Christian churches virtually compelled their congregations to split up into two groups and answer each other. Everything conspired to encourage the sequence-writers to turn their irregular melodic sentences into syllabically corresponding strophes.

From the first, then, sequences were invested with an element of regularity, one that derived from external features and conventions, but which itself became a determining characteristic if the text happened to be separated from the music. Almost all sequences composed up to the middle of the eleventh century exhibit this form, with syllabic responsion but only rudimentary features of rhyme, and this type has become known as the 'classic' sequence.[12] Some texts were however composed without parallelism. Such sequences were generally assigned to days without a special celebration during festal seasons or to the octaves of great feasts. Most of them are short, although a few examples of substantial length were written.[13] But absence of parallelism was a dead end, since in order to provide artistic satisfaction the text had to conform to recognisable canons of structure. At the other extreme, however, a few sequence-composers, having discovered and exploited the principle of responsion, chose to embellish it with extraordinary refinements of elaboration. In nine early examples of the sequence the author, after composing a text to be sung to the melody in the normal way, with syllabically corresponding strophes, begins again, using either all or part of the melody for a second time. These so-called *da-capo* sequences, or sequences with double cursus, look like the work of a circle of specialists parading their virtuosity for its own sake. Several of them stress the power and importance of music; and although the majority of them commemorate particular saints, liturgical considerations seem not to have played a dominant role in their composition.[14] A piece such as the *Rex caeli domine*, quoted in the ninth-century musical treatise *Musica Enchiriadis*, reveals how enormously the double cursus expanded the author's opportunities for the display of artistry both in detail and in overall effect.[15]

One might have expected that such sophistication would reveal itself only after a long initial period of development, and that in its turn it would prompt further subtleties of composition. In fact the sequences with double cursus make their appearance within fifty years of the origins of sequence-writing (if we regard the starting-point as around 800), and they fade out early. The sequence-writers presumably placed a higher value on improving the internal pattern of individual strophes than on creating large-scale compositions; and the melodic material that they used was in most cases sufficiently long to prevent them, except in special circumstances, from feeling obliged or even inclined to cover it twice. The 'classic' sequence thus comes to exemplify the *via media*, and after the mid-tenth century it stands unchallenged and begins its steady progress towards perfection in metrical regularity and rhyme.[16]

The names given to the melodies of many early sequences, particularly those originating from or influenced by 'St. Gall, pose some intriguing and probably insoluble questions about the antecedents of the sequence-form and the melodies that the writers drew upon. Notker was perhaps being a little disingenuous when he spoke of the difficulty of remembering very long melodies. The practice of writing sequences to the *jubili* of *Alleluias* had been established for a generation or more by the time the refugee priest from Jumièges appeared at the gates of St. Gall carrying his precious antiphonary. We possess some of these very early sequences, and we also in many cases know the titles of the melodies to which classic sequences were set, even if the melody itself is lost. Quite often the melody survives without the text. It is clear that although the *Alleluia-jubilus* provides the musical material in the majority of instances, secular melodies were also used. The well-known *Clangam filii*[17] clearly has a religious theme, and is an allegory of fallen mankind's search for God; but it is not intended for any particular occasion in the church's calendar, and need not have been written for liturgical use at all. The title of the melody is *Planctus cygni* — 'The Swan's Lament' — and it is natural to assume either that the text and the tune were composed together, or that a secular version of the sequence already existed and that the composer of *Clangam filii* took it over when he wrote his allegorical poem. A number of melody-titles indicate that they were associated with particular musical instruments, for example *Fidicula, Lyra, Organa, Symphonia, Tuba*; and others have feminine names that suggest that they derive from love-songs: *Aurea, Gemebunda, Puella turbata*, and the intriguing *Hypodiaconissa*. One cannot rule out the possibility that in addition to taking over secular melodies (as composers of sacred music continued to do for centuries) the sequence-writers adopted the formal patterns of earlier and now lost popular verse-forms. Certainly once the sequence-form had become established it exerted a great influence on secular lyric: it would be surprising if at the outset the composers of sequences had not themselves exploited at least some of the literary as well as the musical aspects of popular verse.

Four motifs can be identified in the majority of early sequences: their order and emphasis may vary, and sometimes they are combined in a way which makes it impossible to isolate them from one another.[18] Sequences generally open with an expression of praise. The word *Alleluia* means 'Praise the Lord', and the sequence usually announces at its outset a theme of worship or thanksgiving. This motif is closely associated with, and often almost indistinguishable from, the desire to celebrate a particular festival. We can see the beginnings of a feeling for special religious occasions in pagan Roman religion, with its favourable and inauspicious days and its scrupulous observance of anniversaries. In literature this outlook is reflected most obviously in the *Fasti* of Ovid, but it can also be seen in the ironic opening of one of Horace's invitations to Maecenas: *Martiis caelebs quid agam Kalendis? (Odes* 3,8,1). Christianity, the basis of whose calendar is derived from the Jewish festivals of the Passover and Pentecost, developed this tendency to a far greater degree. Each festival assumed its own special character. The central mysteries of the redemption, or the virtues of a particular saint, evoked their individual associations and sentiments. The word *hodie* is one of the most common and characteristic in the entire tradition of sequence-writing. From the commemoration of its festival a sequence normally passes to what may be called the legend associated with it. In the case of a feast of Our Lord this usually involves some poetic comment on the scriptural passages narrating the event, often embroidered with extensive use of Old Testament passages, interpreted in a prophetic or allegorical sense. The profound knowledge and love of the scriptures revealed by the composers of so many sequences need scarcely be stressed. For feasts of the Blessed Virgin this feature is modified into an exploration of the imagery and symbolism associated with the virgin mother. Sequences for saints'–days nearly always contain a description of at least one famous event in the saint's life. A good example is provided by one of the poems in honour of St. Nicolas of Myra,[19] where we find references to his refusal as a baby to take his mother's milk on fast-days, his academic distinction and blameless life, his election as bishop, his charity, exemplified by his gift of money to save three girls from a life of shame, and his calming of a storm at sea.

The final motif characteristic of the sequence is the element of prayer, or more precisely of supplication. A high proportion of sequences end with a sentence including the words 'we pray' or 'let us pray', asking to be associated with the celebration in heaven of whatever event is being commemorated, and also often imploring favour or mercy from God. In a sequence like Notker's poem for Whitsun, *Sancti Spiritus assit nobis gratia*,[20] this aspect takes priority over the others, so that the sequence has an unusual form, and contains much clearer reminiscences of the formal features of Greco-Roman pagan prayers: the 'Du-Stil', with successive stanzas beginning *Tu*, and the relative pronoun introducing a reference to one of the deity's special characteristics.[21]

The sequences of the twelfth century, and particularly of their most accomplished master, Adam of St. Victor, mark the final stage in the liberation of the texts from their music.[22] No one can fail to acknowledge the consummate technical brilliance of many late sequences. At the same time, however, they have lost the element of freshness and spontaneity that provides one of the constant rewards of the earlier poems. However impressive their formal perfection, however subtle their imagery, however profound their theological insights, the late sequences generally fall short of the highest standards of poetic inspiration. One wearies eventually of the endless succession of stanzas made up of rhyming eight-syllable trochaic lines rounded off by a catalectic line, and occasionally varied by a complete stanza of catalectics. From this time onwards sequences could be and often were set to several different melodies: the tunes simply had to cater for the metrical pattern of the sequence, which had by that time become almost uniform. Despite their beauty the sequences of the second period have a feeling of the assembly-line about them. All religious sequences need to be read with the eye of faith in order to be appreciated fully: but the early sequences have a capacity, deriving partly from their irregular construction, to take the reader by surprise and make him wonder what is coming next. The later sequences have sacrificed this quality in the interests of formal beauty and order.

*   *   *   *   *

In essences the sequence was a liturgical chant. It was intended to function as an adornment to the eucharistic worship of the church. It probably made use of secular elements, at least on the musical side, and certainly provided a model for popular art-forms once it had become established. But what were the factors that brought it into existence? How did an unofficial and informal chant come to achieve universal acceptance and wide diffusion in western Europe? Did it decline naturally or was it arbitrarily killed by papal decree?

The close alliance established between the Frankish kingdom and the papacy in the second half of the 8th century marks one of the decisive shifts in the history of Europe. In the ecclesiastical field its principal effect was to bring the Gallican rite into much closer contact with Roman practice: in fact to bring about before long the demise of Gallican forms of worship. Charlemagne adopted Roman liturgical practice even more enthusiastically than his father had done, since he saw in it an important factor in welding his domains into a cultural unity. The Frankish empire came to enjoy the benefits of order and stability, at least for a while; and its members gained a sense of being members of a genuinely civilised community. The ninth century witnessed a huge outburst of creativity in all fields of art, but perhaps pre-eminently in both poetry and music. One theory holds that the corpus of what we call Gregorian chant represents the achievement of monks under the Carolingian empire in blending and refining the traditions of both Roman and Gallican chant during the eighth and ninth centuries.[23] Certainly the earliest extant MSS containing the accepted Gregorian melodies date from around 900. The sequence should be seen in the context of this outpouring of artistic energy. It was complemented and paralleled, at a far lower artistic level, in the tropes to the Mass.

A trope was a text added to a prescribed liturgical prayer. It could be interpolated before, during or at the end of an official text.[24] Some tropes, like the earliest sequences, were composed as syllabic settings of a *melisma:* this is true particularly of those set to the *Kyrie* chants. Others simply introduced new material at various points in the official texts. From the musical point of view the newly composed tropes gave a new lease of life, albeit a precarious one, to the now established style of chant. Their melodic character did not diverge to any marked degree from that of the chants which they embellished.[25] The texts themselves, however, multiplied and become elaborated to an astonishing extent. Virtually no part of the liturgy remained exempt from their ramifications: troping was applied to both the Ordinary of the Mass, that is the parts that remained unchanged — the *Kyrie, Gloria, Sanctus* and *Agnus Dei* (though not the Creed), and to the Proper, that is those sections that varied from day to day, the Introit, Gradual, Alleluia-verse, Offertory and Communion-antiphon; also occasionally to the 'Epistle' — the so-called 'Epîtres farcies'.[26] Not only were tropes added to and inserted within the official texts, but they themselves could provide the basis for further interpolations. The use of liturgical tropes reached its apogee in the early 11th century;[27] and it seems to have gradually declined not because the additional texts were considered to be intrinsically unsuitable but principally as a result of a shift in the preoccupations of the people who used them, namely the monks, who turned their attention to more purely musical developments, above all to polyphony. The new horizons that certain tropes themselves opened up can be gauged from the influences of the celebrated *Quem quaeritis* trope on popular drama.[28]

Although sequences make their appearance in surviving MSS somewhat earlier than the first tropes, it is safe to regard them as a specialised form of trope, one that held a far greater potential for artistic development and allowed its writers much more creative scope than the normal tropes, which led an essentially parasitic life, dependent on the standard prayers of the liturgy. The sequence embedded itself firmly at one of the most obvious interstices in the structure of the liturgy, between the two readings from Scripture, and had sufficient strength to lead a virtually independent existence: tropes were never able to establish themselves as a viable artistic form or to break free from the musical and liturgical conditions that brought them into being. The sequence retained its place in the western liturgy until the end of the Middle Ages, although by about 1300 it had lost all its vitality and become merely one more fossilised element in liturgical worship. In the sixteenth century the church, faced with a frontal attack on the very concepts that underlay the eucharistic sacrifice, understandably decided to return to fundamentals. The sequence had become *de trop*.

NOTES

1. I am grateful to Professor P.G. Walsh and to Professor R.A. Markus for helpful criticism of the original form of the paper.

2. The literature on the sequence is now immense, but the following works are indispensable: W. von den Steinen 'Die Anfänge der Sequenzendichtung' *Zeitschr. für schweizerische Kirchengesch.* 40 (1946) pp.190-212, 241-268; 41 (1947) pp. 19-48, 122-162; *Notker der Dichter* 2 vols. Bern (1948); J. Handschin 'Trope, Sequence and Conductus' in *New Oxford History of Music* II Oxford (1954) pp.128-174; B. Stäblein 'Sequenz' *Die Musik in Geschichte und Gegenwart* 522-548; J. Szövérffy *Die Annalen der lateinischen Hymnendichtung* Berlin (1964-5) I pp.282-312.

3. Complete text in von den Steinen *Notker der Dichter* II pp.8,10; also in his *ed.min.* of the *Liber Ymnorum* Bern (1960) pp.6,8. The date of the *prooemium* is established by its dedication to Liutward, bishop of Vercelli and chancellor to Charles the Fat from 881 until his disgrace in 887. For speculation over a more precise date see von den Steinen *Notker der Dichter* I p.507.

4. See any example of an *Alleluia*-verse in the *Graduale Romanum* or *Liber Usualis.*

5. See the *Antiphonale missarum iuxta ritum sanctae Ecclesiae Mediolanensis*

Rome (1935). An example is provided by E. Wellesz in *Eastern Elements in Western Chant* Oxford (1947) pp.179f.

6. Examples of *jubilus* melodies, which often exist without word-settings, are found in numerous MSS from shortly after Notker's time. See A. Hughes *Anglo-French Sequelae* Burnham (1934).

7. *De Ecclesiasticis Officiis* 3,16 (*PL* 105, 1123).

8. *De Ordine Antiphonarii* 52 (*PL* 105, 1295).

9. The term was applied to texts composed to pre-existing music: in the case of tropes the diminutive *prosula* was used. Poetic compositions were also designated *prosa* by early medieval writers who were unfamiliar with the ancient rules of metre, before new rhythmic conventions became established. See further E.R. Curtius *European Literature and the Latin Middle Ages* New York (1953) pp.150f.

10. Philo *De Vita Contemplativa* 84.

11. Plin. *Ep.* 10, 96, 7. For a discussion of this and other views of Pliny's account see A.N. Sherwin-White *The Letters of Pliny* Oxford (1966) pp.704f.

12. The early sequences found in the MSS originating from the abbey of St. Martial at Limoges were collected by G.M. Dreves and published as Vol. 7 of *Analecta Hymnica Medii Aevi (AH)*. Later C. Blume and H. Bannister issued a newly-edited collection of early sequences in Vol. 53 of the same series; but this is unfortunately by no means exhaustive.

13. E.g. *Age nunc, die, camoena* for Christmas (*AH* 53, 11), the two Notkerian sequences *Christe domine laetifica* and *O quam mira sunt* for the Tuesday after Easter and the Sunday after Ascension respectively (*ibid.* 48 and 69), and the extensive Eastertide sequence *Praecelsa admodum* (*AH* 7, 71). See also von den Steinen 'Anfänge' (1947) pp.161f.

14. See von den Steinen 'Anfänge' (1946) pp.241-252.

15. Text printed and discussed in P. Dronke 'The Beginnings of the Sequence' *Beitr. zur Gesch. der deutschen Sprache u. Lit.* 87 Tübingen (1965) pp.45-47, with discussion of date *ibid.* pp.70-73. Text and melody printed in *MGG* 12 *s.v. Sequenz* Beisp.I.

16. Consideration of the three forms of early sequence brings out clearly the vital and determining role played by antiphonal performance. The immediate repetition of each musical sentence by means of syllabically corresponding strophes gave the composition an instantly recognisable structure. A pattern combining absence of strophic responsion (as in the sequences cited in n.13) with an iterated cursus would make perfect aesthetic sense, but is not found. It would inevitably reflect an academic approach rather than the demands of performance.

17. *AH* 7,230; *OBML V*[2] (Raby) 68. See von den Steinen 'Anfänge' (1947) pp.139-141.

18. In *Notker der Dichter* von den Steinen identified two principal motifs characteristic of the sequence, *viz.* 'Fest–' and 'Liedmotiv', but did not treat them systematically. He also referred at one point to a 'Pflichtmotiv' (not included in his index). See *op.cit.* I pp.135, 163f., 213-215.

19. *AH* 54,66; *OBML V*[2] (Raby) 116.

20. *AH* 53,70.

21. See E. Norden *Agnostos Theos* Leipzig (1913) pp.149-160, 168-176. These features are also strongly marked in Notker's sequence for the Assumption *Congaudent angelorum chori* (*AH* 53,104).

22. The transitional and rhyming sequences are collected in vol. 54 of *AH*.

23. See W. Apel *Gregorian Chant* London (1958) pp.79-83.

24. The fundamental study of tropes (from the textual point of view at least) is still L. Gautier *Histoire de la Poésie liturgique au moyen Age: I Les Tropes* Paris (1886, repr. 1965). See also Szöverffy *op.cit.*(n.2 above) I pp.275-281; Stäblein *s.v. Tropus MGG* 13, 797-826.

25. See B. Stäblein 'Zum Verständnis des "klassischen" Tropus' *Acta Musicologica* 35 (1963) pp.84-95, esp. 91f.

26. For verse tropes to the Ordinary see *AH* 47; to the Proper *AH* 49.

27. See Gautier *op.cit.* (n.27) pp.49, 84 and cf. 77.

28. *AH* 49, *Vorwort*, 3; *OBML V*^{2}(Raby) 99. See further K. Young *The Drama of the Medieval Church* Oxford (1933) I pp.201ff.; W.L. Smoldon *New Oxford History of Music* II pp.177-189.

DANTE'S LATIN *ECLOGUES*

by

MARK DAVIE

(University of Liverpool)

Dante Alighieri, besides the *Divine Comedy* which was probably the product of the last fifteen years of his life, wrote some ninety lyric poems in Italian, two prose works, also in Italian, which take the form of extended commentaries on selections of his lyrics, three Latin prose treatises on more specialised topics, and thirteen Latin prose epistles. In prose, his Latin and Italian writings are almost equal in volume; his verse production is entirely Italian, with the exception of two compositions in hexameters, of sixty-eight and ninety-seven lines respectively, written in the last years of his life in response to two verse epistles sent to him by Giovanni del Virgilio, an otherwise little known teacher of rhetoric at the University of Bologna[1]. These poems[2] are in every way so exceptional among Dante's works that there have been persistent, though almost certainly unfounded, doubts about their authenticity[3]: they are the only works (apart from the short scientific *Quaestio de Aqua et Terra*) which can definitely be assigned to the last two years of Dante's life, and which therefore postdate the greater part of the *Divine Comedy*; the decision to write in Latin verse runs counter to all Dante's pronouncements on the status and purpose of his poetry elsewhere in his works; and the literary challenge which Dante sets himself to overcome, the revival of Vergilian Eclogue as a vehicle for the discussion of the poet's craft, is altogether more characteristic of the succeeding generation, when following Dante's lead both Boccaccio and Petrarch wrote full-scale *Bucolica Carmina*, than of Dante's own.[4] These two poems are therefore something of an enigma to Dante scholars, and although by no means neglected they have been less generally known among readers of Dante than the rest of his works. But they are recognisably the work of the poet who wrote the *Divine Comedy*, and this alone, quite apart from their significant place in the history of Medieval and Neo-Latin Pastoral, makes them worthy of the attention of students of Latin poetry, and indeed of poetry in general.

Dante's two *Eclogues* are the second and fourth poems in the correspondence which was initiated by Giovanni del Virgilio some time during the year 1319[5], and terminated by Dante's death in September 1321[6]. It is naturally essential to consider the correspondence as a whole, and in the discussion which follows the four poems are numbered consecutively (nos. 1 and 3 being by Giovanni, 2 and 4 by Dante) as in the Wicksteed and Gardner edition.

Giovanni's first poem, *Pieridum vox alma*, addresses Dante as a revered master, though not without a hint of academic complacency, as he praises the exalted themes of Dante's poetry (lines 1-5) but regrets that he chooses to cast such pearls before swine (21) by writing in the vulgar tongue: how can he expect the mere *gens idiota* to follow him as he penetrates mysteries which perplexed Plato himself (10f.)? Meanwhile, scholars who would appreciate the profundities of his thought wait in vain for a poem addressed to them: *nos pallentes nihil ex te vate legemus* (7). Giovanni therefore proposes several themes from contemporary history which await worthy commemoration in verse (26-9); and the classical garb in which he alludes to these events, as well as the events themselves (the death of the emperor Henry VII in August 1313, in the course of his unsuccessful attempt to re-establish the imperial overlordship in Italy, and various episodes in the ensuing struggle for control of the northern and central parts of the country) indicates clearly enough the kind of work which he had in mind: a poem which would confer epic[7] dignity on the great issues of contemporary or recent history and preserve them for posterity. Such a poem had, indeed, been written only four or five years before, by the Paduan Albertino Mussato; his *Ecerinis* had celebrated the downfall and ejection from Padua of the Veronese tyrant Ezzelino da Romano (1194-1259), in terms which explicitly invited his fellow citizens to take note of the parallel in their own day, when once again a lord of Verona, Can Grande della Scala, was attempting to assert his overlordship of Padua. The Della Scala family, however, had been Dante's patrons for many years, and Giovanni here suggests Can Grande's exploits against the Paduans[8] as a possible theme for Dante's work. It seems likely that Giovanni intended to recall Mussato's poem and to invite Dante to counter its Guelph republicanism with an equally forceful celebration of the Ghibelline, imperial, cause; and this probability is strengthened by the fact that Giovanni here (35ff.) offers Dante precisely the honour which the Paduans had conferred on their poet, when in 1315, in the first such ceremony recorded in modern times, he had received the traditional laurel crown of the poet. The promise of coronation, indeed, provides one of the persistent images which is never far from the surface throughout the rest of the correspondence; although Mussato is never named in these poems[9], it is clear that Dante ardently hoped for the recognition which the Paduan humanist had gained. Giovanni invites him to equal or surpass Mussato in the same poetic genre; but Dante will insist in his reply that not only his political outlook, but the source of his whole inspiration and, inseparable from this, the language and style of his poetry, is utterly different from Mussato's. It is this underlying theme of the correspondence – the language and function of poetry and the recognition due to the poet – which will be the particular concern of this paper.

Giovanni concludes by apologising, with a Vergilian allusion (Vergil *Eclogue* 9,36), for his temerity in presuming to offer advice to so great a poet in lines *quos strepit arguto temerarius anser olori* (50) (which the goose cackles at the clear-voiced swan). And one needs only a slight acquaintance with Dante and the bold claims which he made for his vernacular poetry to recognise that Giovanni's anxiety is well founded: what will be the reaction of the proud Florentine exile, putting the finishing touches to what he had called "the sacred poem to which both heaven and earth have set their hand" (*Paradiso* 25, 1f.), to this good-natured if somewhat patronising promise of academic recognition once he has abandoned the *sermo forensis* and written verses *quae te distinguere possint* (1,18;23)? To answer this question, it will be necessary to digress briefly and to consider some of Dante's statements on the relationship between Latin and vernacular poetry elsewhere in his works.

In the *Vita nuova*, compiled when Dante was about thirty and the first work in which he collects and discusses his own poetry, his basic contention is already clear: vernacular verse, although a relatively recent phenomenon in European poetry, is based on exactly the same principles as Latin verse, and vernacular poets can claim the same poetic license as their Latin predecessors: *... chè dire per rima in volgare tanto è quanto dire per versi in latino, secondo alcuna proporzione ... onde, se alcuna figura o colore rettorico è conceduto a li poete, conceduto è a li rimatori.* (*Vita nuova* 25) (for writing in rhyme in the vernacular is the same, *mutatis mutandis*, as writing in metre in Latin ... so if any figure or colour of rhetoric is allowed to Latin poets, it is allowed to vernacular composers of rhyme)[10]. Nonetheless, the situation in which a vernacular poet finds himself is a special one; although his language has the potential qualities for any kind of poetry, there are no principles laid down to guide him in his choice of subject, style, and metrical form. In Dante's words, he is obliged to write *casualiter*, not, like the Latin poets, *regulariter*. It was to make good this deficiency that, probably in the years 1304-6, Dante began his treatise on vernacular poetics, *De Vulgari Eloquentia*; here he reiterates his claim for the potentialities of the vernacular, and specifically of the Italian vernacular, as a language for the highest style of poetry, and undertakes to "throw open the workshop" of the poet's craft (*qui* *hucusque casualiter est assumptus, illius artis ergasterium reseremus*) by providing the theoretical framework, the *poetria*, which has hitherto existed only for Latin poetry (*De Vulgari Eloquentia* 2,4). The rhetorical principles which he then goes on to state are in themselves unremarkable enough: the poet should establish the level of style appropriate to his subject matter (*utrum tragice, sive comice, sive elegiace sint canenda*) and adapt his language accordingly; the novelty lies in his assumption that there will be a vernacular language appropriate to each style, even the highest: *Si tragice canenda videntur, tunc assumendum est vulgare illustre... si vero comice, tunc quandoque mediocre, quandoque humile vulgare sumatur;... si autem elegiace, solum humile oportet nos sumere* (*ib.*). The choice of Latin or vernacular has no bearing, Dante claims, on the stylistic level of a poem; the poet is free to exploit the full range of styles in either language.

So in the *Divine Comedy* Dante is able to greet Vergil as a master, certainly, but also as a fellow-poet whom he knows intimately, and whose example he claims as the source of his own *bello stilo* (*Inferno* 1,82-7); and he can make the thirteenth-century troubadour Sordello, who wrote poetry in Provençal although he was a native of Vergil's own territory of Mantua, greet the classical poet not only as a fellow-townsman but as a poet in a shared tradition: *O gloria di Latin... per cui/mostrò ciò che potea la lingua nostra* (*Purgatorio* 7,16f.) (o glory of the Latins, through whom our tongue demonstrated its power). The tradition which unites Dante to Vergil is, in his mind, an unbroken one; the difference of language is of minor importance compared to the deep affinity which Dante felt with his predecessor and model in writing on what he saw as their common theme, the destiny of Rome.

But in the *Divine Comedy*, Dante does not only regard himself as Vergil's heir. Through no merit of his own, and no fault of Vergil's, he sees his poem as destined to penetrate into realms of revealed truth where neither Vergil nor any other poet has preceded him. Even in the *Inferno*, divine punitive justice gives rise to prodigious sights, of a purely physical and indeed grotesque kind, which Dante challenges Lucan or Ovid to match: *Taccia Lucano omai la dov'e' tocca/ del misero Sabello e di Nasidio,/ ... /Taccia di Cadmo e d'Aretusa Ovidio;* (*Inferno* 25, 94-7). (Let Lucan now be silent where he speaks of wretched Sabellus and Nassidius ... Let Ovid be silent about Cadmus and Arethusa). How much more, then, will the spiritual experiences of the *Paradiso* transcend any possible models; and at the outset of his third canticle, Dante pauses to apostrophise his readers and warn them to consider whether they will be able to follow him through the uncharted waters he is now entering: *L'acqua ch'io prendo già mai non si corse;/Minerva spira, e conducemi Appollo . . . (Paradiso* 2,7f.) (The water I am entering was never sailed before; Minerva breathes, and Apollo guides me . . .). To those few who will be able to persevere, he promises: *Que' gloriosi che passaro al Colco/non s'ammiraron come voi farete,/quando Iasón vider fatto bifolco.* (*ib.* 16-18) (Those glorious ones who crossed to Colchis were not amazed as you shall be, when they saw Jason turned ploughman).

The reference to Jason is significant in more than one respect; primarily, Dante clearly intends to compare his own unprecedented poem to the voyage of the Argonauts, the first men to venture across the open sea in a ship — and as we shall see, the reference recurs in the last canto of the *Paradiso*, making it clear that this is no casual boast but a deliberate and considered claim for the status of the poem. But more than one of the early commentators on this passage[11] also noted the contrast between the stupendous nature of the task which Jason successfully completed (the yoking of Aeetes' oxen, sowing of the dragon's teeth, and defeat of the warriors who sprang from them) and the humility of the means which he adopted (the noble warrior "turned ploughman"). And it is precisely this contrast which pervades the *Paradiso*, and makes Dante's attitude to his work much more than simply one of pride. For his subject — to some extent throughout the poem, but above all in the last four cantos, where his journey is complete and he is in the presence of God himself — is such that any effort of human language must inevitably be insufficient to recall it. Confronted with such a theme, any rhetorical notion of matching style to subject is doomed to failure; the poet's art may reach unprecedented heights, but it will still be hopelessly inadequate to match the reality which he seeks to describe. So he must acknowledge: *Da questo passo vinto mi concedo/più che già mai da punto di suo tema/soprato fosse comico o tragedo; (Paradiso* 30,22-4) (I confess myself beaten at this pass more than ever comic or tragic poet was surpassed by a point in his theme)[11]. In the last hundred lines of the poem, where Dante makes his supreme effort at visualising the ineffable as he contemplates the mystery of the Trinity, he again refers to the Argonauts, as the basis of a difficult simile comparing, not the two "voyages" themselves, but the impression they have left on the human memory: *Un punto solo m'è maggior letargo/ che venticinque secoli a la 'mpresa/che fe' Nettuno ammirar l'ombra d'Argo. (Paradiso* 33, 94-6) (A single moment produces in me greater oblivion than twenty-five centuries have brought on the enterprise which made Neptune wonder at the shadow of the Argo). The theological point which Dante makes here — that his momentary supernatural experience of God transcended the power of the intellect to comprehend it, so that the incapacity of the memory to retain it was greater than that produced by even the longest lapse of time[12] — does not directly concern us; but, quite apart from the implied comparison, once again, of Dante's enterprise with that of the Argonauts, it clearly has a direct bearing on the theme of the necessary inadequacy of human language. So, ten lines later, as he reaches the culmination of his vision, Dante again breaks off to remind his readers: *Omai sarà più corta mia favella,/pur a quel ch'io ricordo, che d'un fante/che bagni ancor la lingua a la mammella.* (*ib.* 106-8) (Now my speech will come more short even of what I remember than that of an infant who still bathes his tongue at the breast). The abrupt lowering of the stylistic level produced by this last interjection — partly by the physical explicitness of the last line, partly by the echoes which it awakes of passages earlier in the *Divine Comedy* where Dante has emphasised his own weakness by comparing himself to a small child[13] — itself exemplifies the point which Dante forces on our attention, even here at the climax of the poem: that this is not a "tragic" work, written in a uniformly elevated style, but a "comedy" which adopts *quandoque mediocre, quandoque humile vulgare.* Giovanni asked Dante to write on a theme and in a style worthy of his talents; the answer of the *Divine Comedy* is that it deals with the worthiest theme imaginable, a theme of which no style attainable in human language can ever be worthy.

How, then, does Dante reply to the well-meaning if tactless suggestions of Giovanni's epistle? As far as Giovanni was concerned, it is clear from his next missive (no. 3) that Dante's poem had surpassed his best hopes; not only did the master reply to him in Latin verse, but he showed his confidence in Giovanni's judgement by addressing to him, without preamble or explanation, the first attempt in modern times to clothe a discussion of poetry in the guise of Vergilian Pastoral. After a brief acknowledgement of Giovanni's letter, Dante's poem (*Vidimus in nigris*) moves straight into the bucolic world: *Forte recensentes pastas de more capellas* . . . (3) (it chanced that, counting as is our wont our well-fed goats . . .). The narrator, *"Tityrus"*, who it soon becomes clear is Dante himself, accompanied by *"Meliboeus meus"*[14], is reading a letter which he has received from *"Mopsus"*, evidently Giovanni. Meliboeus asks to know its contents, and is not to be dissuaded by Tityrus' protestations that Mopsus inhabits *pascua . . .ignota tibi* (11) and sings *ignota carmina* (25). Tityrus relents, and explains that Mopsus, richly endowed by the Muses, though alone in his devotion to them in Bologna, *dum satagunt alii causarum iura doceri* (29) — Bologna being famous for its law school —

writes to invite him to receive the laurel crown: *me vocat ad frondes versa Peneide cretas* (33). Will he accept, Meliboeus asks? Tityrus acknowledges that the pastures would ring with a great *balatus* if he did accept and raise his song before a gathering such as Mopsus proposes, his head crowned with leaves (39f.); but, in lines which strongly recall a famous and moving passage in the Paradiso[15], he insists that if he ever accepts such a form of public recognition, it must be in his native Florence when the *Divine Comedy* is completed – when . . . *mundi circumflua corpora cantu/ astricolaeque meo velut infera regna patebunt* (48f.) (the star-dwellers and the bodies which flow round the world are, like the lower realms, made known in my song). Perhaps then he may hope for such recognition, if, he adds, Mopsus does not object (*Concedat Mopsus*, 51). Why should Mopsus object, asks Meliboeus? To which Tityrus replies: *Comica nonne vides ipsum reprehendere verba...?* (52) (do you not see how he blames the words of comedy?) How then, pursues the practical Meliboeus, are we to overcome his hostility? Tityrus proposes to send him ten measures of milk from a certain *ovis gratissima* of his flock, *nulli iuncta gregi, nullis assuetaque caulis* (61) (part of no flock, familiar with no pen). Clearly Dante is alluding to some examples of his most highly prized poetry; and it would seem reasonable to suppose that these are ten cantos of the *Paradiso*[16]. This was known only fragmentarily, if at all, in Dante's lifetime, and, if anything could, it would persuade the most sceptical classicist of the value of *comica verba*, vernacular verse. And Dante's *Eclogue* ends on a note of rustic simplicity, with Meliboeus told to content himself with *duris crustis...infigere dentes* (66) and a meal of barley cooking for the two shepherds in their *parva tabernacula* (68).

This final note is of course appropriate to the Pastoral genre, traditionally the genre of the *stilus humilis* – what Dante, as we have seen, calls *comedia*. And a number of other qualities in the poem become clearer when it is considered in this light[17]. Tityrus' companion Meliboeus, for instance, is evidently one of the *gens idiota* on whom Giovanni had told Dante he was wasting his efforts, and this status frees him from the obligation of behaving with the *gravitas* and decorum of his betters; and his conversation – the insistent questioning of line 6 (*"Tityre quid Mopsus, quid vult? edissere" dixit*), the disjointed exchange of line 51 (*"... /Concedat Mopsus". "Mopsus" tunc ille "quid?" inquit*), and his resigned gesture in lines 56f. (*... Tunc ille humeros contraxit, et "Ergo/quid faciemus" ait...*) – consistently has the effect of bringing the style down to a concrete, almost banal level. There is surely a gently ironical note, too, in Tityrus' words in line 39, when he presses the pastoral allegory to the point of describing the academic plaudits of Bologna as a great *balatus* echoing round the pastures. It is difficult to avoid the impression that Dante, in replying to Giovanni, deliberately does so on a lower stylistic level, implicitly rejecting Giovanni's appeal to him to raise his verse to the highest level of "tragedy". And this gives a new perspective to his paraphrase of Giovanni's argument in line 52; Giovanni had urged him to abandon mere *comica verba*, by which he evidently meant poetry in the vernacular; any composition in the *sermo forensis* must, in his view, necessarily be *comicus*[18]. But is not Dante in his reply giving him precisely *comica verba*, a composition in the *stilus humilis* – but one which Giovanni will not reject, because it is in Latin? It is the point which Dante was at pains to make in the *De Vulgari Eloquentia*: that the choice of style is quite independent of the choice of Latin or vernacular; any level of style is equally possible in either language.

Giovanni, at any rate, was as we have seen delighted when he received the poem, and in his reply (*Forte sub irriguos*) he enthusiastically acclaims Dante for sounding a note which has not been heard in Arcady for so many years (20ff.), and takes up the challenge to reply in the same vein: *depostis calamis maioribus... arripio tenues* (31f.) (laying aside the greater reeds, I take up the slender ones). He hails Dante as a second Vergil, perhaps even Vergil himself reincarnate (33-5), shares his indignation at the rejection and exile which he has suffered from his native city, and sympathetically echoes, perhaps sensing that this was the emotional centre of Dante's poem, the lines in which he had confessed to his dream of receiving coronation there (44-6)[19]. Nonetheless, he presses Dante not to despise the hospitality which he offers in Bologna, of which he gives a delightful picture (52ff.), equally delightfully allegorised in the *Laurenziana* gloss (see note 6), so that every detail, from the *fons humidus* (52) and the *virgulta* (53) to the *herba papavera... oblivia.../grata creans* (55f.) corresponds to an aspect of their intellectual pursuits. But Giovanni then reflects that he cannot hope to entice Tityrus away from the patronage of *"Iolas"* – clearly Guido Novello da Polenta, at whose court at Ravenna Dante spent the last years of his life – where he already has all that he could wish for (80ff.); and finally he resolves to return Tityrus' compliment and to send him ten measures of milk from his own herd – *tot.../vascula quot nobis promisit Tityrus ipse* (94f.).

Several points in this poem reveal Giovanni's slight unease in his adoption of the Pastoral convention. Although he responds to Dante's initiative by taking up in his turn the *calamos tenues* of Pastoral, he still expects Dante, if he accepts his invitation to join him in Bologna, to sing with greater *gravitas* than Giovanni himself, as befits his age: . . . *simul cantabimus ambo,/ipse levi calamo sed tu gravitate magistrum/firmius insinuans, ne quem sua deserat aetas.* (49-51) (We shall both sing, I with a light reed, but you gravely and with more authority showing yourself a master, that we may each observe our age). Again, following Dante's example, he adopts a "rustic" style, asking himself *quia nam civile canebas/urbe sedens carmen* . . .?(27f.) (why did you sing an urban song, dwelling in the city?); but although he knows that, according to the convention, *rusticitas* is preferable to *urbanitas* in pastoral poetry, his instinctive sympathy for the latter reveals itself when he reasons that he will never be able to rival the hospitality of Iolas, and he tells himself that Iolas is *comis et urbanus, dum sunt tua rustica dona* (81) (courteous and urbane, whereas yours are rustic gifts). One senses that, for all his enthusiastic acceptance of the Pastoral mode in which Dante had addressed him, Giovanni is as anxious to heighten the style of the correspondence as Dante was to lower it.

Before moving on to Dante's final contribution to the correspondence, we should note one further point in Giovanni's poem which will be taken up by Dante. Giovanni begins with a topographical periphrasis indicating the location of Bologna: . . . *ubi Sarpina Rheno/obvia fit, viridi niveos interlita crines/nympha procax* . . . (1-3) (where Sarpina, a sportive nymph, goes to meet Rhenus, her snowy locks interspersed with green). These two rivers (in Italian, the Sàvena and the Reno) partially enclose the city between them, coming near to each other but not actually merging; and Dante himself had described the city as lying, simply, *tra Savena e Reno* in a canto of the *Divine Comedy* (*Inferno* 18, 61) where Bolognese characters are particularly prominent. Giovanni almost certainly knew the *Inferno*[20], and may well have had Dante's phrase in mind; but there was certainly nothing there to suggest the description of the water of the Sàvena, *viridi niveos interlita crines*, apparently indicating a basically white colour (its "snowy locks" − foam?) flecked with green (the underlying colour of the water, or of vegetation beneath the surface?). What this expression does recall − and one can only assume that the resemblance is fortuitous, since the contexts are so entirely different − is Dante's image, in 2, 43f., of his own white hair hidden under the green leaves of the laurel − *abscondere canos/fronde sub inserta*. The coincidence, however, is not lost on Dante, who in his second *Eclogue* takes up the image and boldly brings the two contexts together.

The evidence for dating this last poem (*Velleribus Colchis*) in the spring of 1321, and hence for assuming a lapse of about a year between this and the earlier part of the correspondence, has already been noted (note 6); and it is confirmed by the marked difference in the tone which now prevails. The whole poem is concerned with the hostility of the city of Bologna to Dante, and the dangers which he would incur if he were to go there. Dante had touched on this danger – almost certainly a political one, since Bologna was staunchly committed to the Guelph cause in Italy as a whole, and to the ruling Black Guelph faction in Florence, to both of whom Dante had by this time made himself *persona non grata* – in a brief reference in his first *Eclogue: Sed timeam saltus et rura ignara deorum* (2, 42) (but let me fear the glades and countryside which are ignorant of the gods); but now the menace pervades the whole poem, and Dante's rejection of the city is bitter and violent. In the traditional pastoral setting of Sicily, Bologna becomes Mount Etna, the home of the dreaded Polyphemus[21]. The poem begins with Tityrus and another companion, Alphesiboeus[22], marvelling that Mopsus should continue to live in such an uncongenial place – *arida Cyclopum . . . saxa sub Aetna* (27) (the parched rocks of the Cyclopes under Etna) – when Meliboeus returns, breathless, from his mission to Mopsus. As soon as he has recovered sufficiently to blow on the flute which he carries, it utters of its own accord the ninety-seven verses of Mopsus' song – that is, of Giovanni's *Eclogue* (28ff.). Alphesiboeus, alarmed at this evidence of the song's supernatural power, fears that it may overcome Tityrus' caution and tempt him to venture, after all, to the Cyclops' den. But Tityrus reassures him, saying that he would indeed be tempted by Mopsus' invitation, if it were not for his fear of Polyphemus which overrides all other considerations (63ff.); and Alphesiboeus reiterates the horrors of the Cyclops' reputation: *"Quis Polyphemon" ait "non horreat" Alphesiboeus/"assuetum rictus humano sanguine tingui . . .?"* (76f.) ("Who would not recoil from Polyphemus", replies Alphesiboeus, "wont as he is to dye his jaws in human blood?"). Finally, he echoes Giovanni's reference to the two rivers encircling the city, as he prays that Tityrus may never seek *"ut Rhenus et Naias illa recludat/hoc illustre caput, cui iam frondator in alta/virgine perpetuas festinat cernere frondes."* (85-7) ("that Rhenus and the Naiad should ever enclose this illustrious head, for which the pruner is already hastening to select evergreen leaves from the noble virgin"). Dante could not resist the hint of coronation in the phrase *viridi niveos interlita crines*, although Giovanni had tactfully omitted any overt reference to this aspect of his invitation in his second poem. Dante's expression, too, is now unspecific: the *perpetuas frondes* are clearly those of the laurel (the *alta virgo* being Daphne); but the reference could be either to a literal laurel crown or to the eternal fame which it symbolises, and Dante leaves this ambiguity unresolved.

This is not the only respect in which Dante's poem, like his first, responds unpredictably to Giovanni's invitation. There is again a "comic" episode in Meliboeus' breathless arrival and the laughter of his companions, but this, as Martellotti has noted (note 17), corresponds to similar details not only in Dante's first *Eclogue* but also in Giovanni's reply. More striking is Dante's response to Giovanni's suggestion that, while he himself might sing *levi calamo*, Dante should show greater *gravitas*, as befits his age (3, 50f.). Giovanni has given Dante the venerable qualities of the Vergilian Tityrus, addressing him as *divine senex, blande senex* (3, 33; 42); and although it is true that Dante in his first poem had referred to his *canos* which he, *solitum flavescere*, would now hide under the laurel (2,43f.), the Tityrus of this last poem is a quite different figure: he is *annosus* (4, 12) and reclines on the ground while his companions stand; he is referred to as *senior* (32) and *longevus* (64), and addressed as *venerande senex* (46) and *fortunate senex* (twice: 55, 61). This insistence on the venerability of a character representing the poet himself is surprising, particularly since this quality was in no way stressed in the earlier poem, and bearing in mind that at the time of writing the poet was approaching only his fifty-sixth birthday and was apparently in good health[23]. I would not wish to press the point of biographical fact too far, because to do so would be to make the mistake which, I suspect, Dante is here tactfully pointing out to Giovanni: that of confusing a literary convention with literal truth[24]. The aged Tityrus is a conventional figure representing the poet; in particular, the respect due to his white hair adds to the dignity of the laurel crown which rests upon it, and the combination of this sign of age with the undying leaves of the laurel vividly represents the immortal fame which outlives the poet. It was surely this, rather than any merely literal reference, which Dante intended to convey when he described his dream of *abscondere canos/fronde sub inserta* (2,43f.) – the image which, as we have seen, recurs so insistently in the rest of the correspondence. It therefore seems reasonable to detect a gently ironical note in Dante's repeated references, in his last poem, to his own senility.

More importantly, and more positively, any suggestion of senility and its accompanying *gravitas* is decisively overridden by the dominant metaphor of this poem. It is a metaphor which recurs constantly throughout Dante's poetry, beginning in some of his relatively early lyrics and becoming one of the key metaphors in the *Divine Comedy*: that of growth and fertility as opposed to hardness and sterility[25]. Dante's situation in Ravenna – in the allegory, the richest pastures of Sicily (70ff.) – is one of *viridis caespes* (32), *roscida rura* (46), *fontes et pabula* (61), *tenera herba* (70), *mollia prata* (94). In contrast, Bologna (allegorically, Etna) is a place of *arida saxa* (27), *Aetneo pumice tectum* (54), *Aetnica saxa* (74). The contrast is of course primarily between the two cities, and Dante's hostility towards Bologna is as we have seen primarily political; but the contrast which emerges so strongly in this poem should also, I think, be seen as the culmination of the contrasts which have been present implicitly throughout the correspondence. In his description of the horrors of the career of *"Polyphemus"*, Dante does briefly adopt the tragic style which Giovanni had recommended to him in his first epistle – recording, in allegorical guise, the violent struggles of contemporary politics. Urging this style upon him, Giovanni had offered him academic recognition and learned conversation; but Dante here defends his humbler muse, not because it is more tranquil (there is no lack of political and moral struggles in his masterpiece), but because it is more fruitful. He knows that his claim to the *perpetuas frondes* of poetic immortality will rest, not on the kind of "tragedy'. which Giovanni wanted him to write, but on the poem which Dante himself called a Comedy, and which by common consent of readers ever since has been called Divine.

NOTES

1. The known facts about Giovanni del Virgilio are conveniently summarised, with bibliography, by G. Martellotti in *Enciclopedia dantesca* III Rome (1972) pp. 193f. The documents recording his presence in Bologna and in the neighbouring town of Cesena all date from 1321-6. Of his other works, there are extant an *Eclogue* addressed to Albertino Mussato (see note 9 below) in which Giovanni tries to continue the correspondence begun with Dante, some other fragments of poetic correspondence and a verse epitaph intended for Dante's tomb; these are all printed in Wicksteed and Gardner's edition (see following note). In addition there is the *Diaffonus*, a verse correspondence with one Ser Nuzio Marchigiano; two partial commentaries on Ovid, a fragmentary translation of *Metamorphoses* 13 into Italian, and an *ars dictaminis*.

2. The first critical edition of the correspondence was that of P.H. Wicksteed and E.G. Gardner *Dante and Giovanni del Virgilio* Westminster (1902, photographic reprint New York 1970), with an English translation facing the text and much useful introductory and explanatory material. The translations given in this paper are based on those of this edition. The text itself has been corrected at a number of points by the editions of G. Albini, Bologna (1903, reprinted with additional material ed. G.B. Pighi, Bologna 1965); and of E. Pistelli in *Opere di Dante* Florence (1921), frequently reprinted.
For an overall introduction to the poems, there is again the article and bibliography by G. Martellotti in *Enciclopedia dantesca cit.* II pp. 644-6. A

useful summary of the main critical problems is given by G. Reggio *Le egloghe di Dante* Florence (1969).

3. The earliest MS of the correspondence (Florence, *Laurenziana* 29, 8) is an anthology of pastoral poems collected and copied by Boccaccio, and the suggestion that the four poems are an elaborate falsification on Boccaccio's part, in order to raise Dante's standing in a generation which undervalued the vernacular, has been most recently made by A. Rossi in a series of articles: *Paragone* 13 (1962) pp. 3-41; *Miscellanea storica della Valdelsa* 49 (1963) pp. 130-72; *Studi danteschi* 40 (1963) pp. 133-278; *Paragone* 19 (1968) pp. 61-125. Rossi's arguments have been authoritatively countered by G. Padoan in *Studi sul Boccaccio* 1 (1963) pp. 528-44, 2 (1964) pp. 475-507, and 5 (1969) pp. 365-8.

4. The adaptation of Vergilian Pastoral to the discussion of contemporary issues from the Carolingian period to the 12th century is described by Professor P.G. Walsh in his contribution to this volume; but the originality of Dante's use of the genre as a vehicle for specifically literary discussion remains striking. See C. Battisti 'Le egloghe dantesche' *Studi danteschi* 33 (1956) pp. 61-111. On Dante's *Eclogues* and their subsequent development by Boccaccio and Petrarch see G. Martellotti 'Dalla tenzone al carme bucolico' *Italia medioevale e umanistica* 7 (1964) pp. 325-36, and 'La riscoperta dello stile bucolico (da Dante al Boccaccio)' in *Dante e la cultura veneta* Florence (1966) pp. 335-46.

5. The exact date depends on the identification of the historical events referred to allegorically in 1, 26-9, and possibly 42-3. The *Ligurum montes et classes Parthenopaeas* of l.29 clearly refer to the siege of king Robert of Naples by a Ghibelline army surrounding Genoa in 1318-19, which was eventually relieved from the sea by the Neapolitan fleet in February 1319. This final action has generally been regarded as the *terminus a quo* for the poem, although E. Chiarini *(s.v.* 'Ravenna' in *Enciclopedia dantesca cit.* IV p. 861) has pointed out that this is not consistent with the other events mentioned in these lines, since it represented a major Guelph victory whereas the others all invite Dante to celebrate Ghibelline successes; Chiarini therefore takes the poem to have been written in the earlier stages of the siege when Robert was under considerable pressure from the Ghibellines. On the other hand, some scholars see ll. 42-3, *quid concitat aequor/Tirrhenum Nereus?,* as an allusion to a storm which damaged Robert's fleet in December 1319, and Reggio *(op. cit.* pp. 13-20) goes on to show that the consequent postdating of this poem to the very end of 1319 or the beginning of 1320 gives a convincingly coherent chronology to the whole correspondence. It is perhaps worth pointing out, with reference to Chiarini's objection, that the battle of February 1319 was by no means the end of the anxieties of the Genoese Guelphs, and that the situation at the end of that year was still one in which a Ghibelline propagandist might find some grounds for encouraging his troops.

6. According to the marginal gloss which accompanies these texts in the *Laurenziana* MS (which may be the work of Boccaccio although they appear to have been added by a different scribe), *stetit Dantes per annum* [after receiving Giovanni's poem] *ante quam faceret Velleribus Colchis* [i.e. no. 4 of the correspondence], *et mortuus est ante quam eam micteret.* Dante's own opening lines indicate the season as April – May (the sun has emerged from Aries) and it is likely that the poem's political allusions (see below, note 21) correspond to the situation in Bologna during these months in 1321.

7. The word "epic" is here used in its generally accepted modern sense; as will

become clear below. Dante and his contemporaries called such poetry "tragic".

8. 1, 28: the *"Phrygios"* are the Paduans, so called because of the legendary founding of the city by the Trojan Antenor; and the *"molossus"* (hound) is Can Grande, with an evident play on the meaning of his name.

9. There may be an indirect reference to Mussato's name in Giovanni's second poem, 3, 88f.: *Me contemne, sitim Frigio Musone levabo;/scilicet hoc nescis, fluvio potabor avito.* Literally, the "Phrygian [i.e. again, Paduan] Muso" is a small river which flows near the city; but the *Laurenziana* gloss sees the phrase as an allusion to Mussato's name, and modern commentators have generally accepted this. The passage remains ambiguous: does Giovanni mean, as Wicksteed and Gardner thought, that if Dante despises him he will tempt him to Bologna with the promise of a meeting with Mussato ("I will quench [your] thirst with the Phrygian Muso")? This assumes that this poem was written before September 1319, when Mussato visited Bologna, and that Giovanni had sufficient prior knowledge of his visit to be able to communicate it to Dante. But as we have seen (note 5 above), it is at least possible that the whole correspondence was not begun until the very end of 1319; and there is the further difficulty that on this interpretation the second line becomes virtually meaningless. The alternative, that, if Dante refuses his invitation, Giovanni will turn to Mussato instead ("I will quench [my] thirst"), seems excessively abrupt, unless one makes the primary reference to Padua as a place, and only secondarily, if at all, to Mussato ("If you decline my invitation, I too will leave Bologna and return to my native place"); the second line then expands and explains this, since (*hoc nescis*) Dante could not be expected to know of Giovanni's Paduan ancestry. See Reggio, *op. cit.* pp. 74-8.

10. Dante's works other than the *Eclogues* are quoted from the following editions: *Vita nuova* ed. M. Barbi, Florence (1931); *De vulgari eloquentia* ed. A. Marigo, 3rd ed. revised by P.G. Ricci, Florence (1957); *La commedia secondo l'antica vulgata* ed. G. Petrocchi, 4 vols. Milan (1966-7). Available English translations are: *Vita nuova* trans. B. Reynolds, Harmondsworth (1969); trans. M. Musa 2nd ed. Bloomington Indiana (1973); *De Vulgari Eloquentia* in *The Latin Works of Dante Alighieri* trans. A.G. Ferrers Howell, London (1904); *Divine Comedy* trans. J. Sinclair, 3 vols. 2nd ed. Oxford (1971); trans. C.S. Singleton, 6 vols. Princeton and London (1971-5). Translations in this paper are my own, although for the *Comedy* I have drawn on those of Sinclair. The phrase *mutatis mutandis* here is a free translation of *secondo alcuna proporzione*, which I interpret, following N. Sapegno (*La vita nuova . . .* Florence (1943) *ad loc.*): *"tenendo conto cioè delle differenti regole, che essi seguono (per gli antichi la misura del verso, per i moderni la rima")*.

11. e.g. Benvenuto da Imola (*ca.* 1380; *Comentum super D. Aldighierii Comoediam . . .* ed. G.F. Lacaita, 5 vols. Florence (1887) vol. 4 p.340): *Vos primo videbitis magnam novam navim, idest, magnum opus novum, quod antea non vidistis; secundo, videbitis, quod ex re vili nascentur milites armati, idest, ex verbis vulgaribus nascentur fortes sententiae;* Francesco da Buti (ca. 1385-95; *Commento . . . sopra la D.C. di D. Allighieri* ed. C. Giannini, 3 vols. Pisa (1858-62) vol.3 p.45): *. . . imperò che maggior fatto è vedere me poeta poeticamente essere intrato a trattare della celeste beatitudine de' beati, che Iasone che era figliuolo di re diventare bifolco: imperò che maggior fatto e maggior fatica è a montare che a descendere. Lo poeta trattare della beatitudine celeste è montare, e lo re arare è descendere.* The incongruity of Jason's ploughing is in any case an element in Ovid's account (*Met.* 7, 118ff.) which was evidently Dante's source.

12. On the theology of this passage, see K. Foster 'Dante's Vision of God' *Italian Studies* 14 (1959) pp. 21-39.

13. The closest parallel is in a corresponding passage at the culmination of the *Inferno* where again Dante stresses the inadequacy of his speech to describe what he has witnessed (32, 7-9). For another parallel in a different context, see the famous encounter with Beatrice in *Purg.* 30, 43-5. It is interesting that in both these passages Dante uses the infantile word *mamma* (and in the former, also *babbo*), which are specifically excluded, as *verba ... puerilia propter sui simplicitatem* from the highest style in *De Vulg. Eloq.* 2, 7, 4.

14. The *Laurenziana* gloss identifies *"Meliboeus"* as one Dino Perini, like Dante a Florentine exile and his companion in Ravenna; but this identification has no direct bearing on the interpretation of the poem.

15. *Par.* 25, 1-12: a passage which is an essential commentary on this *Eclogue*. The context is the confirmation of Dante's declaration of faith, in the Heaven of the Fixed Stars, by the apostle Peter; thus, this is one of several passages where Dante explicitly claims prophetic authority for his poem. His brow has been encircled (l. 12) by the embrace of Peter himself; can he not hope for a similar gesture of recognition on earth? Yet recognition of his poem must imply acceptance of his message; and his message was nowhere more bitter, because it was nowhere more deeply felt, than when it was directed against the corruption which he saw in his native city. In his lifetime, Dante remained "a prophet without honour in his own country"; but this passage explains the importance which he attached to Florence itself, and his indifference to mere academic recognition.

16. It is difficult to imagine any poetry other than the *Paradiso* holding such a special place in Dante's affections at the end of his life as he gives to this *ovis gratissima* in ll. 58ff.; and a reference to the *Paradiso* would follow logically from the expression of his hope for recognition in ll. 48-50. Nonetheless, the *Laurenziana* gloss and a significant minority of modern scholars have taken the allegory to refer to the pastoral poetry which Dante initiates with this poem, and the *decem vascula* as a promise to extend the series to the Vergilian total of ten. But this sudden conversion to Giovanni's preference for Latin verse would represent a complete *volte-face*, not only from his own earlier position but from the whole logical progression of the poem up to this point. The most recent summaries of the argument on each side are Reggio *op. cit.* pp. 21-33 (in favour of the *Paradiso*), and E. Chiarini 'l "Decem vascula" della prima egloga dantesca' in *Dante e Bologna nei tempi di Dante* Bologna (1967) pp. 77-88 (in favour of the *Eclogues* themselves).

17. This aspect of all three *Eclogues* – Dante's two, and the second poem of Giovanni – has been noted by G. Martellotti, 'La riscoperta dello stile bucolico' *cit.* note 4 above.

18. M. Pastore Stocchi 'Dante, Mussato e la tragedia' in *Dante e la cultura veneta* Florence (1966) pp. 251-62, suggests that Dante is similarly paraphrasing the view which he rejects when, in a notorious *crux* in his letter dedicating the *Paradiso* to Can Grande, he explains that his work is a "comedy" because its language is *remissus ... et humilis, quia locutio vulgaris in qua et mulierculae communicant* (*Dantis Alagherii Epistolae* ed. P. Toynbee 2nd ed. Oxford (1966) p. 177). The questions raised by the letter to Can Grande are beyond

the scope of this paper, but Pastore Stocchi's article gives a convincing account of it in relation to the *Eclogues.*

19. Compare these two lines with ll. 42-4 of Dante's poem: i.e. 3, 44 and 2, 43 *si quando;* 3, 44 *iterum flavescere* and 2, 44 *solitum flavescere;* 3, 45 *canos . . . ab ipsa Phillide* [Florence itself?] *pexos* and 2, 44 *pexare capillos.*

20. Of the various suggested allusions to the *Divine Comedy* in Giovanni's poems 1, 17-19 at least seems a clear reference to *Inf.* 4, 102.

21. No single identification has been firmly established for the person of *"Polyphemus";* the most likely figure is Fulcieri de' Calboli, who was about to assume the office of Capitano del Popolo at Bologna (and had probably already been elected) in April – May 1321 when Dante wrote this *Eclogue.* Dante already had good reason to fear and dislike Fulcieri, who had held the office of Podestà in Florence in 1303, and whose reign there is described, in bloodthirsty terms similar to those used for Polyphemus here, in *Purg.* 14, 58ff. See Reggio, *op. cit.* pp. 35-47.

22. The *Laurenziana* gloss offers more information on the minor characters in these poems than on those whom it would be most interesting to identify: although silent over the identity of *"Polyphemus",* it names *"Alphesiboeus"* as one *magister Fiducius de Milottis de Certaldo medicus qui tunc morabatur Ravenne.*

23. Dante's final illness was apparently quite short; in August 1321, less than a month before his death, he travelled to Venice as Guido Novello's ambassador, with the responsibility of conducting difficult negotiations in a dispute between Venice and Ravenna over the right to levy customs dues.

24. The importance of this distinction in interpreting these poems has recently been emphasised by R.W. Carrubba 'The Color of Dante's Hair *Medieval Studies* 33 (1971) pp. 348-50.

25. To cite only the most obvious examples: rock, with its associated qualities of hardness and sterility, is the underlying metaphor, recurrent to the point of obsessiveness, of the group of poems known as the *rime petrose* dating from 1296-7; the same qualities are symbolised by ice in the lowest depths of *Inferno.* In contrast to this, the Earthly Paradise which Dante reaches at the summit of Mount Purgatory is a place of perpetual fruitfulness (*Purg.* 28, 109ff.; 143), corresponding to the healthy growth which should be attained by the individual soul (*ib.* 30, 118-20). Paradise itself is similarly represented in terms of the fruit of man's redemption (*Purg.* 32, 73-5) and the souls of the blessed form a celestial rose (*Par.* 33, 7-9) which is Dante's point of arrival, and the measure of the distance he has travelled from the chaotic, uncultivated *selva oscura* which was his point of departure.

THE CAMBRIDGE SONGS

by

ALLAN B.E. HOOD
(University of Edinburgh)

1.   The external circumstances of the collection

This early lyric anthology forms one section of a bulky volume copied at the monastery of St. Augustine, Canterbury, in the 11th century, and now in Cambridge University Library. The songs are an integral part of the manuscript, but derive from a Rhenish collection. The lyrics range widely, from hymns and sequences, imperial and ecclesiastical panegyrics and laments to ballad-like narratives, love poems and excerpts from classical poets. Though only two pieces are neumed, formal features and numerous musical references indicate that music was an important factor in selection; and the excerpts from Horace, Vergil and Statius correspond with the rare neumed passages in manuscripts of classical poetry.

Such Latin songs would be accessible to a restricted audience; the collection may have originated among the Emperor's courtier-clerics, or from a religious house with imperial connections like Hrotsvitha's Gandersheim, or from some worldly episcopal court like that satirised by Sextus Amarcius. Despite the local and transient interest of some of the Rhenish material, the anthology was copied at Canterbury; some poems would serve as models for panegyric and *planctus,* and musical entertainment was popular with the monks of Christ Church.

2.   Four permutations of amatory themes

(a)   no. 40 (*Levis exsurgit zephirus*) provides a very early instance of two recurrent themes in medieval lyric, the juxtaposition of spring and love, and the lament of a love-sick woman; these are interestingly exploited, with the increasing personification and animation of the nature-introduction, and the open-ended, suggestive conclusion.

(b)   no. 48 (*O admirable Veneris idolum*) is a North Italian poem, which may have reached the Rhineland through scholars, such as Rather of Verona, who were drawn from Italy to the Ottonian court. In this clever and erudite paederastic poem, learned word-play and evocation of classical mythology are framed by reference to God

199

and the devil in the first stanza and by wry Old Testament allusion in the last.

(c)   no. 14 (*Advertite, omnes populi*), the tale of a Swabian merchant, his adulterous wife and her bastard son, is plausibly attributed to Heribert, bishop of Eichstatt. The snow-child motif does not belong to folk-tradition but is a witty cleric's tale, in complex sequence form and with reminiscences of Horace and Sallust; the theme has a varied subsequent history, in such diverse literary contexts as Geoffrey of Vinsauf, Hans Sachs and even the N-town mystery cycle.

(d)   no. 27 (*Iam, dulcis amica, venito*) is extant also in two other manuscripts. After an almost identical invitation to a girl, in stanzas 1-5, to come to a splendid banquet, the versions diverge, and medieval censorship makes the Cambridge manuscript illegible. In a collection of tropes and sequences from St. Martial, Limoges, the poem is most explicit in its echoes of the Song of Solomon; it may be devotional rather than amatory and portray in dialogue form the love-affair between Christ and the human soul. The version in a Vienna manuscript also uses Solomonic language, but the physical urgency and erotic tendency are clear; it should be read as a monologue, not a dialogue. Since composite reconstruction may produce a poem which never existed for any medieval reader, each version should be interpreted independently; and the variant versions illustrate the interdependence of secular and devotional poetry, in which the Song of Solomon is crucial.

3.   Conclusion

The Cambridge Songs anticipate types of lyric common in later medieval poetry, Latin and vernacular: for example, love-lyrics with spring introduction, the melancholy *chanson de femme, fabliaux*. A comprehensive view of the history of early medieval poetry is impossible, given the precarious transmission of medieval Latin secular lyric and the lowly literary status of the Romance vernaculars in particular before the 12th century; but the Cambridge Songs at least provide clues for that literary history.

PERSONA IN TWELFTH CENTURY LATIN POETRY
(With special reference to Walter of Châtillon)

by

MICHELLE LEVY
(Somerville College, Oxford)

In the works of some twelfth century Latin poets we discern a use of *persona* in a manner new to the Middle Ages, allowing a more personalised type of poetry. Conditions of publication did not favour poetic collections which could be unified by a single personality, in the manner of Horace's *Odes*. But an individual voice can be perceived behind single poems, contributing to their coherence of structure.

We should not seek such personal qualities principally in terms of autobiographical truth. Even the Archpoet, whose *persona* is unusually monolithic, expresses contradictory views. Compare *Confessio* 37–40 (Raby no. 183)[1] with *Archicancellarie, vir discretae mentis* 41–44 (Raby no. 185): inconsistent *topoi* deriving from Horace *Epistles* 2, 2, 51f. and 1, 19, 1ff. Walter of Châtillon adopts different *personae* in different poems. Raby is wrong to claim that in the satires we are 'nearer to the man himself':[2] satire naturally seeks to create an impression of verisimilitude.

'The discovery of the individual' in this period,[3] the interest in personality and autobiography, is thus insufficient to account for the development of a more personal poetry. More important is the influence of classical models. Walter in particular responded sensitively to the literary qualities of different Roman poets, recreating them in his own work.

Verna redit temperies (Raby no. 192) shows the influence of Horace's *Odes*. Lines 19f. allude directly to *Odes* 2, 13, 1f. proving Walter's acquaintance with an ode, itself significant as the *Odes* were then relatively unfamiliar (see e.g. Dante *Inferno* 4, 89: *Orazio satiro*). The poem's structure is more complex, the tone more personal than is normal in Medieval lyric. The spring-song, a popular Medieval genre (cf. Raby no. 212), is transformed into something unexpected. The springtime opening does not predict future developments. Spring is first shown as the season of birth and growth. There follows a conventional contrast between the seasonal rejoicing and the poet's misery. The *topoi* deliberately lead in a false direction (cf. *Odes* 1, 4): for it next emerges that the poet's misery springs not from unrequited love but from the birth of a daughter. This he regards with mock-serious ruefulness, but comforts himself with the thought that she will be more useful than a boy. The self-mockery and urbanity are Horatian; a piece of autobiographical information is developed into a complex work of art (cf. *Odes* 2, 13).

Walter's pastourelles reproduce the slickness of Ovid's love elegies: Walter adopts the *persona* of the sophisticated lover. The *locus classicus* for seduction poems is *Amores* 1, 5. Allusions to this appear in *Declinante frigore* (Raby no. 194) 48 (cf. *Amores* 1, 5, 25); *Sole regente lora* (Raby no. 195) 12-14 (cf. *Amores* 1, 5, 19ff.); *ibid.* 52 *pressi* (cf. *Amores* 1, 5, 24).

Walter learned from Juvenal how to intensify satiric attack by depicting the poet as an outsider. He found a Biblical equivalent for the 'outsider' in the Old Testament prophets. His 'prophetic' *persona* allows him to express outrage authoritatively. At the beginning of *Propter Sion non tacebo* (Raby no. 196) he takes on three successive prophetic mantles (l. 1 cf. *Isaiah* 62, 1; ll. 7f. cf. *Lamentations* 1, 1; l. 13 *Vidi, vidi* cf. openings of prophetic visions, e.g. in *Revelations*). In *Versa est in luctum* (Raby no. 200) he adopts the sorrowing *persona* of Job (lines 1f. cf. *Job* 30, 31), like himself an outcast because of disease.[4] The poet's connection with Job enhances his moral stature.

NOTES

1. F.J.E. Raby *Oxford Book of Medieval Latin Verse* Oxford (1959), henceforth simply Raby.

2. F.J.E. Raby *A History of Secular Latin Poetry in the Middle Ages* Oxford (1934) II p.195.

3. See Colin Morris *The Discovery of the Individual, 1050–1200* London (1972).

4. The evidence for Walter's leprosy is found in John of Garland's *Aequivoca*; see Hauréau *Notices et Extraits des Mss.* XXVII, ii, 62.

THE REVISION OF THE BREVIARY HYMNAL UNDER URBAN VIII

by

KEVIN MAGUIRE
(University of Liverpool)

Before the Council of Trent (1545-64) there were already several movements for the reform of the Breviary. One of these, the extreme humanist movement, sought to purify the latinity of the texts to a *stylus quo meliora nitebant saecula*. Encouraged by Leo X, Zaccaria Ferreri produced in 1525 a completely rewritten Hymnal, which was, however, never propagated. Ferreri turned all the hymns into pseudo-classical odes, a few of them splendid, but most of them rather naively "pagan", and all of them lacking the simple strength or charm of Ambrose, Prudentius or Gregory. For example the popular lines:

> Ave maris stella
> Dei mater alma
> Atque semper virgo
> Felix caeli porta.

became in Ferreri's version:

> Ave superna janua,
> Ave beata semita
> Salus periclitantibus
> Et ursa navigantibus.

There were other revised Breviaries, notably that of Quiñones in 1535, and that of Carafa (Paul IV) and the Theatines which became largely embodied in the new Roman Breviary of Pius V in 1568. These, however, attempted no revision of the latinity of the texts, and left the hymns completely untouched. Subsequent revisions under Sixtus V, Gregory XIV and Clement VIII emended many of the Breviary texts, but it was not until 1629, when Urban VIII set up a congregation for the definitive reform of the Breviary, that the Hymnal was finally tackled.

The revised hymns were the work of a sub-committee of four Jesuits: Famiano Strada, Tarquinio Galuzzi, Girolamo Petrucci and Matthias Sarbiewski. The four worked directly under Urban himself, and the Pope was ultimately responsible for many of the final versions. It is known that he submitted to Strada's criticism several versions which Strada emended, but which nonetheless passed into the final text in Urban's own version. In some 130 hymns the Jesuits found no fewer than

952 errors, mostly of prosody, but many of these were allowed to stand, chiefly on account of the high standing of their authors. The hymns of Ambrose, Gregory, Sedulius and Prudentius were therefore eventually left untouched, except for a word or two, but with those of Fortunatus, Rabanus Maurus and the anonymous authors of the 8th, 9th and 10th century hymns, the reformers felt at liberty to make considerable and sometimes drastic alterations. Thus the fine concrete imagery of Fortunatus:

> Vexilla Regis prodeunt:
> Fulget Crucis mysterium,
> Quo carne carnis Conditor
> Suspensus est patibulo.

is weakened, for prosodic reasons, to the following version of the last two lines:

> Qua vita mortem pertulit,
> Et morte vitam protulit.

There are many examples of this kind of unhappy change. Compare, for example, these lines from the anonymous *Urbs beata Jerusalem:*

> Angularis fundamentum
> Lapis Christus missus est,
> Qui parietum compage
> In utroque nectitur,
> Quem Sion sancta suscepit,
> In quo credens permanet.

which the revisers have completely rewritten, to read:

> Alto ex Olympi vertice
> Summi Parentis Filius,
> Ceu monte desectus lapis
> Terras in imas decidens,
> Domus supernae et infimae
> Utrumque junxit angulum.

One may likewise compare the splendid hymn for St Michael of Rabanus Maurus, *Tibi, Christe, splendor Patris*, with the laboured iambics of the revisers' version, *Te, splendor et virtus Patris*; or his hymns for All Saints, *Jesu Salvator saeculi* and *Christe Redemptor omnium*, with their versions, *Salutis aeternae dator* and *Placare, Christe, servulis.*

Certainly by this century's standards of taste, most of the work of Urban and his Jesuits is a pointless and tasteless exercise. Much that was simple, strong and exemplary of its own culture, or at least picturesque, has been thrown away to be replaced by a tawdry collection of schoolboy exercises, whose only merit is that they might well collect an alpha-plus for scansion. The twentieth century would not think of putting a neo-classical facade on a gothic or romanesque cathedral, but it is interesting to see that the seventeenth century had no such scruples, to judge by what was carried out in this revision of the medieval hymns, in the name of good Latin and good taste. Most interesting of all is that the revisers were men of tolerance and restraint who, in their final revision, only changed what they regarded as intolerable.

SAPPHO *FR.* 16 (LP): SELF-CONSOLATION AND ENCOMIUM[1]

by

J.G. HOWIE

(University of Edinburgh)

ο]ἰ μὲν ἰππήων στρότον, οἰ δὲ πέσδων,
οἰ δὲ νάων φαῖσ' ἐπ[ὶ] γᾶν μέλαι[ν]αν
ἔ]μμεναι κάλλιστον, ἔγω δὲ κῆν' ὄτ–
4   τω τις ἔραται·

πά]γχυ δ' εὔμαρες σύνετον πόησαι
π]άντι τ[ο]ῦτ', ἀ γὰρ πόλυ περσκέθοισα
κάλλος [ἀνϑ]ρώπων Ἐλένα [τὸ]ν ἄνδρα
8   τὸν [πανάρ]ιστον

καλλ[ίποι]σ' ἔβα 'ς Τροΐαν πλέοι[σα
κωὐδ[ὲ πα]ῖδος οὐδὲ φίλων το[κ]ήων
πά[μπαν] ἐμνάσϑη, ἀλλὰ παράγαγ' αὔταν
12   [   ]σαν

[   ]αμπτον γὰρ[
[   ]... κούφως τ[   ]οη.[.]ν
..]με νῦν 'Ανακτορί[ας ὀ]νέμναι–
16   σ' οὐ] παρεοίσας,

τᾶ]ς κε βολλοίμαν ἔρατόν τε βᾶμα
κἀμάρυχμα λάμπρον ἴδην προσώπω
ἢ τὰ Λύδων ἄρματα καὶ πανόπλοις
20   πεσδομ]άχεντας.

].μεν οὐ δύνατον γένεσϑαι
].ν ἀνϑρωπ[..(.)π]εδέχην δ' ἄρασϑαι
[   ]
24   [   ]
[   ]
[   ]
[   ]
28   προσ[

ὠσδ[
..].[
.].[.] ωλ.[
32   τ' ἐξ ἀδοκή[τ

207

1	(Some say a force of cavalry, some say a force of infantry,
2	Some say a fleet of ships is over all the black earth
3	The most beautiful thing, but I say it is
4	Whatever one loves.
5	It is wholly easy to make this understandable
6	To anyone. For she who far excelled
7	Mankind in beauty, Helen, left the man
8	Who was the (best?),
9	And went sailing to Troy.
10	And neither children nor dear parents
11	Did she remember, but instead ⟨noun or name⟩ led her astray
12	⟨participle referring to Helen⟩
13	For (pliable?) . . .
14	. . . easily/rashly . . .
15	. . . now reminded me of Anactoria,
16	who is (not?) here.
17	Her beautiful way of walking I might wish to see
18	And the bright gleam of her face
19	Rather than the chariots of the Lydians and their armoured soldiers
20	Fighting on foot.
21	. . . not able to happen
22	. . . mortal . . . but to pray for a share.
. . . .	
32	And unexpectedly.)

There is great uncertainty about this poem. Three principal points of difficulty may be identified. In order of occurrence these are:

(i) The sense of the priamel in lines 1–4. Precisely how is the poet contrasting cavalry, ships and infantry, on the one hand, and 'whatever one loves' on the other hand?

(ii) The poet's attitude to Helen in the myth (6–12). Does the poet approve or disapprove of Helen's action or does the poet indeed consider that the question of human moral responsibility does not arise?

(iii) The length of the poem. Does the poem end at line 20 or does it continue into the fragmentary lines 21 ff.? Could the *coronis* at line 32 be marking the end of this poem?

These three points are logically related. One cannot offer a solution to any of them without taking all of them into account. The most important of the three is the second, the interpretation of the myth. The solution of this difficulty would clear the way for the solution of the other two. The myth is introduced as an explanation of the gnome at the end of the priamel. The solution of the problem of the myth ought therefore to point towards a correct interpretation of the priamel as a whole. The question of where the poem ends depends on whether Sappho is drawing a parallel between Helen and Anactoria or between Helen and herself[2] and on whether the myth is critical of Helen or not.[3] We shall see that the parallel Sappho draws is between the myth of Helen and her own feelings for Anactoria and desire to see her. If Sappho shows disapproval of Helen in the myth, it is unlikely that she ended the poem with an eloquent declaration of her desire to see Anactoria. Such an ending would give undue prominence and a wholly unqualified form to feelings that were at variance with a moral view of the myth. It would be more likely that the poem continued in the next stanza in the papyrus. The eloquent declaration in lines 17–20 would then be tempered by other considerations. Thus if the myth shows disapproval of Helen, it is unlikely that the poem ended at line 20; if the myth shows no disapproval, it is possible that the poem ended at line 20.

The view taken in this study is that Sappho's myth of Helen is a negative moral exemplum set in an encomium of Anactoria. The demonstration of this view has three stages. The first is to show that the poem is an encomium and that there is a place for a negative exemplum in its encomiastic structure. The second is to demonstrate that the myth does take a negative view of Helen and to account for the apparent restraint of its language. The third is to show how Sappho uses self-consolation to enhance the encomium and to give it moral importance.

1. **The Encomiastic Structure of Sappho's Poem and the Place of the Myth within it.**

The encomiastic poetry of Pindar and Bacchylides often approaches the personal object of its praise (the *laudandus*) by stages before it finally identifies that person as the principal theme of the poem. This approach is employed not only at the beginning of poems but also at other points where a new object of praise is introduced for the first time or an earlier one is reintroduced. These encomiastic poets have a great variety of approaches and often combine several of them before at last introducing the proper object of praise. Among these approaches are contrasts, analogies, and generalisations. Rhetorically, such structures are *prooimia* and their purpose is *auxesis.*

E.L. Bundy[4] has investigated these structures and has classified the typical stages by which the subject of praise is approached. His general term for these approaches is 'foil'[5] and his general term for the identification of the subject of praise is 'climax'.[6] He has further shown that these typical stages are signalled by typical forms of expression. Foils not offering detailed items, so-called 'summary foils' or 'summary priamels' contain terms like πολλά (many) and ἄλλοι ἄλλα (some ⟨say or do⟩ one thing, some another).[7] Climaxes introducing the subject itself ('concrete climaxes')[8] often have first or second person pronouns ('pronominal caps') denoting the poet and the *laudandus* respectively and temporal expressions like νῦν denoting the present occasion of the poem.[9] 'Pronominal caps' also occur in statements of general truths ('gnomic climaxes'),[10] which the subject is then said to exemplify.

The typical groupings of sentences which Bundy's studies expose are in fact a form of parataxis. The practice of prefacing one's main point by lengthy preliminaries goes back to the speeches in Homer. J. Classen[11] in the nineteenth century considered that such structures formed a syntactical unit and were compound sentences. He maintained that the stages of approach to the main point constituted a paratactic parenthesis and that the statement of the main point was the principal clause in the compound sentence.[12] This view was upheld more recently by E. Schwyzer.[13] If this view is extended to the encomiastic structures of Pindar and Bacchylides, the 'foils' are species of paratactic parenthesis and the 'concrete climaxes' are principal clauses in what are often very extended paratactic compound sentences.[14]

The sense-relationships between the parts of such compound sentences in Homer are often comparable with the relationship between 'foil' and 'climax' in Pindar and Bacchylides; and the linguistic signals are often the same. Forms of the adjective πολύς occur in paratactic concessive clauses[15] comparable with Bundy's 'summary priamel'; principal clauses sometimes have prominently placed personal pronouns denoting speaker and addressee, functioning in the same way as Bundy's 'pronominal caps', or they have νῦν denoting the present occasion;[16] and principal clauses are introduced by ἀλλά after a clause comparable with a 'foil'.[17]

The typical sentence structures and typical signals are thus not an invention of encomiastic poets but a specialised form of Greek parataxis.[18] The principal characteristic of this specialised form is the regular assignment of topics to fixed syntactical roles. The employment of such structures for praise goes back to Homer. In *Odyssey* 4,267–289 Menelaus praises Odysseus:

> "Before now I have learnt the counsels of many heroes
> and I have travelled over much land (267f.),
> but never yet have I seen with my own eyes (269)
> such a heart as the dear heart of enduring-minded Odysseus was (270).
> What a thing that was that the mighty man did and endured (271)
> in the wooden horse . . . (272)"

This passage can be analysed in Bundy's terms:

267–268: Summary priamel employing forms of πολύς.
269–270: 'Concrete climax' with 'pronominal name-cap' i.e. naming of the subject in association with personal pronoun.[19]
271–289: Exemplum.

Sappho *Fr.* 16 (LP) has been examined by Bundy. He has shown how Sappho uses encomiastic structures and verbal signals comparable with those used by Pindar in *Olympian* 11.[20] In his analysis, Sappho's poem opens with a priamel (1–4) with a 'gnomic climax' (3f.) which has a 'pronominal cap' (ἐγώ, 3). The mention of Anactoria later forms the 'concrete climax' (15). It is signalled as the 'concrete climax' by the subject's name and the adverb νῦν (15) — and also by the pronoun με in the same line, which Bundy has not mentioned. These indications are certainly enough to show that Sappho's poem is formally an encomium. Another typical feature one can mention is the use of the relative pronoun (τᾶς, 17) after the name to introduce the detailed praise of the subject.[21] There are, however, two other questions about the structure of Sappho *Fr.* 16(LP) which Bundy does not deal with. These are the place of the myth of Helen within an encomiastic structure, and the way in which Sappho effects the transition from the myth to the naming of Anactoria. The answers to both questions are to be found in a passage of Pindar analysed elsewhere by Bundy. This is *Nemean* 8, 19ff.[22]

Nemean 8 contains two encomiastic structures.[23] The first climaxes with the local hero Aeacus, the victor Deinis, and his father Megas (1–18).[24] The second climaxes with Megas, now said to be dead, and his family the Chariadae (19–48). The double function of celebration and consolation is stated at the end of the poem (48–52). The second of these structures contains an exemplum-myth on the suicide of Ajax. The position, form, and purpose of this myth are all comparable with Sappho's myth in *Fr.* 16(LP). Here is a translation of the relevant part of the poem:

I am standing poised on light feet and taking my breath before I speak. For many things have been recounted in many ways, but to find new things and submit them to the touchstone for trial is a risk in every respect. Accounts(i.e. of great deeds)are only meat for the envious. Envy always attacks good men and has no quarrel with the bad. (19—22)

Envy feasted upon the son of Telamon and twisted him round his own sword. If a man is not gifted in speech though brave in heart, ⟨others'⟩ forgetfulness pins him down in any vile dispute and the greatest prize is held up for devious deceit. Thus by a secret vote the Greeks served the interests of Odysseus; and Ajax, having been deprived of the golden arms of Achilles, wrestled with death. (23—27)

There was no comparison between the wounds that each cut in the enemy's warm flesh while hard-pressed by defensive spears over Achilles' body and in other destructive days of battle. But, then, even long ago hostile Misrepresentation existed, the companion of seductive tales, deviser of trickery, evil-working disgrace, she who oppresses the brilliant and raises on high the rotten fame of the obscure. (28—34)

Father Zeus, may such a character never be mine. May I tread plain paths of life so that I may die with no disreputable fame attaching to my children. Some pray for gold, others for boundless land, but I pray that when I hide my limbs in the earth I may have pleased my fellow-citizens by praising what is fit for praise and sowing blame upon wrong-doers. (35—39)

Pindar *Nemean* 8, 19—39

This encomiastic structure has clear affinities with Sappho *Fr.* 16(LP). It begins with a priamel (in this case a 'summary priamel') with a 'gnomic climax' (20—22). This 'gnomic climax' states in general terms the problem which troubles the poet and causes him to brace himself before speaking. The 'gnomic climax' is then exemplified by a myth (23—32). The myth is rounded off by a gnome on Misrepresentation (32—34). The poet then introduces himself with a 'pronominal cap': he is uttering a prayer in gnomic terms on the course of life a poet should follow (35—37); and this leads ultimately to the praise of Megas.

The myth of Ajax, like Sappho's myth of Helen, is located between an opening priamel with 'gnomic climax' and the 'concrete climax' where the person to be praised is identified. This parallel is sufficiently close to suggest that *Nemean* 8 can help with the question of the transition from the myth in Sappho *Fr.* 16(LP). Pindar's long myth ends with a gnome (32—34). The function of this gnome is clearly to put the myth back on to a general basis from which the poem may proceed to the particular praise of Megas. The lines in Sappho's poem which would correspond in position to this gnome are 13f. and these are fragmentary. The remnants of them, however, would be consistent with a gnome. The explanatory γάρ is a suitable introduction for a gnome. The adverb κούφως is suitable too.[25] It could denote either the ease of a god's action or the rashness of a mortal's action.[26] The fragmentary αμπτον is clearly the remains of a verbal adjective. Verbal adjectives can be used in generalisations. Compare Homer *Iliad* 24,49: τλητὸν γὰρ Μοῖραι θυμὸν θέσαν ἀνθρώποισιν (For the Fates made for mortals a heart able to endure). On both typological and linguistic grounds, therefore, it is highly probable that lines 13f. contained a gnome.

The myths in Sappho *Fr.* 16(LP) and Pindar *Nemean* 8 thus occupy a similar position in the poets' approach towards their personal objects of praise. This position in the encomiastic structure has a vital bearing on the purpose of both myths. Both are introduced to explain the encomiastic poet's own position. For this purpose they are both placed in their respective encomiastic structures at a point earlier than the naming of the *laudandus*. These myths thus differ in both position and purpose from a laudatory mythical parallel following the praise of the *laudandus*, such as the myth of Antilochus in Pindar *Pythian* 6, 28ff.

Nemean 8, unlike Sappho *Fr.* 16(LP), is completely preserved. It is therefore worth seeing how a negative exemplum serves the encomiastic purpose of that poem. In fact, Pindar's poem provides insights not only into the position and purpose but also into the internal construction and concepts of Sappho's myth. The second of the two encomiastic structures in *Nemean* 8 begins with a hesitation-formula (19). The priamel, the myth of Ajax, and the gnomic lines on hostile Misrepresentation are all an explanation of the poet's hesitation (hence γάρ in line 20). The hesitation and its explanation serve as a 'foil' and are dismissed by lines 35ff. This is Bundy's view of the overall structure.[27] In the priamel (20f.) there is a contrast between already established stories of varying degrees of credibility (= 'summary foil') and new praise such as a poet dedicates to a *laudandus* (= 'gnomic climax').[28] Such new accounts, says the poet, are exposed to danger. He then defines the danger as that caused by envy towards good men (21f.).

These considerations in 20—22 explain in general terms the poet's own position, which he has stated in the hesitation-formula in 19. The myth, however, presents the iniquities caused by envy as they affect the man who merits the praise. This view is summed up by the first part of gnome within the myth in 24f. There is then a further shift marked by the second part of that gnome: not only is the good man deprived of recognition but the inferior man is glorified instead. Thus as the poet examines the grounds for his feelings and considers a myth illustrating these grounds, he reveals other, compelling, reasons why he ought to overcome these feelings and adopt a different position. It will be argued below that Sappho uses the myth of Helen in a similar way.

The form of the myth of *Nemean* 8 and the forces which it shows at work in human life are also relevant to an interpretation of Sappho's myth of Helen. In his *synkrisis* of Ajax and Odysseus, Pindar states in weighty language the many services that Ajax had rendered in battle (28—33). These important considerations are forgotten however (24). Misrepresentation, an entity with divine powers (34), is responsible for this.[29] It will be argued below that Sappho's exemplum-myth had a similar form. *Nemean* 8 has thus shown how a negative exemplum-myth can be used in an encomiastic structure comparable with Sappho *Fr.* 16(LP). The next question is whether Sappho's myth is indeed a negative exemplum.

2. Sappho's Moral View of Helen

Despite the gaps in lines 12—14, it can be established that Sappho says that Helen made a wrong decision and that Sappho compares Helen's position with her own. It is true that the myth nowhere explicitly condemns Helen herself; and it does not criticise her action until it says in the final part that she was 'misled' (11). Before then, however, the very terms describing her departure invite the audience to arrive for themselves at a judgment which is then confirmed by the word 'misled'. There are four points that would lead Sappho's audience to be critical of Helen. In order of occurence, these are:

(i) the contrast between Helen's beauty and her action and state of mind.

(ii) Helen's abandonment of an excellent husband.

(iii) her voyage to⟨far away⟩Troy.

(iv) her failure to remember her children and her parents.

For purposes of demonstration, I begin with the third point, her voyage to Troy, a place far away. The point is picked up in a decisively explicit form in the sentence which draws a parallel between Sappho's own position and the myth (15f.). 'Who is not here' does more than report that Anactoria was elsewhere. It puts her into the realm of things which it is folly to seek or desire. The point is strengthened when Sappho says that she might want to see her (17) and when the word 'lovely' is used in a description of her beauty (17). Sappho is invoking a widespread moral theme in early Greek literature, the theme of the Near and the Far. Greek writers often represent the choice between the possible, advantageous, and morally right course and the impossible, dangerous, and morally wrong course figuratively, speaking of the former as near and the latter as far away. Often they combine this conceptual distinction with the notion of physical distances.

D.C. Young has examined the use of this theme in Pindar *Pythian* 3.[30] An exemplum-myth in this poem tells of Coronis, a Boeotian woman, who slept with a stranger from Arcadia while already pregnant by Apollo. Pindar's criticism is an instructive specimen of this theme:

> She fell in love with things that were elsewhere. Many have been afflicted in this way. There exists among mortals a most vain breed, the sort of person who disgraces what belongs to his own country and gazes at what is far away, chasing after wind-borne things with unfulfillable hopes.
>
> Pindar *Pythian* 3,20-23

Sappho's terms οὐ παρεοίσας (16), βολλοίμαν and ἐρατόν (17) together correspond to Pindar's ἤρατο τῶν ἀπεόντων (20). The moral force of these terms is guaranteed in *Pythian* 3 by the context.

These terms connecting Sappho's own position and the myth confirm an impression already created in the myth. Sappho says that Helen sailed to Troy. In itself this statement simply follows tradition. In Sappho's myth, however, the statement is combined with two other statements which invite judgement and give the physical distance between Greece and Troy a moral significance. These statements imply that Helen abandoned both advantage and obligation. She left the husband she had. Sappho's phrasing implies a mistake. Compare the proverb: νήπιος, ὃς τὰ ἕτοιμα λιπὼν ἀνέτοιμα διώκῃ, Hesiod *Fr.* 61 (Merkelbach-West).[31] (Foolish is the man who leaves what is available and pursues what is not available.) Helen's mistake was all the greater since, as Sappho says, Menelaus was 'the most outstanding of men'. In not keeping in mind her children and parents, Helen ignored her obligations. The verb μέμνημαι is used to express the notion 'to be mindful of an obligation'. For a Greek audience, it is obviously not good that a mother should forget her children.[32] In the case of her parents the adjective 'dear' is used to emphasise her obligation. Compare Achilles' feelings for Patroclus: εἰ δὲ θανόντων περ καταλήθοντ' εἰν Ἀίδαο, /αὐτὰρ ἐγὼ καὶ κεῖθι φίλου μεμνήσομ' ἑταίρου (Homer *Iliad* 22,389f.) (Even if in Hades men forget the dead, nevertheless even there I will remember my dear comrade).

These considerations of advantage and obligation tell against Helen's action. Flanking on either side the statement that she sailed to Troy they suggest that she wrongly chose the Far and left the Near. There is evidence, too, that the verbs Sappho uses in expressing these considerations, 'to leave'[33] and 'not to keep in mind',[34] are themselves familiar in connection with the theme of the Near and the Far. The impression that Helen made a mistake is then confirmed when Sappho says that Helen was led astray (6). In a poem which is explicitly critical of Helen – *Fr.* 283 (LP) – Alcaeus makes the same point, namely that Helen abandoned both obligations and advantage (ll.7ff.). I shall be dealing with this poem in a later article (see n.1).

Because of the state of the papyrus, we do not know precisely who led Helen astray in Sappho *Fr.* 16 (LP). There can be little doubt, however, that it was a superior power, either an established personal god such as Aphrodite or a personified abstraction, rather than the mortal Paris.[35] The verb παράγαγ(ε) belongs to a class of verbs used of superior powers when they mislead mortals.[36] The position of the statement towards the end of the exemplum-myth is closely comparable with Pindar's words on Misrepresentation in *Nemean* 8, 32ff. – the power which led the Greeks astray in his myth.

Some have argued that lines 6ff. of Sappho *Fr.* 16(LP), which say that Helen was led astray, exonerate her, and that the myth therefore has no moral significance.[37] This is unlikely. The prefix παρα– means that Helen took the wrong course. If she was led astray by an outside force, this does not make her action any more righteous or her example any less bad.[38] In *Pythian* 3 Pindar condemns Coronis and yet he describes her love for the Far as a great *atē* (line 24) and says that an evil *daimōn* turned her to wickedness and caused her destruction (*Pythian* 3,34f.).[39] If the myth invites moral disapproval of Helen, both Helen's own beauty and her judgement of what is most beautiful have a recognised place in the exemplum. Early Greek literature teaches that a beautiful thing may also be dangerous and that a beautiful person may not have a character or prowess to match his beauty; and Sappho is combining the two teachings.

The danger of beautiful things is taught by both Hesiod and Pindar. Hesiod describes how Zeus had woman created and decked out. The poet calls her καλὸν κακόν, 'a beautiful evil' (Hesiod *Theogony* 585). Pindar, in his story of Ixion who tried to ravish Hera, describes the cloud which Zeus made in her likeness to deceive Ixion as καλὸν πῆμα 'a beautiful misery' (*Pythian* 2,40). Statements that a person's beauty was or was not matched by his deeds or character are common. Pindar praises the beauty of young victors in close association with praise of their achievements.[40] He says of one that his achievements did not belie his appearance (*Olympian* 8,19f.). Already Homer attempts an elaborate treatment of this theme in Odysseus's rebuke to the insolent young Euryalus:

> "Stranger, you said something not beautiful. You look like a reckless man. In just this way the gods do not give graceful things to all men alike, neither stature nor wits nor public eloquence. One man is inferior in appearance, but a god wreathes his words with form and the people gaze at him with delight as he speaks without a slip and with winning modesty. He is outstanding in the assembly and when he goes about the town the people look upon him like a god. Another, again, resembles the immortals in his appearance, but no grace is wreathed about his words; and in that way you, too, have an outstanding appearance, which not even a god would fashion differently, but in mind you are useless."
>
> *Odyssey* 8, 166–177

Euryalus's beauty is thus belied by the absence of beauty in his speech, his resemblance in this respect to a reckless man, and the worthlessness of his mind.

In Sappho's myth both the beauty Helen saw in what she loved and Helen's own beauty have moral importance. For Helen the most beautiful thing was what she loved — Paris — and she chose it without regard for either advantage or obligation. Helen's own beauty was belied by such a wrong choice. In giving beauty a multiple significance Sappho is aiming at an effect comparable with that achieved by Homer in the speech of Odysseus. Sappho herself elsewhere shows interest in the relationship between beauty and good character: ὁ μὲν γὰρ κάλος ὄσσον ἴδην πέλεται 〈κάλος〉, /ὁ δὲ κἄγαθος αὐτίκα καὶ κάλος ἔσσεται. (*Fr.* 50 (LP)). (For while the handsome man is handsome so far as appearance goes, the man who is actually good will at once also be handsome.) The elements of the myth up to the sentence stating that Helen was led astray are thus all relevant in a moral version of the myth of Helen.

The form of the myth, too, is appropriate for a negative exemplum. There is a significant resemblance between the way Sappho lists the people Helen abandoned or forgot and the way Pindar stresses the many great services Ajax performed for the Greeks (*Nemean* 8,28ff.). This similarity reflects a standard motif in the composition of exemplum-narrative: the heaping up of patently important considerations which the offender ignores. Compare Meleager's rejection of the pleas of his relations and fellow-citizens in Phoenix's exemplum (Homer, *Iliad* 9, 575ff.). Compare also the exemplum-myth of Asclepius in Pindar *Pythian* 3. Pindar catalogues the ailments that confronted Asclepius and the varied methods of legitimate medicine by which he cured them in accordance with Chiron's teachings (47—53). He then says that skill is not free from greed (54) and tells how the appearance of gold in Asclepius' hand brought him to raise the dead, with fatal consequences for himself (55—58). For Asclepius all that he had been taught by Chiron was not enough.

3. Sappho's Choice of Motifs in the Construction of the Myth

Although the myth in Sappho *Fr.* 16(LP) is a negative exemplum, there is a certain restraint about its treatment of Helen. It will be shown later that this restraint is required by the encomiastic purpose of the poem. Two points will be established here: how much Sappho says and how much she has avoided saying. The lacuna in line 12 leaves it uncertain what power led Helen astray and what was ascribed to her by the unknown participle agreeing with αὔταν. The lacunae in 13f. permit no more than the probable guess that the lines contain a gnome (see above § 2). In essence, what is left in doubt is Helen's motives: we have in the surviving text what Sappho said about Helen's actions and their effects (6—11).

There are two remarkable omissions in these fully preserved lines: the wider ill consequences of Helen's action and the identity of her beloved, Paris. Comparison with two similar treatments of such a love affair shows that Sappho's account of Helen belongs to a type admitting within its framework certain standard motifs; and that Sappho has made a choice among these motifs while still adhering to and exploiting the underlying type. The underlying type is the story of a young and good-looking person who meets another young and good-looking person of the opposite sex belonging to another country. They fall in love; they consummate their love without any regard for their families; for at least

one of the two the affair causes disgrace and ruin, even death, and his or
her family or even whole community may also be affected. The type has
obvious exemplum-value. It readily admits the theme of the Near and the
Far. It is capable of modification in terms of the motivation of the parties
and the extent of the ill-effects of the affair.[41]

Two elaborate treatments of the type are: Hector's denunciation of
Paris in *Iliad* 3, 39ff.; and Pindar's exemplum-myth of Coronis in *Pythian*
3, 8–37. When Hector sees Paris shrinking back from Menelaus he calls
out:

> "Evil Paris! Best in appearance! Mad for women! Deceiver! Would
> that you had been sterile and died unmarried. I might wish for just
> that. It would have been far better so than that you should be such a
> bane and object of others' contempt. The long-haired Achaeans must
> surely be laughing and saying that you are an excellent champion to
> have as leader since you have a beautiful appearance but no strength
> or fighting quality in your mind. (39–45)

> Were you like this when in sea-faring ships you sailed across the sea
> with a chosen band of trusty companions and mingled with foreign
> people and brought back a woman with a fine appearance from a
> far-away country, who was already married into a family of warriors,
> a great disaster for your father and the city and all the people, a joy
> to the enemy and an embarrassment to yourself? (46–51)

> Would you not stand your ground against Menelaus dear to Ares?
> You would find out then what sort of man it is whose glorious wife
> you are holding. Your lyre would not save you, nor those gifts of
> Aphrodite, your hair and your appearance, as you mingled with the
> dust. The Trojans are cowards indeed. Otherwise you would have
> been stoned to death for all the evil you have wrought. (52–57)
> Homer *Iliad* 3, 39–57

Paris admits the truth of Hector's words, makes what excuse he can and
offers to fight Menelaus in a duel:

> Alexandros with his godlike appearance replied, "Hector, you have
> rebuked me rightly and not more than is right. Your heart is like an
> unwearing axe . . . Do not blame me for the lovely gifts of golden
> Aphrodite. One cannot cast away any of the gods' famous gifts that
> they themselves grant and no one would choose them of his own
> free will. Now, then, if you wish me to fight . . . "
> Homer *Iliad* 3, 58–66

Though Hector ironically adduces Paris's elopement as evidence of greater courage than he now shows, he leaves him in no doubt that it was wrong (50). Paris's admission of the truth of Hector's words means that Homer's audience is intended to accept them as correct.

In Pindar *Pythian* 3, 8—37 the stories of Coronis and her son Asclepius, the healer-hero, serve as an introduction to a consolation addressed to Hieron in time of sickness. Their moral is the folly of seeking the unattainable and the inevitability of death for all mortals:

> Before she could be delivered of Asclepius with midwife Eileithyia's aid the daughter of horse-raising Phlegyas was killed by the golden arrows of Artemis and in her own chamber went down to the house of Hades. This was by the design of Apollo.   (8—11a)

> The anger of the children of Zeus is not idle. She, however, made light of it in the sinfulness of her mind and consented to another union in secret from her father, although she had already had intercourse with Apollo and was carrying the pure seed of the god.
>   (11a—15)

> She did not wait for the wedding feast to come nor for the full-toned call of the hymeneal songs, which maiden companions of the bride's own age love to tease her with in evening songs. (16—19a)

> No. She fell in love with things that were elsewhere. Many have been afflicted in this way. There exists among mortals a most vain breed, the sort of person who disgraces what belongs to his own country, and gazes at what is far away chasing after wind-borne things with unfulfillable hopes.   (19b—23)

> Such was the great infatuation which the wilful spirit of beautiful-robed Coronis had. She lay down in bed with a stranger who had come from Arcadia.   (24—26)

> However, she did not escape the notice of a watcher. In sheep-receiving Pytho the lord of the temple happened to be present and there he heard of it, persuading his intellect in concert with the straightest witness, namely his own all-knowing mind. He does not touch lies and neither god nor mortal can deceive him in deeds or plans.   (27—30)

> Knowing then, therefore, that Ischys, the son of Eilatus, had lain with the daughter of his foreign host and perpetrated a lawless trick he sent his sister raging with overwhelming might to Lacereia, where the maiden lived by the banks of the lake of Boebe. Another (i.e. a

bad)god turned her towards evil and caused her to be killed. Many of her neighbours were affected and perished with her. Fire from a single spark can leap into a great wood and destroy it. (31–37)

Pindar *Pythian* 3, 8–37

These two specimens of the type have in common several of the elements of Sappho's myth of Helen. Like Helen, Paris and Coronis seek the geographically far in a love-affair (*Iliad* 3, 46–49; *Pythian* 3, 25f.). Their action is not advantageous to themselves (*Iliad* 3, 51; *Pythian* 3, 16–19; 35). Their parents are disregarded or adversely affected (*Iliad* 3,50; *Pythian* 3,13) – neither yet having a spouse and children like Helen. Like Helen, both are good-looking themselves (*Iliad* 3,39; 44f.; 55; *Pythian* 3,25) and their looks are belied by their characters (*Iliad* 3.45; *Pythian* 3,25). Given that beauty is naturally a motive in the affair, it is appropriate that the offenders' beauty should be contrasted with their wrongful deeds and bad character. This contrast is only to be expected in such stories. This can be seen from Pindar's very compressed reference to it in a myth to whose exemplum-value beauty is not relevant (*Pythian* 3,25, καλλιπέπλου λῆμα Κορωνίδος, a contrast between εἶδος and νοῦς). It is likely therefore that Sappho's audience would be ready to see the same contrast in Helen's case.

The most important differences between Sappho's treatment of the type and the other two are the omission in Sappho of the disgrace (*Iliad* 3,42ff.; *Pythian* 3,22), of the widespread ill effects of the offenders' actions (*Iliad* 3,50; *Pythian* 3,35–37), and of the explicit and harsh condemnation of their motives (*Iliad* 3,39; *Pythian* 3,13;19–23). These elements belong together. If the ill effects of the offenders' actions and the disgrace are stated, they attract condemnation and the attribution of discreditable motives. Conversely condemnation and the attribution of discreditable motives need a statement of the ill effects as evidence. Sappho has avoided this whole set of motifs.

Pindar and Homer differ in two respects in their treatment of the beloved (Ischys, Helen). (i) Pindar names Ischys and blames him along with Coronis (*Pythian* 3,31f.); Homer does not mention Helen by name and does not blame her. This suggests that naming the other party in the typical story-form requires that his part in the affair should also be indicated and condemned. Here may be one reason why Sappho does not name Paris. Naming him would have meant blaming him. This would have been contrary to the encomiastic requirements of the myth (see below § 4). (ii) Pindar makes no mention of Ischys' own beauty but Homer

221

speaks of a 'beautiful woman' (*Iliad* 3,48). In Pindar's myth Ischys' beauty
would have suggested a new motivation not covered by the important
gnomic lines in 19—23. Homer, however, chooses to mention the beauty of
the beloved without naming her. Sappho does not even use such a phrase
as this, saying e.g. 'for love of a handsome man'. She avoids even this sort
of reference because it would give undue prominence to the fact that Paris
was a man. Such a reference would also be contrary to the encomiastic
requirements of the myth (see below § 4).

4. The Encomiastic Purpose of Sappho's Myth of Helen

The place of the myth in the encomiastic structure makes it clear
that Sappho introduces it in the first instance to illustrate her own
position. On the other hand, the beauty and the love Sappho speaks of are
paralleled by the beauty of Anactoria and the love Sappho feels for her.
The connection between myth and *laudandus* is therefore closer than in
Nemean 8. Greater care is therefore required to avoid unpleasant
implications in the myth.

Helen's position in the myth is parallel to Sappho's. For Sappho
Anactoria's beauty is such that she could wish to see her with the same
intensity as Helen desired Paris. The exemplum is a negative one however,
and Sappho later rejects this wish (21ff.). Helen's decision and action were
wrong. Sappho's choice of motifs in the myth (see above § 3) ensures that
no guilt or disgrace is associated with Anactoria through any parallel
between Anactoria and Paris. It also ensures that Sappho's feelings for
Anactoria are not made parallel to those of a woman for a man. That
would impugn Anactoria's femininity.[42] The omission of the dire
consequences of Helen's action and of any harsh, explicit criticism of her
has a more delicate effect. It ensures that Sappho's love for Anactoria is
not given an exaggerated importance.

It has been argued above that the myth of Helen is a negative moral
exemplum. The question therefore arises how, if Helen's judgment under
the influence of love was wrong, Sappho's judgment under the same
influence can be any better; and also whether Anactoria's beauty is only
skin deep. Sappho's ability to see the dangers of her own feelings have
encomiastic value here. If Sappho can see the danger in her feelings, her
judgement is superior to Helen's. Indeed the quality of the feelings
Anactoria inspires in Sappho reveals Anactoria as a better object of love
for Sappho than Paris was for Helen. The morally correct attitudes of the
poet thus guarantee the truthfulness of the praise. This is an aspect of

encomiastic poetry common to Sappho and Pindar.[43]

5. Consolatory Elements in Sappho *Fr.* 16(LP)

It has been argued above that Sappho's myth is a moral exemplum set in an encomiastic scheme and that an encomiastic scheme at this point can contain a serious negative exemplum. Unlike *Nemean* 8, however, the moral of Sappho's poem is not simply that one should praise the *laudandus*. It is a consolation. The 'concrete climax' with the naming of Anactoria is followed by praise (17ff.). However, this praise is followed by defective gnomic lines (21f.). These say that something is 'not possible' (21), stress that someone is a mortal and not a god (22) and recommend that someone should pray instead for a share, presumably a share of what is open to one as a mortal (22).[44] These lines continue the theme of the Near and the Far. They are similar to the gnome Pindar uses after his exemplum-myth of Coronis and Asclepius at *Pythian* 3,59f. (see below). Thus after her praise of Anactoria Sappho resumes the moral view already expressed in the myth and in the gnome following it. She is rejecting her wish to see Anactoria as impossible. The praise of Anactoria has served only to explain why the wish was so strong.

In fact, not only does Sappho's gnome resemble Pindar's in content; it also occupies the same place in the argument. In *Pythian* 3, Pindar consoles Hieron in time of sickness. He begins by saying that he would have wished that Chiron, the teacher of Asclepius, was still alive (1—8); but after recounting the stories of Asclepius's mother, Coronis, and Asclepius himself (8—58), he rejects the wish outright (59—77):

> One must seek from the gods those things that are appropriate for mortal hearts, recognising what is available, given that we have the lot we have.   (59—60)

> Dear soul, do not strive for an immortal life. Rather, use to the full the means that are practicable.   (61—62)

> If wise Chiron were still living in his cave and our sweet-voiced hymns could put some love-philtre into his heart, I would even now have persuaded him to provide good men with a healer of hot diseases, be it one called the son of Leto's son (i.e. Asclepius, son of Apollo) or son of his Father (i.e. Apollo, son of Zeus); and I would have come by ship, cleaving the Ionian sea, to the stream of Arethusa and my host at Etna, who reigns in Syracuse as king, gentle to citizens, without envy towards the noble, and a wonderful father to men from abroad.   (63—71)

If I had disembarked bringing him as twin joyful favours golden
Health and a celebratory chorus for his Pythian victories to brighten
the wreaths which Pherenicus the race-horse once won for excellence
at Cirrha, I declare that, for him, I would have come as a light more
brilliant than a star in the heavens once I had crossed the deep sea.
(72–76)

Instead, however, I want to pray to the Mother of the Gods, that
holy goddess, whom together with Pan maidens often sing of at
night at my own porch. (77–79)
Pythian 3, 59–79

Pindar rejects the wish despite the joy that its fulfilment would have
brought to his patron and despite the abundant grounds he has for good
will towards him (70f.). Instead he will pray to the Mother of the Gods
(77–79). Here, as in Sappho's poem, the wish is rejected and a legitimate
prayer substituted. Here too the praise of the *laudandus* is introduced not
as the purpose of the poem but as a ground for being tempted to wish for
the impossible. An important difference between the two poems is that,
while Sappho's is a self-consolation, Pindar's poem is a consolation
addressed to his patron. However, Pindar's poem begins with the poet
apparently consoling himself and this impression is maintained until his
patron is introduced in 66. The direct consolation of Hieron only begins at
80ff. and the naming of Hieron has been reserved for that point. Pindar's
opening self-consolation, which is framed like Sappho's, is intended to
emphasise his sincere concern for Hieron, which affects his own feelings.

The rejected wish as a form of consolation already occurs in Homer.
In Book 3 of the *Odyssey*, when Nestor exhorts Telemachus to follow the
example of Orestes, Telemachus replies,

"Would that the gods would invest me with such great power
As to take vengeance for the cruel trangression of the suitors,
Who abuse me and contrive wicked things against me.
But the gods did not spin such good fortune for me,
For my father or for me, and now I must endure nevertheless."

Homer *Odyssey* 3,205–209

Telemachus is treating vengeance against the suitors as an
unfulfillable wish and represents endurance as the wise course. He is
setting his argument forth in the form of a self-consolation. First there is
the wish (205f.). Then comes a relative clause giving the grounds for the
wish (207). Then the wish is rejected by a sentence introduced by the
particle ἀλλά and the preferable course is signalled by the verb χρή and

the temporal adverb νῦν. This Homeric example is instructive in its clarity and represents a simple arrangement of self-consolation employing a rejected wish. The choice of sentence-arrangement and sentence-signals show that the wish is, in Bundy's terms, a 'foil' stated only so that it can be decisively rejected in the main clauses in 208f. This is the form of the Sapphic and Pindaric examples. In them, the relative clause stating the grounds for the wish is made the vehicle of praise (Sappho lines 17ff.; Pindar lines 70f.), a well-established role for the relative clause. Pindar's example is much more elaborate. He safely lays a foundation for this elaborate treatment in lines 59–61 which reject such a wish and hint at a preferable course of action. He is then free to elaborate the rejected wish in the guise of unreal conditional sentences which describe in moving terms the joy which the fulfilment of such a wish would have given Hieron and state in a relative clause the good and laudable grounds for being tempted to wish for the impossible. The wish is then decisively rejected again in 77ff. and a preferable course of action, a legitimate prayer, pleasingly described.

Two other points of Sappho's rejected wish may be clarified by comparison with the Homeric and Pindaric examples. These are the modality of the wish and the imagery used in praise of Anactoria. The three examples of the form examined here show that the form left room for a variety of modalities. The wish may be either remote and presumably unlikely or it may be completely ruled out as impossible, Furthermore the state of mind itself which tends to lead one to make a wish may also be treated in different ways. In Homer's example, the wish is simply voiced aloud and the choice of mood (optative) shows that it is not completely impossible that the gods might give Telemachus such power, however remote he may consider that possibility to be. In Pindar's example, on the other hand, the very making of the wish is ruled out (1) and all its ramifications are similarly ruled out by the modality of the verbs (63–76). In Sappho's example, making the wish is not ruled out. In the relative clause she says κε βολλοίμαν (17). With Sappho's choice of expression here we might compare Hector's words after he has expressed the now impossible wish that Paris might have been born sterile and died unmarried: καί κε τὸ βουλοίμην, καί κεν πολὺ κέρδιον ἦεν (Homer *Iliad* 3,41f.) (I might well wish that and it would certainly have been better ...). This is a wish that Hector might well make, a wish he is tempted to make.

To judge from the Pindaric and Homeric examples, there appears at first sight to be an anomaly in the Sapphic poem, since in Sappho (17) both the wish and the grounds for making the wish are contained within the relative clause (i.e. both the wish to see Anactoria and the praise explaining this wish); in the Homeric and Pindaric examples, however, the relative clause contains only the grounds for the wish, and not the wish as well. Fortunately, lines 15f. of Sappho's poem are sufficiently well preserved to let us see that the poet's state of mind prompting such a wish was already described before the relative clause. Sappho was reminded of Anactoria. Such a sudden recollection (15) produces a rapid response. Compare *Iliad* 3,139ff., where the goddess Iris fills Helen with yearning for Menelaus, and she responds at once. The relative clause in Sappho *Fr.* 16,17ff. (LP) then brings out the wish already implied before the relative clause as well as explaining in detail the grounds for the wish.

The imagery used to explain these grounds would appear to be traditional. Sappho uses terms suggesting brightness (line 18, κἀμάρυχμα λάμπρον ἴδην προσώπω) and makes a comparison between Anactoria and the chariots and infantry in Anactoria's favour (lines 19f.). Pindar uses the same sort of imagery in his description of the joy that the fulfilment of the wish would have brought Hieron. Health is described as golden (73), the chorus is described as brightening the wreaths won in the past (73) and the poet's arrival would have been a brighter light than a star in the sky (75). This last piece of brightness imagery is a favourable comparison like Sappho's comparison of Anactoria with the chariots and infantry; and like Sappho's it is placed for emphasis at the end of the section. It is likely that Sappho still had the imagery of brightness in mind when she reintroduced from the opening priamel the chariots and the foot-soldiers (19f.). The gleam of the arms of land-forces is familiar in Homer. The ships are not reintroduced. One can see that they would have distracted from the suggestion of a gleam commonly associated with land forces. The choice of the Lydians is apt. They were well known for their land forces, especially their cavalry, but they were not a naval power (Herodotus 1,27). The mention of the Lydians would therefore make the omission of the ships for the sake of implicit brightness imagery less surprising and perfectly appropriate.

The construction of Pindar's myth in *Pythian* 3 is also instructive. It confirms the earlier analysis of the myth of Ajax in *Nemean* 8 and the myth of Helen in Sappho *Fr.* 16 (LP). The wish in *Pythian* 3 is stated as a conceivable state of mind for the poet. Though not introduced as an exemplum, the myth supplies the grounds why the wish should be rejected. It exemplifies the folly of seeking what is not within a mortal's grasp (19–23). The audience is therefore ready to see for itself the grounds for rejecting the wish when it is reintroduced as something desirable but not possible (63ff.).

The results of the discussion so far may be summarised as follows: Sappho *Fr.* 16 (LP) is an encomium of Anactoria. The myth of Helen is a negative exemplum. This exemplum illustrates not the virtue of Anactoria but the position of Sappho the encomiastic poet. Care is taken in the choice of motifs in the myth so that no negative aspect of Helen should affect the praise of Anactoria. While the poem's encomiastic form makes it clear that Anactoria is the personal object of praise in the poem, the occasion of the poem is presented not as the need to praise Anactoria but as the poet's need to console herself in Anactoria's absence. The poem did not end at line 20 but continued at least into the following stanza (21–24).

6. The Priamel

Two further points raised at the beginning of this paper may now be considered. These are the significance of the priamel (1–4) and the possibility that the poem ended at line 32. As far as the priamel is concerned, there is a choice between two interpretations. On the first interpretation 'whatever one loves', because it is 'the most beautiful thing on earth', is more beautiful than cavalry, infantry and ships and is quite distinct from them. Hence those who say that cavalry, infantry, or ships are the most beautiful thing cannot be feeling any *erōs* for them. If the admirers of such things do not feel any *erōs* for them, the question arises what sort of thing can be put under the heading of 'whatever one loves'. It is unlikely, for example, that a fine house could be put under this heading any more than cavalry etc. Therefore those scholars who interpret the priamel in this way conclude that 'whatever one loves' can only refer to human beings. For them, the point which Sappho says she will make in the myth of Helen is that whatever human being one loves is the most beautiful thing. On the second interpretation, 'whatever one loves' is not something distinct from cavalry, infantry, or ships. Rather Sappho is proposing a comprehensive definition of 'the most beautiful thing' as opposed to the narrow definitions of the others. According to this interpretation, people who say, for example, that the most beautiful thing on earth is cavalry, are led to say so because they feel *erōs* for cavalry. Each individual's opinion as to what is the most beautiful thing is determined by his *erōs*. This comprehensive definition embraces all the individual views mentioned in the first three items of the priamel by identifying *erōs* as the common element in them all.

The only helpful indication in the priamel itself is the neuter gender of κῆνο, which suggests both personal and impersonal objects of *erōs* rather than only personal objects of *erōs.* [46] This points to the second interpretation. The 'gnomic climax' is explicitly explained by the myth of Helen. In it, Helen chooses the man she loves (Paris) in preference to an outstanding husband (Menelaus) and forgets both her children and her parents. She thus chooses between two possible personal objects of *erōs* and forgets other persons to whom she was bound by affection — her children and her 'dear' parents. The myth has been interpreted above as taking a negative view of Helen's choice and therefore also of the object of *erōs* pure and simple. If the second interpretation is correct, the cavalry etc. ought to be open to a similar negative view. Indeed this would be part of the poet's argument. The negative aspect of cavalry etc. would corroborate the negative view of Helen's choice in the myth. This is in fact so: it is a commonplace of early Greek literature that men feel 'erotic' feelings for such things as warships and such activities as warfare. For example, the Argonauts are filled with πόθος for their ship and are unwilling to stay behind free from danger:

> "Hera kindled in the demi-gods that all-persuading sweet yearning (184, πόθον) for the ship Argo so that none should be left to digest a life without danger at his mother's but should rather, even at the cost of death find a most beautiful (187, κάλλιστον) preservative for his own prowess together with others of his age."

Pindar *Pythian* 4, 184–187

Thucydides makes such a feeling contribute to the disastrous Sicilian expedition and associates it with the theme of the Near and the Far:

> A desire (ἔρως) to sail out fell into all alike. The older men expected that either they would conquer what they were sailing against or that a great armament could not come to any harm. The young men were affected by a yearning for distant sights and spectacles (τῆς τε ἀπούσης πόθῳ ὄψεως καὶ θεωρίας).

Thucydides 6,24,3. [47]

Thus warfare is attractive and leads to danger in distant places and sometimes to disaster. This view of warfare is, as we shall see shortly, as old as Sappho's time. These beautiful military forces, which are all mobile (on horseback, on foot, and by sea), and the last of which, the ships, foreshadows Helen's voyage, thus begin that unfolding of a negative view of 'whatever one loves' which has already been observed in the myth of Helen.

Sappho echoes the opening priamel in her praise of Anactoria (17–20). She says that she would rather see Anactoria than the Lydians' chariots and infantry. Here she is certainly saying that she prefers the personal object of her own *erōs* to impersonal things. This contrast ought not to be used as evidence that, in the priamel too, she makes a contrast between a personal object of *erōs* and impersonal things not themselves the objects of *erōs*.[48] Sappho is making a different contrast in lines 17ff. She is expressing her own specific *erōs* for Anactoria and saying that she prefers Anactoria to what are likely objects of *erōs* for others. The common factor of *erōs* in both Sappho's choice and the military splendour of the Lydians is kept in view by the fact that both are distant: Anactoria is absent (16) and this military splendour is to be seen in foreign Lydia. Though the contrast in 17ff. is thus a different one from that in 1ff., the thematic overlap of the passages suggests that the theme of the Near and the Far is present in the reference to military forces in the priamel.

Odysseus's false tale of the Cretan adventurer (Homer *Odyssey* 14, 159–359) shows that the elements exposed in the examination of Sappho's priamel are already present in the poetry of Homer. Furthermore its description of the dangers of the love of the Far is comparable with Sappho's myth of Helen. The Cretan was illegitimate but through his prowess in war he made a good marriage and had children. However, warships and fighting were what was 'dear' to him:

> "Work was not dear to me nor husbandry, which raises fine children, but for me it was always ships that were dear and battles and well-polished javelins and arrows, dreadful things that make other people shudder. I suppose that what was dear to me was what a god had put into my mind. For different men take pleasure in different things."

Odyssey 14, 222–228

The warlike equipment and activity is described in such a way as to convey its attractions (224f.). These are dear to him. His feelings are therefore like those of the people in Sappho's 'foil' (1–3) who say that cavalry, infantry, or a fleet of ships is the most beautiful thing and who feel *eros* for them. Like Sappho in the 'gnomic climax' (3f.), the Cretan recognises that such preferences are subjective and vary from person to person (226–228). This man generally disregarded the advantageous and Near, the improvement of his own property and the rearing of fine children (223). Twice in his career he was led to seek the Far, with disastrous results. Only a month after returning from Troy he set off again. Through his own strong feelings he disregarded the children, spouse, and property which he had just been enjoying. Personal obligations and advantage were thus abandoned by him just as they were by Helen in Sappho's myth:

> "However, Zeus the Planner devised evil things for me. I only stayed a month enjoying my children and wife and estate. After that, my heart commanded me to voyage to Egypt".

Odyssey 14, 243–247.

The expedition was a disaster but he entered the king of Egypt's service. He settled and became wealthy. Egypt was now the Near. After seven years he was persuaded by a deceitful Phoenician to go first to Phoenicia and then to Libya, where the Phoenician planned to sell him as a slave (287–297). These journeys led to further adventures and to the state of privation he is in when he tells his story.

The Cretan's story thus shows that the points raised in the interpretation of Sappho's priamel are within the scope of early Greek thinking. It further shows that after such an opening Sappho's audience would be prepared for a negative treatment of the exemplum-myth.

7. The Possible Ending at Line 32.

It is not known whether the *coronis* at 32 marks the end of the present poem; and little or nothing is known of the content of lines 23–31. Since, however, the sense of line 32 is clear, it is worth considering whether, if it were the conclusion, it would square with the interpretation of lines 1–22 offered above.

In a poem with consolatory elements, 'unexpectedly'(32), could well be expressing a notion which is familiar in Greek theology. This is the notion that nothing is impossible for the gods provided it is not against fate and that, as a result, things may happen against all expectations. Archilochus draws this moral from the eclipse of the sun: one cannot expect that anything will not happen or swear that it will not happen (Archilochus *Fr.* 74,1 D). Pindar announces the taming of the winged horse Pegasus in similar language: 'the god fulfils even a rash enterprise undertaken in defiance of all one would swear or expect would happen.'

(*Olympian* 13,83).

This belief can be used in consolations. A clear instance is the conversation between Nestor, Telemachus, and Athene in the guise of Mentor (*Odyssey* 3,210ff.). Nestor suggests that Odysseus may return and later expresses the wish that the gods may help Telemachus as the goddess Athena once manifestly helped his father Odysseus (211–224). Telemachus replies: "Sir, I do not think such words will ever be fulfilled. You said far too much. I would not expect these things to happen even if a god wished it so." (*Odyssey* 3,226–228). At this point Athena intervenes: "Telemachus! What are you saying? If a god wished, he could easily save a man even from afar." (*Odyssey* 3,230f.) The moral is clear: the great power of the gods is a ground for not giving up hope altogether.

If Sappho is using this topic, that the gods can do things unexpectedly, she must somehow be integrating it into her self-consolation and ending her poem on a note of hope. Hope is a common topic in consolation. The question remains how hope could be added to this self-consolation, the preserved portion of which is negative. Pindar's *Pythian* 3 shows that a consolation containing a rejected prayer or wish may proceed to an expression of hope. In it, Pindar rejects a prayer for a miraculous cure (1–79) and teaches that man is mortal and his blessings always mixed (8–109). He ends the poem, however, with the consoling hope that his addressee's wealth will provide a different kind of immortality through song, such as the Homeric heroes Nestor and Sarpedon enjoy: 'If a god were to grant me glorious wealth I hope I would find lofty fame far off . . .' (Pindar *Pythian* 3, 110ff.). What hope Sappho consoled herself with and how the transition was effected is unknown. Possibly her hope was that she might nevertheless see Anactoria somehow at a time when she was not expecting it.

If this is how the poem ended, there is no contradiction between that ending and the more fully preserved part of the poem as expounded above. Such an ending is conceivable for the poem both as a consolation and as an encomium. With such an ending the consolation would have a form comparable with Pindar's consolation to Hieron in *Pythian* 3. There would be no contradiction if Sappho said on the one hand that she ought not to desire to see Anactoria and on the other hand, that she might see her unexpectedly. The two sides of the moral teachings of such a poem may be summarised as follows. On the one hand, if one feels a desire for something unattainable, one should not wish or pray for it. This only intensifies the longing and tempts one to pursue it rashly. Rather, one should pray for what is attainable for a mere mortal. On the other hand, a mortal cannot dismiss anything as impossible altogether. If a god wishes it and it is not contrary to fate, it may come about unexpectedly. Therefore one should not entirely despair. Rather one should console oneself with the hope that one's desires may one day be fulfilled unexpectedly and without one having sought actively or desired too fervently for them. With such an ending, too, the encomiastic value of the poem is not diminished. It means that Anactoria's beauty is such that the desire to see her never entirely passes and that an elaborate meditation is required to contain this desire safely.

If the poem continues to 32 and 'unexpectedly' has the significance suggested above, then a guess may be hazarded about the contents of some of the missing lines. It is possible that they contained an exemplum illustrating how things can happen unexpectedly, perhaps how someone returned unexpectedly from afar. If hope is being enjoined, it is natural that some exemplum offering proof of the possibility should be offered. We have seen that Pindar, when ending his consolation on a note of modified hope, instances Nestor and Sarpedon as men who survived in men's memories after death through poetry. Nicias in his exhortation to his men to keep up their hopes briefly refers to men who have won safety out of dangers greater than those facing his men now (Thucydides 7,77). In the conversation between Nestor, Telemachus, and Athena in *Odyssey* 3, mentioned above, Telemachus's self-consolation is countered by Nestor with the example of the help that Athena manifestly gave to his father Odysseus in the Trojan War (216ff.). It is possible therefore that Sappho balanced her negative exemplum of Helen with a second exemplum that was, perhaps in some modified sense, optimistic. There is nothing to help in lines 23–28. At the beginning of line 29, however, at the beginning of what would by this hypothesis be the last stanza, the letters ὦσδ appear. These may stand for ὣς δ(έ) (and in that way) or for ὡς δ(έ) (and as). They might then mark the beginning or the end of a comparison between a second exemplum and Sappho's own position.

NOTES

1.   This article is based on part of a paper given in the School of Classics of the University of Liverpool in March 1975 at the invitation of Professor Francis Cairns. The theme of that paper was the traditional moral teachings embodied in four poems of Sappho – *Frr.* 5,16,94,96 (LP) – and in one poem of Alcaeus – *Fr.* 130 (LP). Studies of the other poems and also of Alcaeus *Fr.* 283 (LP) are now in preparation.

I wish to record my thanks to Professor O. Reverdin and to the Fondation Hardt for a profitable period of study there. I wish also to thank my colleagues who have read and criticised drafts of this paper including

Professors A.J. Beattie of Edinburgh, F. Cairns of Liverpool, K. Deichgräber of Göttingen, T. Krischer of Berlin, and Mr. C.W. Macleod of Oxford. Professor Cairns first drew my attention to the importance of *Iliad* 3,39ff. for the discussion.

For the first twenty lines of Sappho *Fr.* 16(LP) I follow D.L. Page's latest text, *Lyrica Graeca Selecta* Oxford (1968) pp.101f. For the remainder of the fragment I follow E. Lobel and D. Page's text as found in *Poetarum Lesbiorum Fragmenta* Oxford (1955). I am indebted to the Delegates of the Clarendon Press for permission to quote the text from these two works.

2. A parallel between Helen and Anactoria is drawn by R. Merkelbach 'Sappho und ihr Kreis' *Philologus* 101 (1957) pp.1ff. (esp. p.15) and C.W. Macleod 'Two Comparisons in Sappho' *Zeitschr. für Papyr. und Epig.* 15 (1974) pp.217ff. (esp.pp.217f.).

3. On this question see: C. Theander 'Studia Sapphica' *Eranos* 32 (1934) pp.57ff.; G. Perrotta *Saffo e Pindaro* Bari (1935) pp.42f.; H. Eisenberger *Der Mythos in der äolischen Lyrik* Diss. Frankfurt am Main (1956), esp. pp.90f.; 'Ein Beitrag zur Interpretation von Sappho Fr. 16 L.P.' *Philologus* 103 (1959) pp.130ff., esp. p.131 n.1 and p.132; C.M. Bowra *Greek Lyric Poetry* 2nd. ed. Oxford (1961) pp.180f.; G.L. Koniaris 'On Sappho fr.16 (L.P.)' *Hermes* 95 (1967) pp.257ff., esp. p.261 n.1 and p.265; G.A. Privatera 'Su una nuova interpretazione di Saffo fr.16 L.P.' *Quad. Urbin.* 4 (1967) pp.182ff., esp. pp.183ff.; E.M. Stern 'Zu Sappho Fr. 16 L.P.' *Mnemos.* 23 (1970) pp.348ff., esp. p.352 n.1 and p.354; M.L. West 'Burning Sappho' *Maia* 22 (1970) pp.307ff.

4. E.L. Bundy *Studia Pindarica* I and II Berkeley and Los Angeles (1962), hereafter referred to as *St.P.* I and *St.P.* II.

5. *St.P.* I p.5.

6. *Ibid.*

7. *St.P.* I p.7. and n.23.

8. *St.P.* I p.5.

9. *St.P.* I p.5 and n.18.

10. *St.P.* I pp.5f.

11. J. Classen *Beobachtungen über den homerischen Sprachgebrauch* Frankfurt am Main (1854).

12. Classen *op. cit.* pp.5ff.

13. E. Schwyzer *Die Parenthese im engern und im weitern Sinne* Abhandlungen der Preussischen Akademie der Wissenschaften (Jahrgang 1939) Philosophisch-historische Klasse Nr. 68 Berlin (1939).

14. I intend to deal further with this matter in a future article.

15. E.g. Hom. *Il.* 5,197 (principal clause in 201); 9,348 (principal clause in 351); *Od.* 14, 281 (principal clause in 283f.).

16. Classen *op. cit.* (n.11) pp.6f. cites a number of examples of sentences with a paratactic parenthesis with γάρ preceding the principal clause, a number of which have similar signals in their principal clauses.

17. See Bundy *St.P.* II, p.36 n.3: 'ἀλλά dismisses the foil', citing numerous examples.

18. The affinities between these encomiastic arrangements and Homeric parataxis are seen to be even closer when other signals of 'foil' and 'climax' are included, such as particles and asyndeton. I intend to treat these correspondences, especially with regard to asyndeton, in the near future.

19. For this term see Bundy *St.P.* I p.5 n.18.

233

20. Bundy *St.P.* I pp.5f.

21. See Bundy *St.P.* I p.8 n.27 and E. Thummer *Pindar, Die isthmischen Gedichte* I Heidelberg (1968) pp.133ff. The latter gives a collection of Pindaric examples.

22. Bundy *St.P.* I p.10; II p.40 n.16.

23. This is, I believe, my own term.

24. Bundy *St.P.* II p.36 n.6.

25. With κούφως in this sense cf. ῥεῖα in e.g. Hes. *Op.* 5—7.

26. This is a common use of κοῦφος. Cf. Solon *Fr.* 13,36 (West); Pind. *Ol.* 8,61; Bacchyl. 1,178 (Sn.—Mae); Soph. *Ant.* 617: κουφόνοοι ἔρωτες. Cf. Aesch. *Ag.* 407f. (of Helen's action): βεβάκει ῥίμφα/διὰ πυλᾶν . . .

27. See n.22.

28. The difference of verb-tense is important for understanding the contrast between the 'summary foil' and the 'gnomic climax'.

29. 'Hostile Misrepresentation' has the powers of reversal characteristic of a divinity. Cf. Hes. *Op.* 5—7; T. Krischer 'Sappho's Ode an Aphrodite' *Hermes* 96 (1968) pp.1ff., esp. pp.5ff.

30. D.C. Young *Three Odes of Pindar* Leiden (1968).

31. Quoted in Young's collection of examples *op. cit.* pp.116ff.

32. Cf. G.L. Koniaris *art. cit.* (n.3) p.265.

33. Hes. *Fr.* 61 (Merkelbach-West), cited above, is among Young's examples *loc. cit.* (n.31).

34. Cf. (with Young) Soph. *El.* 392.

35. The subject is taken as Paris by C. Theander *art.cit* (n.3) p.70.

36. Cf. Pind. *Pyth.* 3,34f.; 55; Hom. *Il.* 9,600f.

37. See above n.3.

38. Theander *art. cit.* 72f.

39. This is how the Scholia take the passage (Σ62b p.72 Drachmann).

40. *Ol.* 9,94; *Pyth.* 9,97—103.

41. The story of Jason and Medea is of this type: in *Pyth.* 4,218f. Pindar takes a moral attitude towards Medea comparable with Sappho's towards Helen. For the omission of Paris and the evil consequences of Helen's actions see also Koniaris *art. cit.* (n.3) p.265; H. Saake *Zur Kunst Sapphos* Paderborn (1971) pp.132f.

42. The converse is of course acceptable and Sappho can compare her feelings towards a beautiful girl with those of a man towards the girl: cf. *Fr.* 31 (LP).

43. Cf. Pind. *Nem.* 8,35—39 (quoted above) and *Pyth.* 3 (see below).

44. J. Sitzler *Philologische Wochenschrift* 47 (1927) coll.999f. offers a supplement which shows how the text might have looked if this interpretation is correct.

45. For literature and theoretical discussion see Bundy *St.P.* I pp.4ff. and T. Krischer 'Die logischen Formen der Priamel' *Graz. Beitr.* 2 (1974) pp.79ff. For a detailed discussion of Sappho's priamel and a different solution from that offered here, see G. Koniaris *art. cit.* (n.3).

46. For the wide inclusiveness of Sappho's formulation see G. Wills 'The Sapphic "Umwertung aller Werte" ' *AJP* 88 (1967) pp.434ff., esp. pp.435f.

47. The two passages are compared by G. Méautis *Pindar le Dorien* Neuchâtel (1962) p.230. Young *op. cit.* (n.30) pp.116f. cites a number of instances of

the theme of the Near and the Far in Thuc. 6, in connection with the Sicilian expedition.

48.   This is what Koniaris *art. cit.* (n.3) p.261 and Privatera *art. cit.* (n.3) p.183 do.

THE PORTRAYAL OF MINOS IN BACCHYLIDES 17

by

GREGORY J. GIESEKAM

(University of Liverpool)

Poem 17 of Bacchylides was written for a Cean chorus (1.130) by a Cean poet.[1] One of the two central figures of the poem, Minos, was the principal ancester of the Ceans, through whom they traced their descent from Zeus. Bacchylides himself had celebrated Minos in poem 1. There he had narrated how Dexithea, daughter of Makelo, one of the Telchines, took refuge on Ceos and was visited by Zeus, who told her that she and the island would have a glorious future. Subsequently Minos arrived in full splendour and bedded Dexithea, 'thanks to glory-giving Zeus' (1.116). Their son, Euxantios, then became the earliest king of Ceos.[2]

In spite of these acknowledged facts and the importance which was given to ancestral myths in Greek communities, the generally accepted interpretation of poem 17, under the influence of its portrayal of the Athenian Theseus, casts Minos in the role of a black-hearted villain. Preuss noted the Cean connection, but commented (p.9): *Cum in fabula illa Cea (1) iussu Iovis adiutor et vindex Dexitheam consolaturus adveniat, hic crudelis Atheniensium vexator describitur.*[3] Recently it has even been claimed that Bacchylides invented the whole episode which shows Minos in such a light.[4] In this paper, I intend to argue against this prevailing view of Minos and to develop a hypothesis about the poem's composition which allows for a more coherent explanation of certain features in Bacchylides' presentation of the quarrel between Minos and Theseus, and which suggests what motivated Bacchylides to treat the story in the first place.

This will require initially a reconsideration of the historical and mythological context of the poem's creation, in which I will not be revealing any new facts, but simply suggesting that what is already known might lead to different conclusions from those which have previously been drawn. What will be of more importance is an analysis of the way in which Minos' behaviour is portrayed in the poem. Central to this, and crucial to any understanding of the poem, is the position we take on the disputed passage, ll.86-9.

The generally accepted view of the poem's circumstances of performance may be easily summarised. The presence of predominantly Athenian subject-matter in a performance of Ceans, and the invocation of Apollo as Δάλιε (1.130), have led most scholars to agree that the poem was intended to be sung on Delos, probably at an Athenian-sponsored festival connected with Theseus.[5] The poem is usually linked with the growing emphasis of Athenian public policy on the cult of Theseus as a pan-Ionian hero in the period 490-470 BC.[6] It is also claimed that the myth used might have been considered relevant for such a festival because it was on his return from Crete that Theseus established the *geranos* dance on Delos.[7] All this, along with Severyns' hypotheses concerning Bacchylides' chronology (p.59), which suggest that the poem was written between 480 and 470 BC, seems as probable a picture as we can obtain from the limited surviving evidence.

There are, however, more grounds for dispute over the origins and development of the story found in the poem. The most recent, and most lucid, account of the problems involved is found in Ellen Wüst's article. She outlines two view of Bacchylides' use of the legendary material in the poem. The earlier and more common one, accepted by Wilamowitz, Preuss, Robert and Jebb, among others, minimises his initiative in handling the story, and regards Bacchylides as simply versifying an already existing legend. Wüst herself argues that Bacchylides invented the quarrel-scene in order to provide a dramatic setting for the already existing tale of Theseus' reception by Amphitrite in Poseidon's underwater palace. She sums up the contrasting positions (pp.532f.): 'Since this combination of the story's elements occurs for the first time in Bacchylides, we may assume that he himself arranged them, that, when he took for his subject the story of the Cretan journey and the Delian dance, he by-passed the related account of the fight with the Minotaur and in its place invented the quarrel with Minos. If he did not, then another poet must have done this before him – and it must have been for exactly the same external reason! – and Bacchylides would have carefully imitated his version of the story.'

In fact we have no firm evidence which forces total agreement with either of these positions. The situation may be briefly presented. During the 6th century process of accommodation between the Athenian and Troizenian accounts of Theseus' birth, it seems likely that a story came to be told of Theseus visiting Poseidon's underwater home to receive recognition as his son.[8] Later, another version came into existence, in which Theseus was received by Amphitrite, Poseidon's wife.[9] In neither case is it likely that the motivation for the visit was that found in Bacchylides, i.e., for Theseus to prove his divine parentage to Minos.[10] Our first surviving piece of vase evidence for the sea-visit, the Euphronios cup in the Louvre, dated *ca.* 500 BC, shows no specific link with the quarrel story, and in fact shows a character extraneous to the

Bacchylidean account, Athena. The other vases discussed by commentators on Bacchylides are all mid-5th century or later, and only the Bologna vase seems to be definitely related to the Bacchylidean story.[11] It seems likely then that the quarrel story is a development of an existing sea-visit legend.

The quarrel-story also depends on a variant account of the Cretan voyage, which involved Minos coming to Athens to collect the tribute. In the most common accounts Minos sent messengers to collect the youths, or the Athenians sent them in their own ship, as is implied in the legend of the sacred ship with its black and white sails.[12] Apart from Pausanias' treatment of the quarrel scene (1,17,3), the only descriptions of the voyage which include Minos on board the ship carrying the Fourteen are Diodorus' (4,61), in which Minos comes with a huge Cretan fleet, and Hellanicus', reported in Plutarch *Theseus* 17. It is then probable that there was a reasonably early, although not generally accepted, variant version, which had Minos take delivery of the victims. This was then used by whoever introduced the quarrel over Eriboea into the story.[13]

The first literary evidence for the combined quarrel and sea-visit stories is Bacchylides' poem, which, as we have seen above, is probably to be dated in the decade 480-470 BC, although it could be later. The first pictorial evidence is Mikon's painting in the Theseion, described by Pausanias and dated *ca.* 470 BC.[14] In view of the steps in the development of the myth needed to provide the basis of the account in Bacchylides, a reasonably late date is to be inferred for the invention of the quarrel story. But, in view of the paucity of solid evidence, both the theories outlined by Wüst are obviously possible. The story may have been invented in the late 6th century or early 5th century, or it may have been Bacchylides' invention. Although I agree with the overall point of Wüst's article, that Bacchylides shows initiative in his use of myth in poem 17, I feel that there are some difficulties involved in her claim that he invented the whole story. First, is it likely that Bacchylides would invent such a story which presented his Cean ancestor in a more or less sinister light? Secondly, if Bacchylides did invent it, for performance in the mid or late 470's, is it likely that this foreign invention would be immediately taken over and depicted on the walls of the Theseion, along with only the two major episodes of Thesean legend, the battles with the Centaurs and with the Amazons?[15] Thirdly, and most importantly, such a view does not take into account the startling dichotomy between the non-Athenian picture of Minos and the Athenian picture of him which developed in the late 6th century and the early 5th century, and which has dominated later interpretations of him.

These factors, along with what will be said in my treatment of ll.86-9, suggest to me a third possibility in discussing Bacchylides' handling of the material here, which involves him in re-working an Athenian tale of the quarrel in such a way as to present Minos in a less evil light. This will be expanded on later. First, however, we should examine the depiction of Minos in literature before Bacchylides' poem was written. For this, Maniet's article provides a useful introduction to much of the relevant material, although he uses it to draw very different conclusions from mine about the portrayal of Minos in Bacchylides.

The best ancient exposition of the contrast between the earlier, non-Athenian, conception of Minos and the 5th century Athenian hostility to him, and a useful starting-point for our discussion, is the pseudo-Platonic *Minos*.[16] The topic is introduced in 318D, when Socrates' companion contrasts the just Rhadamanthys with Minos, who, he says, was 'savage, harsh and unjust'. Socrates replies, 'What you say, my friend, is a fiction of Attic tragedy.' He proceeds to point out that Homer described Minos as a confidant of Zeus and judge of the dead, quoting *Odyssey* 19,178f., 'Among them (the 90 cities of Crete) is the mighty city of Knossos, where the king was Minos, with whom Zeus had counsel every nine years.' and *Odyssey* 11,568-71, 'And there I saw Zeus' glorious son, Minos, sitting, holding a golden sceptre and dealing out justice to the dead, who sat around him pleading their cases.' He also quotes (320D) a Hesiodic passage — *Fr*.144(M-W) — which is alluded to in Plutarch (*Theseus* 16), describing Minos, 'who was the most kingly of mortal kings,/and ruled over more neighbouring peoples than any,/holding the sceptre of Zeus; and with that he ruled as king over the cities.'

Socrates goes on to stress what a wise law-giver Minos was and impresses on his companion that he should not be misled by the Athenian poets into maligning a hero who was the son of Zeus. When the companion asks how Minos came to be slandered so, he replies that Minos' mistake was to have been at war with Athens, a city whose poets had great influence. He than makes the traditional point about the dependence of a man's posthumous reputation on his portrayal in poetry (320D), 'For poets have great influence over opinion, according as they create it in the minds of men by either commending or vilifying.'[17]

Similar views of Minos' fate at the hands of the Athenian tragedians are taken by Plutarch and Strabo. The latter (10,4,8), giving an account of Ephorus' favourable description of Minos, quotes *Odyssey* 19,178f. and comments, 'But again the earlier writers have given a different account of Minos, which is contrary to that of Ephorus, saying that he was tyrannical, harsh and an exactor of tribute, representing in tragedy the story of the Minotaur and the Labyrinth, and the adventures of Theseus and Daedalus.' We should also note Plutarch's statement (*Theseus* 15f.) that most writers agreed that the Athenians treacherously killed Minos' son, Androgeos, thereby provoking Minos' attack and the wrath of heaven, which manifested itself in drought and pestilence. He also says that the god (presumably Apollo) ordered them to appease Minos by sending the tribute, and cites Philochorus and Aristotle's no longer extant *Constitution of the Bottiaeans* in support of the view that the Fourteen were not sent to Crete to be killed, but to become servants.

Another account of Minos which is contrary to the Athenian version is to be found in a reference by Athenaeus (*Deipnosophistae* 13,601) to the shadowy Chian historian Zenis, who, in his history of his native island, reported that Minos befriended Theseus and freely gave him his daughter, Phaedra, in marriage.[18] We should also remember the account of Thucydides mentioned in note 2, which depicted Minos as the destroyer of pirates and someone who made the Aegean safe for sea-faring. A further indication of the survival of his good name amongst the islanders can be seen in a description by Apollodorus (3,15,7) of a festival on Paros which even in his day was celebrated in a mournful fashion commemorating the fact that it was on Paros that Minos heard of Androgeos' death.

If we then turn to the surviving evidence of Attic tragedy, a brief survey seems to support the theory developed in the *Minos*. Apart from treatment of the Minotaur story,[19] various other tales detrimental to Minos' reputation are found. Aeschylus (*Choephori* 612ff.) uses the case of Skylla being persuaded by Minos to betray her father as an example of the evil behaviour caused by love. The story of Polyidos[20] seems to have been recounted by Aeschylus,[21] Sophocles,[22] and Euripides.[23] Minos was also attacked in the *Kretes* of Euripides.[24]

The theory of the *Minos* perhaps should be modified a little in one respect. We should note that Socrates in fact went on to regard tragedy as including the whole Athenian poetic tradition before Thespis as well as what we think of as tragedy (321A). Wilamowitz may have had this in mind when he wrote, 'Minos was changed from the 'counsellor of Zeus' into an evil king by the poets (not first by the tragedians).'[25] In view of the existence of 7th century vases which depict the Minotaur story and the probable compilation of the *Theseis* in the Peisistratean period, with the likelihood of a hostile picture of Minos in it, this may be so, in spite of our lack of solid literary evidence. It does not, however, invalidate the view that attacks on Minos were primarily Athenian and reached a peak in 5th century tragedy.[26]

It would appear then that there were two very different traditions of Minos in the ancient world. The older one, which probably originated in Crete and was developed among the islanders and the Ionians of Asia Minor, who traced their ancestry from Minos, held that he was a great and just king who had brought about a *Pax Cretica* in the Aegean. The other, which, through the dominant influence of Athenian tragedy on later literature, has totally conditioned our modern view of Minos, portrayed him in a much nastier light. The contention of this article is that Bacchylides' poem was written at the time when this denigration of Minos was beginning to gain ground, and that it is a subtle attempt to undermine a recently invented slander of Minos which accused him of trying to rape Eriboea. I would suggest that the evidence discussed above allows, and perhaps demands, the hypothesis that the general outline (but not necessarily some specific details) of the quarrel-story used by Bacchylides was an Athenian invention. The rest of the discussion will aim to show how specific details of Bacchylides' treatment suggest that he is modifying such an Athenian version of the affair.

The first reaction of upholders of Jebb's view of ll.86-9 will be amazement that anyone could claim Bacchylides is making a defence of Minos in this poem. That is why we must now turn to a close examination of that passage in particular and of Bacchylides' depiction of Minos throughout the poem.

The lines in question are printed by Snell-Maehler as:

> τάφεν δὲ Διὸς υἱὸς ἔνδοθεν
> κέαρ, κέλευσέ τε κατ' οὖ-
> ρον ἴσχεν εὐδαίδαλον
> ναˆα· μοῖρα δ' ἑτέραν ἐπόρσυν' ὁδόν.

Jebb translates: 'The son of Zeus felt a secret awe in his heart, and gave command to keep the cunningly-wrought ship before the wind; but Fate was preparing a different issue.' In l.87, however, Housman proposed printing κάτουρον, and translating, 'He ordered them to stop the ship which was running before the wind.' (p.139 = *Collected Papers* II p.468).

The passage is the most vexed in the poem, yet it is crucial to any understanding of it. Does Minos intend to abandon Theseus in the middle of the sea, or does he try to stop the ship? When Minos made his challenge to Theseus in ll.58ff., did he intend to bring about Theseus' death, as Snell-Maehler claim in their apparatus: *cur enim in mare misisset, nisi perdere eum voluisset?*[27] Or does he simply attempt to intimidate him into acquiescence, without really believing that Theseus will make the proposed jump? Housman argued for this: 'He believed of course that Theseus was the son of Aegeus, and expected him to shrink from the test.'[28] How will our answers to these questions suit the rest of the characterisation of Minos in the poem, and should they be affected by the Cean provenance of the poem? The difficulties are not as easily solved as the black and white categorisations of some critics imply.

Since the question of the Greek is in fact fairly clear-cut, and in Housman's favour, I will leave aside discussion of it until after we have confronted the principal fallacy which has led scholars to accept its distorted sense — the conception of Minos as a melodramatic black villain in the poem.

As we have seen above, the obvious and principal aim of the poem is the glorification of the Athenian Theseus by a Cean chorus, probably at an Athenian-sponsored festival on Delos. In effecting this, Bacchylides uses a story which was linked with the voyage which resulted in Theseus' establishing such a festival on Delos. We have also noted the likely recent nature of the quarrel story and the freedom which this would allow Bacchylides in his treatment of details of it. It is also clear that Minos' main function in the poem is as the means of bringing about the leap into the sea which displays Theseus' bravery and confirms his divine parentage. This does not, however, require a wholly evil Minos: he is a foil.

In fact, an examination of the narrative sections will show how Minos' heroic standing is carefully upheld in the poem. He is a 'steadfast hero' (1.73), 'Knossian war-lord' (1.120),[29] the 'dear son of Zeus' (1.69, and constantly referred to, in ll.20; 29f.; 53f.; 86), the 'son-in-law of Helios' (1.50); his passion is described in terms of him being the reluctant victim of the 'dread gifts of Aphrodite' (1.8),[30] and only takes the form of a desirous touch of Eriboea's cheeks;[31] Zeus willingly extends 'pre-eminent honour' to him in response to his 'blameless prayer' (1.68).[32] The only pejorative description occurs in Theseus' blustering attack on him: 'No more within your breast do you steer your spirit aright. A hero restrains his powerful might ... But you, keep in check your harsh intent ... I bid you curb your harmful insolence. For I would not wish to look a moment on the lovely light of immortal Dawn once you had forced, against her wish, any one of these young girls' (ll.20ff.). But this is to be expected from an angered adversary, and should not be taken as the total characterisation of Minos, just as the attacks of Achilles on Agamemnon in *Iliad* 1,225ff. and Theseus on Hippolytus in Euripides *Hippolytus* 943ff. could not be interpreted, even by the harshest critics of them, as full pictures of the persons assailed. It may also be noteworthy that in Bacchylides there seems to be a deliberate avoidance of any mention of the original purpose of the journey, which, according to the Athenian accounts, was to provide the Fourteen as human sacrifices to the Minotaur.

Given these considerations regarding Minos' portrayal and his structural role in the poem, along with its Cean context, it would perhaps be surprising to find Minos foully abandoning Theseus in the middle of the sea, so that he can get away with the girl, like some villain of melodrama. Once Theseus intervenes, in fact, the girl drops out of the picture entirely, and, as Hyginus noted, the argument revolves purely around the question of divine parentage.[33] The sailors are amazed (1.47) and Minos angered (1.50) that some Athenian upstart of a boy should reproach him, Minos, the son of Zeus, lord of the Cretans, etc. His 'newly woven plan', which results, is simply aimed at putting Theseus back in his place by a triumphant display of his own divine parentage, coupled with what he expects will be Theseus' humiliating inability to accept the challenge. Here we should note some aspects of his challenge which have not been sufficiently taken into account in the past. First, we should observe the surface irrelevance of his prayer for lightning. Theseus had plainly admitted Minos' claim to be the son of Zeus in his first words, 'Son of mighty Zeus' (1.20), and again in ll.29ff: 'Even though the noble daughter of Phoenix, famed for her loveliness, lay in bed with Zeus beneath Ida's brow, and bore you, most mighty of mortals . . .' Here it should be noted that εἰ καί is to be translated, 'even though', and is not meant to raise any doubt.[34] There is therefore no 'implied doubt of Minos' divine parentage', which Jebb (p.224) assumed to exist in Theseus' speech. If this is the case, then Minos' call for lightning has two purposes, outside its structural balancing of the Theseus miracle: it emphasises Minos' own glorious nature (both to Theseus and to the contemporary audience), and it is aimed at intimidating Theseus. The attempt to intimidate Theseus is maintained in the tone of his demand to him, with its elements of irony and the use of grandiose epithets: 'Cast your body boldly (θράσει)[35] into your father's realms. But you will soon know if Kronos' son hears my prayer, the all-ruling lord of thunder (ἀναξιβρέντας ὁ πάντων μεδέων)' (ll.63-6) and 'Now you leap into the loud-roaring (βαρύβρομον) sea. Kronos' son, the father, lord Poseidon, will bring about for you the highest glory through the well-forested earth' (ll.76-80).[36] The view of Minos' intentions expounded here is strengthened too by his amazement at Theseus' leap. He did not expect it.[37]

Now to the Greek. First we must understand ll.89ff., before considering what the sense of l.87 was. If the order in l.87 was to stop the ship, then μοῖρα δ' ἑτέραν ἐπόρσυν' ὁδόν./ἵετο δ' ὠκύπομπον δόρυ, will mean, 'but fate provided a different course, for the swift-moving ship sped on ...'[38] Jebb's objection to this type of interpretation is hardly compelling. He says: 'But, if Minos told his men to stop the ship, why did they not do so? Or if the helmsman obeyed Minos, and put his helm hard up, did fate forbid the ship to answer it? In either case the operation of fate was of such a remarkable kind that we might have expected the poet to say something about it' (CR p.153). But Bacchylides does just that in describing the winds driving the ship on, 'a northern blast blowing astern rushed it on' (ll.90f.). Fate helps magnify the miracle, by having the winds force the ship on, despite the will of Minos.[39] If the order had been to keep the ship on course, we must ask why the poet places such emphasis on describing this, after we have already been told that 'northern winds were hurtling against the sail' (l.6). The improbability of Jebb's answer to this, that an Athenian helmsman had tried to halt the ship, is clear, especially since it is almost certain that Minos is sailing on one of his own ships.[40] If, on the other hand, Minos did try to stop the ship, line 6 may have been intended by the poet to prepare the ground for the plausibility of Minos' excuse for speeding on.[41]

If the order in l.87 had been to keep the ship on course, we have to overcome a certain awkwardness in the use of ἑτέραν ὁδόν, in a situation where the ship is described as continuing on the same course which Minos supposedly ordered. When ὁδός is used metaphorically, as it would have to be here according to Jebb's interpretation of it as 'issue', it is usually qualified in some way which indicates what 'path' is in question.[42] In its immediate nautical context here it could only refer to the physical course of the ship, not to some vague 'issue' or 'result' of the events. If Minos in fact wished to change the course of the ship by bringing it round, then the Greek is clearly comprehensible.

If the above interpretation of the scene, which is basically an elaboration of Housman's, is accepted, then we need to explain the papyrus' KATOYPON, or be prepared to look for some emendation which supplies the proper sense. Housman argued that it should be construed as a previously unknown adjective, meaning 'running before the wind'. For the formation, there is the analogy of ἔπουρος (Sophocles Trachiniae 954;

Clemens Alexandrinus *Paedagogus* 1,7,54), meaning 'blowing favourably'.
The sense can be paralleled by the use of κατουρόω in Polybius 1,44,3 and
1,61,7, and in Lucian *Lexiphanes* 15, meaning 'run before the wind'.
Anyone who doubts the propriety of suggesting a *hapax legomenon* should
be read here might note that well over a hundred *hapax legomena* have
been found in Bacchylides' work.

If this reading is accepted, ἴσχεν will have its regular meaning of
'stop, check'. Jebb objected, however, that even if κάτουρος can mean
'running before the wind', the phrase would have to mean, 'keep the ship
running before the wind', on the analogy of certain usages of ἔχω applied
to ships (p.384). But in the analogous use of ἴσχω in 1.23, where an
adjective qualifies the noun governed by the verb, ἴσχε μεγαλοῦχον ἥρως
βίαν, he does not try to claim the meaning is, 'he keeps his might
powerful.' It clearly means, 'he stops his might from being overweening.'
And so in the present passage the meaning is, 'he ordered them to stop the
well-made ship from running before the wind.' In view of the presence in
the poem of a careful symmetry, which Stern has noted includes the
tendency of elements in the first half to be picked up in the second, we
might feel that the use of ἴσχεν in 1.87 was intended to recall Theseus'
admonition in 1.23. Minos now tries to exercise the restraint which
Theseus had claimed was the duty of a hero, but this time fate trips him
up by pitting the winds against him.[43]

If the above picture of Minos' behaviour is correct, certain questions
arise, concerning Bacchylides' handling of the story in the poem. We must
re-assess his motives in treating it, and attempt to suggest what
innovations, if any, he made in it.

In a recent discussion of Pindar *Nemean* 7, Hugh Lloyd-Jones cites
numerous examples in support of the following contentions: 'It would not
be surprising if its (i.e. *Paean* 6) presentation of Neoptolemus as a savage
killer, true as it was to the standard version of the cyclic epics, angered the
Aeginetans. It is true that in early times the violent and savage actions of
heroes did nothing to diminish their heroic status, or their right to be
venerated... Yet as early as the archaic age we discern the tendency to
censor stories about heroes in places where they received worship, just as
we discern the tendency to censor stories about the gods... There is no
doubt that in Pindar's time hero cult was an important factor in religion,
and consequently in politics; and it followed that treatment of cult heroes
by poets was matter of legitimate public interest.'[44]

I have quoted this at length because it is just such an outlook which I would suggest is at work in Bacchylides' treatment of Minos in poem 17. We have seen above the likelihood that the tale told in the poem is based on a story invented some time in the period 525-475 BC, and that it is linked to the development in Athens of an extremely hostile picture of Minos, especially in the works of the tragedians, but also probably in other poems, including the *Theseis*. Let us imagine then the situation when Bacchylides was asked to write a song for the Ceans to sing at an Athenian festival honouring Theseus. If the choice of subject was left to him,[45] we should surely have expected him to treat some other of the plethora of myths about Theseus, and to steer clear of any which continued the Athenian denigration of Minos. He could, however, have decided to confront one of these stories with a slightly different version of Minos' behaviour, which, while it fulfilled the requirement of honouring Theseus, also served to show Minos in his full glory again.

The extent to which Bacchylides may have modified the story might be seen by focussing on several supposed oddities in his treatment, and contrasting what Bacchylides has done with what we might have expected from an Athenian account of the events. Attention has been drawn to the absence of any mention of the Minotaur in the poem. We have seen that the idea of it as a man-eating monster was an Athenian one, so that it would be natural, if Bacchylides were trying to rehabilitate Minos' reputation, for him to omit it. A purely Athenian account would surely have included some reference to it, so evoking the Athenian memory of Theseus' glorious battle to overcome it. Another case of Bacchylides underplaying Minos' behaviour is in the description of the 'assault' on Eriboea. The use of $\delta\alpha\mu\acute{\alpha}\sigma\epsilon\iota\alpha\varsigma$ in Theseus' speech (l.44) and Hyginus' statement that Minos wished to rape Eriboea (*comprimere*) suggest that in the original version of the story Minos' intentions were much more passionate than is envisaged by Bacchylides' picture of him stroking the girl's cheeks. The building towards the high point of Minos' sexual assault is deliberately brought down to earth, and this is stressed by the following inflated drama of Theseus' reaction. Next we should note the call for lightning. Surely an account which was aimed at simply satisfying Athenian patriotic sentiments would not have made such play of this manifestation of Minos as the extraordinarily favoured ($\acute{\upsilon}\pi\acute{\epsilon}\rho o\chi o\nu\ \tau\iota\mu\acute{\alpha}\nu$ in l.68) son of Zeus. What is perhaps most important, however, is the attempt to stop the ship. We have seen what great stress Bacchylides has laid on external reasons for Minos' ship speeding on, and how he even describes it as the work of fate. If a previous Athenian account of the quarrel and sea-leap were to be discovered, it should cause no surprise if it depicted Minos deliberately and disgracefully deserting Theseus in the middle of the sea. If this were the case, then Bacchylides will have accepted that a given element of the story was true — that Minos' ship went on — but he will then have tried to exculpate Minos, by showing that this was contrary to his intentions.

We might now return to the starting point of Wüst's article. On p.527 she makes it clear that it is intended to combat the claims of Wilamowitz (p.11) and others that Bacchylides was unimaginative in his use of myth. I would suggest that if Bacchylides' handling of the material in poem 17 is as I have described it, Wilamowitz's criticism cannot be applied to this poem. On the contrary, Bacchylides shows, in the potentially difficult and ambiguous situation of having to provide the Ceans with a song in praise of Theseus, a great subtlety in adapting his sources in such a way that he could satisfy the demands of both Athenian and Cean pride in their ancestral heroes.[46]

NOTES

The following editions of Bacchylides will be referred to by author's name only: F. Blass, 3rd edn, Leipzig (1904); R.C. Jebb, Cambridge (1905); H. Jurenka, Vienna (1898); B. Snell, rev. by H. Maehler, Leipzig (1970), cited as Sn.-M. References to the text are taken from Sn.-M.

Reference to the following works will be by author's name and page number: H. Herter 'Theseus der Athener' *Rh.M* 88 (1939) pp.244-326 (cited as 'T d A'); 'Theseus' *R–E* Suppl. XIII (1973) pp.1045-1238 (*R–E*); A.E. Housman 'Notes on Bacchylides' *CR* 12 (1898) pp.68-74, 134-40, 216-8, reprinted in *Collected Papers* Cambridge (1972) vol.II, pp.442-69; R.C. Jebb 'Notes on Bacchylides' *CR* 12 (1898) pp.123-33, 152-8 (cited as *CR*, to distinguish from his edn.); A. Maniet 'Le Caractère de Minos dans l'Ode XVII de Bacchylide' *Et. Class.* 10 (1941) pp.35-54; H. Preuss *De Fabulis apud Bacchylidem* Diss. Könisberg (1902); C. Robert 'Theseus und Meleagros bei Bakchylides' *Hermes* 33 (1898) pp.130-59; A. Severyns *Bacchylide, Essai Biographique* Liège (1933); A.H. Smith 'Illustrations to Bacchylides' *JHS* 18 (1898) pp.267-80; J. Stern 'The Structure of Bacchylides XVII' *Rev. Belg. Phil.* 1967 pp.40-7; U. von Wilamowitz-Möllendorff *Bakchylides* Berlin (1898); E. Wüst 'Der Ring des Minos: zur Mythenbehandlung bei Bakchylides' *Hermes* 96 (1968) pp.527-38.

1. Note Bacchylides' emphasis on his Cean origins in 3,97f.; 5,10-12; 19,11; *Epig.* 1,4. We should also observe that he was employed by Cean victors for poems 1,2,6,7 and 8.

2. See also Bacch. 2,8, where Ceos is called 'the island of Euxantios', and Pind. *Pa.* 4,32ff. where Euxantios turns down the inheritance of his share of Minos' Cretan kingdom, in favour of remaining on Ceos. Thucydides (1,4) tells how Minos cleared the Aegean of pirates and settled most of the Cyclades islands.

3. Cf. Maniet p.47, 'Les Athéniens du temps de Bacchylide se représentent Minos sous des traits odieux. Or, Bacchylide écrit en l'honneur des Athéniens. Donc, il ne peut prêter a son personnage des sentiments forts délicats.' He later supports such an outlook by the jibe that Bacchylides, unlike Pindar, knew how to flatter the dedicatees or hearers of his poems (p.51).

4. Cf. Wüst's article.

5. The Delian connection is not a necessary conclusion, since Apollo can be, and often is, called 'Delian' in poems which have no special link with Delos. But the political considerations about to be discussed, especially the use of Delos as the centre of the Athenian Confederacy and the presence of the annual festival there, lend weight to the suggestion. It is difficult to find a more suitable occasion; there are no parallels for a foreign chorus competing in Athens, which is the scenario proposed by D. Comparetti 'Les Dithyrambes de Bacchylide' *Mélanges H. Weil* Paris (1898) p.35 (reprinted in W.M. Calder III and J. Stern *Pindaros und Bakchylides* Darmstadt (1970) p.399.)

6. The Athenians claimed to have seen Theseus at the Battle of Marathon and, in thanksgiving for their victory, they decorated their newly-built treasury at Delphi with a frieze depicting Theseus' Labours (Plut. *Th.* 35; Paus. 1,15,3). Delos, which had been wrested from Minos' control by Theseus, was made the centre of the Confederacy. (For a discussion of Theseus' connections with the island, cf. Herter *R–E* § § 77-9.) The high points of the Thesean policy were Cimon's removal of Theseus' bones from Scyros to Athens, following instructions from Delphi, in 476-5 BC. (Thuc. 1,99; Plut. *Th.* 36), and the rebuilding of the Theseion in the late 470's or early 460's, in a *temenos* supposedly established by Theseus after his return from Crete (cf. Herter *R–E* § 131). For the Athenian emphasis on Ionianism at the time, see Thuc. 3,86 and 6,87; also note l.3 of this poem and 18,2; the inclusion of the Megarian Eriboea (mother of Telamonian Ajax in Pind. *Isth.* 5,45 and Soph. *Aj.* 569) among the Athenian offerings may also be significant. Plutarch *Th.* 25 tells us that Theseus in fact married her and annexed Megara for Athens.

7. Cf. Call. *Hymn* 4,300ff.; Plut. *Th.* 21. It seems to be illustrated by the 6th century François vase (Beazley *ABV* 76.1), on which Theseus leads off a dance by the Fourteen (headed by Eriboea, holding his hand). See Robert p.144.

8. For the divergent accounts of Theseus' birth and their resolution, see Herter 'T d A' p.274 and *R–E* § 10, and Wüst pp.530f.

9. Most scholars accept that the Amphitrite version followed the Poseidon version, although Jane Harrison *CR* 12 (1898) p.85, thought the reverse was true. S. Wide's discussion of the ritual origins of the sea-leap (Meeresprung) in the *Festschrift für O. Benndorf* Vienna (1898) pp.13-20 supports the traditional view. Amphitrite's gracious reception of Poseidon's bastard son has been contrasted with 'the Dorian legend of Hera's relentless enmity to the son of Alcmena' (Jebb p.225). It may also be paralleled by a scene on the reverse of the Agrigento vase which is usually brought into discussion of the Bacchylides poem (Beazley *ARV* 260.2; cf. Smith p.278, and *Mon. Inst.* I.52 and 53). On one side Theseus is shown being welcomed by Poseidon and a woman, probably Amphitrite. On the reverse it would seem another of Poseidon's bastards, Glaukos, is being received by Amphitrite. Smith thought this figure was simply another portrayal of Theseus; but his appearance is different from Theseus' on the other side, and the fact that he is carrying the famous 'Wunderblume' of Glaukos has persuaded scholars that this is Glaukos (cf. R. Gaedechens *Röscher Lex.* I,1679-82; J. Hind *Dict. des Ant.* II,1612; S. Reinach *Rep. Peint. Gr.* p.213). For Glaukos' reception by Poseidon and Amphitrite, see Ov. *Met.* 12,948f.: *corpusque sub aequora versi; / Di maris exceptum socio dignantur honore.* I would suggest that the coupling on this vase, of the underwater reception of Glaukos and Theseus, is a reflection of a common theme, whereby Poseidon's sons by mortal mistresses were introduced to and welcomed by his goddess wife. For such thematic coupling on early vases, see J. Harrison *JHS* 19 (1899) pp.239f.

10. Cf. Wüst p.532, against Herter 'T d A' p.272 and *R–E* § 49, where he suggests that Bacchylides' story was already found in the 6th century epic *Theseis.* Cf. also Wide *art. cit.* p.20.

11. For discussion of these vases, see Smith's article. A better reproduction of the Euphronios cup, which, unlike Smith's, shows Amphitrite holding a wreath, is found in R. Fagle's translation of Bacchylides, New Haven and London (1961).

Incidentally, the presence of dolphins on the Euphronios cup, where Triton is Theseus' means of transport, need not be a hang-over from an earlier version in which they carry Theseus to the sea-bottom, as Wüst seems to suggest (p.531). They may be simply a decorative device aimed at supplying the underwater atmosphere. For the use of a tortoise on Skiron vases to indicate a coastal setting, see T. Ely *JHS* 8 (1888) p.274; and for a similar purpose in the presence of a crab on a 7th century engraving of Herakles and the Hydra, see G. Kirk *The Nature of Greek Myths* London (1974) p.185. It is therefore still possible that Bacchylides was the first to use dolphins.

12. Cf. Plut. *Th.* 15.

13. Cf. Wüst p.532.

14. Cf. Herter *R–E* § § 131f.

15. Cf. Paus. 1,17; Herter *R–E* §131.

16. For a discussion of the dialogue's authenticity, see the Budé edition of J. Souilhe, Paris (1962) pp.75-85. It is generally thought to be a work of the late 4th century BC. The attitude of Socrates in it may be owed to the possibly historical statement of Socrates in Plat. *Apol.* 41A that he was looking forward to having discussions in Hades with such just and true judges as Minos.

17. Compare the reverse situation in Pind. *Nem.* 7,20ff., where the poet claims that Odysseus' reputation benefited from poetry out of all proportion to his worth, because of Homer's sweet words.

18. *FHG.* IV,530. Jacoby dates Zenis to the 4th century.

19. Found, for example, in *P.Oxy.* 2452, possibly by Sophocles (cf. H. Lloyd-Jones *Gnomon* 35 (1963) p.453).

20. Recounted by Hyginus *Fab.* 136.

21. In the *Kressai* ? Cf. Nauck on *TGF Fr.*116.

22. Cf. *P.Oxy.* 2453, and *Gnomon* 35 (1963) p.436.

23. Cf. *TGF Frr.*634-46, especially 640f., in which Minos is seen as an example of wanton luxury.

24. Cf. C. Austin *Nov. Frag. Eur.* 82,32ff.

25. *Der Glaube der Hellenen* Berlin (1931) I p.112.

26. Maniet (p.47) may have been right in attributing this to the influence of the renewed Athenian naval policy in the early 5th century, which we have seen was also connected with the increase in Theseus' national role at this time.

27. Cf. Jebb p.384 and *CR* p.153; such an interpretation is supported by Kenyon (edn. London 1897 p.168), Jurenka (*ad loc.*), H.W. Smyth *Greek Melic Poets* London (1900) p.438, Maniet p.53, and most recent commentators.

28. *CR* p.218 (*Coll. Pap.* II p.468); this interpretation is supported by Wilamowitz p.28, H. Herwerden *Mnem.* 27 (1899) p.30, Blass (*ad loc.*), N. Festa (edn. Florence 1916 pp.106f.), H. Mrose *De Syntaxi Bacchylidea* Diss. Leipzig (1902) p.22, E. Schwartz *Hermes* 39 (1904) p.641, and P. Maas *Die Neuen Responsionsfreiheiten bei Bakchylides und Pindar* Berlin (1921) II p.87.

29. Cf. the honorific address to Hieron in 5,1f., Συρακοσίων . . .στραταγέ.

30. Reading α(ὶ)νά rather than ἀ(γ)νά which is printed by Sn-M. I have discussed this, along with some other textual problems in poem 17, in a forthcoming article in *Classical Quarterly*. Minos' reluctance is brought out in the phrase, χεῖρα δ' οὐκέτι παρθενικᾶς ἄτερθ' ἐράτυεν, which implies that he had in fact tried to restrain his passion. The fact that he is the victim of Aphrodite does not of course exculpate him from responsibility, but it is a claim to audience sympathy.

31. Cf. Stern's article for the humour engendered by Bacchylides' mounting description of Minos' passion which ends in such an anti-climactic action, followed by the exaggerated description of Eriboea's and Theseus' reaction.

32. Blass' conjecture ἄμεμπτον, for the reading of Pap. A, AMEΠTON, has been confirmed by Pap. O (*P. Oxy.* 1091). Jebb's view of Minos even led him to confusing his reports of the text here. On p.178, in his reproduction of the unedited text of the Pap., he prints AMEΠTON; on p.382 he claims the Pap. has AMEITPON, and that 'the conjecture ἄμεμπτον is against the Ms., and gives a weak sense.' He naturally preferred the prayer to be ἄμετρον, 'immoderate'.

33. *Poet. Astron.* 2,5: *cum iam non de puella, sed de genere Thesei controversia facta esset, utrum is Neptuni filius esset necne . . .*

34. Cf. Denniston *Greek Particles* 2nd edn. Oxford (1954) p.299, remarking on εἰ καί: 'it represents the fulfilment of the condition as immaterial' and is used in certain conditions 'in which the present or past indicative expresses an admitted fact: 'even though, obwohl'.'

35. The slightly pejorative θράσει in Minos' words picks up the more favourable θάρσος of the narrative in l.50, and takes on an ironical tone. For Bacchylides' effective use of such verbal recollections, see my discussion of ἴσχεν below and the use of τελεῖται in 18,30; 45. In the latter case, Aegeus' anxious 'I fear how these events will be brought to an end (τελεῖται as future)' is picked up by the chorus' words in the same metrical position, 'In the long course of time all things are brought to an end (τελεῖται present).'

36. In ll.77f. there seems to be some teasing from Minos in the ambiguity of the reference of τοι (strictly with τελεῖ, but also able to define πατήρ), played off against the delay in identifying Κρονίδας . . . ἄναξ πατήρ as Poseidon, not Zeus. Jebb noted that when Κρόνιος or Κρονίδας is used of Poseidon, he is always named or indicated, which gives point to the delay here, after Zeus had earlier been referred to as Κρόνιος (l.65).

37. Cf. Schwartz *art.cit.* p.641, 'Minos' demand is one of those demands of folk-tale which involve an impossibility; he does not think that Theseus will fulfil it, and so is amazed that Theseus does leap into the water.'

38. I translate the second δέ as 'for'; Denniston *Greek Particles*[2] p.169 discusses such usages and says, 'δε is not infrequently used when the context admits or even demands γάρ. In such cases the writer is content with merely adding one idea to another, without stressing the logical connection between the two, which he leaves to be supplied.' He cites numerous examples from poetry.

39. For any who might find this inability to stop the ship a trifle far-fetched, although the poet lays such stress on the winds, Housman provided a neat example from poetry:

> He shouted, nor his friends had failed
> To check the vessel's course,
> But so the furious blast prevailed,
> That, pitiless perforce,
> They left their outcast mate behind
> And scudded still before the wind.

> Cowper *Castaway* 19-24

40. This point needs to be stated since Jebb's assumption (p.384) that Minos is on board an Athenian ship has been followed by later scholars, including, most recently, H. Kriegler *Untersuchungen zu den optischen und akustischen Daten der bakchylidischen Dichtung* Diss. Vienna (1969) pp.57, 109, who repeats Jebb's qualms over the supposedly careless use of τηλαυγεῖ to describe the sail in l.5. As Housman and Festa (p.106) noted, the use of an Athenian ship to transport the victims is only relevant in the tradition which does not include Minos coming to collect them.

41. This view of line 6 is supported also by the use of πελεμαίγιδος (aegis-shaking) to describe Athena. It is not merely an ornate epithet, but has implicit in it the idea of the αἰγίς as a rushing storm, found in, e.g. Aesch. *Cho.*592, and in words such as ἐπαιγίζω (used of winds in *Il.*2,148 and *Od.* 15,293), καταιγίζω and καταιγίς (on which cf. the references in *LSJ*). This description of Athena's function here reinforces the feeling of the irresistible nature of the winds in the poem.

42. Cf. Housman p.218 (*Coll.Pap.* II p.468), 'The Greek word ὁδόν, between the words ἴσχεν νᾶα and ἴετο δόρυ, means the course of the ship.'

43. If this interpretation of ll.86-9 is correct, we shall also need to accept Wilamowitz's interpretation of ll.120f. οἴαισιν ἐν φροντίσι Κνώσιον/ ἔσχασεν στραταγέταν, as meaning 'From what anxieties he released the lord of Knossos' (p.29). This allows φροντίς its usual sense of 'care, worry', rather than the stretched sense provided by Jebb, 'exultant thoughts'. Compare Bacch. *Fr.* 26, again involving Minos, κρύπτουσα σύννομον Μίνωα τοξοδάμαντα/ Κνωσσίων στραταγέταν. ὁ δ' ἐπεὶ μάθε μῦθον / σχέτο φροντίδι. Furthermore, σχάζω will be allowed its more literal meaning, 'release, let go', rather than Jebb's 'check'. Cf. Ar. *Nub.* 740, σχάσας τὴν φροντίδα, 'having relaxed your thought'.

44. 'Modern Interpretations of Pindar: The Second Pythian and Seventh Nemean Odes' *JHS* 93 (1973) pp.136f.

45. We cannot be certain how much control a Greek lyric poet had over the selection of the subject for works commissioned for public performance. We therefore cannot be certain whether the initial decision to treat the subject matter of poem 17 was Bacchylides' or that of his Cean employers. For a general discussion of Pindar's and Bacchylides' adaptation of myth to suit the conditions of performance for their songs, cf. C.M. Bowra *Pindar* Oxford (1964) pp.278ff.

46. I should like to thank Professors H. Lloyd-Jones, A.A. Long and H.D. Jocelyn, and the members of the Manchester University seminar, Topics in Current Research, for their discussion of various points raised in this article.

THREE ALEXANDRIAN EPIGRAMS· APl. 167; CALLIMACHUS EPIGRAM 5(Pf.); AP.12,91

by

GIUSEPPE GIANGRANDE
(Birkbeck College, London)

In *APl.* 167 (= Gow-Page *Hellenistic Epigrams* 464ff.) we read:

Φάσεις τὰν μὲν Κύπριν ἀνὰ κραναὰν Κνίδον ἀθρῶν
ἅδε που ὡς φλέξει καὶ θεὸς εὖσα λίθον·
τὸν δ' ἐνὶ Θεσπιάδαις γλυκὺν Ἵμερον οὐχ ὅτι πέτρον
ἀλλ' ὅτι κἠν ψυχρῷ πῦρ ἀδάμαντι βαλεῖ.
τοίους Πραξιτέλης κάμε δαίμονας ἄλλον ἐπ' ἄλλας
γᾶς ἵνα μὴ δισσῷ πάντα θέροιτο πυρί.

What has hitherto caused difficulty to interpreters is the preposition ἀνά in line 1. The parallelism between τὰν μὲν Κύπριν ἀνά . . . Κνίδον and τὸν δ' ἐνὶ Θεσπιάδαις . . . Ἵμερον shows that ἀνὰ Κνίδον, corresponding as it does to ἐνὶ Θεσπιάδαις, must denote the notion of the statue of Aphrodite being in Cnidus. The commentators however have not been able to account for ἀνά meaning 'in'. Gow-Page *ad loc.* observe that 'ἀνά should mean *distributed over*, not *in*, but these meanings are often not far apart (e.g. Xen. *An.* 7.4.2. ἐστρατοπεδεύοντο ἀνὰ τὸ Θυνῶν πεδίον) and in Anyte 666 ⟨=AP 6, 123, 3⟩ ἀνά probably means simply *in*'. At AP 6, 123, 3 ἀνά in Anyte's line does certainly not mean 'in', as my colleague D. Geoghegan has demonstrated.[1] The meanings 'distributed over' and 'in' are always very far apart, inasmuch as in passages like the one quoted by Gow-Page the specific notion of a plurality of persons or objects being 'distributed over' a place is always explicit; at Xenophon *Anabasis* 7, 4, 2 the point is that the soldiers' tents are scattered, distributed, over the plain.

A solution to the problem will be obtained by considering the nature of Cnidus, a factor already well known, and a peculiarity of Hellenistic poetic syntax, a factor not recorded by the common Greek lexica. The town of Cnidus,[2] as everybody will recall, was located 'on the slopes of the mainland', which were 'terraced'; on account of 'the high slopes of the mainland' Cnidus received the epithet αἰπεινή (Homer *Hymn to Apollo* 43). Such 'terraces . . . stretch horizontally through the town, rising one on top of the other from the sea upwards' and are connected by vertical transversal roads, which cut at right angles the horizontal roads'. Such 'vertical roads ... climb ... gradually upwards'. The various temples and public buildings were situated 'in great numbers' along these streets which climb upwards, in a steep gradient from the sea level. The temple containing Praxiteles' Aphrodite was, in sum, in an elevated position with respect to the sea level; this is confirmed by Lucian *Amores* 11, where it appears that the visitors first reached the porticos of Sostratus, which supported a terrace used as a promenade, and then went further to the temple of Aphrodite.

The preposition ἀνά governing the accusative can denote in Hellenistic poetry not movement upwards, but the notion of being located on something elevated.[3] The statue of Aphrodite, being situated high up, at a certain height over the sea-level, on steep Cnidus, is therefore aptly described in the epigram by the words τὰν μὲν Κύπριν ἀνὰ κραναὰν Κνίδον which means 'Aphrodite situated, located, on rocky[4] Cnidus'.[5]

Boissonade (quoted by Dübner *ad loc.*) has already explained line 2; only certain details need clarifying. There is no need to alter θεός into λίθος, as suggested by Fr. Jacobs *Animadversiones in Epigrammata Anthologiae Graecae* II, 1 (= VIII) pp.39f. The point is that Praxiteles' Aphrodite, inasmuch as she is a real goddess (θεὸς εὖσα, that is, a goddess in flesh and blood, not a mere statue[6]), produces so much ἐρωτικὸν πῦρ[7] that she will set fire 'even to the rock on which she stands' (φλέξει καὶ λίθον),[8] the implication being 'let alone to humans'.[9] The poet, by way of a climax, then goes on to say that Praxiteles' Eros in Thespiae will set fire not only to the stone of which the mountains are made, but also to steel.[10]

*   *   *   *   *

I should like now to clarify two epigrams in which the meaning of the adjective περίσκεπτος has been misunderstood. The error, in the case of the first of these two poems, is over two thousand years old, because it must be laid at Didymus' door. Ancient critics of Homer agreed[11] that the Homeric adjective περίσκεπτος meant either 'that can be seen, is seen, from all sides' or 'from which one can see all sides' (e.g. Hesychius *s.v.* περισκέπτῳ: πάντοθεν ὁρωμένῳ· οἱ δὲ μόνῳ, κεχωρισμένῳ, ὥστε ἀπ' αὐτοῦ περισκέψασθαι).[12] Callimachus in *Epigram* 5 (Pf.) (= Gow-Page *Hellenistic Epigrams* 1109ff.) wrote:

Κόγχος ἐγώ, Ζεφυρῖτι, παλαίτερος, ἀλλὰ σὺ νῦν με,
    Κύπρι, Σεληναίης ἄνθεμα πρῶτον ἔχεις,
ναυτίλον ὃς πελάγεσσιν ἐπέπλεον, (εἰ μὲν ἄηται
    τείνας οἰκείων λαῖφος ἀπὸ προτόνων,

εἰ δὲ Γαληναίη, λιπαρὴ θεός, οὖλος ἐρέσσων
ποσσὶν †ἰν᾽ ωσπεργῳ† τοὔνομα συμφέρεται)
ἔστ᾽ ἔπεσον παρὰ θῦας Ἰουλίδας ὄφρα γένωμαι
σοὶ τὸ περίσκεπτον παίγνιον, Ἀρσινόη,
μηδέ μοι ἐν θαλάμῃσιν ἔθ᾽ ὡς πάρος (εἰμὶ γὰρ ἄπνους)
τίκτηται ψοτερῆς ὤεον ἀλκυόνης.
Κλεινίου ἀλλὰ θυγατρὶ δίδου χάριν· οἶδε γὰρ ἐσθλά
ῥέξειν καὶ Σμύρνης ἐστὶν ἀπ᾽ Αἰολίδος.

By way of anticipation and explanation of the text printed I should like to observe now that the MSS reading ναυτίλον (3) is perfectly sound (cf. Prescott *CPh.* 16 (1921) p.332 n.1); that the parenthesising given above will be explained later, note 30 below; and that the form ἀλκυόνης (10) is sound, being a vulgarism for ἀλκυόνος.[13]

Didymus, who was notoriously stupid when he produced ideas of his own, could not fit either of the two above meanings to περίσκεπτος as employed by Callimachus in this epigram, and so he concluded that the adjective must have been used by the poet in a new sense, i.e. 'wonderful' (ὅ τις ἂν κατανοῶν θαυμάσειεν).[14] Didymus' error has been perpetuated to this day: in *LSJ s.v.* we are told that Callimachus' περίσκεπτος means 'worth seeing'; Cahen renders τὸ περίσκεπτον παίγνιον as 'bibelot qu'on admire'; and in *Thes. s.v.* περίσκεπτος Didymus' hypothesis is accepted. Indeed the editors add, and they are in this completely mistaken, as we shall see below, *AP* 12, 91, 3 as a further example of the meaning 'wonderful'.

There are several reasons why περίσκεπτος in Callimachus' epigram cannot have the sense suggested by Didymus. First of all, the shell of the nautilus was, in itself, nothing to marvel at (ἂν θαυμάσειεν): it was, and is, 'common in the Mediterranean' (Prescott *art. cit.* p.328). Nor does Callimachus say anything to indicate that this particular specimen was in any way different from ordinary nautilus shells; nor could we think that the presentation of a shell was in itself anything worthy of admiration, because shells were commonly dedicated (cf. Gow-Page *ad* 1116, quoting an epigram of Theodoridas and a fragment of Hedyle).[15] For this reason, *LSJ* prefers the less emphatic rendering 'worth seeing', which however does not alter things: a nautilus shell, being a common object, was not any more 'worth seeing' than it was 'wonderful'.

This semantic difficulty is accompanied by a syntactical one: according to Greek and indeed Callimachean[16] usage the phrase τὸ περίσκεπτον παίγνιον, inasmuch as the adjective is attributive, means obviously enough not 'the toy which is' but 'the toy that is . . . ', i.e. the phrase necessarily implies a distinction between the toy that the shell has become and another toy. If περίσκεπτον meant 'wonderful' or 'worth seeing', the sense would be 'the toy that is wonderful (worth seeing)'; but in opposition to which toy that was not wonderful, not worth seeing? This syntactical difficulty has been either swept under the carpet, through neglect of the article τό: 'bibelot qu'on admire', Cahen; 'thy admired toy', Mair in his Loeb edition of Callimachus, and Gulick in his Loeb edition of Athenaeus; or it has been removed by conjecture: editors eliminated τό by changing it to τι, or by transmuting σοὶ τό into σεῖο (cf. Schneider's apparatus).

A further difficulty resides in the fact that the meaning 'marvellous' runs counter to Callimachus' compositional method. When a Homeric word such as περίσκεπτος caused ancient critics of Homer to debate whether it had one or other of two senses, Callimachus' method was to employ the word in one of the two debated meanings, thereby intimating his opinion on the matter.[17] In such cases of Homeric interpretation on the part of Callimachus the context in which Callimachus uses the relevant Homeric word is intended by him to indicate which Homeric meaning he accepted with respect to the word concerned.

The context of the epigram under discussion leaves us in no doubt that Callimachus sided with those scholars who took Homer's περίσκεπτος to mean 'that can be seen from all sides'. The poet means that, when the nautilus was sailing and floating on the surface of the water (πελάγεσσιν ἐπέπλεον) only the top and the sides of the animal could be seen, i.e. only the part which was above sea-level. Now that the nautilus has become a toy in Arsinoe's hands, she can see, when playing with it, all the sides of the animal, including the part which was previously invisible, inasmuch as it was under the sea-level when the nautilus was floating on the water. The sense is in sum: 'so that I might become for you the toy that can be seen from all sides'.

It remains now for us to explain the attributive nature of the adjective περίσκεπτον in its context. We shall in fact find a welcome confirmation of what I have just demonstrated: the attributive nature of the adjective fully corroborates our explanation of it as having the sense 'that can be seen from all sides' instead of 'wonderful'. Apart from the nautilus, there is in the epigram no other object that could be called a toy, nor indeed any other object at all. On the other hand, there exists in the epigram only one object other than the περίσκεπτον παίγνιον, and that is the object which the nautilus itself was before becoming (γένωμαι) the περίσκεπτον παίγνιον: it was a ship sailing on the surface of the water (πελάγεσσιν ἐπέπλεον),[18] a ship having its own forestays (οἰκείων προτόνων), cf. Aelian *De Natura Animalium* 9,34, τὴν συμφυῆ ναῦν.

Now this very object, the ship, was precisely a παίγνιον according to a proverbial saying common enough to have been recorded by Secundus *Sententiae* 17: πλοῖον ἀνέμων παίγνιον.[19] We know that Callimachus, like all Hellenistic epigrammatists, was fond of alluding, in order to obtain witty effects in his epigrams, to common proverbial sayings;[20] and this is a case in point. According to the proverb every ship was a toy, i.e. a toy of the winds; the nautilus therefore, inasmuch as it was a ship before becoming a toy for the goddess, was a toy of the winds. To put it another way: περίσκεπτον, in so far as having an attributive force, must oppose the περίσκεπτον παίγνιον to another παίγνιον; the only παίγνιον to which the περίσκεπτον παίγνιον can be opposed in the epigram is the ship that the nautilus was before becoming the περίσκεπτον παίγνιον that it is now; the ship that the nautilus was before becoming the περίσκεπτον παίγνιον was not only a παίγνιον, but in particular a παίγνιον that could not be περίσκεπτον, inasmuch as its lower side could not be seen, submerged as it was in the water. The sense is now totally clear: 'so that I might become for you the παίγνιον that is visible from all sides (*scil.* as distinct from the παίγνιον that I was before and which I am capable of being. the ship, which is a παίγνιον that cannot be seen from all sides insofar as its lower side is immersed in the water)'. The point achieved by Callimachus is of the type 'à intégration mentale'. The pronoun σοί, coupled with the attributive περίσκεπτον, has an obvious point: 'so that I might become for you the toy that can be seen from all sides, as distinct from the toy that I was for the winds, the toy that could not be seen from all sides, i.e. the ship'. The allusion to the 'lieu commun' is obtained by means of the article τό, which give attributive power to περίσκεπτον.[21]

Now to the textual difficulties presented by the epigram. First of all, a minor one. ἀλλά in line 1 evidently expresses a contrast; but a contrast between which two factors? Bentley saw himself compelled to change the MS reading παλαίτερος to παλαίτερον in order to obtain a contrast between the adverbs παλαίτερον and νῦν. To produce an opposition with νῦν Schneider created the adverb πάλαι by suggesting πάλαι τέρας, but his τέρας is contextually inappropriate, as Gow-Page correctly underline. A.W. Mair, in his Loeb edition of Callimachus, preserves παλαίτερος, but his rendering ('an old shell am I, o Lady of Zephyrium, but now, Cypris, I am thine') fails to account for the contrast which ἀλλά necessarily presupposes.

There is no need for any change: the epithet παλαίτερος is pointed and has deliberate relevance to two topical factors which are unknown to the modern critics but were very much present to the mind of Callimachus' readers. The solution to the problem is simple, if we remember the two factors. First, opposing the ϑεοὶ παλαιότεροι to the ϑεοὶ νεώτεροι or ϑεοὶ νέοι (e.g. Aeschylus *Eumenides* 721, 778; *Prometheus Vinctus* 955) was a literary *topos* not unknown to Callimachus (cf. Pfeiffer *ad Fr.* 177,8f.) and fashionably alluded to by '*Alexandrini poetae, pro sua eruditione*'.[22] Second, the goddess to whom the κόγχος παλαίτερος is dedicated is the newest goddess of all, i.e. Arsinoe Aphrodite Zephyritis. Arsinoe II Philadelphus was in fact deified during Callimachus' lifetime.[23]

It has thus become clear that Callimachus has cleverly utilised and elegantly alluded to the then fashionable and topical opposition between the old gods and the new gods. The contrast expressed by ἀλλά is, in other words, not between παλαίτερος and νῦν, but between παλαίτερος and the emphatically placed σύ. The sense is 'I (emphatic ἐγώ, personal pronouns being, of course, always emphatic in Callimachus) am an old (παλαίτερος emphatically placed at the end of the colon) shell, but (ἀλλά) I am dedicated to you, who are the newest goddess, now (νῦν), instead of having been dedicated in olden times to one of the old gods, as would have been chronologically appropriate, seeing that I am old myself and therefore was in existence already in times of old, when the old gods ruled the earth'. The pointed force of παλαίτερος as a topical allusion is now, I trust, completely clear. Neither Bentley's παλαίτερον, nor παλαίτερος taken as an adjectival equivalent of the adverb παλαίτερον, is acceptable, not only because the opposition is, as I have underlined, between the two emphatic personal pronouns ἐγώ and σύ, but in particular because the κόγχος 'did not cease to be a κόγχος when it was dedicated in a temple' (cf. Gow-Page *ad* line 1109).

Professor Verdenius and Professor Parasoglou have independently of each other drawn my attention to the fact that my explanation of the passage throws light on πρῶτον in line 2, whose force in relation to ἀλλά in line 1 had hitherto not been accounted for (cf. Schneider *Callimachea ad loc.*). The opposition between *primum* and *nunc autem* was felt by scholars to be baffling. πρῶτον means here 'for the first time' in the sense that the shell, although very old, had never been offered before as a dedication. Both Professor Cairns and Professor Parasoglou have independently suggested that ἄνϑεμα πρῶτον might mean 'first dedication' in the sense that the brand-new goddess, Aphrodite Zephyritis, received as her first offering the nautilus presented by Selenaea. This of course would not enable us to take περίσκεπτον as 'wonderful', in the sense that the shell was to be marvelled at *qua* first dedication. The poet explicitly underlines that the epithet περίσκεπτον refers to the toy that the shell had become, not to the shell *qua* ἄνθεμα.

Now to the great difficulty in line 6. None of the solutions proposed satisfies, so much so that Pfeiffer places the corruption between *cruces*. Bentley has already put line 10 in order: I shall now do the same for line 6, so that between the two of us we can claim to have restored Callimachus' poem to its pristine beauty. What has so far proved the stumbling block in †ἰν'ὡσπεργῳ† is the group of letters σπερ. Schneider's ἰδ' ὡς τώργῳ does not account for them. Remembering that σπέρχω is the verb traditionally associated with a ship progressing on the surface of the sea by sail or by oars,[24] we shall immediately recognise that the MSS reading σπέργῳ is nothing but a corruption of σπέρχω. The original χ became γ either as a scribal error (confusion between the letters is common) or as a result of the phonetic confusion which seems to have existed in Ptolemaic Egypt between them (as Professor Bogaert suggests to me[25]).

As for the iota, σπέργῳ is either a pseudo-dative born after χ was corrupted to γ and the resulting –εργῳ was misinterpreted as the dative of ἔργον; or, more probably, it could well be that the original indicative σπέρχω used by Callimachus was spelt σπέρχωι (on this very common spelling in Egypt cf. Mayser *Gramm. Pap.* 1[1], p.134,6). The equation ἐρέσσων . . . σπέρχω (Callimachus) and εἰρεσίη σπέρχοντες (Oppian) is neat. What about the letters ιν'ω, now that we have explained σπεργῳ? Three factors will enable us to solve the problem.

First of all, we shall consider the zoological factor: the nautilus was described by the ancients as capable either of sailing on the surface of the sea or of diving from the surface of the sea down to the bottom, when threatened. Cf. ἐπιπλεῖ γὰρ ἐπὶ τῆς θαλάσσης . . . ἐὰν δὲ φοβηθῇ, καταδῦναι τῆς θαλάσσης κ.τ.λ. (Aristotle *Historia Animalium* 622b, 5ff.); ἀναπλεῖ . . . γενόμενος . . . ἐπὶ τοῖς κύμασιν . . . ἐρέττει . . . ἐὰν μέντοι φοβηθῇ τι . . . βυθίσας κ.τ.λ. (Aelian *De Natura Animalium* 9,34); *in summa aequorum . . . naviget . . . si quid pavoris interveniat, hausta se mergens aqua* (Pliny *Historia Naturalis* 9,103); ἀναπλώσῃ ῥοθίων ὕπερ Ἀμφιτρίτης . . . ναυτίλλεται . . . ἀλλ' ὅτε ταρβήσῃ . . . βαρυνόμενος . . . καθέλκεται κ.τ.λ. (Oppian *Halieutica* 1,340ff.).

The second factor to be considered is that the adverb ἄνω, when used of fish and the like, means 'aloft, on the surface of the sea'. Cf. e.g. Oppian *Halieutica* 3,101; 5,189; 5,357; also Callimachus *Hymn* 1,24, where it is used as a preposition in the sense 'on the surface of the river-water'. The third factor is that the verb σπέρχω can also mean, of fish, 'proceed downwards, diving to the bottom', as opposed to 'proceed on the surface of the sea'. σπέρχω, when used of fish, was usually accompanied by words specifying in which direction, vertical or horizontal, the fish was moving. As examples of vertical downwards motion we might quote Oppian *Halieutica* 2,438 (σπερχόμενον ποτὶ βυσσόν); 4,542ff. (σπερχόμενον . . . καταρρεπὲς . . . ἐς ῥίζας); 5,170f. (σπερχόμενος . . . δύεται).

Callimachus, who is describing the nautilus as sailing or rowing on the surface of the sea and not diving, found it expedient to use σπέρχω accompanied by the adverb ἄνω, which specified that the motion was a horizontal one. The poet, in sum, wrote ποσσὶν ἄνω σπέρχω 'I proceed aloft with my feet': ἄνω corresponds, that is,[26] to ἐπ– in ἐπέπλεον in line 3, to ἐπι– in Aristotle's ἐπιπλεῖ or to ἀνα– in Aelian's ἀναπλεῖ.[27] I need hardly add that the error whereby ΑΝΩ became ΙΝΩ is a text-book case of 'assimilation'.[28] The AN– of ΑΝΩ became IN– because of the preceding –IN of ΠΟΣΣΙΝ. Such cases, as here IN and AN, often involve two syllables, each composed of one vowel and one consonant, the letter common to both syllables, in this case N, acting as 'amorce'. In our case the 'amorce' which prompted the error was the N of –IN, which caused (type "après l'amorce") the AN– of ΑΝΩ to be altered into IN–, thereby creating ΙΝΩ.[29]

The presents σπέρχω and συμφέρεται are intended to explain a scientific fact, and the sentence containing these presents is a parenthesis.[30] Callimachus, as is well known, was fond of long parentheses.[31] In sum, the epigram can be restored as follows:

Κόγχος ἐγώ, Ζεφυρῖτι, παλαίτερος, ἀλλὰ σὺ νῦν με,
  Κύπρι, Σεληναίης ἄνθεμα πρῶτον ἔχεις,
ναυτίλον ὃς πελάγεσσιν ἐπέπλεον (εἰ μὲν ἄηται
  τείνας οἰκείων λαῖφος ἀπὸ προτόνων,
εἰ δὲ Γαληναίη, λιπαρὴ θεός, οὖλος ἐρέσσων
  ποσσὶν ἄνω σπέρχω· τοὔνομα συμφέρεται)
ἔστ' ἔπεσον παρὰ θῖνας Ἰουλίδας, ὄφρα γένωμαι
  σοὶ τὸ περίσκεπτον παίγνιον, Ἀρσινόη,

260

μηδέ μοι ἐν θαλάμῃσιν ἔθ᾽ ὡς πάρος (εἰμὶ γὰρ ἄπνους)
τίκτηται νοτερῆς ᾤεον ἀλκυόνης.
Κλευίου ἀλλὰ θυγατρὶ δίδου χάριν, οἶδε γὰρ ἐσθλά
ῥέξειν, καὶ Σμύρνης ἐστὶν ἀπ᾽ Αἰολίδος.

The sense of lines 3—6 is: 'I am the nautilus who used to float upon the sea — if there is wind, I progress aloft by stretching my sail on my own forestays, if there is calm, by rowing with my feet: my name is apposite[32] — until I fell . . . '. The presents in the parenthesis describe what the nautilus is capable of doing, i.e. its ability to act as a sailor. To be more precise, σπέρχω is necessary in line 6 because πελάγεσσιν ἐπέπλεον in line 3 merely means 'I floated upon the sea' (cf. Cahen on Callimachus *Hymn* 4,36; *LSJ s.v.* ἐπιπλέω § VI): to say that his name (ναυτίλος = sailor) is apposite and that he can sail (as distinct from merely floating) by means of his λαῖφος or rowing with his feet, the nautilus must use a verb denoting the act of sailing.[33]

Arsinoe's nautilus is, of course, imagined by the poet as being still alive inside its shell, so much so that the animal speaks. This is confirmed by the adjective ἄπνους in line 9. ἄπνους cannot possibly mean 'dead', on two grounds. First of all, for a Lapalissian reason: the animal is very much, like M. De Lapalisse, 'encore en vie', witness the fact that it speaks. The nautilus is of course envisaged as a 'seaman', ναυτίλος, a living being, capable of skilfully sailing, and not as an inanimate object (on these latter cf. M. Burzachechi 'Oggetti parlanti nelle epigrafi greche' *Epigraphica* 24 (1962) pp.3ff.). Secondly, whether the nautilus was dead or alive would be irrelevant as an explanation (εἰμὶ γάρ) of the fact that the halcyon laid her eggs inside the nautilus' shell. For this reason, Lentz proposed ἄπλους (cf. Gow-Page on ἄπνους in line 1117). In reality, ἄπνους is perfectly sound. We must remember that the nautilus is talking about the eggs of the halcyon hatching inside the shell of the nautilus.[34] Gow-Page correctly comment on line 1117 'the shell is no doubt meant'; cp. 'the nautilus' shell was obviously a good substitute' for 'the halcyon's normal nest' (Prescott *art. cit.* p.333[35]).

Now, as we have already emphasised, the nautilus was known to have the habit of regularly diving from the surface to the bottom of the sea when it wanted to avoid a danger; 'the fact of the nautilus' sinking from apprehension' was commonplace in ancient literature (cf. Prescott *art. cit.* p.331, with texts). In view of this habit, the hatched young of the halcyons would have drowned, had it not been for the fact that, as Callimachus pointedly emphasizes, the innermost part of the shell was 'air-tight', ἄπνους. The adjective ἄπνους, cf. most recently *CR* N.S. 24 (1974) p.33, can mean in Greek, and does mean in Callimachus' line, *'flatum non emittens'* i.e. 'not leaking air'. The real nest of the halcyon, for which the nautilus' θαλάμαι acted as a substitute, had to be water-tight to prevent the danger of the hatched young drowning.36

Now we can understand the relevance of γὰρ ἄπνους. The explanatory parenthesis εἰμὶ γὰρ ἄπνους explains the words that immediately precede it, i.e. ὡς πάρος: previously (πάρος), when the nautilus was in the water, it was possible for the halcyon's eggs to hatch inside the shell, because the nautilus is watertight. The young halcyons could safely hatch (τίκτηται) inside the nautilus' shell, because (γάρ) its innermost part (the θαλάμαι) was ἄπνους, *flatum non emittens* , 'not leaking air' so that, when the nautilus dived, the air contained in the θαλάμαι did not leak out, but was kept therein, and could be breathed by the young of the halcyon. In other words, those who accepted the 'supposedly scientific fact' of the 'halcyon's hatching in the chambers of the nautilus' (Prescott *art. cit.* p.328) believed, naturally enough, that the part of the shell where the eggs hatched was just as airtight as the normal nest of the bird had to be. The nautilus speaking in the epigram is, as I have just said, envisaged by Callimachus as being alive and capable of sailing: hence the present εἰμί in the parenthesis at line 9 exactly parallels the presents σπέρχω and συμφέρεται in the parenthesis at lines 3–6.

To sum up: the two parentheses as indicated by Prescott constitute an explanatory interruption in the narration in the past tense (ἐπέπλεον, ἔπεσον) and explain what the nautilus is capable of doing, insofar as it is still alive. Each of the two parentheses contains one finite verb in the present (σπέρχω, εἰμί). The present εἰμί indicates that the nautilus is still very much alive; the finite present σπέρχω is needed because the parenthesis after ἐπέπλεον cannot be a mere amplification of ἐπέπλεον, in that ἐπιπλέω governing the dative πελάγεσσιν, as I have indicated, means 'float, drift afloat', whereas the nautilus wants to emphasise that he is capable of sailing (as opposed to merely 'drifting', 'floating' as a piece of flotsam would do) propelled by his sail or by his oars.

What is the point of the poem? ἐσθλὰ ῥέξειν (11f.) has been correctly elucidated by Kaibel (cf. now Gow-Page *ad loc.*). The phrase καὶ Σμύρνης ἐστὶν ἀπ' Αἰολίδος is, of course, intended to offer 'a second reason why the goddess should regard' Selenaea with favour (Gow-Page *ad loc.*). Wilamowitz suggested that being a native of Smyrna may have endeared Selenaea to Arsinoe because the latter had been married, before becoming Ptolemy's wife, to Lysimachus, who had together with

Antigonus 'refounded the Hellenistic Smyrna' (so Gow-Page *ad loc.*).

Gow-Page hesitatingly follow Wilamowitz. However, an allusion to Lysimachus would be most undesirable for many reasons. To begin with, it is unlikely that Ptolemy would have been pleased by an allusion to his wife's first husband instead of to himself; secondly, the marine animal, the nautilus, is offered to Arsinoe in her capacity as Aphrodite Zephyritis, i.e. as a goddess, and any allusion to her past as a common mortal, as she was when she was married to Lysimachus, would have been both indelicate in itself and inappropriate to the dedication.

The solution to the problem is simple and has to do with two facts: first that old Smyrna had been destroyed about four hundred years before and had recently been refounded; and second that Aphrodite Zephyritis was the goddess concerned with harbours in a storm and safe anchorages (cf. Gow-Page on line 3119). Now Aeolean Smyrna = old Smyrna, the name Selenaea pointedly gives to the town of which she declares that she is a citizen, was known to be the safe harbour *par excellence*, so much so that it was called Naulochon. Any citizen of old Smyrna could therefore expect to be regarded with favour by Arsinoe Zephyritis. The epithet Αἰολίδος, which does not seem 'appropriate' to Gow-Page *ad loc.* is, in the light of the equation Aeolean Smyrna = Naulochon, highly functional: for it was Aeolean Smyrna, as distinct from the new town, that was called Naulochon.

The epithet Αἰολίδος is fully justified and doubly expedient. It is justified because, in spite of its destruction, the town of Smyrna never formally ceased to exist: the proud Smyrnaeans had their own mint and struck their coins in the fourth century BC (cf. *RE s.v.* Smyrna 745,48ff.), so that the new Smyrna where Selenaea was born could also be called Αἰολίς inasmuch as there was, at least in the eyes of the Smyrnaeans, no break in continuity between the old town and the new. The epithet is expedient because on the one hand it suggests that Selenaea expects in so far as she is a native of Aeolean Smyrna = Naulochon, to be regarded with favour by the goddess Aphrodite Zephyritis; and on the other it sweeps under the carpet the fact that the town in which Selenaea had been born was, architecturally speaking, a new town.

This fact had to be swept under the carpet because, whereas Aphrodite Zephyritis had every reason to like old Smyrna, Queen Arsinoe had every reason to dislike the new town founded by Lysimachus. Arsinoe was given as presents several towns by her husband Lysimachus (Heracleia, Tios etc., cf. *RE s.v.* Arsinoe 1282). But the new Smyrna, also perhaps called Eurydikeia (cf. *RE s.v.* Smyrna 745f., 763 and *s.v.* Eurydikeia) was presented by Lysimachus to his daughter Eurydike; the latter had been born to him by one of his previous wives, not by Arsinoe.[37] We know that there was no love lost between Arsinoe and her husband's children by previous marriages. Selenaea discreetly disguises new Smyrna as the old Aeolian town, as such not connected with Eurydike, because the mention of Eurydike's new town would have irritated Arsinoe.

Dealing as we are with Ptolemaic toponymy, we may also treat the problem of the relevance of ϑῖνας Ἰουλίδας in line 7. Schneider has already shown *ad loc.* that there is no need to alter Ἰουλιδας into Ἰουλίδος. Nobody however has been able to see how the shores of Iulis could be relevant. But a solution is easy if we remember certain factual points which modern literary critics, not familiar with Hellenistic affairs, have forgotten. The town of Iulis is of course known to Callimachus, cf. *Fr.* 75,72ff. (Pf.). It was the capital of the island of Ceos (so Passow *Wörterbuch*[5]*s.v.*), the 'bedeutendste' town on the island (*RE s.v.* Iulis 2,104). Its sea-front, 'Hafenort' (*RE s.v.* Iulis *ibid.*), which was originally called Koressos or Koressia, had become the most important sea-harbour in the area facing Asia Minor in Ptolemaic times. Callimachus is no doubt alluding to the sea front of Iulis (ϑῖνας), i.e. the harbour. This harbour had been, of all things, renamed Arsinoe (cf. e.g. *RE s.v.* Poieessa 1274,31ff.).

We may now conclude: Kaibel and Prescott had assumed from the context that Selenaea had acquired the shell in the island of Ceos whilst on her voyage from Smyrna to Alexandria. This is contested by Gow-Page, who state *ad loc.* that 'since Ceos is in the Cyclades, it is not evident, as Kaibel and Prescott assumed, that Selenaea acquired the shell on her way from Smyrna to Alexandria'. On the basis of Ptolemaic sea logistics we can now see that Kaibel and Prescott had made a correct assumption: given the fact that Ceos was the most important harbour facing Asia Minor, what could be more natural than that the voyage made by Selenaea, aboard either one and the same ship, or several ships, one for each leg of the voyage, should have been effected via Ceos? The relevance of the words ϑῖνας Ἰουλίδας is now evident: they denote the harbour called Arsinoe. A nautilus which came from a harbour called Arsinoe and which was being offered by a girl whose native town was called Ναύλοχον, 'Safe Anchorage', was destined to be doubly welcomed by the goddess who was called Arsinoe and who had safe anchorage at heart. Note Callimachus' typical *arte allusiva*: neither place, Naulochon or Arsinoe, is overtly named; but both are discreetly and far more effectively brought into play by means of the phrases Σμύρνης Αἰολίδος and ϑῖνας Ἰουλίδας.

*   *   *   *   *

At *AP* 12,91 (= Gow-Page *Hellenistic Epigrams* 3040ff.) we read:

Διασὸς "Ερως αἴθει ψυχὴν μίαν. ὦ τὰ περισσά
ὀφθαλμοὶ πάντη πάντα κατοσσόμενοι,
εἴδετε τὸν χρυσέαισι περίσκεπτον Χαρίτεσσιν
'Αντίοχον λιπαρῶν ἄνθεμον ἠϊθέων.
ἀρκείτω· τί τὸν ἡδὺν ἐπηυγάσσασθε καὶ ἀβρόν
Στασικράτη, Παφίης ἔρνος ἰοστεφάνου;
καίεσθε, τρύχεσθε, καταφλέχθητέ ποτ' ἤδη,
οἱ δύο γὰρ ψυχὴν οὐκ ἂν ἕλητε μίαν.

The adjective περίσκεπτον in line 3 is taken to mean 'admired' in *LSJ s.v.*
Gow-Page *ad loc.* take Χαρίτεσσιν as a causal dative and περίσκεπτον as
equivalent to θαυμαστόν. In this they follow Jacobs (*Animadversiones* II,1
(=VIII) p.1) who rendered the phrase '*venustate conspicuus*' and Dubner,
who rendered it '*conspicuus Gratiis*'. However, the dative accompanying a
verbal adjective in —τος is as a rule a dative of agent.[38]

   This consideration and the fact that περίσκεπτος, as we have seen,
means normally 'looked at from all sides', lead us to conclude that
περίσκεπτον Χαρίτεσσιν means, in the context, 'looked at from all sides
by the Graces'. Such a conclusion is fully confirmed by two Hellenistic
motifs and by the context of the epigram, as indicated in particular in line
2. The first motif concerns the Graces: it was their function to bestow
beauty on whomsoever they looked at when he was born, cf. e.g. *AP*
12,122 for the motif. The motif of total beauty is well known: complete
beauty was envisaged as extending either from head to toes or all around
the body.[39]

   In the epigram under discussion, Polystratus means that Antiochus'
body was beautiful 'all around': the boy had been made beautiful at birth
by the Graces, who had looked at him from all sides, περίσκεπτον
Χαρίτεσσιν. Accordingly, the poet lets his eyes rove all around Antiochus'
body (πάντη πάντα κατοσσόμενοι (2), cf. *APl.* 160,3 (πάντη
... περισκέπτῳ) just as Philodemus and Ovid look all around the body of
their beloved,[40] a body which is beautiful all round, not only frontally.
Antiochus was, in sum, to use Meleager's phrase, ὅλος καλός (*AP*
12,154,3).

   The final two lines contain, as usual, the point. It has eluded the
critics, but we can easily understand it on the basis of Hellenistic *Motivik*.
First of all, we must note that the text is sound. In the phrase οὐκ ἂν

ἕλητε, the subjunctive ἕλητε should not be changed into ἕλοιτε, as Jacobs does, followed by Dübner: the subjunctive with οὐκ and ἄν is an overt Homerism.[41] Syntactical Homerisms are, of course, legion in the epigrammatic genre. Ψυχὴν μίαν in line 8 cannot but denote the poet's own ψυχὴν μίαν mentioned in line 1; οἱ δύο cannot but denote the poet's two eyes, as is shown by the 'verb in the 2nd person' (so Gow-Page *ad loc.*). The second person forms καίεσθε, τρύχεσθε, καταφλέχθητε correspond to the second person forms εἴδετε, ἐπηυγάσσασθε in lines 3 and 5. This is confirmed by the parallel motif in Meleager *AP* 12, 92,7 (= Gow-Page *Hellenistic Epigrams* 4620ff.). In Meleager's poem 'the eyes must endure their own share of the roasting', as correctly indicated by Gow-Page on lines 4624 ff.

Now to the verb ἕλητε. The verb is, in itself, not out of place: it was used to denote the notion of 'appropriating', 'making one's own slave'[42] the soul of the person who had fallen in love. Such 'appropriating' is, of course, normally achieved by the eyes of the person who conquers the poet.[43] Normally, that is, the poet is enslaved by the eyes of the person he falls in love with. How could, now, the poet's own eyes be envisaged as enslaving the poet himself?

Polystratus has ingeniously achieved a neat 'Umkehrung' of the motif we have so far discussed. There existed the opposite motif to the one just mentioned: the poet's own eyes, in so far as they received the ἀπορροή, the ἐρωτικὸν πῦρ produced by the beauty[44] of the person loved by the poet, were the instruments whereby the poet's soul was captured by love, so that the poet was consumed by fire ἐρωτικῶς (Aristaenetus 2,7,18), was melted down.[45]

In the light of such a motif, therefore, the eyes of the poet were traitors, because they betrayed the poet by siding with the enemy and by making the poet prisoner of his enemy, i.e. of his beloved. Polystratus, in his final couplet, is alluding to this latter motif: the poet's own eyes, in so far as they receive the fiery ἀπορροή emitted by the beauty of the boys the poet loves, are traitors to the poet: they hope to 'capture' –ἕλητε– his soul by siding with his enemy. He makes it clear, however, that his treacherous eyes will not get the better of him. Although he is admittedly burning (αἴθει), he will not be consumed by the fire of love; it will be his eyes which will be consumed (καταφλέχθητε) by the ἀπορροή they are receiving, because they are two and therefore cannot both appropriate the poet's ψυχή, which is only one. Polystratus' ψυχή, because it is one, can only be owned, appropriated (ἕλητε), as distinct from shared, by one conqueror. Polystratus is elegantly alluding to a Hellenistic *topòs*, i.e. the question whether it is possible to love two persons at the same time.[46]

In order to have his say on this debated *topos*, Polystratus has dexterously employed the complex *Motivik* of fire and love-warfare which I have illustrated. Polystratus takes the view that true love, the kind of love that conquers the lover's soul, can only be felt towards one person: to this end he utilises the grammatical argument that the act of appropriating, as distinct from sharing, can only be done by one individual. His two eyes have, by betraying the poet, identified with the cause of his two loves, for Antiochus and for Stasicrates, so much so that the poet says ἕληπε to his two eyes instead of to his two loves. The two treacherous eyes cannot, on behalf of the two loves, individually appropriate the poet's soul, which is only one. His eyes, who have betrayed him, will be punished because their attempt, being vain, is protracted. The present imperatives καίεσθε, τρύχεσθε, followed by the aorist imperative καταφλέχθητε, mean 'go on being burnt, go on being worn out, be consumed'.[47] They will consequently be consumed by their prolonged exposure to a double fire, since exposure to one fire alone would be enough (ἀρκείτω, 5).

I hope that I have demonstrated in detail that this epigram, far from being 'frigid' (Gow-Page on line 3046), is sharply pointed and skilfully employs specific Hellenistic literary *topoi*. It remains to be added that Meleager, who in *AP* 12,92 imitated Polystratus' poem, fully understood Polystratus' point as I have illustrated it here. Meleager calls his own eyes προδόται ψυχῆς, accusing them of deserting (αὐτομολεῖν) to the enemy who wants to conquer Meleager, and emphasises that they will be 'roasted alive' (ὀπτᾶσθε) by the fire of Love, whom the poet calls ἄκρος μάγειρος. For the motif, cf. also Gow-Page *Hellenistic Epigrams* 3654ff. (τρισσοὺς ἰούς, ἐν δὲ μιῇ ψυχῇ).[48]

NOTES

1. 'An Epigram of Anyte' forthcoming in *Quad. Urbin.*: in Anyte's phrase ἀνὰ ...δόμον ...αἰπύν, the preposition ἀνὰ indicates the Homeric notion 'des Erstreckens von unten nach oben hin' (A.C. Capelle *Vollständiges Wörterbuch über die Gedichte des Homeros und der Homeriden* Darmstadt (1968) *s.v.* ἀνὰ 3 *a*) i.e. it refers to the spear resting vertically and stretching upwards on the wall of the tall, αἰπύν, building.

2. *RE s.v.* Knidos 915,62ff.; 916,68.

3. Cf. M.M.F. Oswald *The Use of Prepositions in Apollonius Rhodius* Notre Dame University Press, Notre Dame, Indiana (1904) p.169, quoting *Arg.* 3,44; P.P. Priewasser *Die Präpositionen bei Kallimachus und Herondas, verglichen mit denen bei Bacchylides und den bereits für Pindar bekannten Resultaten* I Hall

(1903) p.10, quoting *Hymn* 6,82 Πίνδον ἀν'εὐάγκειαν, 'on Pindus'. (For *Hymn* 4,280, quoted by Priewasser *loc.cit.*, cf. V. Loebe, *Commentationis de elocutione Callimachi Cyrenensis poëtae* Pars II Putbus (1874) p.13.)

4. Epithets in Hellenistic poetry are never otiose: cf. αἰπύν n.1 above. Κραναάν, "rocky", entails the notion of being elevated, as opposed to mud-flats which are low.

5. The expressions τὰν Κύπριν ἀνὰ κραναὰν Κνίδον and τὸν ἐνὶ Θεσπιάδαις Ἵμερον are cases of 'partiziplose Konstruktion'. On this common feature of Hellenistic poetry cf. e.g. *Quad. Urbin.* 14(1972) p.38 n.2 and 15 (1973) p.31.

6. On this motif cf. *APl.* 159; 161 etc.

7. The erotic fire produced by the sight of a beautiful body made of flesh and blood was, of course, a commonplace (cf. e.g. *Rev. Et. Gr.* 81 (1968) pp.53ff.).

8. Stone was proverbially resistant to fire: cf. *AP* 12,61.

9. The artificial word-order whereby καί, referring to λίθον, is separated from it by the phrase θεὸς εὖσα is typical of the epigrammatists' style: cf. e.g. Fr. Lapp *De Callimachi Cyrenaei Tropis et Figuris* Diss. Bonn (1965) p.35 (*trajectio*); Gow-Page *The Garland of Philip* II p.266 'artificiality of word-order'; 268, 'the sentence structure and word-order are uncommonly elaborate'; 387, on the 'extraordinarily harsh displacement' of a καί; 265, 'the word is oddly placed in this sentence'. Jacobs *loc.cit.* recognised the grammatical structure of the sentence (*sensus est: 'haec vel lapidem incendat, cum dea sit'*) but then contended that the '*sensus*' was '*subabsurdus*'. But Boissonade's explanation of the text makes sense in itself and is a neat allusion to the ancient motifs indicated in nn.7 and 8.

10. Antipater is employing commonplace proverbs. Mountains are made of rock or stone, not of soil: on the *proverbialis locutio* involving steel cf. Dübner *ad loc.* and also Gow-Page *ad loc.*, 'proverbially hard substance'.

11. Material in *Thes.* and in H. Ebeling *Lexicon Homericum* Hildesheim (1963) *s.v.*

12. At *APl.* 160,3 περισκέπτῳ ἐνὶ χώρῳ means 'that can be looked at from all sides', as explained by O. Benndorf *De Anthologiae Graecae epigrammatis quae ad artes spectant* Diss. Leipzig (1862) p.23 (cf. Dubner *ad loc.*). Pliny *NH* 36,4,21 says: *aedicula eius (scil. Veneris Cnidiae) tota aperitur, ut conspici possit undique effigies*; cf. also *APl.* 166,3 πανωπήεσσαν, 169,1 περιδέρκεο.

13. ˌFor ἀλκυόρη˙ = ἀλκυών cp. σωδόνη = σινδών, ἁρπεδόνη = ἁρπεδών etc.; the type is very common (cf. C.D. Buck and W. Petersen *A Reverse Index of Greek Nouns and Adjectives* Hildesheim (1970) pp.288ff.). Callimachus used many vulgar forms in his epigrams, as is well known (cf. *Maia* 26 (1974) p.230 n.10). Professor Kamerbeek tells me in a private communication that, just as I have shown the bird-name ἀλκυόνης to be correct in Callimachus' epigram, so the bird-name ἀηδόνης is correct at Aesch. *Suppl.* 62.

14. Cf. *Et.Magn.* 664,48ff.; *Didymi Fragmenta* (ed. Schmidt) pp.184f.

15. Gow-Page on 1119 note that Selenaea's offering is certainly 'not splendid'.

16. Cf. L.A.A. Aulin *De elocutione Callimachi quaestiones* Diss. Upsala (1865) pp.74f.; Loebe *op.cit.* II pp.10f.

17. Cf. Fr. De Ian *De Callimacho Homeri Interprete* Diss. Strassburg (1893) for such problems. For the reproduction of undecided alternatives cf. *CR* 18 (1968) p.165. It is well known that Hellenistic poets often indulged in the 'reproduktion homerischer Zweideutigkeiten' as a *timatissimum artificium* : cf. *Hermes* 98 (1970) p.267 n.4; *Eranos* (1970) p.90 with n.40.

18. Ἐπιπλεῖ δίκην πορθμίδος, Ael. *NA* 9,34 (cf. Prescott *art.cit.* p.331).

19. This meant that the ship was at the mercy of the winds: cf. *AP* 7,665,1, μήτε ναυτίλλεο . . . κρατεῖ παντὸς δούρατος εἷς ἄνεμος.

20. Cf. E. von Prittwitz-Gaffron *Das Sprichwort im Griechischen Epigramm* Diss. Giessen (1912).

21. On this type of point, very common in Hellenistic poetry, cf. my *L'humour des Alexandrins* Amsterdam (1975) pp.1–21. By way of appendix, it may be noted that in Theodoridas' imitation of Callimachus' epigram (*AP* 6, 224, = Gow-Page *Hell.Epigr.* 3524ff.) Callimachus' witty employment of the attributive epithet περίσκεπτον had to fall out, because the λαβύρινθος described by Theodoridas is εἰνάλιος, i.e. is always totally immersed in the sea-water and could not be opposed to a ship floating on the surface of the sea. Sailing as a ship on the sea was, amongst shellfish, peculiar to the nautilus; the λαβύρινθος is therefore described by Theodoridas as a mere παίγνιον, without any attributive epithets.

22. Cf. especially K. Kuiper *Studia Callimachea* II, *De Callimachi Theologumenis* Leiden (1898) pp. 120f.

23. Cf. Mair, in his Loeb edition of Callimachus, n.c on the epigram under discussion; Prescott *art.cit.* p.334; and especially P.M. Fraser *Ptolemaic Alexandria* Oxford (1972) I pp. 239f., 587.

24. From Hom. *Il.* 13,334 to Opp. *Hal.* 5,295 εἰρεσίη σπέρχοντες. Cp. also Hom. *Od.* 13,22 σπερχοίατ' ἐρετμοῖς with Opp. *Hal.* 5,544 νῆα κατασπέρχουσιν ἐρετμοῖς.

25. Cf. E. Mayser *Grammatik der griechischen Papyri aus der Ptolemäerzeit* I Berlin-Leipzig (1923) p.164 'spirantische Aussprache des γ'; 2nd. ed. rev. H. Schmoll, Berlin (1970) p.142.

26. Cf. Prescott *art.cit.* p.331.

27. Apollinarius' ἄνω σπέρχουσαν (*Ps.* 50,38) is a neat *imitatio* of Callimachus' ἄνω σπέρχω (with *variatio:* ἄνω in Apollinarius' line means 'upwards').

28. On all this cf. L. Havet *Manuel de critique verbale* Paris (1911) § § 483ff.

29. Cf. in particular Havet *op.cit.* § § 483, 488.

30. See Prescott *art.cit.* p.327f. on the 'parenthesizing' and the 'parenthetical shift'; cf. also Gow-Page on l.1114. Ἀῆται (3) is nom.plur. of ἀήτης, not the present of a verb, as Prescott thought (cf. Gow-Page on 1111); we must understand εἰ μὲν ἀῆταί εἰσιν, εἰ δὲ Γαληναίη ἐστίν, cf. Arist. *HA* 622b 5ff. ὅταν πνευμάτων ᾖ and Ael. *NA* 9,34 (quoted by Prescott himself *art.cit.* p.331) ὅταν ᾖ γαλήνη . . . εἰ δὲ εἴη πνεῦμα.

31. Cf. Lapp *op.cit.* n.9 above, pp. 52ff.

32. Συμφέρομαι is used by Callimachus absolutely, in the sense 'be apposite', as e.g. in Eur. *El.* 527: cf. *Thes. s.v.* συμφέρω 1141, A–B. The sentence τοὔνομα συμφέρεται is added in asyndeton. This is typical of Callimachus' style (cf. Lapp *op. cit.* pp.80f.) and of epigrammatic poetry in general. I have indicated many cases of asyndeton in 'Vierunddreissig hellenistische Epigramme' *Graz. Beitr.* (forthcoming).

33. On σπέρχω, σπέρχομαι of sailors, ships, and animals envisaged metaphorically (like Callimachus' nautilus) as sailing cf. Nic. *Ther.* 814; *Lycophr.* 23; *Thes. s.v.* σπέρχω 586 A–B.

34. Cf. Prescott *art.cit.* pp.238 and 333. The plural θαλάμῃσιν is of course 'poetical' (cf. Gow-Page on 1117f.). Such plurals are very common in Hellenistic epigrams (cf. e.g. *Mnemos.* 25 (1972) p.297 n.1). I have collected many examples in 'Quelques aspects de la technique littéraire des epigrammatistes Alexandrins' *Graz. Beitr.* (forthcoming).

35. Cf. also Prescott *art.cit.* p.329 n.1.

36. τυφλός, Plut. *Mor.* 983D = *Soll.Anim.* 35,8; στεγανός Ael. *NA* 9,17: οὐκ ἂν δὲ ἐσρεύσειε δι' αὐτοῦ οὐδὲ τῆς θαλάττης ἔσω οὐδὲ ἕν· οὕτω τοι στεγανόν ἐστιν.

37. Cf. J. Seibert *Historische Beiträge zu den dynastischen Verbindungen in hellenistischer Zeit* Wiesbaden (1967) p.93.

38. Cf. e.g. Eur. *Herc. Fur.* 508: περίβλεπτος βροτοῖς; and, to quote a compound in –σκεπτος, Arat. *Phaen.* 1134: ἄσκεπτος ἀνθρώποις. Liddell and Scott 8th ed. *s.v.* render περίσκεπτον Χαρίτεσσιν as 'admired by the Graces' – grammatically accurate but meaningless, because the Graces would certainly not have admired merely human beauty.

39. On this motif cf. *Maia* 25 (1973) p.65 n.4. Gow-Page misunderstand both *AP* 12,121,4, where ἡλίκος ἐσσί means *totus quantus*, i.e. from head to toes, and *AP* 12,96, which varies the motif by excluding the toes of a beautiful boy. Gow-Page *Hell. Epigr.* II p.576 find this exclusion 'somewhat puzzling': in fact it is the whole point of the epigram, since the feet of the boy or girl were normally included in the catalogue of beautiful features. Cf. *AP* 5,132,1, ὦ ποδός, and cf. n.40 below.

40. *AP* 5,132; Ov. *Am.* 1,5,19; cf. *Maia loc.cit.* n.7.

41. Cf. e.g. P. Chantraine *Grammaire Homérique* II Paris (1963) § 306b.

42. On the motif which describes the poet as 'taken captive' when he falls in love, cf. Gow-Page *Hell. Epigr.* II pp.661, 619 (Introduction to Meleager ciii, xx). Love is seen as a war between the poet and his beloved: cf. *AP* 12,144,3, δύσμαχος.

43. Cf. e.g. *AP* 12,101,1 = Gow-Page *Hell.Epigr.* 4542: ὄμμασι τοξεύσας . . . εἷλον; Prop. 1,1,1: *me cepit ocellis* with Rothstein's note *ad loc.* Such a motif is 'in der erotischen Dichtung geläufig': cf. in particular Rothstein on Prop. 2,3,14.

44. The ἀπορροή was usually emitted by the eyes of the poet's beloved: cf. Gow-Page *Hell. Epigr.* 4550; 4556 σὲ . . . αἴθει, and esp. 4296f.

45. Cf. *AP* 12,83,3ff.: ἐμοῖς ὄμμασι πῦρ ἔβαλεν . . . ἔτηξε . . . πῦρ ψυχῆς; and *AP* 12,92; on the motif, see in particular Ludwich's note on *Mus.* 94 and E. Rohde *Der Griechische Roman und seine Vorläufer*[3] Leipzig (1914) pp.158ff.

46. Cf. *AP* 12,88; 89; 94;95; for neat variations by Ovid on this theme see *Am.* 2,10,1ff.; 2,4,47ff.; cf. *Emerita* 42 (1974) pp.15ff.

47. Cf. for such an employment of the imperative forms *op.cit.* n.21 above, p.8 n.19.

48. H. Akbar Khan, in *Hermes* 97 (1969) pp.375ff., suggests οἱ δύο γὰρ ψυχὴν οὐκ ἂν ἔχοιτε μίαν, but his proposal is untenable: ψυχὴν μίαν, in lines 1 and 8, denotes the poet's soul, and ἕλητε is a *terminus technicus*, denoting the poet's soul being made prisoner.

ASPECTS OF APOLLONIUS RHODIUS' LANGUAGE

by

GIUSEPPE GIANGRANDE
(Birkbeck College, London)

Hellenistic epic poetry[1] is erudite poetry, i.e. it consists in the manipulation and interpretation, on the part of the Hellenistic poet, of Homeric linguistic material. In order to understand and enjoy Hellenistic epic poetry we must not only be thoroughly familiar with the content of Homer's works, but also, indeed especially, with Homer's text, as it was constituted in the Hellenistic period, and with the ancient critics' theories concerning Homer's text, Homeric variants and the nature of Homer's language. The Hellenistic age marked the climax of Homeric criticism: the text of Homer was sedulously edited, annotated, disputed upon by scholars like Zenodotus and Aristarchus, and as a consequence of this the epic poetry produced by Apollonius, Callimachus or Rhianus, each of whom was a Homeric philologist in his own right, reflected precisely the extraordinary grammatical interest in Homer's works that was characteristic of the Hellenistic age. Callimachus, Rhianus and Apollonius were, as has been rightly emphasised, *poetae grammatici*, and their Hellenistic readers have been rightly called *sermonis Homerici peritissimi*, i.e. readers fully able to understand the subtle linguistic points which Apollonius and his fellow epic poets, through their allusive utilisation of Homeric diction, were driving at.[2] It is from the angle of a Hellenistic reader — after all, the only angle to be historically justified — that I should like to illustrate the methods which Apollonius followed in creating and employing his poetic diction — illustrate, that is to say, the fundamental principles governing Apollonius' art, which was first and foremost linguistic art, as such centred upon the employment of diction rather than characterisation or skilful development of a plot.

First of all, however, a few introductory words on the relationship between the Hellenistic poets and their model, Homer. When Apollonius set about writing his poem, the epic genre had made a come-back. The reasons for this are well known, of course. Tragedy and Comedy, which had dominated the literary life of the *polis*, were too inextricably interwoven with the political and religious life of the *polis* to be able to survive its dissolution — we must not forget that nothing could be more different from the *polis* than the Hellenistic state. Lyric poetry, too, had faded out. The causes of this eclipse are not unknown: although we know

271

next to nothing about ancient music, we do know that, towards the end of the Attic period, music seemed, in the eyes of the ancient public, to have exhausted its possibilities in the same way as was the case with, say, opera after Wagner and Verdi. Lyric poets tried new, unorthodox approaches, just as the 'twelve-tone' school endeavoured in recent years, but the ancient public appears not to have responded favourably to this, as we can learn from Aristophanes.[3]

So poets were left with few options open. There were some who tried new experiments with the 'verismo' approach, that is, they studied and depicted the life of the lower orders (Herodas, Leonidas Tarentinus, Theocritus). This was a fruitful approach, but limited in scope. Others cultivated and developed minor forms of Epic, i.e. the Epigram and the Elegy (which both were regarded by the ancients as sub-species of the Epic genre), but most poets (Theocritus with his epyllia, Callimachus with his *Hymns*, Rhianus with his long epic poems devoted to the exploits of local heroes) preferred to revive the Epic genre, the unsurpassed master of which was universally recognised to be Homer.

The attitude of Hellenistic epic poets towards Homer, however, was not one of pure imitation, but far more complex: it could be best described as a 'love-hate' relationship. This is most clearly exemplified by Theocritus' words (*Idyll* 7, 45-48) 'Much I hate the builder who seeks to raise his house as high as the peaks of Mount Oromedon, and much those cocks of the Muses who lose their toil with crowing against the bard of Chios'. In other words, Theocritus, who in his epyllia sedulously alluded to, echoed and imitated Homer,[4] recognised that mere imitation of Homer, such as was indulged in by those Hellenistic poets who wrote Epic intended to be of so pure a Homeric kind as to be compared with Homer's ('crowing against the Bard of Chios') was futile. Theocritus himself tersely expresses the opinion of the members of the public, by making one of them say (*Idyll* 16,20): 'Who would listen to another? Homer is enough for all'. Callimachus, who imitated Homer no less closely and elegantly than Theocritus,[5] explicitly says —*Epigram* 6 (Pf.) — that 'the Homer-like' ('Ομήρειον γράμμα) that is to say, poetry which imitates Homer in so unoriginal, mirror-like fashion as to be capable of being mistaken for Homer's, is worth nothing.[6] In sum, Hellenistic epic poets wanted on the one hand to imitate Homer, echo his words and allude to them at every step, but on the other they wanted to imitate him in such a way as to assert their own originality vis-à-vis their model.

272

Unlike Callimachus or Theocritus, Apollonius has given us no explicit statement concerning his attitude to Homer, his model,[7] but from the very outset he makes it clear that he will follow on in Homer's footsteps. In the very first line of his poem, where every epic poet traditionally makes his statement of intent, he says Ἀρχόμενος σέο, Φοῖβε, παλαιγενέων κλέα φωτῶν / μνήσομαι, that is, he states that he is going to sing παλαιγενέων κλέα φωτῶν, the exploits of heroes of old, just as Homer had done. Apollonius' choice of words is no less Homeric than his choice of subject: παλαιγενής is a Homeric adjective, and κλέα φωτῶν is a Homeric phrase (Hymn 32,18f.: σέο δ᾽ ἀρχόμενος κλέα φωτῶν/ἄσομαι ἡμιθέων, κ. τ. λ.).[8] Apollonius, in sum, tells us in his very first line that he has chosen a subject of Homeric type (the exploits of heroes of olden times), and that he will sing this subject in Homer's language, as is made evident by Apollonius' choice of the first words he employs. However, Apollonius immediately intimates to us what his poetic programme will be, because he has modified the meaning of Homer's παλαιγενής: whereas in Homer this adjective means 'annosus, old, full of years, aged', in Apollonius' line it has pointedly acquired a different signification, and means 'of old, belonging to ancient times'. Moreover, whereas Homer (Hymn 32,18f.) says σέο ἀρχόμενος κλέα φωτῶν/ἄσομαι, Apollonius has, in his line, reversed Homer's words into ἀρχόμενος σέο.

This observation leads us to state the cardinal principle followed by Hellenistic poets in their imitation of Homer: it was *imitatio cum variatione*, i.e. there always was an element of variation involved in the process of imitation. Pure and simple imitation was avoided. The element of variation served to enable the Hellenistic poet to assert his own originality vis-à-vis his model, Homer. When the element of variation was pushed to the extreme, the principle under discussion led to *oppositio in imitando*, to a process whereby the poet who imitates, in our case Apollonius, reverses what his model, Homer, had written. In this manner, plain imitation, which would have brought forth a worthless kind of 'Homer-like' (Ὁμήρειον) product, was avoided, and originality was achieved. The Hellenistic poet succeeded at one stroke in emphasising his originality (by means of the *variatio* or *oppositio*) and his erudition (by means of his precise allusion to Homer's words, which he had altered whilst alluding to them). The accusation dreaded by Theocritus ('Homer is enough for all!') was thus forestalled.

Before examining a few cases of such methods of *imitatio cum variatione* and *oppositio in imitando* let us briefly examine the material with which the poet operates — his own language, his vocabulary. Also in this respect Hellenistic poets (including Apollonius) avoided the danger of plain imitation, that is to say, refrained from employing purely and simply Homer's stock of words. They adopted two principles, namely analogy and the reproduction of Homeric rarities.

In adopting the principle of analogy, they succeeded in simultaneously achieving two aims: on the one hand, they brought out their own originality, in so far as the words coined by analogy were new, and added to the stock of traditional Homeric vocabulary; and on the other their originality could not be regarded as arbitrary, since the process was perfectly legitimate, in so far as the coining of words was done according to the morphological rules given by none other than Homer himself.

For instance, the ancient critics[9] knew that Homer was fond of coining abstracts in $-$ ίη and $-$ σύνη: Apollonius (and indeed any other Hellenistic poet, cf. my observations in *Classical Review* N.S. 21 (1971) p.354) not only used abstracts of these two types already employed by Homer, but coined his own, such as ἐπιδρομίη, ἀτημελίη, παλιντροπίη, ἀμβολίη,[10] ἀλιτροσύνη, κηδοσύνη, λαθιφροσύνη, μαργοσύνη, δαημοσύνη.[11] In some cases, Apollonius did not forget the principle of *imitatio cum variatione*: for instance, he pointedly employed in the singular (*Argonautica* 1,560) the word φραδμοσύνη, which Homer had used exclusively in the plural. Another method which Apollonius followed in order to enrich his epic vocabulary was to borrow words or meanings of words from Tragedy (e.g. θεήλατος, *Argonautica* 3,939; πανήμερος, 3,251; πορσύνομαι, 'be accomplished', 1,802, which is a tragic meaning, cf. Ardizzoni *op.cit. ad loc.*). This method, which Apollonius shares with Callimachus,[12] has perplexed certain critics. In reality it is perfectly explainable. To the Greeks, Homer was: τῶν τραγικῶν πρῶτος διδάσκαλός τε καὶ ἡγεμών (Plato *Republic* 595c); αὐτῆς (scil. τραγῳδίας) ἡγεμών (Plato *Republic* 598d). This view lasted down to Aristotle (*Poetics* 1148b, 35f.) and Diogenes Laertius (*Vitae Philosophorum* 4,20); indeed many Hellenistic papyri present the *Iliad* and the *Odyssey* arranged in dialogue form as though they were tragedies, [13] a circumstance particularly significant with respect to Hellenistic authors like Apollonius or Callimachus.

The ancient critics, whose theories Apollonius followed, taught that Homer's language was a mixture of dialects: the background was Ionic, but there was an infusion of Doric and Attic elements. Apollonius deliberately reproduced such a mixture in his own poem. For instance, Homer uses, as a rule, the form ϑεά, which the ancients regarded as a 'Doric form' (cf. *Classical Review* N.S. 21 (1971) p.356 n.3), but uses once, as an *unicum*, the form ϑεή (Rzach *op.cit.* p. 437). Apollonius uses in his own poem now the form ϑεά, now ϑεή, thereby reproducing the Homeric oscillation and, at the same time, 'developing' what was in Homer an *unicum*. Homer uses, as a rule, κούρη, but once he uses the Attic form κόρη. Apollonius promptly reproduces the Homeric oscillation by using κόρη at 1,811, whereas he uses κούρη in all the other passages of his poem. It is interesting to see that Callimachus does just the same: he uses the Homeric *unicum* at *Hymn* 4, 67, cf. *Hermes* 98 (1970) p.265 n.2. Homer uses, as a rule, the Ionic form νηῦς, νεός (Rzach *op.cit.* p.508). However, at *Odyssey* 10,127 he uses the Attic form νεώς, and Apollonius promptly follows Homer by using νεώς at 4,208, whereas otherwise he uses the Ionic forms. In the same way, Apollonius normally uses the non-Attic form Ἄρεος; but at 2,404 he uses Ἄρεως, the Attic form, because this Attic form is a Homeric rarity which occurs in *Iliad* 14,485 and 18,100 (Rzach *op.cit.* p.516). He usually uses the non-contracted form κληΐζω (e.g. *Argonautica* 4,1153), but at *Argonautica* 3,993 he uses the contracted form κλήσουσιν because this contraction occurs once in Homer (*Hymn* 31,18 − Rzach *op.cit.* p.459 − κλήσω). He normally uses the syllabic augment in ἐ −, but there is one exception: at 1,1309 he writes ὣς ἤμελλε, because in Homer this irregular augment occurs once, at *Iliad* 12,34, ὣς ἤμελλον (cf. Rzach *op.cit.* p.550). Apollonius usually employs the augmented forms εἷλκον etc., but at 1,1162 he uses, as an exception, the unaugmented form ἐϝέλκετο because this form occurs, in the same *sedes*, once in Homer, at *Iliad* 13,597.

We may thus conclude: Apollonius strove to reproduce Homer's mixed vocabulary, and, more often than not − this is a typically Hellenistic procedure − reproduced, or even 'developed' Homeric *unica*. Before we examine the technique of reproducing *unica*, by means of a couple of examples, let us observe, however, another aspect of Apollonius' technique of enriching the dialect element of his vocabulary, i.e. analogy. Homer was full of Ionic forms. Apollonius felt therefore justified in admitting Ionic forms which were not in Homer. For instance, the form ἐξεαγεῖσα (4, 1686), which had puzzled the critics − they even thought it was corrupt! − is an impeccable Ionic specimen, which the poet has borrowed from Hippocrates (cf. Boesch *op.cit.* p.23; *Classical Quarterly* N.S. 19 (1969) p.184 n.5.). Hellenistic critics underlined the fact that Homer had used a certain number of Doric forms: accordingly, Apollonius carefully introduced a few Doric forms into his poem, such as γᾱτομέοντες at 2, 1005. Modern critics, who did not know the theories of Hellenistic grammarians to the effect that Homer did use Doric forms, were horrified at Apollonius' γᾱτομέοντες, which they branded as *ab epico sermone prorsus abhorrens*; but now, in the light of the said Hellenistic grammarians' theories, Apollonius' γᾱτομέοντες has been shown to be the typical product of Apollonius' striving to imitate Homer. In the same way, the isolated Doric genitive "Ῡλᾱ at 1, 1350 is not a strange anomaly, as certain modern critics thought, but an impeccable feature in Apollonius' epic poem, in so far as it is modelled on Doric genitives in − ᾱ, such as Ἑρμήᾱ at *Odyssey* 12,390, which the ancient grammarians recognised as attested in Homer.[14]

Another way followed by Apollonius in order to imitate Homer without boring his readers with a monotonous repetition of what was usual or common in Homer was the reproduction of Homeric textual *unica*. Apollonius' public was composed, as I said, of learned readers, who were expected to recognise and savour such erudite allusions to one specific recondite or debated Homeric variant reading. For instance, at *Argonautica* 3,15 we read μειλιχίοις; ἤ γὰρ ὅγ' ὑπερφίαλος πέλει αἰνῶς. These words seemed to offer metrical difficulties, and were modified by certain modern critics: in reality, **Apollonius'** text is sound, in so far as his words are an overt allusion to one line of Homer, to *Iliad* 1,342, τοῖς ἄλλοις. ἤ γὰρ ὅγ' ὀλοῇσι φρεσὶ θύει : the group − οις ἤ γὰρ ὅγ' − occupies the same *sedes* in Homer's line and in Apollonius', and in both cases γάρ has the same irregular quantity,[15] so that Apollonius' allusion to Homer's line could not be more patent.

Another example: at 4,1572 the words στόμα λίμνης are not accidentally used: the reading στομαλίμνης occurred, as a debated variant, in the same *sedes* as in Apollonius' line at *Iliad* 6,4 and Apollonius, by reproducing it, wants to tell his readers that he sides with those critics who read such a variant in the Homeric text (other critics read a different text at *Iliad* 6,4: cf. *Journal of Hellenic Studies* 90 (1970) p.214). Apollonius has, of course, not neglected the canon of *imitatio cum variatione*: in Homer's line, στομαλίμνης is the genitive of an 'erstarrt' form ἡ στομαλίμνη, which the ancients recognised to be derived from στόμα λίμνης.[16] Apollonius, following the epic canon whereby words were to be 'reduced' to their etymological meaning,[17] has 'reduced' Homer's compound word to its two etymological components στόμα and λίμνης. When Apollonius was himself not sure which of two debated Homeric readings or forms he preferred, he reproduced both alternatives: this technique was, of course, common to all Hellenistic epic poets. For instance, at *Iliad* 17,571 the MSS hesitate between ἐργομένη, ἐεργομένη and εἰργομένη. Apollonius used ἐεργομένη at 3,649 and εἰργομένη or ἐργομένη (the MSS of the *Argonautica* show both these forms!) a few lines afterwards, at 3,653. The MSS hesitate, at *Odyssey* 5,385, between ἔαξε and ἄξεν: Apollonius reproduced both these rival forms, so that we find ἄξεν at *Argonautica* 1,1168, but ἔαξε at 2,1109. Ancient critics were not in agreement as to the significance of διέτμαγον in Homer.[18] Since Homer uses, at *Odyssey* 7,276, διέτμαγον as the first person singular of a transitive aorist of the type ἔλιπον, certain ancient critics decreed that διέτμαγον could only be a transitive aorist, and Apollonius accepts their theory at 3,343, where the third person singular of the transitive aorist in question is used (διέτμαγεν, 'it cut'). Apollonius' choice of a verbal person other than Homer's (the third instead of the first) is a common feature in epic: Oppian, in *Halieutica* 3,146, uses the third person plural διέτμαγον, 'they cut'. On the other hand, there were those who maintained that διέτμαγον could also be an intransitive form, meaning 'they parted': Aristarchus rejected this thesis, but Apollonius evidently accepted it, because we find διέτμαγον in the sense 'they parted' at *Argonautica* 3,1147. In spite of its being opposed by Aristarchus, this latter theory appears to have been followed not only in Hellenistic times, but also until late, witness Nonnus, who uses διέτμαγον in the sense 'they parted' at *Dionysiaca* 7,108.

Reproduction of Homeric *unica* was by no means limited to forms: it was extended to syntactical features.[19] For instance, at 3,377 we find εἰ δέ κε . . . ἥψασθε. κε is used with the indicative in the protasis of a condition contrary to fact. Such a construction is 'irregular' (so Gillies *op.cit. ad loc.*), and nowhere else attested in the *Argonautica*. Apollonius' irregularity is explained by the fact that the syntactical feature in question occurs in Homer as an *unicum*, at *Iliad* 23,526, which Apollonius wanted to reproduce as an *unicum* in his own poem. At 3,481 we find μή with the optative after a primary tense. This construction, not paralleled in the *Argonautica*, is employed once by Apollonius because Homer had used it once (*Iliad* 9,245) as a variant. At 3,404 we read ἤν κ᾽ ἐθέλησθα, instead of the regular αἴ κε. This construction, unparalleled in the *Argonautica*, is undoubtedly irregular, but the fact is that certain ancient critics accepted it in Homer at least once, at *Iliad* 4,353: ἤν κ᾽ ἐθέλησθα. I could easily produce many more cases, but I hope that this would be unnecessary, in the sense that the point has been sufficiently illustrated. Apollonius strove to imitate and reproduce not what was the trivial, the regular, the normal in Homer, but rather the exception, the rare, the *unicum*. In this way, he

277

avoided mere imitation of the obvious, and followed the Hellenistic canon which recommended avoidance of what was the common, the ordinary — τὰ δημόσια, as Callimachus put it.[20]

The tendency to achieve imitation with a difference, which we have seen in Apollonius' striving to imitate the rare and the unusual, becomes even more evident when we consider the techniques of *imitatio cum variatione* and *oppositio in imitando*. These features can be effected in various ways. First of all, there is the conceptual reversal. Homer says ἐς ἠέλιον καταδύντα — it is a common formula, — and Apollonius will pointedly say ἐς ἠέλιον ἀνιόντα *(Argonautica* 1,725). Homer uses the formula νῶτα θαλάσσης, and Apollonius, utilising the proverbial opposition between sea and land, will say νῶτα χθονός (4,1246).[21] This kind of opposition was practised between Hellenistic poets themselves, of course: so Callimachus says Ἐφύρηνδε *(Hymn* 4.42) and Αἱμονίηθεν *(Aetia Fr.* 304, 1 (Pf.)), but Apollonius pointedly says Ἐφύρηθεν (4,1212) and Αἱμονίηνδε (4,1034). Then there is the reversal of the word-order: Homer says *(Iliad* 11,77) κατὰ πτύχας Οὐλύμποιο whereas Apollonius writes *(Argonautica* 3,113) Οὐλύμποιο κατὰ πτύχας. Antimachus *Fr.* 39 (Wyss) has πεπονήατο δίφρον, and Apollonius says δίφροι πεπονήατο (1,752), thereby effecting a double reversal. He has inverted the word-order which Antimachus had employed, and has transformed Antimachus' πεπονήατο, which is a transitive middle as it is in Homer, into a passive.[22] Homer says κώεσιν ἐν μαλακοῖσιν *(Odyssey* 3,38), and Apollonius reverses this into μαλακοῖς ἐνὶ κώεσιν *(Argonautica* 1,1090). Homer says σὺν ἀσπίδι δουρί τε *(Iliad* 5,297) whereas Apollonius reverses this into ξὺν δουρὶ καὶ ἀσπίδι *(Argonautica* 3,1279).[23] Even such minutiae as the augment were utilised for purposes of *oppositio*: if Homer has the augmented ἔχευον *(Iliad* 3,270), Apollonius will use χεῦον *(Argonautica* 1,565). If Homer has φαάνθη *(Iliad* 17,650), Apollonius augments this form into ἐφαάνθη *(Argonautica* 2,449).[24]

This selection of morphological data, tedious as it may be, is nevertheless necessary if we want to get an insight into the way in which Apollonius operated, i.e. into his style. Apollonius' efforts at achieving originality in his imitation of Homer, and of his other epic predecessors such as Antimachus, are also apparent in the semantic field. Here, too, Apollonius' efforts at differentiating himself from his model can be observed in abundance. I shall confine myself to one relevant feature only, the semantic opposition between humans and animals.[25] Φθέγγομαι in Homer is said of humans; Apollonius at 3,1217 uses it of dogs (ὑλακῇ . . . κύνες ἐφϑέγγοντο). In Homer, ὁμοκλή is used of humans shouting, but Apollonius employs it of dogs at 4,13, κυνῶν ὁμοκλή. Αὐλίζομαι is used of cows and pigs by Homer (e.g. *Odyssey* 12,265): Apollonius uses it of no lesser beings than his august heroes (2, 1284; 4, 1689). Ὁμαδέω means 'speak all together', and is used of people by Homer (e.g. *Odyssey* 1,365); Apollonius uses it of bulls (3, 1304). Ἔϑειραι in Homer, as a rule, is used of horse-hair, whereas Apollonius uses it of human hair (1, 223; 3, 829; 4, 1303). This particular word will soon lead us to observe an interesting phenomenon, i.e. Apollonius' sense of humour. But before we proceed to this, I shall quote one particularly significant case of *oppositio in imitando*. In Homer *Odyssey* 11, 571 the opposition between the notions ἥμενοι and ἑσταότες is brought into relief. In Callimachus *Hymn* 3, 49, we see that the Cyclopes working at the anvils are ἑσταότες; in Apollonius we find the very same Cyclopes, at the very same anvils, but ἥμενοι (1, 730). Unless we are familiar with the technique of *oppositio in imitando*, we risk stating with a certain critic that ἥμενοι, in Apollonius' line, is an 'insignificant' detail, which should be removed by conjecture![26]

And now to Apollonius' humour. We know that humour is not extraneous to the epic genre, from Homer down to Nonnus: in Hellenistic poets, who were first and foremost grammarians, it tended, not unexpectedly, to be of a grammatical nature.[27] I shall examine here a couple of cases from Apollonius. At *Argonautica* 1, 671 ff. we read:

τῇ καὶ παρϑενικαὶ πίσυρες σχεδὸν ἑδριόωντο
ἀδμῆτες λευκῇσιν ἐπιχνοάουσαι ἐϑείραις.
στῆ δ᾽ ἄρ᾽ ἐνὶ μέσσῃ ἀγορῇ, κ.τ.λ.

The stupidities which have been written on the λευκαὶ ἔϑειραι of the παρϑενικαὶ ἀδμῆτες are an amusing legion, which can be found collected in Ardizzoni's commentary *ad loc*. The παρϑενικαὶ ἀδμῆτες are young, not old: none other than Apollonius, in order to avoid any doubt on this point, tells us that they are κόραι (line 811). How could such κόραι ('young girls') have white hair (λευκῇσιν ἐϑείραις)? Wilamowitz bewailed our inability to understand what Apollonius was driving at; Fränkel[28] performs disconcerting acrobatics, and says that the poet is guilty of 'eine kleine Übertreibung', in having given white hair, typical of old age, to girls who have not yet reached such old age, and wonders whether the ἀδμῆτες might perhaps be, if not old, at least 'on the way to becoming old' (!). The critics, who, very unchivalrously, would like to transform into old ladies the girls who are openly stated to be young by Apollonius, have not paid

279

attention to the text. It is true that Apollonius uses ἔθειραι in the sense 'human hair' in all the other passages of his poem, but we must remember that Apollonius likes to use words in different meanings at different points of his poem.

The context and Apollonius' *usus* will help us to solve the problem. First of all, the context: the poet has underlined that the girls in question are wearing their full armour (τεύχεα, 635). Now, part of the full armour was the helmet, which was decorated with a white horse-hair crest (such crests are called ἵππειοι λόφοι λευκοί, cf. Xenophon *Cyropaedia* 7,1,1f.; Alcaeus *Fr.* 357, 3f. (LP). Ἔθειραι denotes regularly, in Homer, the horse-hair crest which decorates the helmet,[29] and this meaning had of course survived in Hellenistic epic poetry (Theocritus *Idyll* 16,81, ἵππειαι ἔθειραι; 22, 186, λόφων ἔθειραι). Secondly, in conformity with his *usus*, i.e. his tendency to employ the same word in different meanings at different points of his poem, Apollonius has here used ἔθειραι in the regular Homeric sense 'horse-hair crest', 'crest consisting in white horse-hair', whereas he employed the same word in the sense 'human hair' in the other passages of his *Argonautica*. In other words: Apollonius has produced a grammatical joke typical of the grammarian that he was. Before leaving the word ἔθειραι, we may observe another point typical of Apollonius' method. We have seen that he has used only here, i.e. once in his poem, the word ἔθειραι in its regular Homeric sense, and we have observed that elsewhere in the *Argonautica* he uses it regularly in the sense 'human hair'. What epic precedent authorises him to use ἔθειραι in the sense 'human hair'? None other than Homer: in one Homeric passage, ἔθειραι was regarded by grammarians as having, by exception, the meaning 'human hair' (*Hymn* 7,4).[30] We may thus conclude that we are faced with a double reversal: the regular Homeric meaning of ἔθειραι (= 'horse-hair crest') is employed by Apollonius only once; the exceptional Homeric meaning of the word (= 'human hair'), attested in Homer only once, has become the regular one in Apollonius.

Another grammatical joke occurs at 1, 1323ff. where we read: Χαλύβων ἐν ἀπείρονι γαίη. It was a *locus communis* that the Chalybes' land was not 'limitless', ἀπείρων, but hard. Since the epithet 'limitless' would be meaningless in the context — the land of the Chalybes was no more 'limitless' than those of other peoples — and since, on the other hand, the fact that the land of the Chalybes was hard, unbreakable, was, as I said, a *locus communis* (Apollonius himself calls it στυφελήν at 2, 1005) the critics have in vain struggled to replace ἀπείρονι by an adjective meaning 'hard'. They have forgotten one important point: there is one passage of Homer, in which the adjective ἀπείρων was said by ancient grammarians to mean precisely 'hard', 'unyielding', 'unbreakable', i.e. *Odyssey* 8, 340. It is precisely this semantic *unicum* ιn Homer that Apollonius has chosen to reproduce here, as a grammatical trap set for the critics. Apollonius' accuracy is remarkable: in the scholia on *Odyssey* 8, 340 ἀπείρων is said to be, in the line of the *Odyssey* under discussion, a synonym of ἄρρηκτος and ἰσχυρός. Now, ἄρρηκτος is the *terminus technicus* used of γαῖα which, like :hat of the Chalybes, was 'not ploughed' (cf. *LSJ s.v.* ἄρρηκτος); ἰσχυρά 'hard' of χθών occurs in Aeschylus *Persae* 310.

A similar case occurs at 2, 467. We read: μειλιχίως ἐρέτῃσιν ὁμηγερέεσσι μετηύδα. Since the Argonauts are not rowing at the moment, the word ἐρέτῃσιν has perplexed the critics, ancient and modern – another trap set by Apollonius. The perplexity caused by the poet to ancient critics is shown by the MSS variants ἑτάροισιν (in D), 'companions' an obvious trivialisation, and ἔτῃσιν (in Y) – one of the many unmetrical 'corrections' in which Apollonius' text, as is well known, abounds. As for the perplexities of the moderns, cf. now Vian's note *ad loc.*[31] The context enables us to solve the problem. In the passage under discussion, in which the Argonauts are described as ἐρέτῃσιν, the heroes are at table, drinking and banqueting: they have been enjoying a μέγα δόρπον (line 304) and stuffing themselves with food and wine (line 307, δόρποιο κορέσσαντ' ἠδὲ ποτῆτος). The Argonauts' propensity to drink and to eat is one of the significant motifs in the poem: in fact, Phineus was so impressed by the heroes' capacity for banqueting that a little later (2, 465) he sent Paraebius to fetch 'the choicest of his sheep' to organise another banquet for them (2, 490ff.). The Argonauts, at the moment described at 2, 467, are still ἐν δαιτί, to put it with the author of the *Melampodia* (p.155 Kinkel). They are not rowing their ship, they are certainly not ναῶν ἐρέται (Aeschylus *Persae* 39), but they are certainly 'sailors of the feast and oarsmen of cups' as Dionysius Chalcus (*Fr.* 5) puts it: . . . ἐν εἰρεσίῃ Διονύσου/ συμποσίου ναῦται καὶ κυλίκων ἐρέται (J.M. Edmonds *Greek Elegy and Iambus* I London (1931) p.455). The Argonauts are not involved in the literal act of rowing their boat at the moment, but they are certainly involved in the εἰρεσίη Διονύσου, in the 'rowing of Dionysus', as Dionysius Chalcus (*loc.cit.*) calls it. In other words, Apollonius has here cleverly employed ἐρέτῃσιν in its metaphorical, not literal, sense. The origin of the metaphor κυλίκων ἐρέται is clear: the movement of the drinker's forearm, in lifting the cup from the table up to his mouth, is equated to the movement of the rower's forearm, in pulling the handle of the oar up to his chin. In conclusion, the word ἐρέτῃσιν, far from being corrupt, is very felicitous and contextually appropriate, in so far as the metaphorical use brought to light by me refers to the banquet in which the drinking Argonauts are involved.

Another example of Apollonius' lexical humour: at 4, 1713ff. we read:

> ... ἠὼς
> φέγγεν ἀνερχομένη· τοὶ δ' ἀγλαὸν Ἀπόλλωνι
> ἄλσει ἐνὶ σκιερῷ τέμενος σκιόεντά τε βωμὸν
> ποίεον, Αἰγλήτην μὲν ἐϋσκόπου εὕεκεν αἴγλης
> Φοῖβον κεκλόμενοι.

The epithet σκιόεντα has caused difficulties to the critics. If the ἄλσος was σκιερόν, surely the βωμός which was in the ἄλσος must have been 'shaded', too: σκιόεντα, therefore, seems at first sight superfluous. The fact is that Apollonius is springing for the reader another grammatical trap based on Homeric interpretation. Once again, the context and our knowledge of the ancient grammarians' theories concerning Homer's diction will enable us to solve the problem. We know that Apollonius was particularly fond of playing with light and shade effects, and this is a case in point. As for the context, the whole passage is concerned with the contrast between light and shade. The altar has been dedicated to Apollo αἰγλήτης (1716), who has shown αἴγλη (1710) in the darkness (σκοτίη, 1698) to the Argonauts. Now, σκιερός means *opacus*, 'full of shade'. Homer uses it of a wood, ἄλσος, and Apollonius does so here (ἄλσει ἐνὶ σκιερῷ). A τέμενος, in order to contain an altar, a βωμός, must be cleared of trees however. The τέμενος which Apollonius mentions, for instance, at 3, 1356f. is clear of trees, so that the light of the sun falls upon the armour of the Argonauts who are in the τέμενος and is reflected. Ἀγλαός could mean, in the opinion of certain ancient grammarians, 'full of light', *non opacus*. Aratus used the adjective in this meaning, and in Apollonius' phrase ἀγλαὸν τέμενος the adjective ἀγλαός has the meaning under discussion: the light, φέγγος, of the sun shone (1714), and the τέμενος, cleared of trees so that it might contain the βωμός, was 'full of light', 'exposed to the light'. Let us leave the context and proceed to Homer's diction. The adjective σκιόεις, in Homer, can mean either *opacus* or 'projecting its long shadow because exposed to the sun-light' and was used, in the latter import, of something tall.[32] It follows that σκιόεντα βωμόν in Apollonius' passage means that the βωμός, erected in a τέμενος cleared of trees (not in the *opacus* ἄλσος) was exposed to the αἴγλη of the sun which φέγγεν (1714), and therefore projected its shadow. The epithet was used, in the sense 'projecting a long shadow', as I said, of something tall, so that we may conclude that Apollonius' σκιόεντα is doubly appropriate: it denotes that the altar, erected to no less a god than Apollo himself, the protector of the Argonauts, was tall,[33] not a contemptible little thing; and that the altar, dedicated to Apollo αἰγλήτης, was appropriately situated in the full sun-light, not in the shade of the ἄλσος.

Let us now examine[34] a passage which shows a double aspect of Apollonius' allusive art, 1, 614ff. :

> . . . ἐπεὶ χόλος αἰνὸς ὄπαζεν
> Κύπριδος, οὕνεκά μιν γεράων ἐπὶ δηρὸν ἄτισσαν.
> ὦ μέλεαι, ζήλοιό τ' ἐπισμυγερῶς ἀκόρητοι.
> οὐκ οἶον σὺν τῆσιν ἑοὺς ἔρραισαν ἀκοίτας
> ἀμφ' εὐνῇ, πᾶν δ' ἄρσεν ὁμοῦ γένος, ὥς κεν ὀπίσσω
> μήτινα λευγαλέοιο φόνου τίσειαν ἀμοιβήν.

The poet is alluding to the legend according to which Aphrodite, not having been honoured by the Lemniads (οὕνεκά μιν γεράων ἐπὶ δηρὸν ἄτισσαν), punished them by casting upon them a δυσοσμία which made them repellent to their husbands. These latter abandoned the Lemniads who, full of mad jealousy (ζήλοιο), killed their husbands and indeed their own children. The critics could not understand how the Lemniads, who were made repellent by the δυσοσμία inflicted upon them by Aphrodite, could possibly have enticed the Argonauts to go to bed with them, as Apollonius narrates in lines 841ff. The fact is that the poet is perfectly accurate in every detail. In order to understand the passage, we must be familiar with two elements of Hellenistic epic technique. First of all, Apollonius, like Theocritus and Callimachus, never relates in detail any given legend. He limits himself to alluding to it, and expects his readers to know every particular of the story which he is hinting at. Now, as we learn from the scholiast commenting upon Apollonius' lines under discussion, Aphrodite had cast upon the Lemniads a δυσοσμία which was intended to make them repellent τοῖς ἀνδράσιν, i.e. to their own husbands, not to all males for all time. Secondly: Apollonius, in his turn, tells us explicitly, by his pointed employment of Homeric diction, that the δυσοσμία had fully served its retributory purpose. He does so by pointedly employing the adverb ἐπισμυγερῶς, which in Homer means ἐπὶ κακῷ τῷ ἑαυτοῦ (scholia on *Odyssey* 4, 672), 'to one's own ruin'. The δυσοσμία, by causing the Lemniads to destroy their own families, caused them to act 'to their own ruin'. In sum, the Lemniads punished themselves by killing their own husbands and their own children. Once the wretched (μέλεαι) Lemniads had paid such a bitter penalty, i.e. when the goddess had exacted the penalty from them, there was evidently no need for Aphrodite to make the δυσοσμία last any longer. The δυσοσμία was calculated to render the Lemniads repellent only to their husbands, who were by now dead, so that the δυσοσμία had lost its *raison d'être*. In particular, the goddess herself, as Apollonius underlines, wanted Lemnos to be repopulated (1, 850ff.), and for this reason she could certainly not wish the δυσοσμία to continue to afflict the Lemniads so as to make them repugnant to the fresh bed-fellows who were needed if Lemnos was to be repopulated. To sum up, Apollonius has been as accurate as ever: the Lemniads could certainly go to bed with the Argonauts, because the δυσοσμία, having fully served Aphrodite's purpose, had lost its *raison d'être* and had ceased to exist.

Apollonius' art is nothing if not precise, both in the employment of his diction and in his allusion to legends, as we have seen. The same holds true of his similes. I shall now examine one simile which has been just as unwarrantably criticised as we have seen to be the case with the passage about the Lemniads. At 2,27ff. we read that King Amycus, surrounded by the Argonauts and offended by Polydeuces, looks at him, singling him out from amongst the Argonauts, as a lion singles out from amongst the hunters surrounding him the one who has wounded him:

> ὥστε λέων ὑπ' ἄκοντι τετυμμένος, ὅν τ' ἐν ὄρεσσιν
> ἀνέρες ἀμφιπένονται· ὁ δ' ἰλλόμενός πέρ ὁμίλῳ
> τῶν μὲν ἔτ' οὐκ ἀλέγει, ἐπὶ δ' ὄσσεται οἰόθεν οἶος
> ἄνδρα τόν, ὅς μιν ἔτυψε παροίτατος.

Certain critics have changed οἶος into οἶον, because, they allege, 'the solitude both of Amycus and of the lion is irrelevant'.[35] Indeed, the opposite is true. Those who have studied Apollonius' similes[36] know that the whole point about these is that the poet strives to obtain a complete correspondence of all the details in the two situations compared, and this is a case in point. The fact is that Amycus had gone to challenge the Argonauts, and had spoken all alone, surrounded by them (line 10, ἐν πάντεσσι). One of the Argonauts who surrounded him had offended him. The King, being all alone and surrounded by the Argonauts, singles out from amongst the Argonauts the one who had offended him, just as a lion, being alone at bay and surrounded by hunters, singles out from amongst them the one who had wounded him. The solitude of the lion and of Amycus is therefore part and parcel of the simile, in that οἶος achieves a complete correspondence between the situation of Amycus and that of the lion.

The point is that, as Homer tells us and as every reader of Apollonius is expected to know, lions go hunting either singly or in couples:[37] when a Homeric simile refers to two heroes, Homer uses the simile of two lions hunting in couple (e.g. *Iliad* 15, 324, cf. Leaf *ad loc.*, and *Iliad* 16, 756). Whereas, when one hero is involved in Homer's simile, only one single lion, without his σύννομος is mentioned. Homer's single lion at bay, surrounded ἐν θηρευτῆρσι (*Iliad* 12, 41) or ἐν ὁμίλῳ (*Odyssey* 4, 791f.) is the model of the single (οἶος, line 28) lion at bay, ἐν ὁμίλῳ (line 27!) in Apollonius' simile, which lion is equated with Amycus alone and surrounded ἐν πάντεσσι (line 10). If we were to destroy Apollonius' οἶος, in sum, we would obliterate the very *clou* of his simile!

And now let us examine a typical case of analogical allusion to Homer. Morphological analogy, as is well known, was extensively utilised by Hellenistic epic poets in order to enrich their diction[38] by creating new forms modelled on Homeric specimens. At *Argonautica* 4,604f. we read ταναῇσιν ἀείμεναι αἰγείροισιν/μύρονται. This is an allusion to the fact that the Heliads, inside the poplars (ταναῇσιν αἰγείροισιν – local dative) cry (μύρονται) whenever the wind blows. This is an aetiological point: the wind blows between the leaves of the poplars, and the noise made by the leaves is considered to be the lamentation uttered by the Heliads. What can ἀείμεναι mean? The critics have tried all sorts of emendations, and even concluded that 'the truth will elude us here'.[39] On the contrary, the text is sound. The participle ἀήμενος 'buffeted by the wind' is in *Odyssey* 6, 131. On the other hand, we know that Homer's text presents variants of the type τιθήμενος/τιθείμενος; τιθήμεναι/ τιθείμεναι. It follows that Apollonius' ἀείμεναι means 'buffeted by the wind', 'around which the wind blows', and is his analogical formation created after τιθείμενος, a formation typical of the *poeta analogeticus* that Apollonius was.[40]

Finally, I should like to mention three instructive cases, which teach us that we cannot try to understand Apollonius' words by starting from the abstract concept of what is 'correct Greek'. Our starting point must always be Apollonius' own words, which we must try to comprehend in the light of his allusions to Homer or his employment of Homeric features. At *Argonautica* 3, 1088f. we read: ὃς πρῶτος ποίησε πόλεις καὶ ἐδείματο νηούς/ἀθανάτοις, κ.τ.λ. Hastily stating that 'Greek does not talk about 'making' cities any more than we do', a critic[41] mutilated Apollonius' ποίησε; but the fact is that Apollonius is pointedly alluding to Homer *Iliad* 18, 490f.: ἐν δὲ δύω ποίησε πόλεις μερόπων ἀνθρώπων/καλάς, κ.τ.λ.

where the phrase ποίησε πόλεις not only occurs, but indeed occupies precisely the same *sedes* as in Apollonius' hexameter. In the Homeric passage, ποίησε can be taken to mean either 'sculptured' (on the shield which Homer is describing) or 'erected', 'built' (metaphorically, in the sense that the sculptor who decorated the shield with towns 'built' such towns on the shield). Apollonius wants us to see that he took Homer's ποίησε πόλεις in the sense 'built towns', and uses the phrase in this latter sense.[42]

At *Argonautica* 4, 634f.,we read: ἑπτὰ διὰ στομάτων ἵει ρόον· ἐκ δ᾽ ἄρα τοῖο/λίμνας εἰσέλασαν κ.τ.λ. The form ἵει was suspected by the same critic just mentioned, who, stating 'the form ἵει for ἵησι is normally found in compounds' proceeded to destroy Apollonius' ἵει. Yet Apollonius is overtly alluding to Homer *Iliad* 12,25f. ἐννῆμαρ δ᾽ἐς τεῖχος ἵει ρόον· ὗε δ᾽ ἄρα Ζεύς/συνεχὲς κ.τ.λ. where the phrase ἵει ρόον not only is attested, but occupies just the same *sedes* as in Apollonius' line. In Homer's line, ἵει can be taken either as an imperfect parallel to ὗε, or as a historical present coupled with the imperfect ὗε. Apollonius, by using ἵει ρόον as an unambiguous present ('sends its stream') wants us to understand that he sided with those who took Homer's ἵει as a historical present.[43]

At 4,1654ff. we read:

Κέκλυτέ μευ, μούνη γὰρ δίομαι ὕμμι δαμάσσειν
ἄνδρα τόν, ὅστις ὅδ᾽ ἐστί, καὶ εἰ παγχάλκεον ἴσχει
ὃν δέμας, ὁππότε μή οἱ ἐπ᾽ ἀκάματος πέλοι αἰών.

Medea exhorts the Argonauts not to fear Talus. Stating that 'παγχάλκεον ἴσχει ὃν δέμας is not Greek for 'he has a body of brass' ', the critic already quoted[44] proposes altering Apollonius' ἴσχει into ἴσκει, to obtain the sense 'even if he claims that his body is of brass'. But the alteration is contextually impossible. There is no question of Talus claiming that his body was of brass: its being of brass was a fact, as such well known to the Argonauts, who had quickly backed when faced with the giant, because they knew that he was χάλκειος (4, 1638) and invulnerable in so far as he was made of brass (δέμας καὶ γυῖα τέτυκτο/χάλκεος ἠδ᾽ ἄρρηκτος, 4, 1645f.). Apollonius is certainly playing with the Homeric line-ending οὐδ᾽ εἰ παγχάλκεος εὔχεται εἶναι (*Iliad* 20,102), just as Quintus Smyrnaeus – *Posthomerica* 8, 216, οὐδ᾽ εἰ παγχάλκεος ἦεν – and Dionysius – *Bassarica* Fr.4, 3 (Heitsch), καὶ εἰ παγχάλκεοι εἶεν – have done. But Apollonius has introduced an important variation: in Apollonius' passage we have business with a real δέμας which is actually made of brass, whereas in the other passages just quoted the adjective παγχάλκεος is used in a metaphor or an impossible hypothesis. At *Iliad* 20, 102 παγχάλκεος means *indefessus*, as explained by van Leeuwen *ad loc.*; in Dionysius *Bassarica Fr.*4, 3 (Heitsch) and Quintus Smyrnaeus *Posthomerica* 8, 216 παγχάλκεος occurs in a purely hypothetical sentence, the implication being that nobody can really be made of brass, cf. Koechly *ad* Quintus Smyrnaeus 8, 216: *nemo mortalis meam hastam effugiet, nec si totus esset aheneus, scil. quod tamen fieri nequit* . The change ἴσκει is therefore a non-starter: how could Medea say 'he claims that his body is made of brass' of a giant, 'dessen ehernen Leib sie aus der Ferne glänzen sah?'[45] Both she and the Argonauts had in front of them the ocular demonstration that Talus' body was of brass. Indeed, Medea underlines this fact: in line 1656, ἐπί means 'in addition to his having a body of brass', cf. Mooney *op.cit. ad loc.*

The truth is that the interpreter has misunderstood Apollonius. The normal construction for saying 'he has a body of brass' is, in Greek, παγχάλκεον ἔχει (ἴσχει) δέμας:cf. e.g. Oppian *Halieutica* 3, 190 (ὅσσοι δὲ δέμας περίμετρον ἔχουσι) or 5, 15 (χαμαίζηλόν περ ἔχων δέμας). No possessive accompanies δέμας. Since δέμας is preceded in Apollonius' line by the possessive ὅν it follows that Apollonius' words have nothing to do with the construction in question. The context, and an analysis of Apollonius' diction, will show us what the poet's words really mean. As regards Apollonius' diction, we must remember that the verb ἴσχω, in the *Argonautica*, as, of course, in any other epic poem, can mean 'hold back', 'hold in check' (e.g. *Argonautica* 4,1723 or 3, 344). As for the context, the *Leitmotiv* is that it is thanks to his invulnerable body of brass that Talus has been able to hold the Argonauts in check; cf. εἶργε, 1639; Κρήτης ἑκάς, 1651; ἔχετ' αὐτοῦ νῆα . . . ἐκτὸς ἐρωῆς/πετράων, 1657f; ἐρυκέμεν κ.τ.λ.,1678, etc. The conclusion is obvious: what Medea says to the Argonauts is, therefore, 'I deem that I alone can subdue the man for you, whoever he is, even though that body of brass of his[46] is holding you in check, unless his life, too, is everlasting.' In other words, although Talus, thanks to his body of everlasting brass, is able to hold in check the Argonauts, who are mere warriors of vulnerable flesh, nevertheless Medea, who is a sorceress, will be able to subdue him by removing life from his invulnerable body. The verb ἴσχει governs the accusative of the personal pronoun, ὑμᾶς, which must be understood from the previous ὔμμι. This feature is common in epic poetry (cf. my observations in *Hermes* 92 (1964) p.488 n.1), and is of course common in Apollonius. Indeed, we have two exactly parallel instances of the feature in the passage we are examining: just as in line 1655 ἴσχει 'holds back' governs an accusative ὑμᾶς which is to be understood and which denotes the Argonauts, the subject of ἴσχει being Talus, so in line 1678 ἐρυκέμεν, 'hold back' (a synonym of ἴσχω) governs an accusative αὐτούς, which is to be understood and denotes the Argonauts, the subject of ἐρυκέμεν being, once again, Talus. Scholars had not been able to understand Apollonius because they had forgotten that Apollonius is particularly fond of 'Subjektswechsel' of verbs in the third person,[47] which is, of course, a Homeric peculiarity. The 'Subjektswechsel' ἐστί (subject: ἀνήρ)/ἴσχει (subject: ὃν δέμας) is one instance of the peculiarity under discussion.

In each of the three passages which I have discussed Apollonius has, we may conclude, written perfectly good Greek. In the first two instances he has pointedly alluded to a Homeric phrase (respectively ποίησε πόλεις and ἵει ῥόον), whilst in the third he has employed the 'Subjektswechsel', a feature of impeccable Homeric lineage which Apollonius was particularly fond of reproducing.

I hope that the present paper has contributed to demonstrate that, in Apollonius (and in any Hellenistic poet), literary creation was based on the grammatical analysis of Homer's diction, and that Apollonius' art was nothing if not precise.[48]

NOTES

The present paper is the text of a seminar lecture which I delivered at the Universities of Leeds, Leicester, Southampton, Amsterdam, Nijmegen, Utrecht, Athens, Ioannina, Thessaloniki, Ghent, Liège, Louvain, Madrid and Urbino: my lecture and the relevant bibliography are published at the request of my colleagues from these Universities. I have freely drawn upon my own research work (published and unpublished) and upon the select bibliography cited in note 1.

1.   Select bibliography:

A. Ardizzoni *Apollonio Rodio Le Argonautiche, Testo, traduzione e commentario Libro I* Rome (1967).

A. Ardizzoni *Apollonio Rodio Le Argonautiche, Testo, traduzione e commentario Libro III* Bari (1958).

G. Boesch *De Apollonii Rhodii elocutione* Diss. Berlin (1908).

G. Giangrande ' 'Arte Allusiva' and Alexandrian Epic Poetry', *Classical Quarterly* 17 (1967) pp.85ff.

G. Giangrande 'Der stilistische Gebrauch der Dorismen im Epos' *Hermes* 98 (1970) pp.257ff.

G. Giangrande 'Hellenistic Poetry and Homer' *L'Antiquité Classique* 39 (1970) pp.46ff.

G. Giangrande 'The Utilization of Homeric Variants by Apollonius Rhodius: a Methodological Canon of Research' *Quaderni Urbinati* 15 (1973) pp.73ff.

G. Giangrande *Zu Sprachgebrauch, Technik und Text des Apollonios Rhodios* Classical and Byzantine Monographs I, Amsterdam (1973).

G. Giangrande *L'Humour des Alexandrins* Classical and Byzantine Monographs II, Amsterdam (1975).

M.M. Gillies *The Argonautica of Apollonius Rhodius Book III* edited with Introduction and Commentary, Cambridge (1928).

A. Haacke *Commentationis de elocutione Apollonii Rhodii Particula* Diss. Halle (1842).

A. Rzach 'Grammatische Studien zu Apollonios Rhodios' *Sitzungsber. Akad. Wien* 89 (1878) pp.429ff.

L. Schmidt *De Apollonii Rhodii elocutione* Diss. Münster (1853).

H. Suchier *Animadversiones de dicendi genere quo Apollonius Rhodius poeta in Argonauticis usus est* Prgr. Rinteln (1862).

In the footnotes which follow, items listed above will be cited in an abbreviated form, whereas other works will be cited *in extenso*.

2. Cf. e.g. Giangrande 'Hellenistic Poetry and Homer' pp.46-48; Schmidt *op.cit.* p.20.

3. Cf. G. Setti *La critica letteraria in Aristofane* Pisa (1877) pp.35ff.

4. Cf. in particular E. Frohn *De Carmine XXV Theocriteo quaestiones selectae* Diss. Halle (1908); G. Futh *De Theocriti studiis Homericis* Diss. Halle (1876); F. Schultz *Die Mischung der Dialekte bei Theokrit* Prgr. Gymn. Culm (1872); H. Stanger 'Homer im Theocrit' Blätter für d. Bayr. Gymn.-Schulw. 3 (1867) pp.201ff.

5. Cf. e.g. V. Loebe *Commentationis de elocutione Callimachi Pars I* and *Pars II* Prgr. Putbus (1867, 1874); Fr. De Ian *De Callimacho Homeri interprete* Diss. Strassburg (1893); F. Williams 'Five Problems in Callimachus' Hymn to Apollo' *Quad. Urbin.* 19 (1975) pp. 127ff.

6. On this point cf. in particular G. Giangrande 'Callimachus, Poetry, Love and Irony' *Quad. Urbin.* 19 (1975) pp.111f.

7. Cf. E. Eichgrün *Kallimachos und Apollonios Rhodios* Diss. Berlin (1961) p.82.

8. The variant κλέα ἀνδρῶν which certain MSS. of the *Argonautica* offer, is a Homeric phrase too (*Il.* 9, 189).

9. And poets, of course: Homer's βριθοσύνη was re-used by Nonnus *Dionys.* 1, 298.

10. Cf. Gillies *op.cit. ad* line 144.

11. Cf. Boesch *op.cit.* p.58.

12. Cf. K. Kuiper *Studia Callimachea I De Hymnorum I-IV dictione epica* Leiden (1896) pp.226ff.; Suchier *op.cit.* pp.12ff.

13. Cf. V. Bérard *L'Odyssée* Paris (1947) *préface* pp.Xff.

14. Cf. Giangrande 'Der stilistische Gebrauch' pp.265, 271ff.; 'Dorische Genitive bei Homer' *Glotta* 51 (1973) pp. 1ff.

15. Cf. most recently G. Giangrande *JHS* 90 (1970) p.214.

16. Cf. *Thes. s.v.* στομαλίμνη and *schol.* Theocr. *Id.* 4, 23 a-b (Wendel).

17. Cf. lastly *CR* 23 (1973) p.87; for such technique in Apollonius cf. Boesch *op.cit.* pp.37ff.

18. Cf. e.g. A. Ludwich *Aristarchs homerische Textkritik* I Hildesheim (1971) p.407.

19. Cf. Giangrande 'Hellenistic Poetry and Homer' p.48.

20. Cf. *Eranos* 67 (1969) pp.33ff.; Apollonius' technique is the same as Callimachus', of course: cf. *Ant. Class.* 39 (1970) p.48 n.13.

21. Cf. *JHS* 89 (1969) p.152 n.14.

22. Cf. B. Wyss *Antimachi Colophonii reliquiae* Berlin (1936) p. XLVIII.

23. Cf. A.S. Haggett *A Comparison of Apollonius Rhodius with Homer in Prepositional Usage* Diss. Baltimore (1902) pp.59-66.

24. Cf. Giangrande *Zu Sprachgebrauch* p.33.

25. Cf. Haacke *op.cit.* pp.16ff.; Schmidt, *op.cit.* pp.24ff.; Suchier *op.cit.* pp.31f.

26. Cf. Giangrande *Zu Sprachgebrauch* p.11.

27. Cf. in particular Giangrande *L'humour des Alexandrins* pp.18ff., and *CR* 24 (1974) p.129 with n.2.

28. H. Fränkel *Noten zu den Argonautika* München (1968) pp.97, 110.

29. Cf. G.W. Mooney *The Argonautica of Apollonius Rhodius* Amsterdam (1964) *ad* 1,672.

30. Cf. Giangrande 'Der stilistische Gebrauch' p.265 n.2.

31. *Apollonios de Rhodes Argonautiques Chants I-II* Texte établi et commenté par F. Vian, Paris, Les Belles Lettres (1974).

32. Cf. Hesych., *s.v.* σκιόεντα: ὑψηλά, ἢ τὰ μεγάλην σκιὰν ποιοῦντα; Apoll.Soph. 142,24; *schol.* BLV on *Il.* 1,157 οὔρεα σκιόεντα: τὸ ὕψος ἐδήλωσε.

33. A βωμός must be ὑψηλός, to be desirable: cf. the passages quoted in *Thes. s.v.* βωμός; a βωμός is 'erected' ⟨ἀναστήσαντες *Arg.* 2,689⟩ and must be 'tall' (μέγαν *Arg.* 2,522, meaning 'long', i.e. 'tall').

34. For details, cf. G. Giangrande *Grazer Beitr.* 1 (1973) pp.137f.

35. Cf. lastly M. Campbell *CQ* 21 (1971) pp.412f.

36. The best on the subject has been written by H. Faerber *Zur dichterischen Kunst in Apollonios Rhodios' Argonautika: die Gleichnisse* Diss. Berlin (1932), M. Schellert *De Apollonii Rhodii comparationibus* Diss. Halle (1885) and A. Clausing *Kritik und Exegese der homerischen Gleichnisse im Altertum* Diss. Freiburg i.Br. (1913), esp. pp.29ff.

37. Cf. W. Leaf *The Iliad* Amsterdam (1960) *ad* 5,554: the dual probably implies a couple, i.e. a lion and a lioness. Apollonius knew this, cf. *Arg.* 4, 1339 σύννομον.

38. Cf. Giangrande 'Der stilistische Gebrauch' pp.263f. and *CR* 21 (1971) p.354, on Hellenistic *neologismi analogici*.

39. Cf. for details Giangrande *Zu Sprachgebrauch* pp.34f.

40. Cf. Giangrande 'Der stilistische Gebrauch' p.264 n.1.

41. *CR* 13 (1963) p.11.

42. Cf. Giangrande '*Arte allusiva*' pp.86f.

43. Cf. Giangrande '*Arte allusiva*' p.87.

44. *CR* 13 (1963) p.12.

45. Cf. Fränkel *op.cit.* in n.28, p.614.

46. The possessive ὅν is emphatic, as always in Apollonius.

47. Cf. Fränkel *op.cit.* in n.28 p.645; R. Merkel *Apollonii Argonautica* Leipzig (1854) p.LXXXVIII (*vicissitudo subjecti*). A couple of examples: *Arg.* 4, 1746 (βάλεν, subj. κραδίη; ὀνόμηνεν, subj. Euphemus), *Arg.* 2, 753f. (λάθον, ἄκουον, ἔθεντο); for Homer cf. Leaf *op.cit.* in n.37 *ad Il.* 7, 186-189; for Callimachus cf. G. Giangrande *CR* 21 (1971) p.355; for Quintus Smyrnaeus cf. F. Vian *Recherches sur les Posthomerica* Paris (1969) p.202 ('changements de sujets'). Such cases of 'Subjektswechsel' occur, as a rule, in the third person of verbs (as is the case with the passage under discussion: ἐστί, ἴσχει).

48. Nowhere is this more evident than in the cases of lexical humour I have examined. Apollonius' lexical traps are usually based on the fact that the relevant word used by the poet at first sight appears to have its current meaning

(ἔϑειραι 'human hair', ἀπείρων 'limitless', ἐρέται 'rowers of ships', σκιόεις 'full of shade'), a meaning which would be contextually absurd, but upon closer examination the word concerned reveals itself to have a rarer meaning, which is precisely the one required by the context. On lexical traps in Callimachus cf. my observations in *Hermes* 97 (1969) pp.451f., and F.J. Williams *Quad. Urbin.* 19 (1975) p.133, with n.26, a particularly instructive case concerning Callim. *Fr.*383, 10(Pf.).

THE DISTAFF OF THEUGENIS – THEOCRITUS *IDYLL* 28[1]

by

FRANCIS CAIRNS

(University of Liverpool)

1. The Genre Anathematikon

Idyll 28 is an anathematikon. Ancient poets recording real or imaginary dedications to gods employed this genre, many examples of which are collected in Book 6 of the *Palatine Anthology*. In addition to dedications to gods, *Anthologia Palatina* 6 also contains a few poems recording a gift to a human being.[2] The presence of these 'dedications' to men in a book of anathematika does not in itself prove that they too are anathematika. But the situation, function and *topoi* of the epigrams concerned with gifts to men are almost the same as those of the dedications to gods; and the phenomenon of a single genre with, on different occasions, human and divine addressees, is well paralleled.[3] So there is no reason to doubt that poems recording gifts to men, including *Idyll* 28, also belong to the genre anathematikon.

Idyll 28 could, if this were appropriate, be analysed as an anathematikon without account being taken of anathematika involving dedications to gods. A sufficient number of anathematika recording gifts to men survive to enable us to recognise from them alone the commonplaces of *Idyll* 28. But there are two reasons why reference will be made in this paper to the ancient anathematika to gods. The first is that in this way a more complete treatment of the genre will be achieved. The second is that many ancient poets, and notably Theocritus in *Idyll* 28, make conscious use in anathematika to men of commonplaces native to or better established in the divine anathematikon. Because a large number of ancient anathematika to gods survive, I shall refer for brevity's sake to H. Kühn's 1906 Breslau dissertation *Topica Epigrammatum Dedicatoriorum Graecorum*. This thesis conveniently summarises the topical content of Greek religious anathematika. Page references to it will thus adequately supplement the examples of the commonplaces of anathematika to men listed below.

The following poems form a satisfactory sample of anathematika to men (GP = Gow-Page *The Greek Anthology, Hellenistic Epigrams*):

Antipater of Thessalonika GP 31 = *AP* 9,93; 41 = *AP* 6,335; 42 = *AP* 9,552; 43 = *AP* 6,241; 44 = *AP* 9,541; 45 = *AP* 6,249; Antiphilus GP 1 = *AP* 6,250; 2 = *AP* 6,252; Crinagoras GP 3 = *AP* 6,227; 4 = *AP*

6,229; 5 = *AP* 6,261; 6 = *AP* 6,345; 7 = *AP* 9,239; 11 = *AP* 6,545; Leonidas of Alexandria *AP* 6,321; 322; 328; 329; 9,353; 355; Agathias *AP* 16,36; Paulus Silentiarius *AP* 5,301(300); Palladas *AP* 10,92; Anon. *AP* 5,90; 91; 12,96; 16,62; Catullus 1; Martial 3,2; 4,19; 5,1; 68; 6,1.

In all these examples the following primary elements can be detected, which together characterise the genre: the donor (A1); the recipient (A2); the object given (A3); the giving of the object (A4). In addition examples of the genre may, but need not necessarily, contain the following secondary elements:

B1   Fuller identification of the donor by family, home town, occupation etc., e.g. Antipater GP 31; Leonidas *AP* 6,321; 328; 9,353;355; Anon. *AP* 16,62 (cp. Kühn pp.1ff.).

B2   Fuller identification of the recipient by family, home town, occupation etc., e.g. Antipater GP 41; Crinagoras GP 3; Leonidas *AP* 9,355; Palladas *AP* 10,92 (cp. Kühn pp.20ff.).

B3   Encomiastic description of the gift, e.g. Antipater GP 41; 42; 43; 44; 45; Antiphilus GP 1; 2; Crinagoras GP 3;4;5;6;11; Leonidas *AP* 6,321; 322; 328; Palladas *AP* 10,92; Catullus 1; Martial 3,2; 4,19 (cp. Kühn pp.52f.).

B4   Modest derogation of the donor or his efforts or the value of the gift, e.g. Antipater GP 31; Antiphilus GP 1; Crinagoras GP 3; 4; Leonidas *AP* 6,329; Agathias *AP* 16,36;Catullus 1; Martial 4,19 (cp. Kühn pp.54ff.).

B5   The occasion of the gift, which is often a birthday, e.g. Antipater GP 31; Crinagoras GP 3; 5; 6; 7(?); Leonidas *AP* 6,321; 9,353; 355. Sometimes it is another occasion, e.g. Crinagoras GP 4 (a feast); Leonidas *AP* 6,322 (the Saturnalia) (cp. Kühn pp.55ff.).

B6   The purpose or function of the gift, e.g. Antipater GP 41; 42; 43; 44; 45; Antiphilus GP 1; Crinagoras GP 3; 4; 6; Leonidas *AP* 6,322; Anon. *AP* 12,96; Agathias *AP* 16,36;Martial 3,2; 4,19; 5,68 (cp. Kühn pp.43ff.).

B7   The donor's sentiments towards the recipient. These are usually simply implied. But they are sometimes stated explicitly, e.g. Antipater GP 41; 42; Antiphilus GP 1; Crinagoras GP 3; 4; 5; Paulus Silentiarius *AP* 5,301 (300); Martial 6,1 (cp. Kühn pp.55ff.).

B8   A request to the recipient to accept the gift or be gracious, e.g. Antipater GP 31; 41; Antiphilus GP 1; Martial 5,1 (cp. Kühn pp.67ff.).

B9 The suitability of the gift to the recipient, e.g. Antipater GP 42; 43; Antiphilus GP 1; Crinagoras GP 3; 6 (implied); 7 (implied); 11; Leonidas *AP* 9,355; Paulus Silentiarius *AP* 5,301 (300); Palladas *AP* 10,92; Anon. *AP* 5,90; 91; Catullus 1 (cp. Kühn p.15.).

B10 Compliments to the recipient, e.g. Antipater GP 31; 41; 42; 43; 45; Antiphilus GP 1; 2; Crinagoras GP 3;6;7;11; Leonidas *AP* 6,321;322; 9,353;355; Paulus Silentiarius *AP* 5,301(300); Palladas *AP* 10,92; Anon. *AP* 5,90;91; 12,96; 16,62; Agathias *AP* 6,36; Catullus 1; Martial 5,1 (cp. Kühn pp.11ff.).

2. The Topical Content of *Idyll* 28

In *Idyll* 28 three of the primary elements are present in a simple form: Theocritus the donor (A1); Theugenis the recipient (A2); and the gift, a distaff (A3). There is a small sophistication concerning the actual giving of the gift (A4). Most anathematika record that the gift has already been given or is in the process of being given. But in *Idyll* 28 the intention to give the gift rather than the actual giving is recorded. Temporal alterations of this kind are common in ancient poetry; [4] but there is good reason to think that this particular sophistication may have a special connection with the anathematikon. In some dedications to gods, the plea to the god for gracious reception of the offering or for general graciousness (B8) is extended to include a request for a specific future blessing. This request is then followed by a vow of a further offering to be made on fulfilment of the request (Kühn pp.64f., cp. pp.67ff.). The presence of such *vota* as an element of some dedications to gods may have prompted some writers to extend the future tense over a wider area of the anathematikon. Two interesting cases of this extension in divine anathematika may be mentioned. The first and more relevant is in Theocritus *Epigram* 1 where a present offering of roses and thyme is mentioned conjointly with a future offering, a goat. The second is in Horace *Odes* 3,13 where gifts to the *fons Bandusiae* are promised, not made.[5] *Idyll* 28 exactly parallels this feature in an anathematikon to a human being. A Catullan dedication to a man also employs the future tense. Catullus 14 is not as a whole an anathematikon but an inverse 'thanksgiving'. However Catullus 14 'includes' an anathematikon, lines 17-24.[6] In these lines Catullus humorously declares his intention of sending as a gift to Calvus a collection of bad poetry.

As well as the primary elements, most of the secondary elements, the *topoi*, of the anathematikon are also found in *Idyll* 28:

B1 The fuller identification of the donor, Theocritus, consists in the description of his native city, Syracuse, in lines 17f.

B2 The fuller identification of the recipient, Theugenis, consists in the description of her native city, Miletus (3f., 21), of her family, in this case her husband Nicias (66ff., 19f.), and of her occupation, housewife (1f., 10ff., 22f.).

B3 Praise of the gift occurs first at line 1. There, before the distaff is revealed as the intended gift of Theocritus to Theugenis, it is first ennobled by a relevant divine association: distaffs in general are said to be the gift of Athena to good housewives. Antipater GP 45, where the rush lamp is Κρόνου τυφήρεα λύχνον (1), may be compared. At lines 18f., Theocritus describes the distaff's costly material and intensive workmanship. Cp. Antipater GP 44; Antiphilus GP 1; Crinagoras GP 3; 4; 11; Catullus 1; Martial 3,2. Then at *Idyll* 28,16ff. an encomiastic description of the distaff's place of origin is given. Cp. Crinagoras GP 4; Antipater GP 31; 32; Leonidas *AP* 6,321; 328; Martial 5,68. In addition its place of origin is declared to be the giver's own native land, and so a place esteemed by him. Cp. Antipater GP 31;32; Leonidas *AP* 6,321; 328.

B4 Derogation of the donor's efforts appears in the belittling of the gift's value at line 25.

B5 The occasion of the gift is conveyed by lines 3ff. It is to be an 'arrival-gift' which Theocritus will give to Theugenis when he comes to Miletus, the home of Nicias and his wife. Arrival was a common occasion of gift-giving in antiquity.[7]

B6 The purposes of the gift are described at lines 10f. and 22f. At both places its practical function is stressed. Cp. Antipater GP 41; 43; 44; 45; Antiphilus GP 1; Crinagoras GP 3; 4; 6; Leonidas *AP* 6,322; Martial 4,19. At lines 22f. its intended role as a souvenir is also mentioned. Catullus 12,13ff. may be compared. There the poet stresses the souvenir function of napkins sent to him as a gift from Spain by Veranius and Fabullus.

B7 The donor's sentiments towards the recipient are expressed explicitly at lines 24f. They are also implicit in the compliments to Theugenis and to her husband Nicias noted below under *topos* B10.

B8 This *topos* is naturally absent, since the gift has yet to be given to Theugenis.

B9 The distaff is a suitable gift to Theugenis because she is a busy housewife.

B10 Since the distaff symbolises wifely probity, skill and industry, Theocritus is able, under the pretence of explaining the relevance of his gift, to compliment Theugenis as a good, tireless wife intent on her spinning (1f., 10ff., and esp. 12ff.). This portrait of Theugenis may be contrasted with another Theocritean character-sketch of a woman, that of Gorgo of Alexandria in *Idyll* 15. Gorgo is a wife who accuses her husband of having bought rubbishy fleeces for her to spin (19f.) when in fact, as Theocritus makes clear, she is simply a lazy and empty-headed woman who does not want to do any spinning (cf. line 20 ἔργον ἐπ' ἔργῳ). As well as praising Theugenis, *Idyll* 28 also praises Nicias (3ff., 19ff.). The praise of Nicias is inserted partly for its own sake and partly to reflect further credit upon Theugenis through her association with him.

3.   The Generic Originality of *Idyll* 28

The above analysis allows an assessment of *Idyll* 28. In the brief anathematika listed above there are many examples of the types of sophistication characteristic of short epigrams: *brachylogia* (compression of *topoi*); apt combinations of *topoi*; and subtle minor alterations of *topoi*[8]. For example, the poet's feelings for his addressee can be compressed into a few brief syllables, as in Crinagoras GP **5**,4 (γηθομένῃ σὺν φρενί) and GP 6,3 (ἐπμειδήσαντα...ἄσμενα). These sentiments may be combined with derogation of the gift in a few words as in Crinagoras GP 3,5f. (ὀλίγην δόσιν ἀλλ' ἀπὸ θυμοῦ/πλείονος and GP 4,5 (βαιὸν ἀπ' οὐκ ὀλίγης πέμπει φρενός). As for minor alterations of standard *topoi* of the anathematikon, these are omnipresent. For example in *AP* 6,321, Leonidas, instead of presenting his book himself, makes his Muse present it. In *AP* 5,301 (300) Paulus Silentiarius, in giving a pearl, represents it as a gift from Aphrodite, the sea goddess, and not from himself. Sometimes the gift itself is the speaker and not the giver: so Antipater has a hat speaking in GP 41, a sword in GP 42 and a helmet in GP 43. Crinagoras makes roses the speakers in GP 6 and assigns this role to five books of Anacreon's poems in GP 7. The object speaking can sometimes express the donor's feelings, as for example in Antipater GP 42 and Crinagoras GP 6. Martial in 3,2 innovates in stating the purpose of his dedication of his book to Faustinus: this, he alleges, is the protection of the book and not the advantage of his friend.

Another group of interesting sophistications of brief anathematika relies on the fact that the same genre is used to make gifts to gods as to men. This enables the poet to give his addressee a flavour of divinity. So Antipater in GP 31 asks Piso to receive the proffered book ἵλαος, as Zeus is propitiated by a little frankincense. Cp. Antipater GP 1,5f. for another divine comparison. A cognate form ἵλαϑι reinforces Paulus Silentiarius' subordination of Aphrodite to his beautiful addressee (*AP* 5,301(300)). Leonidas *AP* 6,321, Anon. *AP* 5,90 and Martial 5,1, the last addressed to Domitian, employ the same device of treating the addressee as equal or comparable to a god.

Idyll 28 is twenty-five lines long. It is thus much longer than any of the other anathematika mentioned. The most important technical achievement of *Idyll* 28 is connected with its length. It consists in Theocritus' elevation of a genre originally and in essence brief and epigrammatic to a higher literary level where it can function as the vehicle for much more serious poetry. At first sight, it might appear that in thus developing the anathematikon into a genre of greater length and dignity Theocritus is doing something quite uncharacteristic of Hellenistic poetry. This, after all, is usually associated with abbreviated and intensified treatment of themes previously handled at greater length. But the treatment in more extensive terms of genres previously restricted to a minor compass is just as characteristic of Hellenistic poetry as is the compression of Epic material into smaller confines. Within the work of Theocritus the same tendency can be observed in *Idylls* 10 and 14, where a minor sympotic genre is given wider range and greater length.[9] The tendency can also be observed in Roman elegy, which continues the Hellenistic tradition, and particularly in the work of Ovid.[10]

Because Theocritus elevates and extends the range of the anathematikon in *Idyll* 28, the most frequent topical sophistication in it is *macrologia*, the very opposite of that *brachylogia* which was found to be the most noticeable characteristic of epigrammatic anathematika. In *Idyll* 28 Theocritus has enlarged the various *topoi* he employs until they have become a series of miniature sketches. These demonstrate typical literary interests of the time, foundation learning (3f., 16f.) and local cult (4). The macrologic nature of *Idyll* 28 compels Theocritus to create a complex formal structure for its contents. The *topoi* are arranged in careful symmetry to produce a pattern of themes which combines 'composition in parallels' and 'ring-composition'. This can be represented as follows:

A[1]   (1–2)   The distaff

B[1]   (3–5)   Miletus

C[1]   (6–9)   Nicias

D[1]   (10–14)   Theugenis

A^2	(15–16)	The distaff
B^2	(17–18)	Syracuse
C^2	(19–21)	Nicias
D^2	(22–23)	Theugenis
A^3	(24–25)	The distaff

Patterns of such types can be found in Greek poetry from Homer on.[11]

Apart from learned ornament and thematic symmetry, Theocritus uses two other devices to maintain his reader's involvement with the expanded commonplaces of *Idyll* 28. The first is the formal sophistication mentioned above, the use of the future tense throughout the idyll. By placing the gift in the future Theocritus creates an atmosphere of anticipation and expectation. This provides a tension which keeps the reader's interest in the poem alive throughout. It would have been much harder for Theocritus to sustain his reader's interest for twenty-five lines in a gift already given or in one actually being given.

The second contrivance to maintain audience involvement is more important. It is in fact Theocritus' chief innovation in his treatment of the genre and consists of heavy emphasis on certain anathematic *topoi* which humanise the idyll and which give to it a strong flavour of personal emotion, friendship and intimacy. Paradoxically not all the *topoi* emphasised by Theocritus for this purpose are frequently found and stressed in anathematika to men. Some of them are much more characteristic of anathematika to gods; and Theocritus' use of them for purposes very different from those for which they were originally employed in the genre is central to the ingenuity and success of *Idyll* 28.

B1 and B2, the fuller identification of the donor and of the recipient respectively, are exemplified very often by Kühn from the divine anathematikon (see above). But in the human anathematikon they occur infrequently; and when they do occur, they are usually handled briefly. The reasons may be conjectured: a donor wishes the recipient god to recognise him among a multitude of worshippers; the fuller identification of the god is usually also complimentary; and ancient religion is characterised by superstitious legalism. None of these factors enters into donations to human beings. Yet Theocritus makes B1 and B2 the foundation for a display of his close acquaintance and friendship with Nicias and Theugenis. These *topoi* thus allow him to express strong personal feelings as well as to introduce learned material.

Two other personal *topoi* given great prominence and used in combination by Theocritus are B9 and B10, the suitability of the gift to the recipient and compliments to the recipient respectively. Unlike B1 and B2, these are commonplaces frequently employed in anathematika to men. Theocritus' ingenuity in his handling of B9 and B10 consists not in using them in a novel context but in combining them for a novel purpose. Combination of *topoi* is of course characteristic of short anathematika, but there the purpose of combining *topoi* is to achieve brevity. Here in *Idyll* 28 the purpose is the opposite: the two themes in combination constitute a concept sufficiently significant and weighty to allow Theocritus to macrologise by returning to it repeatedly without running the risk of appearing repetitious.

4. The Occasion of *Idyll* 28

The intense personal feeling expressed by Theocritus in *Idyll* 28 has another function in addition to giving humanity and importance to the lengthened anathematikon. It plays a part in providing a 'pretext' for the composition of an encomium of Theugenis and Nicias.

Up to the end of the fifth century BC encomiastic poets frequently used recognised public occasions for encomium, such as agonistic victories and similar religious and social events. Private pretexts were also available: a journey could be a means of introducing someone in encomiastic terms; so could a profession of the poet's friendship or love. Hellenistic poets also employed public events as pretexts for praise. But because of contemporary increased interest in private life, they made more use of private occasions.

Idyll 28 may in fact have been written for some public reason. It may be that the distaff is connected with the very old cult of Athena which existed at Miletus.[12] Theugenis may have been priestess of Athena at Miletus just as Nicias may have been connected with the cult of Asclepius there.[13] εὐσφύρος(13) or εὐαλάκατος (22) may be or may allude to Milesian cult-titles of Athena. But, if there was a public motive, Theocritus rejected it as a pretext for encomium, or was not permitted to use it.

This then is one reason why Theocritus makes so much of the friendship and the guest-host relationship between himself and Nicias. These links are represented as the cause of a journey by Theocritus to Miletus which in turn explains his bringing there the distaff as an arrival gift. In this way Theocritus combines three important private pretexts for encomium – friendship, a journey and a gift. Thus his anathematikon is placed within a social and personal context identical with that of the four epideictic travel genres which play such an important part in ancient encomiastic literature.

5. The Literary Background of *Idyll* 28

Much of Greek poetry relies heavily for its intellectual appeal upon the allusions it contains to the poetry of its own past. This literary allusiveness is at no time so vital to poets as in the Hellenistic period. So important is their literary past to these poets that we can often feel no confidence in our understanding of a Hellenistic poem's significance until we have identified its literary substratum.

Sometimes this is impossible because the relevant earlier texts are lost. In the case of *Idyll* 28 it is not impossible, merely difficult. The reason is this: the metre of *Idyll* 28, Greater Asclepiad, was used before Asclepiades by Sappho and Alcaeus; and the dialect of *Idyll* 28 is an attempt by Theocritus to reproduce or to evoke the archaic Aeolic of Lesbian poetry. It is therefore likely that Theocritus is directing our attention to the older lyric poets, those of Lesbos. But no work of Sappho or Alcaeus parallel to *Idyll* 28 survives. However this does not mean that we must remain totally ignorant of what Theocritus had in mind. Some parallel material survives in Pindar and Bacchylides; and from these later representatives of the lyric tradition we can derive a useful if tentative notion of Theocritus' Lesbian antecedents.

Pindar contains much ostensible autobiography, which modern scholars regard as conventional commonplace material directed at praise of the patron.[14] One 'autobiographical' theme is the poet's journey. This journey is a metaphor for writing poetry and is self-referent, that is, the poem referred to in the metaphor is the poem in which the metaphor occurs.[15] The poetic journey can, on occasion, be made from the games to the patron's home town, as in Pindar *Nemean* 9,1–3. Another epinician 'autobiographical' theme is the gift metaphor. In *Nemean* 3,73–77 the poem is a drink sent as a gift by the poet to his patron at the latter's home in Aegina (cp. 1–3). A comparable concept appears in Bacchylides *Epinician* 4,9–14 where the poem is a piece of woven-work sent by the poet from his own home Ceos to the Sicilian home of his patron Hiero. In these two cases the poets emphasise that they and the recipients are friends, a relationship which is of course a standard convention in this type of poetry.[16]

301

Sometimes the two concepts are combined. In *Olympian* 7 Pindar first speaks of sending his poem, under the image of 'nectar, gift of the Muses, the sweet fruit of my mind', to winners at the games (7–10). Then a little later he talks of accompanying Diagoras, the victor celebrated in this particular ode, on the voyage back to the latter's Rhodian home (13–17). At *Pythian* 2,1–5 Pindar speaks of going from his own home town Thebes to Syracuse, home of Hiero the victor, bringing with him the song. Later in the same ode the theme of Pindar's voyaging recurs (62f.) and later again Pindar describes his ode as merchandise being sent across the sea (67f.).

Perhaps most interesting of all, Pindar in one such metaphorical journey not only mentions the possibility of bringing the poem as a gift to his patron-friend's home but also of bringing another gift as well, health:

καί κεν ἐν ναυσὶν μόλον Ἰονίαν τάμνων θάλασσαν
Ἀρέθοισαν ἐπὶ κραναῦ παρ᾽ Αἰτναῖον ξένον,
ὃς Συρακόσσαισι νέμει βασιλεύς,
πραῢς ἀστοῖς, οὐ φθονέων ἀγαθοῖς, ξείνοις δὲ θαυμαστὸς πατήρ.
τῷ μὲν διδύμας χάριτας
εἰ κατέβαν ὑγίειαν ἄγων χρυσέαν
κῶμόν τ᾽ ἀέθλων Πυθίων αἴγλαν στεφάνοις,
τοὺς ἀριστεύων Φερένικος ἕλεν Κίρρᾳ ποτέ,
ἀστέρος οὐρανίου φαμὶ τηλαυγέστερον κείνῳ φάος
ἐξικόμαν κε βαθὺν πόντον περάσαις.

Pythian 3, 68–76

These epinician concepts, the poet's journey to his patron-friend's home and the poet as a giver of gifts to his patron-friend, are clearly akin to those of *Idyll* 28. But Theocritus seems to be referring not to later, 'Pindaric', versions of these concepts, in which the journey and the gift are metaphors. Rather Theocritus' antecedents must be earlier versions in which the journey is a literal, although possibly not real, journey and the gift is quite distinct from the poem itself. This view is consistent with what little we know of Lesbian poetry: the only metaphorical journey which can be detected with any certainty in its surviving portions is the voyage of the ship of state.[17] Other journeys are apparently literal, as are gifts.[18]

To say that Theocritus is imitating these earlier Lesbian ideas does not mean to say that *Idyll* 28 is a straight imitation of Lesbian poetry. It is rather a characteristically Hellenistic synthesis of lyric 'autobiography' and of anathematic material; consequently the 'autobiographical' material has a more complex functional role in *Idyll* 28 than anything similar in Aeolic lyric. Here the question raised in §4, that of the 'pretext for encomium', is again relevant. In the Pindaric passages mentioned above, neither the poet's gift nor indeed his friendship with his patron were 'pretexts' for the poem. In each case the occasion was simply a victory. Mentions of friendship, journey and gift were made simply to honour the patron further. It cannot be argued from this that in Lesbian poetry the same was true. Journeys, although not the poet's journeys, do clearly provide pretexts for the composition of some extant Aeolic fragments.[19] But in *Idyll* 28 something much more complex can be seen. The three concepts, friendship, journey and gift, which together provide the occasion for the idyll, are themselves arranged by Theocritus in a causal chain. That is Theocritus' own contribution to this conceptual area and it is an advance on all lyric antecedents.

It is characteristic of Theocritus' art to make such new uses of lyric conventions. *Idyll* 16[20] is ostensibly a request to Theocritus' contemporary Hiero of Syracuse for future patronage. Theocritus advances as the main ground for his request Hiero's need for a poet to celebrate his great military achievements. This thought-pattern is exploiting another convention of lyric poetry. Pindar sometimes proffers counsel to or makes a request of his patron, either in direct imperative form or in some indirect fashion.[21] On occasion the injunction has to do with expenditure upon poetry.[22] All such passages are intended as indirect praise of the patron, since the advice coincides with the patron's actions. By offering it the poet is putting on record his assent to the patron's prior decisions in a way which creates an illusion of free speech.[23] In cases where expenditure on poetry is commended, credit is reflected on the patron, since by commissioning the poem he has already shown generosity to poetry. In *Idyll* 16 Theocritus has taken this lyric convention which was originally used simply to praise the patron. He has developed it by making it the occasion of his poem and the pretext for his praise of Hiero. Theocritus' reader knew that by convention such requests were already fulfilled. So he would see in *Idyll* 16 not a genuine plea for patronage but a commissioned poem ingeniously posing as a request for a commission.

Mention of *Idyll* 16 suggests another question which can also be answered by comparison with it. This is the question why Theocritus wanted in *Idyll* 28 to allude to the archaic poets of Lesbos rather than, for example, to later choric poets, as in *Idyll* 16. The ruler of Syracuse in Theocritus' day was a Hiero homonymous with the fifth century BC Hiero who also ruled Syracuse and was sung of by Pindar, Bacchylides and Simonides. Theocritus takes advantage of this in *Idyll* 16 to eulogise the second Hiero in an idyll full of echoes and conventions from this area of earlier poetry. By doing so he elevates Hiero into a realm of grandeur in which he becomes one of the fabled rulers of the early fifth century, whose eternal fame was sung and guaranteed by the greatest lyric poets.

Theocritus' design is to some extent parallel in *Idyll* 28. On one level of meaning the allusion to the very distant world of ancient Lesbos has a romantic effect. Nicias and Theugenis are removed from their everyday station in the Miletus of Theocritus' day. They are endowed with the flavour of an extremely remote and colourful period; and they are implicitly guaranteed the distinction and immortality won by the patrons of Sappho and Alcaeus.

But the encomiastic design works on another level differently from that of *Idyll* 16. Nicias and Theugenis are not tyrants but citizens of Miletus. Milesian democracy was, at least in formal constitutional terms, restored in 313/12 BC. It continued up to a two year tyrannical interlude around 260 BC and was restored again thereafter.[24] The date of *Idyll* 28 is not known. But the whole Theocritean corpus was composed, as far as we know,[25] within the period of Milesian 'democracy'. This is why Theocritus does not recall in connection with Nicias and Theugenis the world of Pindar, Bacchylides and Simonides, where the most munificent patrons of poetry were tyrants. He chooses rather to allude to archaic Lesbos because Sappho and Alcaeus, unlike the later choric poets, were untainted with tyrannical associations and indeed were famous for their opposition to tyranny. In this way Theocritus, while implying that his patrons share the elevated social status of the clients of Sappho and Alcaeus, can simultaneously ensure that the implication carries with it no hint that these distinguished persons have political sympathies out of keeping with Miletus' democratic constitution.

A second reason for Theocritus to avoid any possible literary reminiscence of tyranny in his treatment of Nicias and Theugenis was the reality underlying Milesian democracy. This was the Ptolemaic suzerainty of Miletus which lasted from 279 BC to 258 BC or later.[26] Ptolemy Philadelphos was a prominent patron of Theocritus (cf. e.g. *Idylls* 14,15 and 17). Nicias was wealthy enough to commission *Idylls* 11,13 and 28 as well as *Epigram* 8. His wealth, his presumed public importance in Miletus and their common patronage of Theocritus suggest that Nicias was a partisan of Ptolemy. It may well be that Theocritus saw in these circumstances another danger in harking back to Pindaric lyric. Had he done so, malicious interpreters might have seen Nicias as a Chromios of Aetna to Ptolemy's Hiero. The cities of archaic Lesbos, on the other hand, were autonomous. The anti-tyrannical poets of Lesbos certainly received commissions from aristocrats; but the society they lived in, in the intervals between tyrants, was ruled through free assemblies, however oligarchic. On all counts then it was much safer for Theocritus to recall archaic Lesbos in his praise of Nicias and Theugenis.

NOTES

1. I am indebted to Prof. G. Giangrande for advice on this paper. He does not necessarily concur with its conclusions.

2. *AP* 6, 227; 229; 241; 249; 252; 261; 321; 322; 325; 328; 329; 335; 345.

3. See F. Cairns *Generic Composition in Greek and Roman Poetry* Edinburgh (1972), hereafter referred to as *GC*, pp.91f., 218. The techniques of generic analysis used in the present paper are explained and exemplified fully in this work.

4. See *GC* pp.127f.

5. For a full generic treatment of Hor. *Od.* 3,13 see my 'Horace, *Odes* III, 13 and III, 23' (*L'Antiquité Classique,* forthcoming).

6. For 'inclusion' see *GC* pp.158ff.

7. E.g. Plaut. *Amph.* 760ff.; *Merc.* 399; *Truc.* 529ff.; Prop. 2,16; Nicodemus *AP* 6,314.

8. On topical originality see *GC* pp.98ff.

9. See F. Cairns *Hermes* 98 (1970) pp.38ff. and *GC* pp.171ff.

10. For Ovidian examples see A.A. Day *The Origins of Latin Love Elegy* Oxford (1938) pp.134ff.

11. On Homeric formal structures see D. Lohmann *Die Composition der Reden in der Ilias* Berlin (1970). Lohmann's introduction (pp.1ff.) refers to prior work on early Greek poetry.

12. See Hdt. 1,19 and G. Kleiner *Die Ruinen von Milet* Berlin (1968) pp.36ff.

13. See Theocr. *Ep.* 8.

14. See e.g. A. Köhnken *Die Funktion des Mythos bei Pindar* Berlin (1971) pp.8ff.

15. E.g. (besides those mentioned below) Pind. *Ol.* 1,110; 6,22-24; 13,49; *Pyth.* 4,247f.; *Nem.* 3,26f.

16. Also e.g. at *Ol.* 9,83f.; *Pyth.* 1,93; 4,1ff.; 10,63ff.

17. See D. Page *Sappho and Alcaeus* Oxford (1955) pp.179ff.

18. *Journeys*: e.g. Alc. *Fr.* 350 (LP); Sapph. *Frr.* 5; 16; 17; 48; 96 (LP). *Gifts*: e.g. Alcman *Fr.* 49 D; Alc. *Fr.* 69 (LP); Sapph. *Fr.* 98 (LP).

19. See n.18 above.

20. I am grateful to Mr. J.G. Howie for discussion of *Idyll* 16.

21. E.g. Pind. *Pyth.* 1,86f.; 4,270ff.; 11,52ff.; *Nem.* 11,13ff.

22. E.g. Pind. *Pyth.* 1,90ff.; *Nem.* 1,31ff.; *Isthm.* 1,64ff.

23. This has long been partially realised (e.g. Gildersleeve on Pind. *Pyth.* 4,279) and is now generally understood: see e.g. E. Thummer *Pindar, Die Isthmischen Gedichte* Heidelberg (1968) I,pp.38ff.

24. See *R−E s.v.* Miletos 1603-7.

25. "The hypothesis therefore that he [Theocritus] was born about 300 BC and died or ceased to write not later than 260 BC, though not necessarily true, would fit the extant evidence satisfactorily." A. S. F. Gow *Theocritus* Cambridge (1952) introd. p.xxix.

26. See P.M. Fraser *Ptolemaic Alexandria* Oxford (1972) II p.301 n.352.

LIVERPOOL CLASSICAL MONTHLY (LCM)   PROSPECTUS

Edited and published from Liverpool by John Pinsent, M.A., D.Phil, Department of Greek, The University, P.O. Box 147, Liverpool, L69 3BX, to whom subscriptions (£3 p.a. of 10 issues in U.K., £4.50 to Europe, $10 to North America by air, $6 by surface mail) and contributions should be sent. A year's subscription at any time entitles to all the issues of that year, and back numbers are always available.

LCM, which appears at the beginning of each of the 10 months of the academic year, October to July, was founded and first appeared on 1 January 1976, in the belief that even, or especially, in a time of financial stringency there was a place for a cheap periodical which provided the opportunity for rapid publication and the circulation of ideas even, though not necessarily, without the full apparatus of learned publication.

The response suggests that this belief was well founded: subscriptions at July 1976 have reached 106 personal, departmental and library from some 42 different institutions in Europe, North America and Australia, and the opportunity now presents for wider publicity.

Contributions on any subject of Classical interest, including Byzantine and humanistic studies and archaeology (with line drawings and perhaps also photographs), are printed in strict order of receipt and in the form in which they are received. They may be of any length, but units of 500 words up to 2000 (1-4 pp.) are preferred, and longer articles may be printed in parts. Changes suggested by the Editor, who does not employ referees, will be submitted for approval unless prior authority is given. The Editor prefers the fullest possible form of reference, initials (but not first names nor titles), volume number as well as date for journals, place as well as date for books, and he hates Roman numerals. He may, then, regularize when preparing copy, but is neither himself consistent or obsessive nor requires it. Obscurities should be avoided and polemic eschewed.

30 free offprints are provided post free: additional copies at 1p a page if ordered before publication, at any subsequent time, 11p a page, in both cases plus postage.

LCM is printed by IBM 82C typesphere, which includes a Greek fount. The contents of the first seven numbers, copyright of which remains in each case with the author and is so secured at the end, will afford the best account of it, and are set out below:

LIVERPOOL CLASSICAL MONTHLY (LCM)

Vol.1 No.1, January 1976

T.P. Wiseman (Leicester): *Factions and family trees* 1–3

H.B. Mattingly (Leeds): *Q. Fabius Pictor, father of Roman History* 3–7

J.C.B. Foster (Liverpool): *Plautus, Bacchides 515ff.* 7–9

M.W. Haslam (Center for Hellenic Studies): *A problem in the history of the transmission of texts exemplified in Demosthenes* 9–10

No.2, February 1976

A.R. Birley (Manchester): *The date of Mons Graupius* 11–14

T.P. Wiseman (Leicester): *Catullus 16* 14–17

G. Giangrande (Birkbeck, London): *Theocritus 1.32* 17–18

N. Horsfall (UC London & Colgate U., Hamilton NY): *Q. Fabius C.filius Pictor; some new evidence* 18

No.3, March 1976

T.P. Wiseman (Leicester): *Senators, commerce and empire* 21–22

A.H. Griffiths (University College, London): *What Syagrus said: Herodotus 7.159* 23–24

P.A. Cartledge (Trinity, Dublin): *Seismicity and Spartan society* 25–28

J. Cressey (Birkbeck, London): *Suetonius as the source of Dante, Inferno 1.62–3* 29

No.4, April 1976

H. White (Birkbeck, London): *Three textual problems in Theocritus: 2.59, 2.144 & 6.29* 33–35

R.J. Seager (Liverpool): *The murder of King Hippoclus of Chios* 36–38

D.W.T. Vessey (University of Florida/Queen Mary, London): *A note on latus* 39–40

J.M. Carter (Royal Holloway, London): *Propertius 2.34C* 41–44

No.5, May 1976

R.J. Seager (Liverpool): *L. Domitius Ahenobarbus and Cicero's election to the consulship* 46

O.P. Taplin (Magdalen, Oxford): *XOPOY and the structure of post-classical tragedy* 47–50

D. Geoghegan (Birkbeck, London): *Some problems in Anyte: AP 9.314, 7.490, 9.745, APlan.291, AP 7.215, 7.202* 51–60

[presented at a meeting of the London Classical Society on 4 February 1976]

E.M. Jenkinson (Durham): *Theocritus 2.59–62 & 144–6* 61

H. White (Birkbeck, London) *replies* 61–62

No.6, June 1976

J.D. Smart (Leeds): *Aristophanes, Wasps 600* 64

R.J. Seager (Liverpool): *Horace, Odes 1.29 as a propempticon* 65–70

F. Cairns (Liverpool): *The philosophical content of Horace, Odes 1.29* 71–77

W. Barr (Liverpool), **F. Cairns** (Liverpool), **O.A.W. Dilke** (Leeds), **I.M. LeM. DuQuesnay** (Birmingham), **G.J. Giesekam** (Liverpool), **A. Hardie** (Foreign & Commonwealth Office), **J.G. Howie** (Edinburgh), **C.W. Macleod** (Christ Church, Oxford), **M.J. McGann** (Belfast), **R.G.M. Nisbet** (Corpus Christi, Oxford), **R.J. Seager** (Liverpool), **C.J. Tuplin** (Liverpool), **A.J. Woodman** (Newcastle), **J.R.G. Wright** (Edinburgh): *Topics in Horace, Odes 1.29* 78–84

[Report of the discussion following the two preceding papers, which were presented at a Colloquium held at Liverpool on 14 May 1976]

J. Pinsent (Liverpool): *Horace, Odes 3.2.13* 84

No.7, July 1976

J. Cressey (Birkbeck, London): *Odyssey 9.390* 86

P.A. Cartledge (Trinity, Dublin): *A new 5th-century Spartan treaty* 87–92

E. Rawson (New Hall, Cambridge): *Homo novus Arpinas ex M. Crassi familia; [Sallust], Cic.3* 93–95

E. Badian (Harvard): *An un-serius Fabius* 97–98

PAPERS

OF THE

LIVERPOOL LATIN SEMINAR

1976

*Classical Latin Poetry/Medieval
Latin Poetry/Greek Poetry*

A R C A

Classical and Medieval Texts Papers and Monographs 2

THE LIVERPOOL LATIN SEMINAR
IS GRATEFUL TO THE FACULTY OF
ARTS OF THE UNIVERSITY OF
LIVERPOOL FOR A CONTRIBUTION
TOWARDS THE COST OF PRODUCING
THIS VOLUME.